Growing Up Jim Crow

Growing Up

THE UNIVERSITY OF NORTH CAROLINA Chapel Hill

Jim Crow

How Black and White Southern Children Learned Race

Jennifer Ritterhouse

Manufactured in the United States of America
Set in Scala and Emma Script by Tseng Information Systems, Inc.

The paper in this book meets the guidelines for permanence
and durability of the Committee on Production Guidelines
for Book Longevity of the Council on Library Resources.

Publication of this book was supported in part by a generous
gift from Eric Papenfuse and Catherine Lawrence.

Library of Congress Cataloging-in-Publication Data
Ritterhouse, Jennifer Lynn.
Growing up Jim Crow : how Black and White southern children
learned race / Jennifer Ritterhouse.
  p. cm.
Includes bibliographical references and index.
ISBN-13: 978-0-8078-3016-1 (cloth : alk. paper)
ISBN-10: 0-8078-3016-x (cloth : alk. paper)
ISBN-13: 978-0-8078-5684-0 (pbk. : alk. paper)
ISBN-10: 0-8078-5684-3 (pbk. : alk. paper)
1. African Americans—Segregation—Southern States—History—20th
century. 2. Southern States—Race relations—History—20th century.
3. Race awareness in children—Southern States—History—20th century.
4. African American children—Southern States—Social conditions—20th
century. 5. Children, White—Southern States—Social conditions—20th
century. 6. African Americans—Race identity—Southern States—
History—20th century. 7. Whites—Race identity—Southern States—
History—20th century. 8. Etiquette—Southern States—Psychological
aspects—History—20th century. I. Title.
E185.61.R59 2006
305.896'07307509041—dc22   2005035087

cloth   10 09 08 07 06   5 4 3 2 1
paper   10 09 08 07 06   5 4 3 2 1

to

Sophie Jane Labys,

and in memory of

Jane Reardon Labys

Contents

Illustrations

Acknowledgments

My debts in this project are many and long-standing. For more than a decade (indeed, a solid third of my life), Jacquelyn Hall has guided my work and helped me to know myself and see who I want to be. I am grateful for her friendship, her steadfast support, the countless hours she has devoted to this and all of my projects, and the inspiring example she so gracefully sets in her own work and being.

I am also indebted to three other mentors, John Kasson, Suzanne Lebsock, and Anne Scott, each of whom has contributed a great deal to my intellectual development, and to a wide circle of friends and colleagues from my graduate school days in Chapel Hill and beyond. Jim Leloudis, Joel Williamson, and Reginald Hildebrand served on my dissertation committee and offered advice and encouragement. Soyini Madison guided me to theoretical readings and was a source of support early on. Many others in the Chapel Hill community, notably Judith Bennett, Stacy Braukman, Gavin Campbell, Peter Coclanis, Peter Filene, Natalie Fousekis, Pamela Grundy, Sandra Hayslette, Jerma Jackson, Joy Kasson, Don Mathews, John McGowan, Beth Millwood, Theda Perdue, and Molly Rozum, suggested readings, provided insights, read chapters, helped with references, or kept my spirits up at various times. G. C. Waldrep has also been a faithful friend and thoughtful reader early and late in this project's development.

Down the road from Chapel Hill, at Duke University, I found other sources of enlightenment and support, particularly through my work on *Remembering Jim Crow*. I enjoyed collaborating with and learned a lot from Bill Chafe, Raymond Gavins, Bob Korstad, Paul Ortiz, Robert Parrish, Keisha Roberts, and Nicole Waligora-Davis. I am also glad to think that *Growing Up Jim Crow* allows more voices from the Behind the Veil oral history collection to be heard.

When I reached the dissertation stage and moved to Philadelphia to live with my husband, Drew Faust was my anchor to southern history, and she and Sheldon Hackney kindly allowed me to sit in on a graduate seminar. Drew also introduced me to Kirsten Wood, who became a good friend and colleague. Kirsten helped organize a dissertation group that proved invaluable for both the insights and the emotional support it provided. Thanks to her and to the group's other members: Jason McGill, Allison Sneider, and Serena Zabin. Beth Clement participated in the group as well and continues to be a valued friend here in Utah. Leigh Edwards is another friend who made my time in Philadelphia enjoyable, as well as productive, and Susan Matt and Marjukka Ollilainen have played that role in my life since I moved west.

My colleagues at Utah State have supported this project in a number of ways, not least by letting me rearrange my teaching schedule and devote time to research and writing. I particularly appreciate the efforts of my department head, Norm Jones, to make my workload manageable. I also value the advice and encouragement I have received from Mick Nicholls and the other members of my tenure and promotion committee: Melody Graulich, David Rich Lewis, Dan McInerney, and Fran Titchener. The fact that my department gave me a surprise baby shower before my daughter Sophie was born is just one indication of what a friendly and nurturing place the USU History Department is. Three members of the department who have since moved on, Anne Butler, Clyde Milner, and Carol O'Connor, embody that spirit of warmth as well, and I appreciate the support that each of them gave me in my first couple of years of teaching.

I have benefited from the insights and advice of a number of scholars who commented on conference papers or otherwise took time to discuss my work. I learned a lot from Karen and Barbara Fields in the course of a shuttle bus ride in Charleston, and Paula Giddings and Nell Painter each offered helpful suggestions in the course of chance conversations as well. John Kasson, Jane Dailey, Patrick Ryan, Fitzhugh Brundage, Nancy Hewitt, Anne Scott, Elsa Barkley Brown, Eileen Boris, Glenda Gilmore, and Edward D. C. Campbell all commented on papers at various conferences, workshops, and symposia. Cliff Kuhn, Rebecca de Schweinitz, and Diana Selig offered suggestions more informally, but no less helpfully. Sandra Treadway, Nancy Essig, and Ted Ownby have all helped me feel my work was important. I also want to thank Vincent Cheng and the other participants in a works-in-progress group at the Tanner Humanities Center, where I spent a final year revising the manuscript: Nadja Durbach, Marian Eide, Dan Greenwood, David Hawkins, Joe Metz, Ronald Smelser, and Carolina Webber. Thanks, too, to Holly Campbell and Beth Tracy for their work keeping the Tanner Center running smoothly.

Throughout my research for this project, librarians and archivists have helped with innumerable questions, large and small. I particularly want to thank John White of the Southern Historical Collection at the University of North Carolina at Chapel Hill and Randall Burkett of the Woodruff Library at Emory University, as well as staff members at those two institutions and at the University of Georgia, the Atlanta History Center, the Atlanta University Center, the Georgia Department of Archives and History, the University of Virginia, the Schomburg Center for Research in Black Culture, and the Rockefeller Archive Center. Thanks also to my two research assistants, Jennifer Hodgkinson and Jennifer Holland.

I have been blessed with a great deal of institutional support over the years, starting with the William N. Reynolds Fellowship that funded my first three years of graduate school at the University of North Carolina. The Department of History and the Graduate School of Arts and Sciences at UNC also supported my work with teaching assistantships, Mowry Research grants, and an off-campus dissertation fellowship. Toward the end of my graduate studies, I received a fellowship from UNC's Royster Society of Fellows, which not only supported the writing of my dissertation but also introduced me to an exciting group of young scholars. My experience as a Royster Fellow and the Ida B. Wells Graduate Student Award I received from the Coordinating Council for Women in History did much to boost my confidence as I made the transition from graduate student to professor.

At Utah State University, I found both a supportive environment and further financial assistance in the form of a generous New Faculty Research Grant. That award, plus a summer stipend from the National Endowment for the Humanities, allowed me to complete additional research and reframe the project in significant ways. A semester of release time from the history department helped me write my new chapters. Finally, a Tanner Visiting Research Fellowship from the Obert C. and Grace A. Tanner Humanities Center at the University of Utah allowed me to finish my revisions even as I read more deeply in the literature on the history of childhood. I am grateful to all of these institutions not only for their financial assistance but also for the confidence it showed and helped to inspire.

I owe many thanks to my editors at UNC Press, particularly Sian Hunter, who guided me through the publication process and shared lunches and laughter along the way, and Mary Caviness, who worked over the manuscript with care and waited patiently for me to write these acknowledgments. I also appreciate the interest that Kate Torrey and David Perry have shown in my work over the years.

Among my greatest debts are those I owe to Jane Dailey and James Marten, who read the manuscript for UNC Press and offered a great deal of constructive criticism. Jane, in particular, has become someone I turn to for sound advice, and I appreciate her insights. I am glad both she and Jim allowed UNC Press to reveal their identities so that I can thank them personally for their perceptive readings.

Thanks are also due to Martha Bewick, who has been an enthusiastic supporter, and to Molly Rozum, who has been there for me in so many ways for so many years. Molly is not only a good friend but also a good reader who has made this book better through her comments.

My parents, Pat and Charles Ritterhouse, and my brother and sister-in-law, Scott and MeLesa Ritterhouse, have supported me throughout my schooling and the many years I have spent on this project. In the last couple of years, Mom and Dad have even flown in several times to take care of Sophie while I attended conferences or got through particularly busy periods. I cannot thank them enough. Becoming a parent myself has helped me to understand how they can be so good to me; I hope I can be equally good to Sophie and thereby live up to their example.

Finally, my greatest debts in all things are to my husband, Paul, who has been my mainstay ever since we met in college. Yes, dear, the book is finally done.

Growing Up Jim Crow

Introduction
Forgotten Alternatives

As a white girl growing up in Virginia in the 1910s, Sarah Patton Boyle learned that she must always "talk a little down" to black people while insisting that they talk "up" to her. She learned that she must never call a black man "Mr." or a black woman "Mrs." She learned that she must never eat with a black person in her family's own dining room, although she might, out of graciousness, share a meal with a valued "Negro 'friend'" in the kitchen or on the back porch. "Day by day," as Boyle put it in her autobiography, these racial rules "grooved their way into my behavior, speech, thought." Blacks' cautious deference seemed to confirm the lessons she received from her parents and other whites, convincing her that most African Americans accepted whites' superiority and approved of "the Southern way of life." Had black opposition been more obvious in her sheltered world, she insisted, "I certainly would not have learned the rules so well, and probably would have rejected them much sooner. As it was, I patiently learned and believed them all." In this, Boyle compared herself to southern ladies of an earlier era who grew so accustomed to wearing corsets that their backs hurt without them. "Thus the confining stays of segregation molded my thoughts and behavior. Yet my heart was never quite bound."[1]

This book is about how people's hearts do and do not become bound. Reading Boyle's autobiography, *The Desegregated Heart*, I became intrigued by the everyday rules of behavior that Boyle described as the "etiquette" of race relations in the segregated South. Because she focused on the minute details of how individuals stood, sat, ate, drank, walked, talked, and even made eye contact with one another, her descriptions brought a new immediacy to my understanding of a Jim Crow system that, as a white, middle-class, southern child of the 1970s, I had experienced only in its decline and with much of the blindness of my privileged social position. To know, as a point of fact, that there had once been separate schools, bathrooms, and water fountains is one thing. To think about the moral and emotional issues involved in habitually denying someone something as ordinary as a "Mr." or "Mrs."—or to think about being so denied—is quite another.

And yet, as fascinated as I was by the whole idea of a regulatory and conformist "etiquette" of race, I could not read a sentence like "My heart was never quite bound" without considering how self-serving and exculpatory it—and perhaps Boyle's whole account of learning the racial rules of her society—seemed. I had picked up *The Desegregated Heart* because I was curious about how, even before the civil rights movement of the 1950s and 1960s, some white southerners had managed to change over the course of their lives, yielding the region's small crop of homegrown white racial liberals. Now I found myself asking how white southerners got to be who they were in the first place, what part racial etiquette played in that process, and what racial etiquette meant for blacks—if, indeed, "racial etiquette" was the best term to use, especially from African Americans' point of view. How did black and white children of the Jim Crow era *learn race*—both the racial roles they were expected to play in their society and a sense of themselves as *being* "black" or "white"?

These are the questions that *Growing Up Jim Crow* explores. They are enormous questions that could be approached in many different ways. Three possibilities would be to analyze adults' prescriptive and descriptive writings about children, to analyze children's literature, and to study children in segregated institutions, especially schools. Although I incorporate elements of all three, none of these is my primary approach. Instead, taking a broad look at the entire South (loosely defined as the eleven states of the former Confederacy) over a long half century, I follow the lead of black and white autobiographers and oral history informants, who often write or talk quite explicitly about how they think they learned race. In many cases, their accounts emphasize childhood interactions across race lines and their own confusions and frustrations with racial etiquette. Thus, like my own curiosity, this book begins with the etiquette of race relations. What was this code of behavior that Boyle described, and how could historians best understand it?

Often, I have pondered whether "etiquette" is even an appropriate term. Especially at first glance, "etiquette" seems too genteel, too much the kind of word white southerners themselves might use to obscure the violence and coercion and fear that they used to keep blacks "in their place." If soft-pedaling the history of racist oppression in the South was not my intention— as it emphatically was not—then perhaps I had better distance myself from a word that I had, after all, first really noticed in the autobiography of a well-intentioned but sometimes blundering white liberal.

But choosing a different word would not necessarily change the concept, and my continued reading told me that many historians had used both "racial etiquette" and related terms frequently over the years, with greater and lesser degrees of self-reflection in doing so. Books like John F. Kasson's *Rudeness and Civility: Manners in Nineteenth-Century Urban America* and James C. Scott's *Domination and the Arts of Resistance* also taught me that etiquette, by definition, involves at least some coercion and, conversely, that power relations operate in a moment-by-moment theater of social interaction just as much as they operate in economic and political realms.[2] Although they were writing from different disciplines about different subjects, both Kasson and Scott drew on a theoretical literature attuned to the everyday and to individual social performance—a literature that I have found helpful as well. Among the founders of this interdisciplinary "performance paradigm" was sociologist Erving Goffman, whose decades-old definition of "etiquette" offers a good starting point for my own efforts to explain what I mean by the term.[3]

The "Etiquette" of Race Relations

According to Goffman, etiquette is "the code which governs ceremonial rules and ceremonial expressions." A "ceremonial rule," in turn, is "one which guides conduct in matters felt to have secondary or even no significance in their own right, having their primary importance—officially anyway—as a conventionalized means of communication by which the individual expresses his character or conveys his appreciation of the other participants in the situation." This is in contrast to a "substantive rule"—for example, the rule against stealing—which guides conduct in an area where following or breaking the rule is seen to have significance of its own, such as the protection or violation of individual property rights and, "only incidentally," of the image of those who possess them. Ceremonial rules and expressions are all about image and social standing. The "character" one expresses when he or she acts according to a ceremonial rule need not be his or her "true" character; indeed, it cannot be, to the extent that it is never one's whole character. As Goffman explains, "In considering the individual's participation in social action, we must understand that in a sense he does not participate as a total person but rather in terms of a special capacity or status; in short, in terms of a special self." In the South, that special self was always a racial self, for blacks and whites alike. Similarly, the "appreciation" that one conveys to his or her interlocutors when he or she follows a ceremonial rule need not be sincere, much less freely given. It can be an appreciation of another's status, rather than his or her worth or deserving of that status. In the South, it could be and often was a black person's appreciation of the fact that if he or she did not say "yes, *sir*" to a white man, that white man might respond with an epithet, a blow, or even lethal force. Goffman acknowledges that rules of conduct can be either "symmetrical" or "asymmetrical," an asymmetrical rule being "one that leads others to treat and be treated by an individual differently from the way he treats and is treated by them."[4] The rules of racial etiquette were determinedly, fiercely asymmetrical, an apt but bloodless term that should be used only in combination with vivid and frequent reminders of the measures white southerners resorted to, including lynching, rape, and other forms of racial violence, when blacks challenged this asymmetry.

After much consideration, my attitude toward the whole terminology of "racial etiquette" is much the same as my attitude toward the word "asymmetrical": it seems an analytically apt language to describe the everyday communications about status between blacks and whites that I am interested in, but only to the extent that I can breathe life into it by connecting it to the tragic, ugly, often brutal history of racism of which daily interactions between black and white southerners were a part.

By reflecting on the connotations of the word "etiquette" even as I continue to employ it, I also hope to get historians thinking about our use of this (and perhaps other) loaded terms. Ideally, the fact that a number of historians have written about racial etiquette allows me to write to and against a tradition of scholarship that will be familiar to some readers. I will begin by saying that I attribute greater significance to racial etiquette than most earlier authors, seeing the unwritten rules that governed day-to-day interactions across race lines not only as a form of social control but also as a script for the performative creation of culture and of "race" itself.[5]

Racial etiquette was also important for individuals, particularly for children who were trying to figure out where they belonged and how they fit into their social world. In the Jim Crow South, questions of place were inevitably questions of race: Why are some people treated one way and others another? How will I and the people I love be treated, and will that treatment be fair? Most often, children asked themselves such questions in response to specific and unsettling events. Taking my cues from autobiographers and oral history informants, I emphasize childhood experiences across race lines and the reworking of those experiences in memory as fundamental to the interior process by which individuals came to think of themselves and others in distinctly racial terms. Etiquette, meanwhile, although sometimes learned as a set of discrete and specific rules, served in practice as a sort of script, guiding interracial encounters and providing a framework within which blacks and whites alike could understand their experiences, albeit from different perspectives.[6] White children might embrace the deference-demanding performance of racial etiquette more or less enthusiastically because it reinforced their own sense of worth. Black children might reject etiquette's lessons of inferiority but not its lessons of difference. As Charles Evers, brother of murdered Mississippi civil rights activist Medgar Evers, explained in his autobiography, "Our mothers began telling us about being black from the day we were born. The white folks weren't any better than we were, Momma said, but they sure thought they were"—which, Evers implied, amounted to much the same thing in practice. "We got it hammered into us to watch our step, to stay in our place, or to get off the street when a white woman passed."[7]

As Evers's remarks indicate, etiquette not only shaped children's experiential learning but was also an important medium for direct adult and peer instruction in racial matters. Both the admonitions of members of their own race and their interactions with people of the "opposite" race (in the South's predominantly biracial model)[8] taught children that they had to follow generally accepted rules of behavior or face the consequences. Depending (primarily) on a child's race, sex, class, and the nature of his or her infraction, these consequences could range from parental, peer, or community disapproval to verbal or physical abuse or even lynching. As a set of rules, etiquette gave individuals a supply of words, phrases, and gestures to use in interracial situations. Yet, like any script, etiquette was always subject to interpretation and improvisation: not only word choice but the precise meanings of the words and gestures individuals used depended on the situation and, most of all, on the people involved. Thus, a boy like Charles Evers might know to get off the sidewalk if an unfamiliar white female approached him, but he might also know that he was expected to speak, with an appropriate and personalized deference, to a white woman of his acquaintance, such as his mother's employer, Frances Gaines. If a woman such as Gaines, whom Evers described as seldom "cheerful" but "always cordial," chose to speak with unaccustomed cruelty or kindness—or if she responded or failed to respond to a word or gesture Evers intended as a challenge—then the nature of the relationship between woman and boy was subtly altered, at least until their next meeting. Although she remained the boss and Evers's mother remained the employee (and thus the material aspects of their power relationship were essentially fixed), Gaines would have been very unusual among white southerners if she did not also measure power and define her own whiteness in terms of black demonstrations of respect.[9] Etiquette, then, was both a set of rules, a script, and part of a *process*, the power-relations process by which a viable relationship between dominant white and subordinate black—and therefore "race" itself—was renegotiated on a day-to-day basis.[10]

Sources, Subjectivity, and Memory

This emphasis on negotiation and interaction has made it crucial for me to try to focus on blacks and whites equally, which is too rarely done in historical writing. Usually, it is blacks who get short shrift because of disparities in sources, but my focus on children has, ironically enough, made this one project in which the sources for African Americans are *better*—both richer and more plentiful—than the sources for whites. Unlike white adults, who generally took white supremacy for granted, black adults worried about how to teach their children about race and racism. Some even discussed their dilemma in articles and speeches that not only provide a window onto black child-rearing practices but also allow us to assess class differences and the extent to which a commitment to bourgeois "respectability" shaped blacks', especially educated or middle-class blacks', racial self-awareness. More valuable still are the accounts of black autobiographers and interviewees who almost invariably describe childhood experiences that taught them painful lessons about race, providing an enormous body of source material.[11] Whites, on the other hand, usually tell us little about the development of their racial sense of self unless they have become uncomfortable with their own privileged social status—that is, unless they are among those I refer to as white "dissenters" from white supremacy, many of whom have been usefully described as white racial "liberals" or "radicals" in other kinds of studies.[12]

Because I hope to capture the subjective experience of racial learning, retrospective sources such as autobiography and oral history have proved by far the richest sources available. Yet my heavy reliance on retrospective accounts also raises questions about memory and the reliability of autobiographical narratives. Like most historians, I view such issues pragmatically, taking my evidence where I can get it and doing my best to interpret it in intelligent ways. Nevertheless, working with autobiography has also encouraged me to take more than a merely pragmatic view. In essence, I accept that individuals telling their life stories are selective at best, that no one can remember past events with instant-replay accuracy, and that autobiographers sometimes even make things up. Whether these elements of fiction (short of a deliberate effort to mislead) make autobiographical accounts of racial learning any less "true" is, I insist, another matter. For what is an individual's sense of self *but* the reworking of his or her experiences in memory, and what is autobiographical writing but the reworking of memories in its most elaborated form? The fact that blacks and white dissenters so often stress the unforgettable quality of their racial learning experiences, as well as the pain and confusion that accompanied these dramatic moments, is further evidence of the link between the experiencing child and the remembering autobiographer. Thus, like a number of literary scholars in recent years, I try to gain a foothold on the middle ground that autobiography as a genre inevitably inhabits.[13]

The larger goals of this project are, however, the goals of a historian and one whose training reflects the burgeoning influence of gender analysis in the 1990s, particularly in its emphasis on questions of identity and connections between public and private spheres. Recognizing that race was something that each generation of southerners had to *learn*, this study revisits fundamental historical questions about continuity and change in the South and about the meanings of segregation within southern culture.

Forgotten Alternatives

I titled this introduction "Forgotten Alternatives" in the hope that I might respectfully redefine a key phrase from historian C. Vann Woodward's 1955 classic, *The Strange Career of Jim Crow*, and in so doing, suggest one of the ways in which focusing on children's racial learning can help us to revise our understanding of the past. Woodward used the phrase "forgotten alternatives" to encapsulate his argument that there was a period of variety and experimentation in southern race relations from the end of the Civil War to the early 1890s in which segregation was not always the rule. He made this argument about discontinuities in the southern past in part to show that the South *could change*. Writing with one eye fixed on the present—namely the breathless, uncertain moment immediately after the Supreme Court declared school segregation unconstitutional in *Brown v. Board of Education* in May 1954—Woodward insisted that segregation was not centuries-old and immutable largely because he wanted to offer hope to those black and white southerners who were beginning to challenge it—a group that, because of a dramatic conversion experience in the early 1950s, included Sarah Patton Boyle.[14] In October 1954, when Woodward presented his thesis about forgotten alternatives in the first of three lectures before a biracial audience at the University of Virginia in Charlottesville, Boyle, the wife of a University of Virginia professor, was drafting a magazine article titled "We Are Readier Than We Think" that would earn her national recognition as a civil rights advocate.[15]

Undoubtedly, Woodward's claims about forgotten alternatives made the most sense in their original setting, as directed to sympathetic listeners in an acceptably presentist forum. Nevertheless, as historian Howard N. Rabinowitz once observed, over the course of its many revisions, "*Strange Career* evolved from a lecture series meant for a local, predominately southern audience, which aimed to provide a historical foundation for hopes that desegregation would be peaceful and successful, into the most widely used survey text on the nature of American race relations since the Civil War."[16]

Even as *Strange Career* gained in popularity, many historians wrestled with the Woodward thesis. A number argued that such forgotten alternatives did not really exist and that, before segregation was written into southern law in the 1890s and early 1900s, *exclusion* was the norm, making segregation something of an improvement for blacks. Both Woodward and his critics were generally circumspect in their claims, recognizing that their disagreement was primarily over matters of law versus practice and making it clear that their analyses chiefly had to do with public accommodations such as theaters, restaurants, hotels, streetcars, and trains.[17] Nevertheless, the impact of their debate has been deep and, to some extent, engulfing. Questions about when, where, and in what forms segregation existed have helped to keep studies of postemancipation southern race relations focused almost exclusively on the public sphere. Only recently have historians begun to look at relations in private—and at connections between public and private—in the post–Civil War era, despite the fact that studies of the antebellum South have long focused on racial dynamics within the plantation household. Indeed, it has been almost twenty years since Elizabeth Fox-Genovese made a compelling case for understanding the white household as *the* unit of analysis for southern history, an observation that has borne comparatively little fruit for the period after 1865.[18]

Only by looking at private, as well as public, life can historians accurately assess continuity and change in southern race relations. By focusing on children's racial learning, I hope to move beyond long-standing debates about the origins of segregation and, indeed, beyond segregation as a singular topic of inquiry. As children's experiences show, segregation was only part of the story of late-nineteenth- and twentieth-century race relations. Or, as I tend to think of it, segregation was only part of "Jim Crow," the total experience of life, for both blacks and whites, in a society structured around racial inequality. Within that total experience, segregation, whether de jure or de facto, was important but not definitive. Racial discrimination and racial hierarchy took many forms. To understand what it was to live Jim Crow, we have to begin by thinking about the nature of race itself.

The Social Construction of Race

That race is "socially constructed" has become a commonplace among scholars. But, as historian Barbara J. Fields has recently lamented, precisely what this *means* is not always clear, particularly as *racism* and, more broadly, "power and the contest over it" become obscured behind ill-defined concepts such as "racial identity" and buried beneath a desire to attribute "agency," however limited it was in practice, to all parties. Fields's emphasis on the primacy of racism is well-founded, although her conclusion that race is "not identity as sense of self, but identification by others, peremptory and binding" seems to dismiss the extent to which identification by others often contributes to an individual's sense of self (and does not merely "nullify" it—a point considered below).[19] That race is a man-made distinction meant to secure and explain material and social inequalities comes into high relief when we consider that every child born into a society has to learn race anew, that every child begins life innocent of the very *idea* that there *are* different "races," much less the idea that "race" ought to matter in certain specific ways as an organizing principle for his or her society. Returning to Woodward's old stomping grounds from this starting point, we see that "forgotten alternatives" abound. The Jim Crow South simply taught its children to forget these alternatives at a very early age.

To be more precise, adult white southerners tried, consciously and unconsciously, to teach both black and white children to "forget" any possible alternatives to white supremacy at the same time they energetically *repressed alternatives* that actually arose in both the public and private spheres. The most familiar of the political alternatives to develop in the postemancipation South is the biracial Populist third-party movement, which appealed to hundreds of thousands of struggling farmers in both the South and the West in the 1890s and which has been the subject of numerous historical studies since its defeat at the turn of the twentieth century. As historian Lawrence C. Goodwyn recognized more than thirty years ago in a case study of Grimes County, Texas, violent political repression of the sort that destroyed the Populists in the South is almost inevitably accompanied by efforts to shape both individual consciousness and historical memory. White Democrats, organized into a local and all-too-appropriately-named White Man's Union, not only drove the Populists out of Grimes County at gunpoint in November 1900 but also succeeded over the next seventy years in supplanting any recollection of the Populist alternative among whites with a history shaped to their own flattering self-image. "In this white oral tradition the general events of 1900 are vividly recounted," wrote Goodwyn in 1971. "Specific events are, however, remembered selectively. The exodus of Negroes from the county is not part of this oral tradition, nor is the night riding of the White Man's Union or the assassination of the Negro Populist leaders." Instead, the White Man's Union, which had maintained its political dominance in the county into the 1950s, continued to enjoy "an uncontested reputation among Grimes County whites as a civic enterprise for governmental reform." Even the elderly niece of a prominent white Populist who had been a target of the Union's violence was able to "recall the racial unorthodoxy of Uncle Garrett" but unable to "participate in such activity herself" in response to the political questions of her own day.

The reason for this, Goodwyn argued, is that "more than a third party passed from Grimes County in 1900; in real political terms an idea died," in this case the idea of black political participation and rights. "A political party can survive electoral defeat, even continuing defeat, and remain a conveyor of ideas from one generation to the next," Goodwyn explained. "But it cannot survive the destruction of its constituency, for the party itself then dies, taking with it the possibility of transmitting its political concepts to those as yet unborn." Clearly, limiting subsequent generations' worldview by encouraging them to "forget" alternatives is a subtler form of political repression than shooting one's political opponents. But it is not a trivial form of repression, as the fact that the White Man's Union faced almost no white opposition, even in the narration of local history, for half a century after 1900 suggests. Here, it is worth thinking about the word "repression" in its psychological, as well as political, sense, for to repress successfully is to *forget* what one is repressing. Considering connections between public contestations over power and the private realm of individual consciousness and behavior helps to explain not only the absence of white counternarratives in Grimes County, but also the extent to which adult white southerners' efforts to inculcate white supremacy in their children could be unthinking and habitual, and not always calculated.[20]

Neither in a psychological nor in a political sense, however, is repression always successful. As Goodwyn was quick to point out, the *black* oral tradition in Grimes County was very different from the white one, with Populist heroes of both races and the exodus of black residents playing "a central role."[21] Similarly, white adults' efforts to make children forget alternatives to white supremacy were far more successful with white children than with black ones. Like black adults, black children resisted white domination in a variety of ways. Adolescents were particularly likely to express a hatred for whites and often wished their elders would do more to challenge Jim Crow. By the 1930s, a comparatively radical youth movement was taking shape within the mostly conservative National Association for the Advancement of Colored People (NAACP)—a foreshadowing of things to come almost thirty years later, when black college students would take the lead in the civil rights struggle and children as young as six would volunteer to march in Birmingham and other cities.[22]

Perhaps more surprising than black opposition is the fact that at least some *white* southerners questioned white supremacy when they were very young, allowing us fleeting glimpses of their early preference for treating at least some black people—usually caregivers or playmates—with a socially unacceptable degree of respect. Thus, while the idea of forgotten alternatives has little meaning for blacks, who never forgot their own innate humanity, it can be usefully redefined in relation to white southerners and the racial power relations that whites, as the region's dominant group, mostly controlled. Consonant with Woodward's core idea that things could have been different in the South, in my usage this phrase describes the socializing process by which individual white southerners learned, both directly from their parents and other white adults and indirectly from observing the nature of their society, to forget nonracist impulses in favor of conventional ideas about racial difference that made life in their communities make sense.

By the Age of Three or Four

In placing so much emphasis on a window of forgotten alternatives that, admittedly, closed for virtually all white southerners at a very early age, I am undoubtedly guilty of much the same kind of optimism that motivated Woodward back in 1954. Like him, I believe that history can have a forward-looking purpose. For how can we hope to see the eradication of racism in this country—a project that has progressed far too little in the half century since *Brown v. Board*—unless we *examine how* (rather than simply insisting that) racism is and always has been something people learn? Nevertheless, the notion that at least some young white southerners considered and then forgot alternatives to white supremacy is all the more problematic because historical sources show us very little of what those alternatives were. All that we can see is what adults taught and how children interacted with one another and with the world around them — and that almost exclusively from the perspective of adults either observing children or looking back on their own childhoods, often in highly crafted autobiographical narratives. Older children do leave historians some sources to work with, but white southerners' youthful writings are not particularly helpful in showing how they learned race because their learning took place at such an early age. By the time they had learned to write, they had also learned to think of white supremacy as natural, simply the way the world worked, no more worthy of comment than salt in the sea.[23]

In fact, recent research indicates that children today understand enough about race and racism to start practicing racially coded behaviors by the age of three or four. In *The First R: How Children Learn Race and Racism*, sociologists Debra Van Ausdale and Joe R. Feagin offer a strong challenge to conventional wisdom that sees young children as "too little" to think in racial terms, a view that has long been supported by theories of cognitive development put forth by Jean Piaget and others that depict preschool-age children as entirely egocentric and incapable of the social awareness that racial thinking requires. Most child-development research is severely limited, in Van Ausdale and Feagin's view, because it examines children's behavior only in the presence of adults. To see children interacting in their own social world, Van Ausdale spent almost a year as a participant-observer at a large, multiethnic preschool, making a point to divest herself as much as possible of adult authority so that the children would not censor themselves. The result was countless instances in which children allowed Van Ausdale to see them "doing race" — that is, noticing and reacting to differences of skin color and other physical features in both positive and negative ways. Although the children sometimes admired or showed unbiased interest in each others' differences, as the school's multicultural curriculum encouraged, they frequently drew distinctions based on race and ethnicity in what can only be described as power struggles over toys, playground equipment, art projects, and games of pretend. Many of the anecdotes Van Ausdale and Feagin record are similar to the everyday social dramas involving children that I analyze in the chapters that follow. Thus, *The First R* has provided welcome validation for my efforts to approach complex questions of identity and social interaction with the tools of a historian, even though I lack those of a developmental psychologist. Two of Van Ausdale and Feagin's conclusions seem particularly pertinent: that "children learn *by doing*, not just by parroting the views of adults" and that "interactive *play* and the experimental world of play are central."[24] Nevertheless, reading *The First R* has also made me all the more aware that the autobiographical and oral history sources from which most of my evidence is drawn cannot show everything. Few informants even claim to remember the earliest days of their childhoods, and most recount stories of racial learning that took place when they were at least six or seven years old, if not older. Thus, the most we can see is how children *continued* to work with racial concepts in their daily interactions and to learn race by doing so. But by the age of six or seven, these children, like the children Van Ausdale and Feagin studied, had already learned a great deal, and most white children had already started to forget any alternatives to white supremacy they may once have pondered.

The Hard Work of Hegemony and the Role of Segregation

Still, to say as I do above that the Jim Crow South "simply" taught its children to forget alternatives is somewhat misleading. Focusing on the socialization of children reveals how much *effort* it took for white southerners to maintain and perpetuate their racist culture. Such is always the case when a dominant group hopes to persuade—and not merely force—a less powerful people to accept their dominance. As George Lipsitz explains, "It is almost as if the ideological dogcatchers have to be sent out every morning to round up the ideological strays, only to be confronted by a new group of loose mutts the next day. Under those conditions, dominant groups can ill afford to assume their own society is wholly pacified, although of course it is in their interest to have others think that all opposition has been successfully precluded or contained."[25] Like other dominant groups in other contexts, whites in the South had to work hard, primarily to counter black resistance but also to co-opt all members of white society, including their own children. To be effective, their efforts also had to extend to all areas of life, including but also reaching far beyond the arena of formal politics that studies like Goodwyn's on the Populists have illuminated so well. An examination of what and how black and white southerners taught their children about race thus sheds new light on the southern past, largely because it broadens our focus to include the private sphere. If, as historians Jane Dailey, Glenda Gilmore, and Bryant Simon have argued, the story of the postemancipation South is one in which "black resistance, not white supremacy, was continuous, while white supremacy remodeled itself to meet any challenge," then this study suggests how many of those challenges were rooted in black family life and how much of that remodeling took place within white southern homes.[26] Whether enforced by law or dictated by custom, segregation is best understood as a public phenomenon. In private, white children learned—and black children learned to anticipate—a white supremacist outlook, a broad worldview (though one that varied in degrees of brutality) that encompassed the developing system of segregation and that inflected all relations between black and white, both in private and in public, with a white demand for deference, for a visible display of acceptance of a supposedly natural racial hierarchy rather than a mere observance of physical separation on the part of blacks. Thus, once we broaden our scope to look at what was taking place in white households and other private spaces, we see that questions about legal segregation, and about racial separation more generally, recede from the singular importance historians have accorded them. Meanwhile, the significance of day-to-day patterns of domination and subordination becomes increasingly clear.

Certainly, we should not underestimate the importance of changes in the southern landscape with the growth of cities and transportation networks and the spread of consumer culture. Nevertheless, it is important to realize that the laws and practices of racial separation that evolved to govern these new spaces were not the only stuff that race was made of. Instead, black and white children alike learned the individual and social meanings of race at home, through the sometimes subtle and sometimes direct instruction of parents and other same-race adults, and through interactions with racial "others," both adults and children, in kitchens, yards, and other spaces that were not subject to either de jure or de facto segregation.

While it is true that segregation eventually became, to many, the defining characteristic of southern culture, separation was never the only impulse among whites in the South, especially not in the late nineteenth century or among those who had experienced firsthand the clear hierarchy and fraught intimacies of the slave system. Even in the twentieth century, many whites, especially middle- and upper-class whites who prided themselves on their "noblesse oblige," desired intimate but demonstrably unequal relations of the sort that Sarah Patton Boyle described more than they desired separation from blacks per se. Social relations of this sort not only fit with their conceptions of a natural racial hierarchy and of themselves as benevolent superiors but were also *necessary*, since whites depended on blacks to work for them as servants, cooking their food, caring for their children, and performing many other physically intimate tasks. As historian Tera Hunter has written of turn-of-the-century Atlanta, segregation and domestic service "represented contradictory desires among urban whites striving to distance themselves from an 'inferior race,' but dependent on the very same people they despised to perform the most intimate labor in their homes."[27]

Segregation has seemed much more coherent and unitary in retrospect than it actually was in prospect, when it reflected white southerners' growing sense that greater separation between the races would be necessary to maintain white dominance. Especially after World War II, segregation became a sort of metonym for the broader realities of racial inequality in *America* and, as such, took on a broad meaning as an index of racial sentiments. This was inevitable, primarily because the expanding civil rights movement had to attack the Jim Crow system where it was most vulnerable to legislative and economic challenges—that is, at the level of laws and practices in public settings. Nevertheless, what the necessary tactics of the civil rights movement have meant for historians is that when we look back from a post–civil rights movement perspective, we see the significance of segregation writ large. However, when we want to ask questions about the development of racial identity among early-twentieth-century black and white southerners, we have to assess the importance of segregation not only from our perspective but also from *theirs*.

Looking forward from the past rather than backward from the present, we see a different picture, especially with regard to white southerners' intentions and desires. Far more than physical separation, white southerners wanted social distance. As Neil McMillen has argued, African Americans' "'place,' as whites defined it, was always more behavioral than spatial in nature.... Valuing hierarchy more than they feared propinquity, whites casually rubbed elbows with blacks in contexts that sometimes startled northerners. Yet the requirements of caste . . . were zealously enforced."[28] In short, given the choice between segregating an anonymous and mobile black population and "integrating" a black population that was familiar, friendly, servile, and devoted, most white southerners would have chosen "integration" every time.

But this was not the choice they had, a fact that became increasingly clear by the 1890s and early 1900s. The end of slavery had upset legal definitions of blacks' social status, while the devastation of the Civil War and the policies of Congressional Reconstruction had shaken the economic and political foundations of white power. Even more important, African Americans were not always agreeably docile and hardworking, nor did they always stay where whites wanted them to, matching labor to land. By the late nineteenth century, blacks were migrating to southern cities by the thousands and there finding new ways to make lives for themselves that were less circumscribed by white dominance, especially as it had been exercised in the largely face-to-face arrangements of the plantation, the small town, and the postbellum tenant farm. In response, whites had to find new means of social control that did not rely so heavily on personal knowledge or personal relationships with individual blacks. Segregation was one solution—indeed, one that had already proven effective in the North and in antebellum southern cities—and it was one that was particularly well suited to the new structures of the southern urban environment and to middle-class Americans' growing tendency to look to government authority to regulate social and economic aspects of life.[29]

Meanwhile, white southerners wrote nostalgically about knowable and lovable blacks, the supposed "good, old-time Negroes" from "before the War." Whites' "glorification of mammy" peaked "from about 1906 to 1912," notes historian Cheryl Thurber, and Grace Elizabeth Hale has argued that the same generation of white southerners who formalized segregation also romanticized interracial intimacy as an impossible ideal, to be experienced only "in an integrated island of time, childhood, and space, the white home."[30] This confluence of political and cultural events is important, especially if we recognize that white homes and white childhoods were not "islands" apart from the ebb and flow of racial politics; rather, what was happening in white homes and among white children were currents within that same tempestuous sea.

As a result, white southern children's racial learning was shaped, over time, both by their elders' craving for intimacy within a white-supremacist framework and by segregation. Perforce, both paternalistic and segregationist impulses shaped black children's racial learning as well. The impact of segregation grew deeper from one early-twentieth-century decade to the next, as younger generations of black and white southerners grew up further apart than their parents and grandparents had. But their greater separateness was only relative; blacks and whites still lived side by side and interacted according to traditional codes of racial etiquette, especially in the private sphere.

While there is much historical work yet to be done, it is clear that dynamics within southern homes did not change as quickly or as much in the late nineteenth and early twentieth centuries as the urbanizing, industrializing world around them (and even that world did not change with equal rapidity in all parts of the South). Although slavery had ended, many white children still grew up in households where blacks did most of the work and received little in the way of compensation or respect—even if they escaped sexual assault and physical abuse, neither of which ended with emancipation. Conversely, although blacks struggled to secure an inviolate domestic sphere, the vast majority of black children still grew up poor and were often hungry for the attention of their overworked parents. Like the children of slavery, they experienced the pain and confusion of watching their mothers, in particular, devote their time, their energy, and often their limited budget of good humor to other children, who also had more material comforts than they did.[31] Thus, any attempt to understand how black and white children came to think of themselves in racial terms must take into account the psychological costs of experiencing or witnessing abuse, of being neglected or being the cause of someone else's neglect.

Racial Identity and Relational Difference

Even more basic, such an effort has to consider how intimately *connected* black and white children's experiences were. In both adult racial teachings and the childhood memories of autobiographers and interviewees, the interdependence of black and white identities is clear. Black and white children came to understand themselves in relation to one another, both through their interactions and by assimilating the complicated lessons of their parents and other adults. While experiences on each side of the color line were also important, racial self-definition seems to have depended most on defining or being defined by racial "others." From infancy, black and white children learned about these "others" from stories, jokes, rumors, and other cultural narratives.[32] By the time they started school, most children had interacted with "others" at some point, and many had done so on an everyday basis either through play or work or fighting or as a result of the widespread presence of black household workers—and sometimes their children as well—in white homes.

The rules of racial etiquette also contributed to both black and white children's racial learning. Black children learned that following generally accepted conventions meant survival, albeit at the price of self-denigration. For many, playing by the rules became a self-conscious performance in which they "put one over on" or otherwise manipulated whites. Other black children, particularly those of educated, middle-class parents, learned to subsume the command performance of racial etiquette in a broader performance of personal dignity. The alternative etiquette of "respectability" their parents taught them was supposed to make the humiliations of Jim Crow etiquette easier to bear. Nevertheless, the penalties for failing to perform according to the rules remained ever in force, demanding that black children suppress (although not entirely "forget") their individual and contrary impulses in a process that inevitably shaped the children themselves.

White children learned to follow the rules of racial etiquette as well, in a process that was differently but no less thoroughly shaping. Demanding deference and using racial keywords to distance and subordinate blacks inscribed white southerners' fundamental lesson of white supremacy all the more firmly in white children's minds. Thus, while historians and other scholars have only recently begun "to move beyond the sense that women have more gender than other groups, that Blacks have more race, and that men have more class,"[33] one could instead argue that whites had a particularly *large* "amount" of race. This is because, for them, concepts of self emanating from within fit together so well with concepts of race emanating from without—concepts that whites were, of course, primarily responsible for creating and enforcing in the first place. Blacks, by contrast, spent much of their time trying to *minimize* the extent to which the social implications of race intruded upon their own and their children's emotional lives. Their self-consciousness was doubled, rather than redoubled or fortified, by their consciousness of the world around them. They experienced, to quote W. E. B. Du Bois's famous phrase, "two souls, two thoughts, two unreconciled strivings; two warring ideals in one dark body."[34]

Of course, any suggestion that whites had more race than blacks, or vice versa, is absurd in the absence of a definition of what "having race" means. While blacks (or women or poor people) may have been compelled to *experience* their race (or gender or class) more self-consciously, race (and gender and class) has always shaped the lives of all people in a given society to precisely the same extent, although in different ways. Thus, when we talk about racial identity, we have to account for at least two interconnecting levels: the level of individuals' subjective experience and the level of positioning, or what Elsa Barkley Brown has called "relational difference." As Barkley Brown has argued for the study of women's history, we need to recognize that white women and women of color "live different lives but white women live the lives they do in large part because women of color live the ones they do." Or, to put it another way, "being a woman is, in fact, not extractable from the context in which one is a woman—that is, race, class, time, and place."[35] Barkley Brown's insight holds true for men and for children of both sexes, as well as for women. The implication is that race operates continuously in all people's lives, whether or not any racial "others" are present and whether or not individuals are thinking about themselves in racial terms.

To suggest that racism, especially in the form of racial etiquette, shaped white children more profoundly than black children, then, is not to suggest that whites had "more race." Rather, it is to recognize that racial etiquette reinforced patterns of self-understanding for white children while it clashed with (but did not thoroughly "nullify") the aspirations and longings of blacks. Black children had strong incentives to resist Jim Crow in all its forms, including not only a desire to be treated with dignity and fairness but also black parents' and other black adults' oppositional teachings. Black southerners' "psychic horizons" may have been "dominated by Judge Lynch," as historian Jacquelyn Hall has written, but the "quality of black life in the region found expression not only in the statistics of violence" or in the rituals of racial etiquette but also in a "vital and sustaining culture."[36]

Although this book is about children, its first two chapters are mostly about adults. Chapter 1 surveys racial etiquette from slavery through the Great Depression, establishing the context and exploring the contours of the Jim Crow South. Chapter 2 examines adults' racial lessons. Looking first at whites, I note that the ideal of an innocent and sheltered childhood took hold in the South in the early twentieth century, although its spread was uneven, particularly among poorer and more rural white southerners who continued to rely on children's labor. Even as childhood became a special and protected time for an increasing number of white southerners, however, a surprising number of families seem to have felt no need to shield their children from the most brutal acts of racism, as the many white children who appear in lynching photographs attest. Children also witnessed the verbal and physical abuse of black domestic workers, much as the children of slaveholders had witnessed the abuse of slaves, and virtually all white southern children learned lessons in racial etiquette, most often from their mothers, who had primary responsibility for child rearing. Indeed, white southerners' autobiographies and oral histories make it clear that racial etiquette was the most common form of *direct* instruction that white children received in racial matters—an indication that teaching racial etiquette was also one of white women's chief forms of collusion in the maintenance of white supremacy.

Black families also taught lessons in etiquette, but often their emphasis was on an alternative etiquette of respectability that ran counter to the humiliating etiquette of Jim Crow. The second half of Chapter 2 picks up the theme of the sheltered childhood as it related to black southerners, exploring the ways in which an emergent black middle class tried to protect its children from the psychological damage of racism by teaching them to maintain a dignified public persona and, with it, their self-respect. To what extent poorer black families embraced this "politics of respectability" with regard to child rearing is a difficult question to answer. Middle-class blacks' desire to reform working-class black family life is evident in articles and speeches published in the black press and in other middle-class sources. But autobiography and oral history suggest that many working-class parents did teach "respectability" and that generational conflicts may have been equally as salient as class differences. Even elite black children often responded to discrimination with anger and tended to favor more straightforward and less patient approaches to combating racism than their parents advised.

That children have minds of their own is something historians too rarely consider. As Chapters 3 and 4 acknowledge, children also have their own social worlds somewhat apart (although never entirely separate) from the world of adults, and they learn just as much by interacting with one another as they learn at home or in the classroom. Chapter 3 focuses on black and white children's first encounters—first encounters not so much with each other as with the social meanings of racial difference. Recognizing the retrospective and highly mediated nature of my sources, I emphasize connections between memory, identity, and autobiographical narratives. I argue that individuals' sense of themselves as being black or white developed largely in response to everyday social dramas that were often scripted by racial etiquette and that were also sufficiently troubling in one way or another to be memorable and thus subject to perpetual reinterpretation throughout an individual's life. As literary critic Jennifer Fleischner has argued, a "compulsion to repeat" often underlies autobiographical writing.[37] It is in this repetition, more than in the "accuracy" of informants' memories, that we find the sense of self *shared* between the remembering adult and the experiencing child.

Chapter 4 pushes still further into children's own social world. One of the ironies of Jim Crow is that, because schools and churches were segregated, children's most meaningful experiences across the color line took place outside the spaces of formal learning and largely apart from adult supervision. Autobiography and oral history allow us to follow children into such interstitial spaces as yards, fields, and kitchens, where they played and fought and tried racial concepts on for size. Because they faced proscriptions and abuse, black children generally developed some understanding of race and racism at a very early age. White children, on the other hand, sometimes struggled to comprehend why black people, particularly beloved caregivers and playmates, were treated differently from whites. Although many seem to have embraced white supremacy quite early, other white children questioned race and racial etiquette, at least until they learned to stop asking questions.

Chapter 5 focuses on black and white adolescents. Here the emphasis is on anger and frustration among blacks and the importance of a developing youth culture among whites as both sexual maturation and increased participation in the worlds of work and schooling altered youths' social status and relationships. Somewhere between puberty and young adulthood, both blacks and whites seem to have reached a fuller understanding of their racial position and what it meant. Most whites completely "forgot" any alternatives to white supremacy they might once have considered. At best, they simply grew apart from black playmates and caregivers; at worst, they grew violent in efforts to assert themselves as racial superiors at an age when their claims to adulthood could not always hold up. Conversely, black adolescents had to come to terms with new kinds and degrees of racism, including vicious assaults on their emergent sexuality. By ending my study at adolescence, when many blacks seem to have been especially frustrated and confused about how best to live their lives in an oppressive society, I highlight the extent to which *age* needs to be factored into any analysis of black accommodation or resistance. A brief conclusion touches on this issue as I survey blacks' changing views on children's place in political struggles in an effort to highlight themes of continuity and change over time.

I *The Etiquette of Race Relations*

On a mid-September evening in 1898, Mrs. J. F. Taylor and Mrs. H. E. Mosley of Winston-Salem, North Carolina, went for a ride on their bicycles. Nearing a tobacco factory, they encountered a crowd of African American workers spilling onto the sidewalk at the end of their shift. "Mrs. Taylor was in front and determined that she would ride ahead anyway, so she brushed past the negroes," the Winston *Free Press* reported. One black woman "then got right in the middle of the path and Mrs. Mosley had to dismount from her wheel and roll it around the impudent negro wench, and all the impudent wenches laughed loudly and clapped their hands," the *Free Press* continued, adding that "such exasperating occurrences would not happen but for the fact that the negro party is in power in North Carolina." Blacks' success in gaining several dozen mostly lower-level political offices in the 1896 elections had supposedly emboldened "bad negroes to display their evil, impudent and mean natures." If white North Carolina newspapers were to be believed, blacks were becoming bolder all across the state that September, just a few weeks before the next statewide election. Newspapers reported all sorts of minor racial incidents, many of which involved white women out for a stroll or a breath of fresh air who were jostled, poked, swatted with umbrellas, and jeered by working-class black women they met on the street.

"What is going on here?" historian Glenda Gilmore asks. She suggests three possibilities. First, the stories might have been totally or partially made-up—"urban legends . . . intended to arouse white male voters" and make sure that the Democrats, with their rhetoric of white supremacy and plans for disfranchisement, regained control after the state's brief experiment with a biracial Republican-Populist "fusion" government. Second, white women might have been inspired by prevailing political bombast to report commonplace, but usually private, complaints. Third, these sidewalk tussles "may represent a departure from normal interaction; the stories may be at least partially true, and the laughter, poking, and physical isolation of white women by black women may constitute political actions using 'weapons of the weak.'"[1] This third possibility compels Gilmore and readers of her *Gender and Jim Crow* to examine these encounters as examples of working-class black women asserting their right to a public presence at a time when whites were moving to eliminate black male voters from the political arena. Bolstered by past successes, they challenged whites' expectations for deference in order to dramatize their opposition to any political arrangement that would privilege leisured white women while denying black women and men visibility and voice in southern society.

Especially since the publication of political scientist James C. Scott's *Weapons of the Weak* and *Domination and the Arts of Resistance*, historians such as Gilmore have paid considerably more attention to street-level wrangles between blacks and whites in the post–Civil War South than ever before. Although observers of the southern past had long been attuned to everyday forms of resistance practiced by slaves and, to a lesser extent, working-class African Americans, Scott and other theorists have encouraged a wide-ranging reexamination of such practices by recognizing that they were not merely individual expressions of frustration or recalcitrance but quintessentially political acts. In perhaps the clearest formulation of the argument, Scott describes the "public performance" demanded of workers, tenants, sharecroppers, serfs, and all others who are "subject to elaborate and systematic forms of social subordination." "With rare, but significant exceptions," he writes, "the public performance of the subordinate will, out of prudence, fear, and the desire to curry favor, be shaped to appeal to the expectations of the powerful." Behind this "public transcript," however, lies a "hidden transcript" crafted by subordinates themselves. Just as much a social performance as the performance of deference, this hidden transcript includes not only "back talk," often expressed in folklore, songs, and jokes, as well as behind-the-scenes conversation, but also a range of dissident practices such as theft, foot-dragging, and sabotage. Such talk and behavior is not simply about individuals blowing off steam, Scott argues. Instead, taken together, the hidden transcripts of an oppressed group comprise an "infrapolitics" that is essential to the development of organized political protest. The reiteration and elaboration of discontent among subordinates lays the foundation for more overt political acts.[2]

For historians interested in the political views and agency of men and women who left few written records, Scott's description of the hidden transcript has opened a wide range of speech and behavior to analysis. Thus, Gilmore can read between the lines of racist newspaper reports and understand working-class black women's verbal and physical battle for precedence on the sidewalk in the context of an electoral battle for control of the North Carolina statehouse. Similarly, Robin D. G. Kelley has applied Scott's concept of "infrapolitics" to his study of working-class black life in the mid-twentieth century to show "how seemingly innocuous, individualistic acts of survival and opposition shaped southern urban politics, workplace struggles, and the social order generally."[3] Meanwhile, interest in slave resistance burgeoned to such an extent in the 1990s that at least one scholar felt it necessary to remind a rising generation of African American and labor historians that "their preferred historical agents . . . got crushed in the nineteenth century, crushed by overwhelming material, institutional, and ideological power that no subaltern formation anywhere in the world could even begin to match."[4]

Such criticisms duly noted, analyses of black southerners' hidden transcripts have added a great deal to our understanding of southern history both before and after emancipation. Yet there is still much to learn by subjecting the *public* transcript of southern race relations to the same degree of scrutiny. Scott and other like-minded scholars have given us a model for examining not only the "weapons of the weak" but also the workings of culture and— once we acknowledge that children participated in both public and hidden transcripts—how culture is perpetuated from one generation to the next. Building on Scott's framework, we can write the history of late-nineteenth- and early-twentieth-century southern race relations as the story of how white southerners fought, with only partial success and against fierce opposition on the part of blacks, to undo the social, political, and economic changes wrought by the Civil War and Reconstruction and to shape a public transcript more to their liking. To do so required not only the subjugation of free black labor and the expulsion of blacks from electoral politics but also the reassertion of a code of domination and deference rooted in slavery—in short, racial etiquette.

This chapter traces the evolution of racial etiquette from slavery through emancipation and its aftermath and well into the twentieth century. I ask what the social code scripting interactions between blacks and whites was and what compelled blacks, in particular, to follow it. What were the relationships between etiquette and racial violence and etiquette and segregation? How does recognizing that racial etiquette shaped social relations both in private and in public (complicating black and white southerners' experience of segregation as a new, essentially public, and largely urban and small-town arrangement of racial power relations) allow us, by looking at racial etiquette, to understand the gendered nature of domination more clearly? While Chapter 2 highlights white women's roles in teaching racial etiquette to their children, in this chapter we see both white women and white men participating in everyday social dramas designed to keep blacks "in their place."

The Role of Racial Etiquette

The fact is that the sidewalk bumptiousness that was so prominent among the weapons of the weak was also among the many and various weapons of the powerful. As historian Jane Dailey writes of 1880s Virginia, whites' "urge for domination" often revealed itself "in small, routine, and seemingly insignificant ways, such as a calculated bump with a shoulder or an imperious demand for an 'explanation' when jostled on the street." Black and white southerners spoke the same language (although with definite class inflections within each racial group) when it came to what was and was not respectful behavior, and whites routinely withheld from blacks all forms of civility that might imply that they were equals. At the same time, whites demanded that blacks display not only civil but often servile behavior, to be manifested in a wide array of verbal and physical cues. The code could be complex and varied, but it outlined a fundamental pattern of white supremacy that both blacks and whites understood. As Dailey notes, it was "the convergence of black and white opinion on markers of status and face in the postwar urban South that turned public behavior into a zero-sum game where one person's gain was another's clear loss."[5] Whenever blacks rejected the command performance of deference—whenever whites lost the zero-sum game of racial etiquette—violence could and often did result. Because small and seemingly insignificant behaviors were not their only weapons, whites were almost always prepared to take the zero-sum game of domination and subordination to the next level.

If racial etiquette was important because breaches of etiquette resulted in violence, it was even more important because etiquette was *not* seriously breached most of the time. Violence was prevalent, and the possibility of violence was always in the back of black and white southerners' minds. But it was not always in the forefront of their consciousness, even if it was a lot closer to the forefront of consciousness for blacks, who had to fear for their safety, than for whites. From one moment to the next, racial etiquette scripted the daily performance of power relations that Scott defines as the public transcript. By acting, at least outwardly, within the limits of the code, blacks avoided verbal or physical assault and whites maintained a sense of dominance that was also rooted in material and institutional power. On a day-to-day level—and especially in the eyes of black and white children who could not so easily see or comprehend the laws and labor arrangements on which white power also rested—etiquette as practiced was the defining idiom of southern race relations. Indeed, the enactment of racial etiquette was how the race line was most often drawn.

As historian J. William Harris observes, despite white southerners' tendency to think of "races" as distinct and biologically determined, "it was not the presence of two races in the South that created a boundary between them, but the presence of a boundary that created two races."[6] The Civil War and its aftermath shook the legal and economic foundations of the boundary that had been built up over the generations of blacks' enslavement. With freedom, blacks gained not only new opportunities for economic and educational advancement but also a new legal and political identity. Congressional Reconstruction, and specifically the Fourteenth Amendment to the U.S. Constitution, ratified in 1868, brought citizenship, due process, and "the equal protection of the laws"—at least on paper. The ratification of the Fifteenth Amendment in 1870 strengthened voting rights for black men, and they would continue to exercise these rights, despite whites' violent opposition, for the rest of the nineteenth century. Only after southern Democrats implemented poll taxes and literacy and understanding tests in the 1890s and early 1900s was the black vote effectively eliminated.[7]

White southerners reasserted their economic dominance more quickly, especially after the federal government abandoned early promises of "forty acres and a mule" and left penniless ex-slaves and their offspring to work out their destiny as sharecroppers, laborers, and—increasingly as the nineteenth century wore into the twentieth—as migrants to southern and northern cities. This migration began within the South as soon as slavery ended, and booming "New South" cities such as Atlanta and Nashville saw sharp increases not only in the numbers but also in the percentages of blacks in their rapidly growing populations throughout the late nineteenth century.[8] Yet 90 percent of black Americans still lived in the South in 1917, and 75 percent of black southerners still lived in rural areas.[9] With mobilization for war providing jobs and the flow of European immigrants cut off, World War I opened a floodgate. Nearly half a million blacks left the South during the war years, a number roughly equivalent to the total number of black out-migrants in the previous four decades. Another 800,000 black southerners moved north in the 1920s, followed by almost 400,000 in the 1930s. Long known as the Great Migration, this population shift planted the seeds for tremendous changes in the nation as a whole by the late twentieth century. The immediacy of such changes, however, should not be overstated, especially not for the South, where, despite three decades of departures, nearly 80 percent of all African Americans still lived in 1940. That black southerners continued to face economic and political oppression, as well as the humiliations of racial etiquette and other hardships, is evident in the fact that another 1.5 million left the South in the 1940s, as opportunities opened up with World War II, and an equal number left in the 1950s, the decade that saw the southern civil rights movement take flight.[10]

Nevertheless, for all the hardships they faced, black men and women had grounds for considerable optimism as they looked ahead from 1865, and white southerners recovering from the Civil War's devastation had reason to feel that, if white supremacy was to be maintained—an absolute necessity, to their way of thinking—then they must act and act fast. "As racial subordination was reimposed in the long process of 'redeeming' the South, racial boundaries had to be drawn in new ways," writes Harris. "A taboo on sexual contact between black men and white women became central to that boundary. . . . Racial subordination also was continually recreated in the routine actions of the everyday world," where "racial etiquette and violence served to mark a new color line."[11]

In fact, what a look at racial etiquette before and after emancipation shows is that white southerners acted to redraw the color line in *culture* long before they were able to "redeem" the South in the areas of law and politics, which were more open to federal oversight. That whites acted as they did was only natural, given not only the force of custom but also their deeply held beliefs that blacks were inferior and must be kept in an appropriately low position within the social hierarchy. Putting blacks "in their place" by enforcing racial etiquette was, in fact, *more natural* from the point of view of most white southerners than segregating blacks and whites, especially by law, as whites would feel compelled to do by the turn of the twentieth century. Black and white southerners had lived in close proximity for hundreds of years and would largely continue to do so in rural areas, where nearly 85 percent of all southerners lived in 1900 and more than 60 percent remained in 1940.[12] Even in the region's developing cities and towns, where the supervision of agricultural work was unnecessary, whites still depended on black household workers to clean their houses, cook their food, and care for their children—all labors requiring intense physical intimacy—within the most private spaces of their homes. The code of racial etiquette was designed above all to create distance and hierarchy within such propinquity, and whites would continue to enforce it in conjunction with segregation laws and practices all the way up to the civil rights era. Had all black and white southerners followed the script of racial etiquette in all situations—had no one ever challenged the assumption that whites were superior and blacks were inferior as they all went about their daily business—white southerners would not have felt that segregation was necessary. Like the supposed "good old-time Negroes" whose disappearance white southerners so often lamented, blacks would have made themselves inconspicuous and ingratiating on streetcars and trains, and they would have stayed away from theaters and restaurants with a white clientele out of their own sense of inferiority and propriety. Fortunately, racial etiquette was an imperfect form of hegemony, as slavery had been and as, it turned out, segregation was also.[13] Nevertheless, we come closer to understanding the South's culture of white supremacy if we think of the enforcement of racial etiquette and the development of legal segregation as first and second steps in white southerners' attempt to create what they saw as a desirable public transcript.

Emancipation and the Etiquette of Slavery

To focus on whites' efforts to dictate the public transcript through racial etiquette is to write the history of postemancipation southern race relations in a way that white southerners would have understood. For many whites, the breakdown of customary social forms was one of the most visible and upsetting indicators of how great a change the Civil War had wrought. "It is hard to have to lay our loved ones in the grave, to have them fall by the thousands on the battle-field, to be stripped of everything," declared a white Savannah woman in February 1865, "but the hardest of all is nigger equality, and I won't submit to it."[14] A former slaveholder from central South Carolina concurred: "In our part of the State . . . the death of slavery is recognized, and made a basis of action by everybody," he informed northern journalist Whitelaw Reid. "But we don't believe that because the nigger is free he ought to be saucy. . . . He's helpless, and ignorant, and dependent, and the old masters will still control him."[15]

Blacks, on the other hand, found ways to resist white control. Many former slaves interpreted freedom to mean that they would no longer have to feign a grinning compliance or put up with the everyday humiliations that even comparatively well treated slaves had always had to bear. As one Georgia freedman expressed it, freedom meant taking "no more foolishness off of white folks."[16] Another ex-slave defined the difference between slavery and freedom in terms of the emotions that lay beneath the mask of compliance: "Don't hab me feelins hurt now. Used to hab me feelins hurt all de time. But don't hab em hurt now, no more." With the exodus of white southerners from the South Carolina Sea Islands where he lived, this elderly freedman could, in fact, escape old patterns of compulsion and subservience. Even his name changed with emancipation; known as "Scipio" under slavery, he became the respected "Dr. Crofts" in the eyes of his fellow ex-slaves.[17]

As historian Leon Litwack has argued, many former slaves tried to project (and protect) a new, more dignified self-image by practicing a new assertiveness. Some did so aggressively, like the freedman who cursed a white man named Powell for calling him "Uncle" when they met on the streets of Helena, Arkansas, in early 1865. When Powell protested that he had only meant to be "civil," the freedman replied angrily, "Call me Mister" and stormed out of sight.[18] Other ex-slaves incorporated new ideas about how they should be treated into older patterns of association. Well-known diarist Mary Chesnut recorded an elderly freedman's promise to watch over his former master: "When you'all had de power you was good to me, and I'll protect you now. No niggers nor Yankees shall touch you. If you want anything, call for Sambo. I mean, call for Mr. Samuel—that's my name now."[19] A Georgia freedwoman named Charity asserted her new status a bit more firmly, informing her former mistress that when she married Hamp, a field hand, she had become "Mrs. Tatom," while he was to be called "Mr. Sam Ampey Tatom." "All these changes are very sad to me," the ex-mistress, Eliza Frances Andrews, wrote in her diary. Although she considered Charity's pretensions "comic," she also understood her desire "to throw off [the] badge of servitude" by insisting on her new name and title. As Andrews saw it, Charity Tatom's assertiveness meant that the paternalistic intimacy of some master-slave relationships would be replaced by a cold distance between black and white. "There will soon be no more old mammies and daddies, no more old uncles and aunties," she wrote. "Instead of 'maum Judy' and 'uncle Jacob,' we shall have our 'Mrs. Ampey Tatoms,' and our 'Mr. Lewis Williamses.' The sweet ties that bound our old family servants to us will be broken and replaced with envy and ill-will."[20] Why the "sweet ties" could not be replaced with respect and equality is something Andrews apparently did not consider.

In any case, Andrews's prediction for the future was only half right: there would be plenty of envy and ill-will in the Reconstruction South, but there would not be any "Mr. Lewis Williams" and especially no "Mrs. Ampey Tatoms"—at least not in most white southerners' minds. Instead, whites acted immediately to inform African Americans that they might be free but they were definitely not equals, that the racial hierarchy of the antebellum South was still in place and was to be preserved in racial etiquette. Furthermore, the distinction between pedestaled white "ladies" and disrespected black "women" or "wenches" was to be particularly strong. Slaves had not been called "Mr." and "Mrs.," and whites were not going to grant freedmen and freedwomen these courtesies either. They would use "Aunt" and "Uncle" or "Mammy" and "Daddy" for esteemed elders as they had during slavery, but for other African Americans' first names, "Boy" and "Girl" would suffice, and "nigger" would become even more common than before.[21] In addition, whites would continue to enforce the well-defined code of behavior to which slaves had been subject.

Although details varied from place to place and from one situation to the next, the essentials of slave etiquette had long been clear. Slaves rarely sat and never kept a hat on in the presence of whites. They walked a few paces behind rather than beside their masters and mistresses. If they had occasion to go into town, they yielded the sidewalk to whites who met or overtook them, stepping completely out of the way and into the street if necessary to let white people pass. On meeting a white person, a slave tipped his hat or bowed her head or nodded but rarely maintained eye contact. Depending on their relationship, an enslaved black and a free white might also hug or kiss, an intimacy that antebellum observers made much of, even though scenes in which white children or adults fell into the arms of their devoted "mammies" must have been far less frequent than the reserved nods and formulaic courtesies expected of the majority of slaves.[22]

If whites sometimes accepted kisses from slaves, they did not eat with them under any circumstances, even if what they ate "came right out of the same frying pan." The food on his place was "all the same," as one Mississippi planter assured northerner Frederick Law Olmsted, "only [the slaves] ate in the kitchen and [the planter] ate in the [dining room] with the door open between them."[23] The separation of blacks and whites at mealtime, however minimal or artificial, was among the most strictly enforced rules of racial etiquette in the antebellum period, a reminder that, as historian John Kasson observes, "eating is a ritual activity, invested with special meaning, in all cultures."[24] In the South, the injunction against eating with blacks was closely related to taboos prohibiting interracial sex, as slaveholder Victoria Clayton suggested in her account of her passage north on a Mississippi riverboat in the mid-1850s. "There was only one thing to make me uncomfortable during my stay on this beautiful steamer," Clayton wrote, "and that was seeing the chambermaid, a neat-looking white woman, sit down to the table to take her meals in company with the black men who were waiters on the boat. I had never seen anything like it. We loved our black servants, but they always had their meals at a separate dining table. The idea of seeing a white woman sit down to the table with those black men was shocking to me."[25]

Most white southerners would have been equally shocked if a slave failed to address them politely. As perhaps the most obvious sign of their subordinate status, slaves used the titles "Master" and "Mistress" (pronounced in various ways) for whites who were known to them, "Boss" and "Captain," as well as "Sir" and "Ma'am," for those who were not. Names and titles have held a particular fascination for observers of racial etiquette. Sociologist Bertram Wilbur Doyle began his influential 1937 study, *The Etiquette of Race Relations in the South*, by focusing on slaves' common use of whites' Christian names along with the titles "Master" and "Miss." This practice made daily life on the plantation or within the household less formal, Doyle suggested, and allowed slaves to "distinguish subtle degrees of intimacy in their relations."[26] Certainly, slaves did use names and titles in a self-conscious and relational manner. Born a slave in Maryland, the great abolitionist Frederick Douglass described the contempt that he and fellow slaves felt for a weak and cowardly but mean plantation owner, adding that "we seldom called him 'master'; we generally called him 'Captain Auld,' and were hardly disposed to title him at all." This manipulation of racial etiquette had its effect on Auld and his more-respected wife, "Mrs. Lucretia." "I doubt not that our conduct had much to do with making [Auld] appear awkward, and of consequence fretful," Douglass wrote. "Our want of reverence for him must have perplexed him greatly. He wished to have us call him master, but lacked the firmness necessary to command us to do so. His wife used to insist upon our calling him so, but to no purpose."[27]

Clearly, the etiquette of slavery was a mode of communication, as well as a code of behavior. In addition to using names and titles in a manner that expressed their opinions, slaves could play upon whites' expectations for respectful submissiveness. Or they could manipulate codes of etiquette in ways that implicitly rejected whites' right to rule. Living up to expectations in form but not in substance, they could exasperate or outwit slaveholders and other whites while appearing humble and obedient. Peter Randolph, a Virginia slave who was manumitted upon the death of his owner, told the story of one such manipulation of etiquette. The owner of a slave named Pompey was preparing to fight a duel. "Pompey," he demanded, "how do I look?"

O, massa, mighty.

What do you mean by "mighty," Pompey?

Why, massa, you look noble.

What do you mean by "noble"?

Why, sar, you just look like one *lion*.

Why, Pompey, where have you ever seen a lion?

I see one down in yonder field the other day, massa.

Pompey, you foolish fellow, that was a *jackass*.

Was it, massa? Well you look just like him.

Randolph's story about Pompey was almost certainly embellished; yet other slaves' recollections suggest a similar deftness with language and social forms. A slave known as Faithful Jack told fellow slaves of his conversation with their dying master. "Farewell, massa!" he had said. "Pleasant journey: you soon be dere, massa—[it's] all de way down hill!" Autobiographer Lunsford Lane remembered a visit from a slave named Derby, whose owner was the North Carolina state treasurer. Derby had gone to the funeral of another state official and reported that the family of the deceased had been very pleased by his decision to put crepe on his hat in mourning. They "thought it evinced great consideration for the family and friends" and that "he deserved great praise." To Lane, however, Derby revealed that he "would be glad to have kept it on his hat until they were all as decently placed beneath the sod as Secretary White, if that would aid him in securing his freedom."[28] By maintaining a respectful demeanor and employing such deferential keywords as "massa," Derby, Pompey, and Faithful Jack all managed to speak their minds without sacrificing their bodies to the certain punishment that awaited slaves who were openly insolent.

Slaves who manipulated racial etiquette were, however, playing a dangerous game. To control one's emotions, much less one's eyes, face, hands, voice, and posture, was difficult, and the least sign of disrespect could instantly enrage many whites. Similarly, any spontaneous or uncontrolled response could bring down penalties for an individual or for the entire slave population. For this reason, slaves themselves usually followed the script of racial etiquette and often distanced themselves from those within the slave community who were inclined to make trouble.[29] They also taught their children to follow the code from a very early age.

Writing about the socialization of children under slavery, historian Wilma King emphasizes parents' efforts to teach submissiveness *and* self-esteem. "Enslaved parents viewed compliance with the deference ritual as a way of avoiding slavery's punitive arm," she writes; "however, they knew that it did not accurately represent their feelings. They juggled public behavior and private convictions without upsetting the routine established by whites." When this juggling act succeeded, it "embodied a major act of resistance and equipped children to defend themselves on the psychological battlefield."[30]

Nevertheless, many slaves' child-rearing practices centered around a strict discipline that could become excessive and brutal and that, in some children, must have engendered resentment rather than a recognition of parental love. Work routines that forced parents to leave their children constantly in the care of others complicated the situation a great deal. Exhausted, short on time, and certain that their children's lives depended on it, enslaved parents "beat children," as historian Nell Painter writes, "to make them regard obedience as an automatic component of their personal makeup that was necessary for survival in a cruel world, a world in which they were to be first and always submissive." In short, slave parents, like slaveholders, "beat slave children to make them into good slaves." Slave parents also taught children to suppress their anger at being beaten and encouraged them instead to feel guilt and shame at having to be punished for their own good. "The question regarding the neglect and physical abuse of slave children is not whether they took place," Painter concludes, "but rather, what they meant to the children and adults who experienced them. Did the whipping that was so central a part of child rearing and the enforcement of discipline among slaves affect them and their families as child abuse traumatizes twentieth-century victims?"[31] Certainly, those who were children when slavery ended remembered their parents as stern disciplinarians who seldom spared the rod in teaching them to be good workers and to practice "good manners," which meant "respect for and deference to parents and all adults, black and white."[32] The next few generations of black parents would be remembered in much the same way.

Thus, it was on pain of punishment that slaves learned to be—or at least to seem—agreeable and even cheerfully submissive in all of their dealings with whites. "Does a slave look dissatisfied? It is said, he has the devil in him, and it must be whipped out," Frederick Douglass wrote in his *Narrative*, suggesting how slaveholders continually reinforced the "good manners" that both they and slave parents had taught. "Does he speak loudly when spoken to by his master? Then he is getting high-minded, and should be taken down a button-hole lower." Violence could await even the slightest breach of racial etiquette, as Douglass made clear: "Does [a slave] forget to pull off his hat at the approach of a white person? Then he is wanting in reverence, and should be whipped for it. Does he ever venture to vindicate his conduct, when censured for it? Then he is guilty of impudence,—one of the greatest crimes of which a slave can be guilty. Does he ever venture to suggest a different mode of doing things from that pointed out by his master? He is indeed presumptuous, and getting above himself." Slaves could be whipped—or struck or shaken or cursed—for a "mere look, word, or motion," Douglass summarized, a "mistake, accident, or want of power."[33] It was violence and the threat of violence, overlaid by habit, that regulated blacks' behavior; whites' behavior, in turn, was regulated by a constant vigilance to how status was being conveyed through gesture, word, and tone.

The Role of Racial Violence

After emancipation, violence continued to enforce these patterns of everyday practice. Indeed, the treatment of free blacks in the antebellum South had already proven that freedom meant neither equality nor immunity from racial etiquette. Whites had an especially hard time maintaining dominance and control over free blacks in antebellum cities, where they could compete economically without having to depend on a white landlord or even a single white employer. "To compensate for their loss of mastery," Ira Berlin has argued, "urban whites tried to legislate the master's role by carefully codifying forms of racial deference often unspoken in the countryside." In Richmond, for example, a city ordinance imbued the etiquette of sidewalk deportment with the force of law. Any slave or free black "meeting, or overtaking, or being overtaken by a white person on the sidewalk shall pass on the outside; and if necessary to enable such a white person to pass, shall immediately get off the sidewalk," the law read, scripting black and white behavior in intricate detail. Other cities made it illegal for blacks to walk in central squares, smoke in public places, or carry canes (a "symbol of white authority").[34] Nor was "impudence" tolerated. Free blacks who challenged *any* white person's authority might find themselves in the position of Esther Fells, a free black woman of Petersburg, Virginia, who ran afoul of a white neighbor named Thomas Tucker in 1856. When Tucker complained about noise coming from Fells's home, Fells stood up to him. Tucker not only whipped her with "three cuts with a cowhide" but also had her carted off to jail. The mayor of Petersburg then sentenced her to fifteen more lashes "for being insolent to a white person."[35]

The only way free blacks could avoid such abuse, whether at the hands of private citizens or public officials or both, was to perform much the same show of humility required of slaves. Lunsford Lane might well admire the dissemblance that his friend Derby practiced in seeming to mourn for the dead North Carolina official, for he knew how important it was to maintain appearances. Even after he managed to buy his freedom, Lane "endeavored so to conduct [him]self as not to become obnoxious to the white inhabitants" of Raleigh, "knowing as [he] did their power, and their hostility to the colored people." He continued, "[I] made no display of the little property or money I possessed, but in every way . . . wore as much as possible the aspect of poverty." In addition, he went on, "[I] never appeared to be even so intelligent as I really was. This all colored people at the south, free and slaves, find it peculiarly necessary to their own comfort and safety to observe."[36] Even if they hid their property and intelligence, however, free blacks were often targets of harassment simply because they were at hand and vulnerable and because whites considered any black person who was not under the direct control of a master to be especially likely to challenge white dominance.[37]

Just as they thought it imperative to keep antebellum free blacks "in their place," white southerners met emancipation with a commitment to preserving racial etiquette. This commitment would outlast all efforts at Reconstruction on the part of the victorious North, and white southerners would be only slightly deterred by military rule. As Leon Litwack has shown, innumerable whites made it clear both in writing and in practice that "the need to maintain the traditional code regulating the relations between the races was now more urgent than ever before."[38] Some were even ready to kill over seemingly trivial matters. Journalist Whitelaw Reid met a Mississippi state legislator who claimed he had threatened to cut an ex-slave's throat because he entered a room without taking off his hat. "This Bowie-knife and pistol style of talk pervaded all the conversations" of ex-slaveholders "about their late affectionate bondsmen," Reid remarked. "Nothing less gunpowdery, it seemed, would serve to express their feelings."[39]

Any number of white southerners proved their commitment to racial etiquette in deed, as well as word. Reid went on to tell the story of a physician near Greenville, Mississippi, who was dissatisfied with the way a freedman in his employ had carried out his instructions for working his land. When confronted, the freedman said that he had received no such instructions. The doctor threatened to kill him on the spot if he dared dispute his word, but the freedman persisted. "Thereupon the doctor, without any other provocation being alleged, drew his revolver." The freedman ran, but the doctor pursued him, fired several times, and killed him. Only the intervention of the doctor's mother saved the dead man's wife from the same fate.[40]

Because federal troops were still in position at the time of the incident, the doctor was taken into custody and would stand trial for his crime. Other murderers escaped punishment altogether or, like another doctor in a widely known case from Rockbridge County, Virginia, were acquitted by sympathetic judges and all-white juries, despite the "black rule" that military Reconstruction had supposedly imposed.[41] "Nigger life's cheap now," white Tennesseans assured Reid, who had perhaps been surprised to learn that African Americans were being shot at the rate of a few a week in the back streets of Knoxville. "Nobody likes 'em enough to have any affair of the sort investigated; and when a white man feels aggrieved at anything a nigger's done, he just shoots him and puts an end to it." Public sentiment in Knoxville led Reid to believe that the freedmen "have more hope from Virginia Rebels than from East Tennessee Loyalists"; yet contemporary Virginia newspapers reported that even some of "the most respectable gentlemen" of the state were guilty of (if not punished for) such crimes.[42]

Wanton killings of this sort continued well beyond Reconstruction and the "redemption" of southern state governments by white southern Democrats in the 1870s. Indeed, perhaps as many as a quarter of the 4,715 lynchings known to have taken place in the South between 1882 and 1946 resulted from breaches of racial etiquette that were seldom crimes even after white southerners rewrote state and local laws in the early twentieth century to incorporate ever more detailed racial proscriptions. As antilynching activist Jessie Daniel Ames observed, white men lynched most readily when the victim had "offended that intangible something called 'racial superiority.'" Despite the chivalric myth of protecting white womanhood that white southerners created to justify their brutality, instances or even allegations of black-on-white rape ignited lynch mobs less often than some sense that blacks were getting "uppity" or out of place—for which rape was, of course, the ultimate symbol.[43]

Precisely how many black men and women died at the hands of whites intent on preserving racial etiquette is something historians can never know. Even less discernible is the far greater number who were whipped, beaten, struck, or verbally assaulted. As early-twentieth-century traveler Clifton Johnson noted, whites' "universal use of the term 'nigger'" was, in each instance, "equivalent to a kick," and no African American who came into contact with white southerners was spared. It was these much-abused survivors who shaped both African Americans' hidden transcripts and, in direct encounters with whites, the public transcript of postemancipation southern race relations. Their refusal to be at all times unmistakably submissive encouraged white violence and repression even as it challenged white supremacy. As Johnson recognized, fear—"superstition"—persuaded average white southerners "that it is not only the negro's due, but that it is necessary to administer these verbal kicks in order to avoid any possibility of his forgetting his inferiority."[44] By reasserting the etiquette of slavery, white southerners administered verbal and symbolic kicks with virtually every breath, look, and motion. Blacks, meanwhile, were supposed to respect, admire, even love their so-called superiors.

Change, Continuity, and Context

The code of racial etiquette that scripted daily life in the postemancipation South resembled the code of slavery in many ways, but it was also flexible enough to adapt as the region slowly modernized between Reconstruction and World War II. Blacks' new legal status and political participation during Reconstruction resulted in some significant, but short-lived, changes, evident in the fact that prominent black men, particularly political leaders, were accorded the courtesy title "Mr." in some white newspapers throughout the 1870s and 1880s.[45] Meanwhile, blacks won a more permanent victory in eliminating "Master" from the South's racial vocabulary—despite the fact that some white southerners wanted so badly to preserve this ultradeferential form of address that they required its use as a condition of postwar labor contracts.[46] Within a few years after 1865, "Boss" and "Captain," as well as "Mister" and "Sir," had replaced "Master," while "Ma'am" and "Miss" (used with either the first or last name) had replaced "Mistress" and "Missy." All of these terms proved acceptable to whites because they marked a clear status distinction that was made all the more apparent by the fact that whites continued to withhold the courtesy titles "Mr.," "Mrs.," and "Miss" from blacks. "Boss," "Captain," "Mister," "Sir," and "Ma'am" were also terms that slaves had used for white strangers and so were particularly appropriate whenever freedom meant moving away from the old plantation or neighborhood and forming new associations across race lines.

When African Americans adopted new titles for old associates, the significance of their choices was presumably greater. To call a former "Master" "Mister" implied a rejection of intimacy much like that Eliza Frances Andrews perceived when her former slave "Charity" informed her that she wanted to be called "Mrs. Tatom." Whites were keenly sensitive to blacks' use of names and titles and considered it a matter of pride if *any* black person continued to call them "Master" or "Mistress" after freedom. In Natchez, Mississippi, Whitelaw Reid met a former slaveholder who boasted of her "little Confederate nigger," a child whose parents had been unable to coax her away from the white household where she had apparently been raised. "Did you notice that she called me 'Missey,' just now?" the white woman asked Reid with obvious satisfaction. "All the niggers have been trying to break her of that, but they can't. They tell her to call me Miss Lizzie, but she says 'she may be your Miss Lizzie, but she's my Missey.'" When the child made a scene in church by getting up from the segregated black seating in order to "sit with my Missey," whites in the congregation were envious: "You should have seen everybody's head turning to see who it was, in these sorrowful times, that was still fortunate enough to be called Missey!"[47] This Natchez woman's pride in the child's loyalty should not, however, obscure the real message in her story: neither she nor any of the other whites in her neighborhood had been spared the awful realization that their slaves did not love and respect them as much as they had assumed. All of her former slaves except one child were distancing themselves from her through a polite but unloving word choice, and they were teaching their children to eschew old titles like "Missy" and adopt new social forms. Less than a year had passed since the end of the Civil War and already her relations with African Americans were changing. Chances were that she would not be able to keep her "little Confederate" for long.

Even as they dropped "Master" and "Missy," however, African Americans found the evolving racial etiquette of the postemancipation South almost as constraining as the code of slavery. They still had to be careful of what they said, how they moved, where they rested their eyes. Moreover, while the old rules of deference were still in force, the new circumstances in which they would play out over the next several decades were more complicated than ever before, especially in the South's growing towns and cities where African Americans had to deal with a wider range of whites in a wider variety of situations than most rural blacks, slave or free, had ever known. That a sharecropper must go to his landlord with hat in hand was, in most cases, obvious, but must a prominent black leader take off his hat to talk with a white business associate on the street? Apparently so, as a former state legislator found out one day in Knoxville, Tennessee, in 1880, when a white real estate agent knocked off his hat with a walking stick. As a testament to the new complexity of social relationships (and to his own self-control), the ex-legislator simply picked up his hat and kept talking, finishing the business that, in a postemancipation world, blacks and whites now had to conduct.[48]

When, how, and how forcefully white southerners would insist on demonstrations of humility was a matter of constant concern for African Americans. Would it be enough for a black man buying farm equipment or a black

Plantation owner with black child, Aldridge Plantation, Mississippi, June 1937. That a share-cropper must approach his landlord with hat in hand was obvious. Whites' expectations of black children were far less clear. (Photograph by Dorothea Lange. Courtesy of the Library of Congress, Prints and Photographs Division, FSA-OWI Collection, LC-USF34-017431-E.)

woman purchasing cloth in a dry goods store to be respectful and polite, or must he or she endure insults or engage in some further ritual of obsequiousness? There was simply no way to know. Some rules, such as those governing the use of courtesy titles, were clear and straightforward, but many aspects of racial etiquette were murkier, subject to variation from place to place and even person to person. Much depended on the situation and the mood, as well as the personality, of each white individual a black person encountered. Some African Americans took no chances. As Neil McMillen writes, black timber workers in the Piney Woods of Mississippi joked about cautious black customers requesting "Mr. Prince Albert" tobacco from white storekeepers.[49] South Carolina educator Benjamin Mays remembered "seeing Negroes go to the back door of a white man's house even when the white people were sitting on the front porch."[50] In a Depression-era interview, one ex-slave described with particular eloquence (despite the transcriber's use of dialect) the stress that resulted from never knowing quite how whites would behave or what the consequences of one's actions, intentional or unintentional, might be. According to Sarah Fitzpatrick, a black person living in the South was "al'ays scaid dat sump'in gonna hap'en all de time; scaid he gwin butt into some white fo'ks an' have trouble, al'ays scaid ya' gwin do sump'in 'rong an' have de white fo'ks beat'cha up." Black southerners lived "under de white man's law," Fitzpatrick concluded, "dat's what keeps him dis'sad'isfied, an' nuverous all de time."[51]

Fitzpatrick's use of the pronouns "he" and "him," although generic in this case, was particularly apropos given the gendered nature of white violence. Certainly, black women who angered whites sometimes suffered greatly as a consequence. Black novelist William Wells Brown recounted an incident in Huntingdon, Tennessee, in 1880 in which a young black teacher, Miss Florence Hayes, accidentally bumped into a white woman named Warren. Because she was unsatisfied by Hayes's profuse apologies, her husband, John Warren, whom Brown described as a "two-fisted, coarse, rough, uncouth ex-slaveholder," went to Hayes's home, "seized the young lady by the hair, and began beating her with his fist, and kicking her with his heavy boots" until she lost consciousness. Hayes was so badly injured that she had to return to her parents' home in Nashville to recuperate for several weeks. Meanwhile, the white Huntingdon *Vindicator* described Warren as a "gentleman" and advised "white men everywhere to *stand up for their rights*" as he had.[52]

Had Florence Hayes been a man, John Warren might not have been satisfied with a beating. Black men had to be especially careful, especially around white women, lest they be accused of sexual impropriety in addition to "uppi-tiness," which whites found more threatening in black men than black women in any case. White southerners' intolerance for any sign of sexual aggressiveness on the part of black men was, of course, abundantly obvious in events such as the Atlanta race riot of 1906—a long weekend of open warfare in which thousands of white men and boys, stirred up by race-baiting gubernatorial candidates, then enraged by false but sensational newspaper reports of a series of black-on-white rapes, attacked blacks on the street and laid waste to black neighborhoods. Among the South's worst racial atrocities, the Atlanta massacre resulted in the deaths of at least twenty-five blacks and one white (and possibly many more of both races; official estimates were "notoriously low"), as well as hundreds of injuries and arrests (mostly of blacks trying to defend themselves) and the departure of more than a thousand black residents from the city.[53] In addition to such stark reminders, there were the suddenly-felt dangers inherent in any encounter, which black men had to assess as quickly as possible from looks, gestures, and other minutiae. Investigating race relations in Atlanta after the riot, Ray Stannard Baker spoke to a white woman who, like John Warren's wife, considered an accidental bump on the street significant, although for a very different reason. She sympathized with the young black man who had brushed against her shoulder as he hurried out of a building and turned onto the sidewalk. When the young man looked back to see whom he had bumped, she explained, "such a look of abject terror and fear came into his face as I hope never again to see on a human countenance. He knew what it meant if I was frightened, called for help, and accused him of insulting or attacking me. He stood still a moment, then turned and ran down the street, dodging into the first alley he came to."[54]

By the turn of the twentieth century, contact between black men and white women had become more limited and constrained than ever before as white men used white women's need for "protection" from sexual assault to justify not only riots like the one in Atlanta but also lynching and disfranchisement. Meanwhile, black men learned prudence as a matter of survival. Alabaman Ned Cobb remembered what it was like to try to collect on a debt. All he wanted was for the white woman in question to chop cotton on his farm as she had agreed to do when he gave her a gallon of cane syrup on credit. Yet, as he sought her at her home, he recalled, "I thought to myself: it just wasn't allowed for a man of my race to mess with a white girl or white woman, and I must consider what would happen if somebody told somethin on me—just like playin with the screws on my coffin." In the end, Cobb wrote off the debt, explaining, "[I]f I'd a kept a runnin over there, no way of knowin what'd been told on me. A colored man got to be scared to hang around a white lady's house thataway. It's dangerous as the devil"[55]—more dangerous by far than casual, or even sexual, contact between white women and black men had been under slavery, when such unions, though not officially sanctioned, had often gone unpunished.[56]

Like the strengthened taboo against sex between white women and black men, taboos against eating and drinking with blacks remained strong in the postemancipation South and, for many white southerners, became deeply ingrained. "If anything would make me kill my children, it would be the possibility that niggers might sometime eat at the same table and associate with them as equals," one woman told Clifton Johnson in 1904.[57] Yet most whites were accustomed to eating food prepared by black hands—a point African Americans made frequently to highlight the hypocrisies of racial etiquette.[58] In addition, in rural areas and especially among those old enough to have experienced slavery, relations between blacks and whites were at times remarkably intimate and included much sharing of food. Ex-slaveholder Victoria Clayton, who had been shocked to see the white chambermaid eat with the black waiters on a Mississippi riverboat, was deeply pleased by the fact that her former cook, Nancy, invited her and her family to dinner frequently after the war. Nancy was a better cook than she was, and her sensitivity to racial etiquette was especially gratifying. She "never for one moment thought of sitting down to the table with 'Master's' folks." Instead, Nancy and her son waited on the Claytons until they had finished eating, then sat down to their own formal dinner with Nancy's husband after the white family had retired to the black family's parlor.[59]

Among poorer whites and blacks, racial distinctions might be drawn with less formality, but they were virtually always drawn. Blacks ate in the kitchen or on the back porch, or they ate after whites had finished. Thus, when some whites did eat at the same table with blacks, it was a practice worthy of comment. Interviewed during the Great Depression, fourteen-year-old Erma Cartwright of Johnston County, North Carolina, suggested just how complex individual relationships among poor rural southerners could be: "White people around here are real nice. . . . They come to the house, sit down and eat with you and are just as nice as can be. One lady comes over here every day. . . . She sits out here and talks to mama most of the day and they sew. Sometimes her husband has to go away overnight, and if she sees a storm coming up she brings the little girl and comes over here and gets right in the bed with any of us and stays all night. . . . When her husband comes home, if she isn't home he comes right up here, 'cause he says he knows just where she'll be."[60] Clearly, some rural white southerners defied racial etiquette when it was in their interests to do so; yet one has to wonder how even this white North Carolina family would have reacted had a member of Cartwright's family gone over to *their* house and gotten into bed.

In cities and towns, white newspaper editors and other public figures encouraged a stricter observance of racial etiquette and frequently chastised whites, especially working-class whites, for crossing race lines. Around 1910, a White Springs, Florida, journalist recorded his disgust at seeing two apparently white couples eating in a black restaurant near the train station. "If a Negro went into a white restaurant in our town and sat at a table and ordered a meal our citizens would want to lynch him, or he would be arrested and a heavy fine imposed upon him. The same should be done to a white person that would go into a Negro restaurant and sit at a table and eat a meal." Whether or not restaurants were segregated by law, this writer implied, racial etiquette ought to keep *both* black and white southerners in their places, which, at mealtime, were far apart.[61]

As racial etiquette adapted to fit new urban environments, strict separation was not, however, always the rule. African Americans could not sit down for a meal at a department store lunch counter or enjoy a Coke at a drugstore soda fountain, yet they were more than welcome to buy anything else these stores had to offer. They could even buy food and drinks as long as they consumed them outside and stood rather than sat as they waited for their orders to be filled.[62] Segregation remained far from complete in the South's ever-expanding commercial spaces for the simple reason that white merchants wanted black dollars. In competitive markets, their desire for black customers was sometimes strong enough to make them offer polite, if not entirely color-blind, service. Thus, more than any other activity, shopping brought blacks and whites together in public places in ways that challenged not only the principle of separation but, at times, the etiquette of domination and subordination itself.

White sellers were most likely to treat black buyers politely in urban settings and least likely to do so in rural areas. Although country stores were sites of racial mixing, they allowed for far less social promiscuity than large department stores or city streets. Instead, storekeepers exercised considerable authority over their customers, most of whom they knew and many of whom also knew each other. Unlike their urban counterparts, country merchants faced little or no competition, especially before mail-order catalogs and rural free delivery became available at the turn of the twentieth century.

Store owners not only decided what to sell to whom but often held crop-liens or played other financial roles, making them powerful figures in the lives of black and white southerners alike.[63]

In both rural and urban areas, white clerks and customers employed various means to demonstrate their sense of superiority over blacks. Writing in the 1930s, sociologists Allison Davis, Burleigh Gardner, and Mary Gardner summarized whites' expectations: "The behavior of both Negroes and white people must be such as to indicate that the two are socially distinct and that the Negro is subordinate. . . . In places of business the Negro should stand back and wait until the white has been served before receiving any attention, and in entering and leaving he should not precede a white but should stand back and hold the door for him."[64] The sociologists' word choice is revealing. African Americans were supposed *to wait to receive* whites' attention, suggesting just how meekly passive whites wanted them to be.

In addition to serving white customers first, store clerks seldom called black men and women "Sir" or "Ma'am" and often refused to let blacks, particularly black women, try on clothes, shoes, or hats. "Sometimes the way they greeted you when you went into a store was embarrassing," an Atlanta physician remembered. "Some would call you nigger. Some would say: How to do boy! . . . Oh, it would make you angry but after awhile you'd get used to it and go about your business."[65] In Atlanta and other cities, African Americans often responded to such treatment by going into business for themselves or seeking out other merchants, including those who were themselves members of ethnic minorities, who offered more civil treatment. As Jewish community activist Josephine Joel Heyman recalled, her father's Bass Dry Goods Co. on West Mitchell Street in Atlanta catered to its poor black clientele not only by underselling the competition by a few pennies per item but by calling black customers "Mr." and "Mrs."[66]

For some, though certainly not all, white businessmen, concern for the bottom line could similarly outweigh a commitment to observing racial etiquette in all its details. In stores that depended on black customers, clerks often served shoppers in order of their arrival and treated blacks with relative politeness. Some also let African Americans try on clothing, although they frequently made distinctions based on class. Some department stores "in competition with others, did let Black women try on items," a black minister from Atlanta recalled. "The better class of Negroes who had charge accounts at these stores didn't have enough trouble to amount to anything, while others did." An Atlanta pharmacist concurred, suggesting that "some of our affluent and well-known people, such as minister's and doctor's wives, didn't feel discrimination as acutely" as the "average Black person."[67] Queried in the midst of the Great Depression, a black professional in Richmond, Virginia, suggested that intense economic competition could make white merchants civil even to poorer African Americans. "Of course, none of them want to give you the same service they give white people," he noted, "but competition for Negro trade is so keen that every store has to make some pretense of fair play."[68]

Still, class was an important factor shaping individual performances of racial etiquette. Even beyond the commercial realm, white southerners often made concessions for African American doctors, lawyers, and other professionals. While they jealously guarded the titles "Mr.," "Mrs.," and "Miss" for white people, most had no difficulty calling black physicians and dentists "Doctor" and black (male) educators "Professor." Famous black educator Booker T. Washington remarked upon "the number of people who have come to shake hands with me after an address, who say that this is the first time they have ever called a Negro 'Mister.'"[69] After he was awarded an honorary doctorate, white southerners no longer had to make this difficult choice. "Now I admire Booker Washington," a white man assured Ray Stannard Baker during his trip through the South after the Atlanta riot. "I regard him as a great man, and yet I couldn't call him Mr. Washington. We were all in a quandary until a doctor's degree was given him. That saved our lives! We all call him 'Dr.' Washington now." Baker's own observations confirmed this: "Sure enough!" he wrote. "I don't think I have heard him called Mr. Washington since I came down here. It is always 'Dr.' or just 'Booker.' They are ready to call a Negro 'Professor' or 'Bishop' or 'The Reverend'—but not 'Mr.'"[70] Indeed, the editors of the white *Augusta Chronicle* were even ready to print a section of "Negro News," but they were not prepared to flout racial etiquette. Instead, they hit upon a compromise, describing the prominent black men and women of Augusta as "Messieurs, Mesdames, and Mademoiselles." As Bertram Wilbur Doyle observed, "no justification for employing the French forms of address was perhaps deemed necessary under the circumstances."[71]

Although a respect for education and refinement led some white southerners to soften *some* of the blows of racial etiquette, few were willing to make concessions in all areas. A wave of resentment swept the South after Theodore Roosevelt invited Booker T. Washington to dine at the White House in October 1901. "The South never got a worse shock than that," a white southern man informed New England traveler Clifton Johnson. "Up to then we'd thought a heap of Roosevelt down hyar. Why, we'd named all our dogs after him and members of his family; but we've changed those dogs' names since that dinner."[72] As historian Joel Williamson notes, Roosevelt himself came to rue the lunchtime meeting as a mistake and found that some white southerners never forgave him.[73]

Whites also had little patience for blacks who treated other blacks with the same respect and politeness that whites demanded for themselves. When "one of your servants announces that a 'gentleman' or a 'lady' want to see you . . . it means a negro man or woman," a white North Carolinian fumed. "But if, instead, they [say] simply 'man' or 'woman,' . . . that always designates a white person, not a black. Evidently, the intent is to assert that the black is not only the equal, but the superior of the white; and tho' I have overheard this sort of thing a thousand times, I cannot recall a single instance in which the servant was reprimanded."[74] This self-styled white "gentleman" was right in thinking that African American household workers employed courtesy titles strategically, but he was wrong when he suggested that they could always do so without repercussions. "My master would kill any-body who called *any-body* but a white person Missis," one Virginia freedwoman flatly declared, describing the postwar period.[75] Such attitudes were still strong in the summer of 1908, when Christopher Brooks of Wilmington, North Carolina, found himself committed to the workhouse for repeatedly using the titles "Mr.," "Mrs.," and "Miss" for other African Americans.[76] Thirty years later, in July 1939, black household worker Eloise Blake was found guilty of disorderly conduct and fined fifteen dollars by a Columbia, South Carolina, court after a white woman named Hadden had her arrested for asking to speak to "Mrs. Pauline Clay"—Hadden's maid—on the telephone.[77] And in Greene County, Georgia, in the early 1940s, *white* sociologist Arthur Raper was brought up before a grand jury for precisely the same offense: using courtesy titles for blacks.[78]

Whites' insistence that blacks not be called "Mr." and "Mrs." paralleled their resentment of black progress, especially any sign of economic gains. Complaints about blacks' "loud" and "extravagant" clothing fit this pattern, as did whites' ridicule of the railroad excursions and other leisure activities blacks sometimes enjoyed.[79] "Really, certain whites didn't like to think you had leisure to do anything but pick cotton and work in the field," South Carolinian Mamie Garvin Fields recalled. "Just generally, if you were black, you were not supposed to have either time or money, and if you did, you ought not to show it."[80] As Leon Litwack notes, blacks who purchased automobiles in the early twentieth century became targets for special abuse. In one case, white residents of a small town in Georgia forced a prosperous black farmer and his daughter to get out of their car at gunpoint, then set the car ablaze. In another case, an Abbeville, South Carolina, mob confronted a black resident who was driving with his wife, mother, and children, then shot him repeatedly as he tried to escape.[81]

Cars, however, were merely a potent new signifier in the decades-old game of domination and subordination—a deadly "zero-sum game," to use Jane Dailey's term. "There was a day when the average Negro householder was afraid to paint his house and fix up his premises because of the attitude of some white man," Mississippi teacher Laurence Jones recalled. An African American "did not always feel as safe in a neat cottage with attractive surroundings as he did in a tumbling-down shack."[82] The same was true of other aspects of racial etiquette. As much as they detested the performance of humility, African Americans could never feel safe—because they were not safe—when they set aside the scripts that racial etiquette supplied.

Hidden Transcripts and the Origins of Segregation

Like the discipline of slavery, the murders and assaults of the postemancipation South convinced most African Americans to follow racial etiquette most of the time. They accommodated whites' expectations at least enough to stay alive in a hair-trigger environment, an environment in which black life remained cheap and unprotected despite economic development and other changes in the region between Reconstruction and World War II. But accommodation was not the same thing as acquiescence. Indeed, it was probably the mental gymnastics they had to go through to anticipate whites' behavior that allowed so many blacks to perceive with such clarity the fact that racial hierarchies were not natural but constructed through an elaborate and deadly social game.

One of Richard Wright's many anecdotes about the "ethics of living Jim Crow" vividly illustrates how energetically blacks' minds had to work to control their faces and bodies even as they inwardly scorned the performance of racial etiquette as a charade. Explaining that it was a southern custom for all men—but especially black men—to take off their hats on entering an elevator, Wright recalled one day when he was unable to do so because his hands were full. "I was forced to ride with my hat on. Two white men stared at me coldly. Then one of them very kindly lifted my hat and placed it upon my armful of packages." Confined in a cramped space with two men who were clearly on the lookout for the least sign of "uppitiness," Wright had to decide instantly how to respond. "Now the most accepted response for a Negro to make under such circumstances is to look at the white man out of the corner of his eye and grin. To have said: 'Thank you!' would have made the white man *think* that you *thought* you were receiving from him a personal service. For such an act I have seen Negroes take a blow in the mouth." Considering the "accepted response" too servile and virtually any other response too dangerous, Wright "hit upon an acceptable course of action which fell safely between these two poles." By pretending that he was losing his grip on his packages, he was able to avoid having to respond to the white man's gesture at all and, "in spite of adverse circumstances, salvaged a slender shred of personal pride."[83] How individual blacks would maintain their self-respect in encounters with white southerners was a matter of moment-by-moment calculation and required constant mental and physical efforts of this sort.

Although we can make some educated guesses about the "hidden transcripts" that black and white southerners brought into their day-to-day interactions, it is extremely difficult to recapture the full psychological complexity of the kinds of performances—by both blacks and whites—that Richard Wright's ride in the elevator required. Analyzing etiquette on a social, rather than an individual, level is far easier. That white southerners enforced racial etiquette as a means of social control is obvious. It is also clear that most southerners, white and black, considered etiquette a better form of social control than the violence that always lay just beneath its surface.

As a shared language for designating status, racial etiquette allowed social relations to proceed relatively smoothly. This was especially true and especially important in the workplaces, including white households, where blacks and whites met every day. When followed, the codes of racial etiquette resulted in maximum productivity and minimum white guilt as whites convinced themselves not only that racial hierarchies were natural but that "good Negroes" accepted their lower status and hence felt more or less the same way whites did about the daily performances of domination and deference whites required. As Sarah Patton Boyle recalled, a standard (though rather genteel) white answer to the question of whether a respected African American ought not to be accorded more dignified treatment was "Oh, no . . . It would embarrass him to death."[84]

For their part, black southerners were far less concerned than whites about maximizing the profits of white-owned farms and businesses and improving the efficiency and quality of life within white homes. More persuasive to them was the fact that following racial etiquette resulted in fewer beaten, burned, and mutilated black bodies than did openly challenging it. As historian Eugene Genovese has written with regard to slavery, "Only those who romanticize—and therefore do not respect—the laboring classes would fail to understand their deep commitment to 'law and order.' Life is difficult enough without added uncertainty and 'confusion.' Even an oppressive and unjust order is better than none."[85] Most blacks considered it best to avoid whites as much as possible and observe racial etiquette when necessary. They might admire those who could successfully manipulate etiquette—those like Mississippian Mark Thomas who "used a lot of psychology on white people," who *"yes sirred"* and *"no sirred"* and thereby "played [whites] for fools."[86] But black southerners had no respect for those whose behavior was too servile, and they lived in fear lest they or their loved ones pay the price for some other African American who was too reckless. Taking the middle ground—anticipating whites' behavior, adapting to whites' expectations, following racial etiquette—was always the safest course.

Nevertheless, it is easy to overestimate how far this "safety first" thinking went. Bertram Wilbur Doyle did so in his 1937 study, which historians would continue to cite half a century later. Influenced by his mentor, University of Chicago sociologist Robert E. Park, Doyle saw accommodation as a temporary stage in a "race relations cycle" that inevitably, if gradually, led to assimilation. However, unlike Park, who believed that conflict was necessary to promote change, Doyle and many other sociologists of his day saw any evidence of antagonism between blacks and whites as a step in the wrong direction. Thus, Doyle emphasized and indeed encouraged racial "adjustment" and peace over racial justice at the price of conflict.[87] He looked for racial harmony while accepting racial hierarchy to a degree that seems remarkable considering that he was himself a black southerner, born in Lowndesboro, Alabama, in 1897.[88]

To find racial harmony required Doyle to overlook contradictory evidence. For example, he "discounted" the complaint of the North Carolinian who thought black household workers were more respectful in announcing black visitors than they were in announcing whites. Doyle understood survival: the African American's "prejudice in favor of an order in which, with all its disabilities, he has been able to gain a livelihood without constant disharmony." But his model provided very little room for resistance and none at all for the aggressive rejection of racial etiquette by any but a criminal class. To his mind, blacks' performances might not be sincere, but neither were they embodiments of a resisting impulse, much less what James Scott would call a hidden transcript. The black man "cannot take the time to determine the class and character of every white man with whom he comes into contact," Doyle argued; "he can only observe those forms which are calculated to allow him to go his way with the least expenditure of thought and energy. And in this way, if perhaps in no other, the etiquette of race relations exerts its most effective control."[89]

Racial etiquette may, indeed, have exerted this kind of control over some African Americans, but it was not nearly so effective as Doyle implied. Just as there were disobedient slaves, there were always black southerners who refused to be subservient, who bought cars or painted their houses or refused to take off their hats. Richard Wright, for one, claimed that, even after years of instruction in racial etiquette, he simply found it impossible to keep up the necessary performance. "I would remember to dissemble for short periods, then I would forget and act straight and human again, not with the desire to harm anybody, but merely forgetting the artificial status of race and class."[90]

The prevalence of racial violence in the South is perhaps the clearest indication that racial etiquette was never wholly effective. "The New South was a notoriously violent place," as historian Edward L. Ayers puts it, and extremely high levels of white-on-black violence gave the region a "poisoned atmosphere" that "permeated life far beyond those counties where a lynching had actually taken place."[91] Certainly, some whites attacked with little provocation, but it would be a disservice to blacks who stood up for themselves or who simply "acted straight and human"—and who often paid the ultimate price for doing so—to suggest that they were merely passive victims caught unawares. As Neil McMillen writes, "If the Afro-American had been by nature the 'servile and contented darky' who . . . cared little for citizenship and nothing at all for suffrage and social equality, force would have not been a requirement of white dominance and, indeed, the color line would have borne less watching."[92] As it was, whites had to expend considerable energy and engage in considerable violence to keep blacks "in their place."

They also had to supplement racial etiquette with legal segregation, drawing the color line in the highly visible form of "Whites Only" signs and separate facilities to make it easier to watch. Just as their grandfathers had found it necessary "to legislate the master's role" to extract deference from free blacks in antebellum cities, white southerners overseeing the tremendous growth of the region's cities and towns found legal devices for regulating blacks' behavior increasingly imperative by the 1890s and early 1900s. As Howard Rabinowitz and others have argued, segregation was foremost an urban phenomenon and one that took hold first and most tenaciously in developing New South cities such as Atlanta and Birmingham that lacked older cities' history of face-to-face, master-servant relationships between whites and blacks. Legal segregation was also the brainchild of moderates and modernizers, who saw it as an alternative to the total exclusion of blacks from public life, on the one hand, and unremitting racial violence, on the other. "Theaters, hotels, streetcars, lunch counters, railway stations, factories—all these are urban phenomena," historian John W. Cell summarizes. "For the very reason that contacts between the races in town were inevitably more casual, because people jostled together much more haphazardly, the rules governing those contacts were defined all the more thoroughly. Precisely because urban blacks were more autonomous and less vulnerable, their place was circumscribed in more detail."[93] Thus, like racial violence, the development of legal segregation is evidence of weaknesses in racial etiquette. Segregating public facilities was a necessary next step whites had to take in order to secure the public transcript of white supremacy they desired.

Nevertheless, weakened as it was by black challenges and by urbanization and other forces of modernity, racial etiquette remained strong enough to convince most white southerners that elaborate codes of domination and subordination were perfectly natural. They saw racial etiquette as a reflection of deeply held prejudices that were entirely justified by blacks' innate inferiority to whites. "That's the way we feel about it," explained the white woman who vowed that she would kill her children before she would allow them to associate with blacks as equals. "And you might as well root up that big tree in front of the house and stand it the other way up and expect it grow as to think we can feel any different."[94] Like most white southerners, she considered any world without white supremacy to be a world upside down.

Social Scientific Views

This was the South that John Dollard, Hortense Powdermaker, and other social scientists found in the early 1930s when they began the research that, along with Doyle's book, established the "etiquette of race relations" as a concept that historians would later employ. Powdermaker, a pioneering anthropologist who had recently completed a study of life in a Melanesian village, was one of the first on the scene. Her analysis of "Cottonville"—Indianola, Mississippi—was based on nine months of field work begun in the fall of 1932 and a three-month follow-up visit in the summer of 1934. The result was a sensitive portrait of African American life in a small southern town, published in 1939 as *After Freedom: A Cultural Study of the Deep South*. Like Doyle, Powdermaker saw racial etiquette as an essential component of southern culture, although "etiquette" was not a word she used. Instead, she alluded to the "well-known Jim Crow arrangements" present in Indianola's railroad station, restaurants, and movie theater, then detailed the "social mechanisms" — the "prohibitions, injunctions, usages" — that over- and underlay segregation in these familiar and expected forms. The use of names and courtesy titles, taboos against eating and drinking and other social contact across race lines, and the withholding of routine courtesies from blacks clearly had deep significance for white southerners, a significance Powdermaker captured by comparing southern culture to that of the Pacific Islanders she had previously studied. To violate the taboo against calling a black man "Mister," for example, was "to arouse the resentment, suspicion, fear, which attend the breaking of taboos or customs in any culture. If a Melanesian is asked what difference it would make if he failed to provide a feast for his dead maternal uncle, or if he broke the rule of exogamy, his attitude is one of complete bewilderment and strong fear at the mere suggestion. . . . The title taboo is sensed as equally essential to the *status quo* in Mississippi. To question either is to question the whole system; to violate either is to violate, weaken, endanger, the entire *status quo*." Indeed, the attitudes that prompted day-to-day injunctions "also underlie the disenfranchisement of the Negro, his exclusion from jury service, and his liability to lynching," in Powdermaker's view.[95]

Psychologist John Dollard emphasized racial etiquette's importance to white southerners with even more force. His *Caste and Class in a Southern Town*, published in 1937, was an instant classic and proved more influential among scholars than Powdermaker's work—which is ironic given that Powdermaker helped Dollard get established in Indianola, which he then chose as the site of his own research. Powdermaker also spent more than twice as many months in the field as Dollard and published what many consider the more insightful study. Yet Dollard's book preceded hers by two years and may have made her work seem less original. Certainly, it was his emphasis on "caste" as the defining feature of southern race relations that came to dominate sociological analyses of the American racial scene for the next two decades.[96] Even more than Powdermaker, Dollard stressed white southerners' unshakable commitment to white supremacy and the "caste etiquette" that upheld it. He thought any change in the South was far off at best and would come through the gradual erosion of white prejudice, not through the efforts of blacks, whom he considered remarkably well adjusted to their limitations, especially among the lower classes. Nevertheless, whites' demands for deference reflected "much fear" of black aggression in addition to a desire to maintain social distance. Attacking blacks' self-esteem through the humiliations of racial etiquette was "a chronic policy of the white caste in the South" that sought "to put [the Negro] on another and lower scale of humanity, and thereby paralyze his aggressive tendencies by making them seem hopeless."[97] How blacks could be both adjusted and aggressive was a contradiction Dollard did not explain. Yet his portrait of southern race relations as a stable caste system unlikely to change anytime soon would be redrawn in several other studies published in the early 1940s, including the second most influential work of this "caste and class" school, Allison Davis, Burleigh Gardner, and Mary Gardner's *Deep South: A Social Anthropological Study of Caste and Class.*[98]

The fact that Dollard, Powdermaker, and other social scientists found racial etiquette alive and well in the 1930s does not mean that nothing had changed in the South since 1865. *Deep South* itself focused on the ways in which the demands of a changing economy could force modifications in traditional racial etiquette, as when white merchants had to compete for black customers.[99] Other social scientists who were less committed to notions of caste and less troubled by racial conflict than Doyle and Dollard found even more reason to expect changes in racial etiquette, and race relations more generally, in the near future. Black sociologist Charles S. Johnson, for example, pointed to such factors as migration, education, the impact of New Deal programs, and the restlessness of black youth as indications that the southern system was not as stable as either white southerners or most social scientists wanted to believe. Etiquette remained strong, but it was not as all-encompassing as the word "caste" implied because of "the attitudes of the participants." "While the southern white traditionalist likes to believe that the race system is accepted as natural and proper, in actuality he and all other participants know that it is not," Johnson wrote in the final sentences of his 1941 study *Growing Up in the Black Belt.* "The race system in the South is preserved by legal sanctions and the threat of physical violence, quite as much as by the mutual acceptance of traditional modes of behavior." The fact that blacks were "struggling against this status rather than accepting it" meant that "in the future, if one cannot safely predict progress in race relations, he can at least predict change."[100] Recognizing the extent to which World War II was a turning point in the South, we can see that Johnson was correct even if the civil rights protests of the 1950s and 1960s remained a generation away.

As much as their views on caste and the prevalence and meanings of racial conflict differed, Johnson, Dollard, and other social scientists writing in the 1930s and early 1940s all tell us two essential things about racial etiquette that should also be clear from the analysis presented above. One is that etiquette remained powerful: that a well-established code of domination and deference inherited from slavery continued to script the public transcript of southern race relations even as the code itself evolved to fit the modern, urban environment that, alongside more traditional agricultural arrangements, characterized the region by the mid-twentieth century. The other is that etiquette was far more powerful among whites than it ever was among blacks. Johnson made this point clearly. Powdermaker implied it by offering sympathetic portraits of black individuals struggling against both major and minor proscriptions.[101] Dollard revealed it by contradicting himself on the subjects of black aggression and dissemblance and by emphasizing the extent to which white southerners tried to teach racial etiquette to *him*. "White friends" in Indianola "tried immediately to instruct me in the etiquette of the situation and to protect me against foolish mistakes," he wrote in the opening pages of his study, later admitting that, when black informants breached racial etiquette, he found himself "in an extremely embarrassing position." He wondered whether one "Negro friend" forced him to shake hands in front of a busy post office "in an excess of enthusiasm, defying custom, or whether he did it 'accidentally on purpose' in order to embarrass me." "Such a situation necessarily breeds many insincerities in the outsider," he concluded. "The white people enforce caste rules with ominous unanimity and one is compelled, by one's white-caste membership, to assist to some degree in the personal derogation of the Negro and the expression of hostile pressure against him."[102]

Perhaps (although Powdermaker seems to have survived in Indianola without embracing racial etiquette nearly so warmly).[103] But if white southerners could compel a well-intentioned northern scholar like Dollard to follow racial etiquette, it should hardly come as a surprise that instruction in racial etiquette was a crucial aspect of white southern child rearing. It was there, among white children, that racial etiquette achieved its greatest degree of hegemony (a hegemony that was still far from perfect), as the following chapter will show.

2 Carefully Taught

In his 1904 travelogue *Highways and Byways of the South,* New Englander Clifton Johnson recorded a scene between a young girl and her grandmother at a private home in Florida where he lodged. "There's a colored lady out on the porch wants to speak to you," the girl told her grandmother. "Colored lady!" the grandmother sniffed, "Colored lady! Say 'that nigger'!" "As she viewed things, her granddaughter had been using fancy and inappropriate language," Johnson explained. He went on to suggest, a little tongue-in-cheek, given his own background and comparatively progressive racial views, that the child had probably learned this "nonsense" from northerners who visited the region in the winter.[1] Certainly, the child had not learned her undiscriminating politeness from her grandmother, who, like almost all white southerners, reserved the word "lady" and the courtesy titles "Mrs." and "Miss" for white women only. In this moment, she taught her granddaughter to do the same.

By itself, this episode may seem like mere ephemera, the splotch of local color that Johnson was offering. Multiplied across the white households of the South, however, interactions like this one take on great significance. Simply put, lessons in racial etiquette were the most common *direct* means that white adults used to teach their children how to be white—the closest thing to a "core curriculum" white southerners had. And, given women's primary role in child rearing, teaching such lessons was also one of white women's chief forms of collusion in the maintenance of white supremacy. Children who learned to treat blacks as inferiors at an interpersonal level were unlikely, as adults, to question laws and institutions that discriminated against blacks at a societal, structural level. Rather, they became all the more receptive to racist imagery and other cultural narratives that assured them that blacks were unworthy of whites' civility because they were themselves uncivilized: dirty, uneducated, immoral, bestial, less than human. Thus, little lessons such as a white grandmother's lesson in naming compounded to perpetuate structures of racism, both material and cultural—and so were not so little after all.

Such lessons were nonetheless reactive. That is, they were usually taught only in response to some infraction of the rules of racial etiquette rather than as part of a self-conscious plan of instruction. As sociologist Olive Westbrooke Quinn perceptively argued in a little-known 1954 article, "For the most part the South does not teach attitudes to its white children. Such teaching is not necessary." Instead, the southern "way of life," particularly racial etiquette, could "have but one meaning for those who diligently practice it," and it was the *practice* of white supremacy that white parents and other adults demonstrated and, when necessary, encouraged, allowing, and no doubt often expecting, racist attitudes to follow.[2] To use Sarah Patton Boyle's metaphor, southern racial etiquette provided the stays of a corset that most white southerners grew to fit.[3]

If white parenting was largely unselfconscious and reactive where race was concerned, black parenting in the Jim Crow South was quite the opposite. Black parents worried about their children, not least about their safety in a world dominated in every way by whites, and they tried hard to shelter their boys and girls not only from racist treatment but also from its psychological effects. Many, especially among the black middle and upper classes, fought etiquette with etiquette, teaching their children an alternative code of respectability—and with it a dual consciousness—that was meant to help them preserve their self-respect. Centered on bourgeois values of temperance, thrift, sexual self-restraint, hard work, and perseverance, as well as conventional good manners, middle-class blacks' "politics of respectability" reflected both an antiracist discursive strategy, as historian Evelyn Brooks Higginbotham and others have argued, and deeply held beliefs that were nowhere stronger than in views on child rearing.[4] Yet "proper" child rearing could also be a focal point for intraracial class tensions, as is most evident in middle-class blacks' concerns that too few working-class blacks were raising their children well.

In addition, even among the comparatively elite, children themselves often struggled with the passivity and repression of emotions that respectability required. Recognizing the burdens that blacks' politics of respectability placed on black children, as well as more familiar issues of class conflict, one has to consider the question that black critics have asked with increasing frequency since the New Negro Renaissance of the 1920s and especially since the Black Power movement: Did black middle-class respectability in fact simply facilitate white supremacy while replicating its racist logic in relation to the black working class? Historian Kevin K. Gaines argues that it did. "Generally, black elites claimed class distinctions, indeed, the very existence of a 'better class' of blacks, as evidence of what they called race progress," Gaines writes. Yet such claims were intrinsically inegalitarian and failed to consider the extent to which "ostensibly universal . . . ideological categories of Western progress and civilization" were in fact "deeply racialized." On a practical, political level, "respectable" blacks' "ethos of service to the masses" could not make up for their failure to demand the full rights of citizenship for all.[5]

Often because they focus on the material progress that did result from black middle-class self-help—the health clinics opened, the clothing distributed, the children fed—a number of other historians have viewed the politics of respectability far more favorably than Gaines.[6] A third view is essentially pragmatic: What choice did blacks, especially in their roles as parents, have?[7] Above all else, black parents in the Jim Crow South had to teach their children to survive. Often, that meant teaching them to avoid whites as much as possible. Always, it meant teaching them to follow racial etiquette enough to get by. Teaching them to be revolutionaries was not an option in a world where any black person who got "uppity," much less openly challenged the power structure, could get killed. Embracing respectability did help many African Americans maintain an inward sense of integrity and self-respect as they lived their lives in the shadow of Jim Crow, and this included many blacks who were poor and uneducated, not just the black middle class. Among those who did not embrace respectability, the pertinent question seems to be whether they taught self-respect at all or, as early black social scientist Allison Davis argued, merely trained their children to be subservient—a possibility that, while not borne out by my research, makes charges that the politics of respectability were elitist and even racist appear in a different light.

One thing that does seem clear is that blacks' strategies of racial socialization changed more over time than whites' did. Nevertheless, change over time is a subject for the conclusion rather than this chapter because, even though some blacks' approach to teaching their children about race gradually became less moralistic and more directly political as early as the 1920s, their commitment to respectability remained and needs to be understood first in its racial and class dimensions. This chapter asks what and how white and black adults, especially parents, taught children about race, keeping class and other variables in view.

To be more precise, my focus is on what white parents taught white children and what black parents taught black children and how in both cases. This leaves out the cultural lessons that many other adults taught through literature, film, advertising, and a variety of media, and it leaves out lessons taught across race lines. Black women and men who worked in domestic service often played a significant role in white children's racial socialization, as examples in this and other chapters suggest, but analyzing that role is beyond my scope here. Instead, I try to capture the range of core teachings on each side of the color line and to put them into the broader context of childhood in America, which changed dramatically between the late nineteenth century and the mid-twentieth, although less dramatically in the South than in other regions.

The Sheltered Childhood

The most fundamental of these changes was the gradual embrace of the ideal of the "sheltered childhood." As historian Mary Ryan argued in an important early study of Oneida County, New York, better-off parents in the North recognized by the 1830s that their children, especially sons, would require more education to succeed in commerce and industry than they themselves had required to work and own farms. So they limited the size of their families and concentrated their child-rearing efforts, including their love and attention, on fewer children for a longer period of time. The upper echelons of the northern working class followed this middle-class example out of similar hopes for their children's advancement, resulting in a gradual abandonment of the long-standing ideal of the "useful child"—the child who contributed to the family economy as an agricultural or industrial laborer—between the 1870s and the 1930s.[8]

As children became economically useless, they became "emotionally priceless." In the words of sociologist Viviana Zelizer, middle-class Americans "sacralized" children's lives at precisely the same time that children were being expelled from the "cash nexus." "While in the nineteenth century, the market value of children was culturally acceptable," Zelizer explains, "later the new normative ideal of the child as an exclusively emotional and affective asset precluded instrumental or fiscal considerations. In an increasingly commercialized world, children were reserved a separate noncommercial place, *extra-commercium*."[9]

In many respects, this sacralization of childhood culminated a trend toward seeing children as innocent and special that had been building in the West for almost two centuries. As historian Steven Mintz has observed, "The new ideal of the sheltered childhood drew upon several sources. These included the enlightened conception of a child as a blank slate waiting to be shaped by parental and environmental influences; the liberal Protestant ideal that granted children innocent souls and assigned parents the task of turning their redeemable, docile wills toward God; and the evangelical stress on childhood development as proceeding through a series of stages, much as religious conversion required." Romantics such as William Wordsworth and Jean-Jacques Rousseau also had a tremendous influence, encouraging a growing acceptance of "the notion that children needed to be sheltered from adult realities, such as death, profanity, and sexuality" (and, one might think, racism or at least racial violence, whether as victims or as perpetrators). By the mid- to late nineteenth century, Americans were establishing schools, Sunday schools, orphanages, children's hospitals, and other new institutions to provide the protection, education, and care that children were now understood to require. Meanwhile, "childrearing became a more intensive and self-conscious activity," a change that went hand in hand with a rapidly declining birthrate, smaller families, and households that were divided more clearly into two generations (whereas a larger number of children had meant wider variations in age).[10]

In the twenty-first century, continued acceptance of the ideas that children are innocent and childhood is sacred makes the sheltered childhood ideal seem normative and natural, constrained only by human frailties and parents' economic and emotional wherewithal. Yet, as historian David Macleod stresses, it is important to recognize that this approach to child rearing is a historical phenomenon and "demanded resources and commitment." Such a commitment was "well established among the urban middle class and increasingly among the upper tier of the working class" by the early 1900s. "Urbanization, declining ratios of children to adults, better living conditions, belief that children needed to develop at a measured pace through different stages—all were helping the sheltered childhood spread. But even in towns and cities it was still contested."[11]

Change came more slowly and was even more contested in the South, but it did come (and would be greatly accelerated by the transformation of southern agriculture after World War II). Although southern children of the early twentieth century continued to work alongside their parents in cotton and tobacco fields, as well as in the region's textile mills and at other paid jobs, and although southern families continued to be larger, on average, than families in other parts of the country, an increasing number of southerners recognized the importance of nurturing each child's potential through education and a prolonged period of economic dependency.[12] For black families, a desire for education and opportunities for the younger generation often meant leaving the South, as an estimated 1.8 million black southerners did between 1910 and 1940.[13] Anxiety and hope for children's futures were, of course, only part of the dynamic of pushes and pulls that mobilized the Great Migration, operating alongside the draw of economic opportunities, the expectation of finding better treatment and a greater political voice outside the South, and the goad of outright fear in response to racial violence. Yet, as historians such as James Grossman have recognized, parental concerns were an important factor.[14]

For those who stayed in the South, both black and white, growing acceptance of the sheltered childhood ideal was reflected most clearly in rates of school attendance, which increased steadily from the late nineteenth century through the mid-twentieth. Working from census data, economic historian Robert A. Margo has calculated the average attendance rate for white children ages five to twenty at 48 percent in 1890 and 63 percent in 1920. "Growth in white attendance continued during the 1920s, slowed during the Great Depression, and then rebounded again in the 1940s," Margo summarizes. "In 1950 about 71 percent of southern white children were attending school" at some point during the census year. Although a racial gap in school attendance persisted throughout the period, black attendance rates grew even faster, from about 30 percent in 1900, to almost 53 percent in 1920 and 69 percent in 1950—this despite the inadequate funding and more limited availability of schools for black children, especially in rural areas. Both black and white children were also staying in school longer. According to Margo, southern whites born between 1886 and 1890 completed about 7 years of school; those born between 1916 and 1920 completed an average of 10.2 years; and those born in the late 1930s averaged nearly 12 years. Meanwhile, southern blacks' average years of schooling increased from about 4 years for those born in late nineteenth century to 7.4 years for those born between 1916 and 1920. Those born in the late 1930s averaged 10.4 years, the equivalent of some high school—although, as Margo points out, census data offers only a crude measure of educational attainment for both blacks and whites because census takers recorded only "years of schooling" rather than grade level obtained.[15] Even with these steady gains in attendance and educational achievement, both black and white southerners lagged considerably behind children in other parts of the country; nevertheless, the fact that more and more black and white southern children were going to school and staying in school longer is an indication that more and more black and white southern parents were coming to value education and the sheltered childhood required to achieve it.

Those southerners who were most dedicated to new child-rearing ideals demonstrated their commitment in the same ways other Americans did, by joining mothers' clubs, following the advice of a new cadre of child-rearing "experts," or promoting "scientific motherhood" in their communities. Analyzing the explosion of women's clubs at the turn of the twentieth century, historians have generally been most interested in how women were able to extend their roles as mothers into the public sphere.[16] Yet it is also worth noting the ideological transformation in parenting that was taking place. As historian Darlene Roth has observed of the black and white Atlanta clubwomen she studied, those who joined organizations founded on women's distinctive maternal roles also "embraced domestic 'science' and the arrival of 'professionalized' home management with a vengeance—as individuals and as groups. They broadcast its virtues and preached its practice through their organizations—not only through the Home Economics League, but also through 'home' demonstrations at the local woman's club, through 'model homes' and 'better baby' contests at fairs and bazaars, through classes and instruction they gave one another, through propaganda in their organizational media, and so on and on and on."[17] These efforts reached something of a high-water mark, at least for the white South, in 1925, when Mrs. Clifford Walker, state chairwoman of the Georgia Parent-Teacher Association, landed a $12,000 grant from the Laura Spelman Rockefeller Foundation for parent training, to be administered through the Georgia State College of Agriculture at the University of Georgia in Athens. "Georgia is the first state in the south to receive a donation from the Spelman-Rockefeller foundation," the *Atlanta Constitution* trumpeted, promising "the beginning of a great health and educational service . . . that may lead to extensive developments along the same lines in the future."[18]

Women in the rural South had less access to information about new "scientific" approaches to raising children than those in urban centers like Atlanta or college towns like Athens. As sociologist Margaret Jarman Hagood found in her study of white tenant farm women in the 1930s, mothers rarely nursed infants on a schedule, for example, despite the fact that most middle-class town and city dwellers knew by this time of experts' preference for scheduled feedings. "The notion was new to some and incomprehensible to a few," Hagood observed.[19] And, indeed, even many rural southerners who were aware of expert opinions had little interest in following them. "People here in the mountains raise [children] very rough and call mine a book baby," a Virginia mother wrote in 1917.[20]

Whether rural or urban, black women had additional reasons to resist expert advice when it came from elite and middle-class whites who had little understanding of the economic hardships most black families faced. As one black mother told an interviewer in Nashville in the 1930s, "I don't need nobody to tell me anything. All I need is a place to leave my William when I go to work. I used to go to that Mother's Club, but shucks, it ain't nothing. White folks just naturally can't tell you nothing about raising children"[21]—a point of view that many black women found all the more persuasive considering the number of white women who left the raising of their own children to black nurses.

As much as working-class black mothers doubted whites' child-rearing advice, they were more willing to listen to middle-class blacks, including teachers, nurses, and social service workers, the vast majority of whom embraced "scientific" approaches to improving children's welfare with great urgency. Thus, in Atlanta, where southern black reformers working in this vein were perhaps most successful, mothers' meetings were held as part of every Atlanta University Conference of Negro Problems, beginning with the third annual conference in 1898.[22] Ten years later, Lugenia Burns Hope, wife of Morehouse College president John Hope, helped to found the Neighborhood Union, the premier social service organization among southern blacks. The women of the NU developed an ambitious agenda, educating black mothers at the same time they established community centers and health clinics and fought for, among other things, improvements in recreational facilities and streetcar and railroad accommodations for blacks, the hiring of black policemen and the extension of police protection in black neighborhoods, and the preservation of the seventh and eighth grades and the development of a high school curriculum in Atlanta's black public schools.[23] This range of activities made the NU, in historian Elisabeth Lasch-Quinn's words, "an eloquent example of the transition from a maternalist philosophy of activism toward one based on the rights of citizenship."[24] Yet this core of maternalism, central to both black and white southern women's organizations in this period, shows how ardently some southerners were embracing the notion that childhood should be a time of sheltering and careful nurture—nurture so careful that it required expert advice and parental training, as well as beneficent public policies.

Even as black and white southerners embraced the ideal of the sheltered childhood, however, they did so in ways that reflected racial hierarchies. For blacks, sheltering necessarily began (although it certainly did not end) with protecting children from racist whites, as the second half of this chapter will show. Meanwhile, even those white southerners who devoted the most attention and material and emotional resources to their own children rarely saw any but the very youngest black children as innocents or extended the ideal of the sheltered childhood to blacks. Future college professor Margaret Jones Bolsterli, born in the Arkansas Delta in 1931, discovered this fact to her horror when she was about thirteen years old. Asked to guarantee the bill for an incubator for the family maid's premature baby, Bolsterli's father, Grover Cleveland Jones, refused "for all the usual reasons: wrong time of year, the crop looked slim, etc." "When I accused him of being a monster," Bolsterli recalled, "he looked at me with genuine hurt and said, 'Why, honey, I never even heard of putting a nigra baby in an incubator.'" As an adult, Bolsterli could reflect knowingly on the fact that "there were things that white people did not think of in terms of black people, and expensive medical care was one of them." But as an adolescent, Bolsterli was bruised. "The incident about the incubator changed things between my father and me," she wrote in her autobiography, *Born in the Delta*. "I never stopped loving him, but I never saw him in quite the same way after that."[25]

"We knew guilt without understanding it"[26]

Thirteen-year-old Margaret's surprise and her father's hurt feelings suggest that, in contrast to some other white parents, Jones did try to shield his daughter from the more brutal aspects of his own and other whites' racism. Many white southerners were far less delicate, failing to protect their own children's innocence in this regard just as much as they failed to extend the ideal of the sheltered childhood to young blacks. "A certain element in the South takes pains to rear the children of the family faithfully in the doctrines of Blease and Vardaman," the *Crisis*, the monthly magazine of the National Association for the Advancement of Colored People (NAACP), observed in July 1912, referring to two of the South's most notorious race-baiting politicians. A poem by Bertha Johnston drove home the point:

I met a little blue-eyed girl—
　She said she was five years old;
"Your locket is very pretty, dear;
　And pray what may it hold?"

And then—my heart grew chill and sick—
    The gay child did not flinch—
"I found it—the tooth of a colored man—
    My father helped to lynch."[27]

More than twenty years later, a *Crisis* account of the lynching of two elderly blacks by 5,000 whites in Gordonsville, Virginia, picked up on the same, still-relevant theme. "If the tradition of American lynchers was faithfully followed," Roy Wilkins wrote, "there reposes now on the mantelpieces of many a Virginia home a bit of flesh or a bone preserved in a jar of alcohol to remind children and grandchildren of the indomitable courage of a brother, father or son of the family who battled to the death to prevent two Negroes from overcoming 5,000 white Virginians." A twelve-year-old boy armed with a .22 rifle was reported to have been part of the mob, Wilkins added, and his "small sister is said to have gone among the 5,000 begging ammunition for her valiant kin."[28]

Although observers such as Wilkins were understandably shocked by white children's presence among lynch mobs, it is difficult to know how commonly and how deliberately white parents exposed their children to lynching and other forms of racial violence (the polar opposite of "sheltering," as far as racism is concerned). Certainly, some white southerners would have been repulsed by the very idea and denounced violence and lawlessness while encouraging their children to treat blacks with a measure of respect. "If I used the word 'nigger' . . . I'd get a licking, and I was taught to regard whites who did use that word as themselves inferior," *New York Times* editor Turner Catledge wrote of his early-twentieth-century Mississippi boyhood in one fairly typical account. Catledge's father despised the Ku Klux Klan and in their "house the name of Bilbo, then a state politician and later the famous racist Senator, was a dirty word." When six fully outfitted Klansman walked into a revival meeting held by a pro-Klan preacher, Catledge's father stood and walked out, with half the congregation following. Yet Catledge himself was never "a crusader" and "thought very little about the plight of Negroes during [his] early newspaper career."[29] His parents had taught him a certain level of decency, not antiracist thinking.

Anecdotal evidence like Catledge's is key to establishing the range of white southern parents' lessons about race because, ultimately, it is the best available. Unlike black parents, white parents thought little—and wrote less—about the issue of teaching their children about race, which they hardly saw as an issue at all. For this reason (and with the exception of autobiography, considered below), white southerners' own writings are less helpful than one might expect. Certainly, there are no white equivalents to black club-woman and Howard University professor Coralie Cook's anguished speech titled "The Problem of the Colored Child," delivered before the annual meeting of the NAACP in 1914, or to W. E. B. Du Bois's musing in the *Crisis* that "in the problem of our children we black folk are sorely puzzled." Both Cook and Du Bois (and others) made black parents' agonizing uncertainty about how to explain race and racism to their children explicit—as, indeed, Martin Luther King Jr. would also do decades later when he wrote in his 1963 "Letter from Birmingham Jail" about the moment "when you suddenly find your tongue twisted and your speech stammering as you seek to explain to your six-year-old daughter why she can't go to the public amusement park that has just been advertised on television, . . . when you have to concoct an answer for a five-year-old son who is asking: 'Daddy, why do white people treat colored people so mean?'"[30] It was one of white parents' racial privileges to be spared such agonies.

White southerners did write proudly of their Anglo-Saxon heritage in the late nineteenth and early twentieth centuries, and many embraced popular versions of scientific racism. In their efforts to end child labor during the Progressive Era (another part of the story of how the sheltered childhood ideal was taking hold in the South), white southerner reformers even connected these strains of thought to what could be called a "problem of the white child": namely, a concern that white children working in southern textile mills might be losing some of their whiteness. As historian Shelley Sallee argues, opponents of child labor played on fears that bad working conditions and a lack of education were degrading white child workers, whom reformers depicted as the youngest and most vulnerable members of "our pure Anglo-Saxon stock," "noble though undeveloped people of the mountains and hills." Although reformers like Edgar Gardner Murphy rooted their arguments in contemporary biological understandings of race, they also implied that biology was not enough and that ignorance and poverty could make whites, in Sallee's words, "lose their race pride," resulting in miscegenation and chaos.[31] Yet even in the specific case of white child laborers, Murphy and his fellow reformers faced an uphill battle. If southern states' weak child welfare laws are any indication, most white southerners were not greatly concerned about poor white children losing their whiteness—a danger that children of the white middle and upper classes would presumably never face because they had not only biology (according to most whites' way of thinking) but also education and social status on their side.

However secure they felt in their own racial identities, elite and middle-class southerners did worry about passing on a distinctively white heritage that they themselves thought of not as white but as "Southern." Many historians have written about white southerners' memorialization of the "Lost Cause" in recent years, and some have focused specifically on efforts to indoctrinate children to a pro-Confederate mind-set. Karen Cox writes of "Confederate motherhood," including the creation of the Children of the Confederacy as a youth auxiliary to the United Daughters of the Confederacy (UDC). Unlike the Republican Motherhood that emerged from the American Revolution, Confederate motherhood was, Cox argues, "motivated in part by fear —fear that textbooks with a northern bias had already accomplished irreparable damage, fear that their ancestors might not be vindicated, and fear that future generations of white southerners may never know the sacrifices" that their forebears, including the women, had made.[32] Fred Arthur Bailey has offered detailed readings of some of the history books that the UDC and other like-minded organizations promoted to counteract other books' supposed northern bias. "Far more than sectional honor" was at stake, Bailey insists. Memorial societies and the textbook authors whose work they supported "were engaged in an intellectual quest designed to confirm the southern aristocracy's continuing legitimate authority as the dominant force in the region's political, social, and economic life." At the same time, they broadcast their assumption that human inequality was natural and inevitable, just as their ancestors had argued in the days of slavery, whereas northerners before and after the Civil War talked of democracy and egalitarianism, even if injustices within northern society belied their rhetoric.[33]

Bailey's emphasis on class and regional intellectual traditions is well-placed, for, if white southerners had only wanted to make sure that their children learned to think of blacks as inferior to whites, they would not have needed to write their own textbooks. As a number of scholars have shown, schoolbooks, and children's books in general, were far more racist than not throughout the late nineteenth and early twentieth centuries (regarded by many as the golden age of children's publishing).[34] White supremacist attitudes even shaped Sunday school literature to a considerable extent, which is why southern blacks of all of the major denominations felt the need to start publishing their own. As historian Sally G. McMillen argues, "black churches, Sunday schools, and publications often attacked racial oppression," while "white children heard only silence." "White superiority was imbedded in the American mindset, and, whether spoken or unspoken, was reinforced in white Sunday schools. In white minds, raising up the South did not include challenging the racial status quo."[35]

As much as we might be able to learn from reading the silences in white Sunday school literature or reading through the "Southernness" in schoolbooks and children's stories authored by southern whites, we would mostly be learning about the reinforcement rather than the initial laying down of white children's racial lessons. Other sources get us closer to this earlier stage (and ongoing pattern) of parental teaching. In most of these sources, an outsider status is critical. For example, it was the fact that he and his family had lived in California before moving to South Carolina that made Thomas Pearce Bailey aware of a change in his two-year-old son. The boy "spoke of Negro women as 'black ladies' when he lived in California, where a Negro was seldom seen and where it was unnecessary to discuss the Negro question," Bailey observed. After a few months in South Carolina, however, the child "had learned to 'discriminate,' and had described a Negro man at the front door as a 'nigger,' not a 'gentleman.'" To Bailey's mind, this incident illustrated "the evident fact that race feeling is not instinctive" but was "a social custom and habit."[36]

Significantly, social scientists writing in the 1920s and 1930s found that many white southerners shared this view of racism as learned rather than innate. In his 1929 study *Race Attitudes in Children*, Bruno Lasker quoted a North Carolina mother and teacher who felt that "adverse attitudes are never shown until the child is old enough to have caught the attitude of older children or adults" and that "young children of their own initiative notice little difference as regards racial characteristics."[37] Anthropologist Hortense Powdermaker found the same sentiment expressed widely in "Cottonville"—Indianola, Mississippi—in the mid-1930s. "Most Whites in Cottonville say that little children have no race prejudice," she wrote.[38]

Unfortunately, whites' recognition that racism was something children *learned* did not encourage them to reflect on their own part in that learning process. Bailey explained the change in his son's word choice by noting that "nothing had been said to him by the adult members of the household; but he had become indoctrinated through the very atmosphere of South Carolina social life."[39] Other parents apparently assumed that their children would learn equally as well by observation and osmosis as Bailey's did, or that, if necessary, they would intervene when a child's lack of racial prejudice really began to matter—that is, at puberty, when any semblance of "social equality" raised the specter of interracial sex.

White adults' laissez-faire attitude toward pre-adolescent children's racial socialization does not mean that they taught their children nothing about being white; rather, it means that the only sources revealing the content and range of their teachings are indirect. Whites' own autobiographies and oral histories are the most detailed and yet among the most problematic of these sources. For a variety of reasons including but not limited to whites' own self-image, autobiography and oral history tell us most often about moderate white parents such as Turner Catledge's. Virtually no white southerners have described their parents as vicious or violent racists—and what incentive would there be for any to do so? Many whites have chosen or been asked to record their lives precisely because they were dissenters against white supremacy, which often meant their parents had been unusually kind-hearted toward blacks as well. Others have sensed, just as white southerners have long sensed, that to defend white supremacy outside the region was to appear backward and provincial, if not immoral and undemocratic. Even proud segregationists like Georgia governor Lester Maddox denied being racists and saw the utility in emphasizing the harmonious aspects of southern race relations in their memoirs. Maddox, for example, explained that the black and white children of his working-class neighborhood "played together without strife—perhaps because we did so by choice and not by decree."[40] Add to this individuals' protective attitude toward their families and it comes as no surprise that white southern parents are generally depicted in white-authored sources as, at worst, "typical" but by no means cruel or even unkind racists. Some whites describe their parents as unprejudiced or "very humanitarian," even if they also acknowledge that their families "lived in the traditional way" and "accepted the traditional pattern in the South."[41] Others mull the inconsistencies at the heart of racially moderate white parenting, which was a reality in many homes even if it is also the image that autobiographers and oral history informants are most likely to project. It is, in fact, the "partial truth" of white parenting that white-authored sources can and do capture, and no white author was more eloquent on this subject than Lillian Smith.

Moderates . . .

Like Catledge, Smith learned that "to use the word 'nigger' was unpardonable and no well-bred southerner was quite so crude as to do so." She also learned to speak "graciously" to black people—"unless they forgot their place, in which event icy peremptory tones would draw lines beyond which only the desperate would dare take one step."[42] As a child, Smith could sense the contradiction between "drawing lines" and practicing the Christian and democratic values that her parents also vigorously taught. Born in the small town of Jasper, Florida, in 1897, Smith had what one biographer describes as a "southern-Calvinistic" upbringing. Her parents taught her to fear God, as well as to love him, to consider her body "a Thing of Shame" that could lead her into sin, and to push away not only black people "but everything dark, dangerous, evil." Nonetheless, her parents' lessons also emphasized service, and she and her five brothers and three sisters were all told that they "owed a 'debt to society which must be paid.'" The result of this combination of lessons was unresolved internal conflicts accompanied by outward conformity to southern social practice. As Smith summarized in her 1949 autobiography, *Killers of the Dream*, "We lived the same segregated life as did other southerners but our parents talked in excessively Christian and democratic terms. We were told ten thousand times that status and money are unimportant (though we were well supplied with both); we were told that 'all men are brothers,' that we are a part of a democracy and must act like democrats. We were told that the teachings of Jesus are important and could be practiced if we tried." Given the difficulty of reconciling such lessons with the patterns of Jim Crow, it is hardly surprising that Smith and other white children learned simply to abide by racial etiquette most of the time. Smith's parents taught her a lesson about this as well: "We were told that to be 'radical' is bad, silly too; and that one must always conform to the 'best behavior' of one's community and make it better if one can."[43]

Exemplifying the "'best behavior' of one's community" made the practice of racial etiquette all the more compelling for some white southerners, especially those with class pretensions. Sarah Patton Boyle is another example of a white southerner whose childhood race training might be described as moderate. On the one hand, she learned a firm commitment to white supremacy and the racial etiquette that upheld it on a day-to-day basis. On the other hand, she learned to be "friendly," "gracious," and even "courteous" to blacks as long as they did not become "familiar" or "uppity" or act the least bit out of their "place."[44] Within these limits, Boyle thought her relationships with black people were "altogether beautiful" and that a "special love and understanding existed between my 'class' and Negroes, and that they had an uncanny ability to recognize 'quality folks.'" Although this "class" of whites who wanted to be recognized as "quality" bore much resemblance to the white middle and upper classes as defined in economic terms, *moving away* from conventional definitions of social status was largely the point. "While any white man was socially above any Negro and accordingly must be treated with respect," Boyle explained, "a Negro of character, sensitivity, and intelligence was humanly above a less decent white. I thought the best Negroes accepted both social and human scales and knew that while our social relationship was unalterably fixed by race, our human relationship was devoid of limitation."[45]

The idea that there was a "human scale" apart from the rigid social arrangements of Jim Crow was also part of former president Jimmy Carter's moderate race training in Depression-era Georgia. And, in contrast to Boyle, who described this notion as an element of her aristocratic heritage, Carter suggested that it was a standard held by many whites in his community, regardless of their class. "In fact, the final judgment of people I knew was based on their own character and achievements, and not on their race," Carter asserted. "There is no doubt that black families had to overcome severe and unfair obstacles, but those who were considered to be honest, hardworking, and thrifty had at least a chance to succeed financially and to enjoy general respect, despite the unalterable social distinctions. This was true even though they still came to the back door of a white family's home, rode in a separate part of the passenger train, sat upstairs in the Americus movie theater and in the county courthouse, and attended their separate schools and churches." Yet, even as he acknowledged some of the injustices of the social scale, such as blacks' inability to vote or sit on juries, Carter left a significant weakness in the "human scale" unexamined. For what did it matter if some whites valued black people as human beings unless they were also willing to defend those human beings against whites who did not share their judgment? This obvious question is one Carter's autobiography does not ask.

Instead, Carter reflects on what it meant to be "white trash," a designation that reveals not only that whiteness, like blackness, was socially constructed but also that civility toward blacks could have as much to do with the social construction of whiteness as economic competition or epithets. "I recall a few instances when disreputable whites had to appeal to the larger community to confirm their racial superiority by siding with them in a dispute," Carter acknowledged, "but their very need to do so confirmed their own low social status." Because it, too, was a judgment based more on a human than on the rigidly fixed social scale, "white trash" was "a greater insult than any epithet based on race."[46] Nevertheless, the very fact that "disreputable" whites could command the support of the white community for their status claims indicates how fragile white southerners' commitment to a human scale was in comparison to their determination to maintain their social system. Whether whites' interest in seeking a separate human scale derived primarily from religion (as for Smith's family), from noblesse oblige (as for Boyle's), or from an ability to appreciate character and initiative (as for Carter's), this double standard seems to have been fundamental to moderating whites' racism. Yet only a handful of whites who were raised this way, including Smith, Boyle, and Carter, managed to move beyond their moderate and seemingly unexceptional childhood training to become true racial progressives as adults.

Thus, while families like Smith's, Boyle's, and Carter's deserve some credit for teaching their children to be more humane (if also more paternalistic) than the dictates of an inherently unjust society required, we should not exaggerate the importance of such moderation. Nor should we fail to recognize that such moderate white child rearing was hardly the whole story. If one were to read only the accounts of white southerners, one might almost begin to wonder whether *any* white children ever learned the word "nigger" from their parents. To capture the full range of white parents' racial lessons, we must turn to other sources in addition to whites' own autobiographies and oral histories. Just as there are no white equivalents to black-authored articles and speeches like "The Problem of the Colored Child," there are no white equivalents to the kind of story black Georgian Albon L. Holsey told in a 1929 *American Mercury* article titled "Learning How to Be Black." Running an errand when he was ten or eleven years old, circa 1893, Holsey passed the home of a white man who was playing on the front porch with his infant son. "Look—nigger," the father said, pointing. "Say 'nigger,'" he repeated again and again.[47]

. . . and Mobs

Black-authored sources such as Holsey's can tell us a great deal about what at least some white southerners taught their children. To get at the bluntest and most brutal of those lessons, a lesson about the cheapness of blacks' very lives, we can also look at lynching photographs. That many white parents saw no reason to keep their children away from lynching scenes is evident in the frequency with which white children appear in such images. For example, white children are visible in photographs of at least ten of the twenty-eight southern lynchings documented in *Without Sanctuary: Lynching Photography in America*, despite the fact that collector James Allen made no special effort to include images with children and rarely even commented on children's presence in his notes.[48] Among these photographs, perhaps none is more disturbing than one taken in Fort Lauderdale, Florida, in July 1935. Three pre-adolescent girls, one with a particularly satisfied smile on her face, stare at the body of Reuben Stacey, a black man in his late thirties whom the *New York*

Times described as a "homeless tenant farmer."[49] Stacey had been arrested after Marian Hill Jones, a white woman, told police that a black stranger who came to her door asking for a glass of water had attacked her, grabbing her by the throat and threatening her with a knife until her screams scared him away. Jones identified Stacey, who claimed to know nothing of the crime, when police brought him to her home in what one historian describes as "a scene of chaos and panic." Jones's children "ran excitedly to inform their mother of the black man's arrival," and one of her daughters "reportedly exclaimed to her mother, 'There he is!'" Satisfied that they had their man, the deputies gave Jones a twenty-five-dollar reward that had been offered for information leading to an arrest. Later that day, officers decided to move Stacey to another county to avoid a lynching. A mob of twenty to thirty armed men in five or six cars overtook the speeding police car and took Stacey from the officers at gunpoint. An even larger mob soon assembled near the Jones family home, where Stacey was shot and hanged. The lynching took place at about 4:30 in the afternoon and brought thousands of curious spectators in addition to the three girls pictured in the photograph, who may or may not have been Jones's three children. While the two younger girls' expressions are hard to read (and the face of a uniformed black maid in the background is, almost symbolically, hidden), the older girl's satisfied look suggests, in a way that only photographic evidence can, her appreciation for the lesson about white men's readiness to "protect white womanhood" that she has just seen acted out.[50]

Certainly, this was a lesson a girl of her age would likely already know — a lesson white southerners had long driven home to their children, though usually by less direct means. Katharine Du Pre Lumpkin's *Making of a Southerner*, published in 1946, describes how the daughters of her no-longer-wealthy but relatively aristocratic family learned the mythology of the black rapist that white southerners used to justify lynching and other acts of racial violence. Although her father, an ex-Confederate officer, spoke openly and bitterly about "Negroes' 'insolence' and 'uppitiness,'" especially during Reconstruction (thirty years before Katharine was born), there were

> worse things he never spoke of, at least to us girls, things not suitable to girls' ears, according to Southern standards, things only to be hinted at. We should fear them, of course, but must only guess at their meaning. Of course we could guess; we even knew quite plainly from headlines of lynchings in our newspapers, or when books like *The Clansman* and *The Leopard's Spots* came spilling from the presses in the early 1900's. We

Lynching of Reuben Stacey, Fort Lauderdale, Florida, July 19, 1935. Stacey was lynched near the home of Marian Hill Jones, a thirty-year-old white mother of three who claimed he knocked at her back door, asked for a glass of water, then attacked her with a knife. (Courtesy of Picture History.)

would read these avidly and in due time come to the cliff scene, for instance—the chase, the hinted-at rape of a white girl. "The leopard cannot change his spots. . . ." Thus was cast the moral."[51]

Presumably, it was the didactic content of Thomas Dixon's books that led one Montgomery, Alabama, mother to instruct her fifteen-year-old daughter to read *The Leopard's Spots* "as you would read your Bible." According to the NAACP's Mary White Ovington, "The girl arose from her reading with a deadly fear of a strange black man, a fear capable of creating a lynching if a Negro so much as brushed her sleeve."[52]

Because parental lessons about the rape-lynch myth were so indirect, it is understandable that children sometimes got confused. In Florence, South Carolina, two girls, ages ten and eleven, falsely accused a man of assault simply to attract attention. "It is understood that the children had been hearing and reading sensational stories throughout the country which have been very frequent in the papers recently and they thought that they would get up a sensation on their own account," the Florence *Times* reported, "so they made up the tale and only the fact that the sheriff was a level-headed man saved that section of the country from an outbreak of lawlessness. The sheriff got the story from the children after some persuasion."[53] These girls were not mistaken in seeing lynchings as "sensations," even if they misunderstood lynching's primary purpose as racial terrorism. Not only headlines but also some parents reinforced the idea that a lynching was foremost a show. In July 1912, for example, the *Crisis* reported the comments of a "recently returned traveler" who noted that a black man had been lynched during the visit "and crowds went out to see what was left of his body." "The people I was staying with," the traveler recounted, "went with the rest and took their children— all but one, who had been naughty and was kept at home as a punishment."[54]

As this anecdote suggests, some white southerners not only failed to regard lynchings negatively as horrors from which innocent children ought to be sheltered but instead regarded them positively as exciting events that neither they nor their children should miss. "The mob 'execution' of a black man, woman, or family was not only a public spectacle but also public theater, often a festive affair, a participatory ritual of torture and death that many whites preferred to witness rather than read about," historian Leon Litwack writes. "Special 'excursion' trains transported spectators to the scene, employers sometimes released their workers to attend, parents sent notes to school asking teachers to excuse their children for the event, and entire families attended, the children hoisted on their parents' shoulders to miss none of the action and accompanying festivities." Litwack goes on to recount several examples of children's responses to what they saw, including that of an eleven-year-old North Carolina boy who injured a (white) playmate during a make-believe lynching and that of a nine-year-old who returned from a lynching "unsatisfied: 'I have seen a man hanged,' he told his mother; 'now I wish I could see one burned.'"[55]

The mutilation of lynching victims' bodies seems to have held particular fascination for some children, and it was even more common for children to see publicly displayed corpses than to witness the lynchings themselves. Photographs document this aspect of children's experience as well. For example, half a dozen boys stand just below the charred remains of a black man named Jesse Washington in one postcard, although only their hats are visible at the bottom of the frame. Washington, who was retarded and only seventeen years old at the time of his death, had been convicted of the rape and murder of a Robinson, Texas, farmwoman and was lynched before a crowd of ten to fifteen thousand spectators on May 16, 1916. Afterward, his body was stuffed in a burlap sack and dragged through the streets of Waco, then transported seven miles back to Robinson, where it was hung from a utility pole for Robinson's black population—and these half-dozen white boys and other white children—to see. White children were also on hand to see the lynching and the remains of Paul Reed and Will Cato, who were burned alive for murdering the Hodges family of Statesboro, Georgia, in the summer of 1904. Digging through the two men's ashes, a couple of boys scavenged fragments of bone, which they wrapped in a handkerchief and presented to the judge who had heard the case prior to the lynching. He refused them.[56]

Although this one judge was apparently nonplussed by the boys' gift, the fact is that white children's exposure to black corpses was commonplace. Indeed, it was commonplace enough that outsider John Dollard apparently felt no need to comment on a white father's decision to take his seven-year-old son to the county prison farm to see a "dead Negro"—in this case, a man who had been shot by the police after he fired at an officer. At least in Dollard's account, the child's observations that the man "had a big hole in his chest and there were stripes on his back as though he had been whipped" were simply matter-of-fact.[57] And in truth, even those parents who might have preferred to protect their children from such horrific sights could hardly keep them from hearing rumors or reading headlines or seeing lynching postcards, which were sometimes sold door to door.[58] Historian Edward Ayers tells the story of young Mell Barrett, a white boy, who paid a nickel to a carnival pitchman for a chance to listen to the first Edison talking machine at a picnic in 1896. "All Right Men. Bring Them Out," were the first words Barrett heard, and they were followed by the anguished pleas of two men confessing to rape and begging for mercy. Next came "sounds of shuffling feet, swearing men, rattle of chains, falling wood, brush, and fagots, then a voice— shrill, strident, angry, called out 'Who will apply the torch?' 'I will,' came a chorus of high-pitched, angry voices." "My eyes and mouth were dry," Barrett recalled. "I tried to wet my lips, but my tongue, too, was parched. Perspiration dripped from my hands. I stood immobile, unable to move." "What's the matter, Son—sick?" a man asked as he took the headset from Barrett. The pitchman, sensing Barrett's trouble, dismissed it with the words, "Too much cake, too much lemonade. You know how boys are at a picnic."[59] Sickened as he may have been, Barrett had, at minimum, learned what the girls in Florence, South Carolina, learned from newspaper reports: that lynching was not only acceptable but *exciting*—the kind of thing that their fellow white southerners would pay to read about or hear.

Like lynch mobs' public display of their victims' bodies, white southerners' perpetuation of lynchings through media and oral narrative was hardly accidental even if it was not part of a self-conscious effort to educate the young. Each retelling was a reaffirmation of communal values—often an end in itself. "I've heard about that lynching a hundred times," a young informant told sociologist Olive Quinn in 1944. "What did I hear? Well, they told me that a nigger shot a policeman and they found him and shot him and hanged him on a telephone pole down there by Link's Cafe. They say the Negroes behaved for a long time after that and they were scared to come out for a week or two. Every time the men at the store start talking about how uppity niggers are now, someone talks about that lynching."[60]

Even if the "men at the store" spoke only to each other and not to the young informant, it would be a mistake to ignore the incidental instruction being offered through such narratives, particularly if children's own parents were on the scene. As Quinn observed, "Ordinarily parents are very careful to see to it that their children hear from them only those things considered appropriate to their years. Perhaps these decisions are not always made at a conscious level; but when adults talk freely about sexual looseness and immorality among Negroes, while maintaining a strict silence before their children on the subject of sexual irregularities among white people, it is difficult to escape the judgment that they make this difference because they want their children to believe the one and to disbelieve the other." White southerners' endless talk about the injustices of Reconstruction were also part of this semiconscious curriculum; such stories were "kept vividly alive not because of historical interest but because they provide the emotional set which any good southerner is supposed to have."[61] Lynching stories worked the same way and, because they were so gruesome, were even more poignant.

Antilynching activist Jessie Daniel Ames, who grew up near Tyler, Texas, in the 1880s and 1890s, captured the ambiguities of the indirect-but-not-accidental parental instruction that Quinn described. On the one hand, Ames's parents raised her "very carefully," drilling her in table manners, for example, to such an extent that she had little appetite until family dinners were over and she could go to the kitchen to eat with the cook and the yard-man, who did not correct her so much. On the other hand, Ames's "careful" parents allowed her to overhear graphic conversations about a lynching that had taken place in Tyler. "The reason I remember it so keenly was because they kept on speaking . . . about burning the Negro's eyes out," Ames recalled. "And it just bothered me so much. . . . That was my first knowing anything about this because . . . race was never mentioned among white people." Al-though Ames attributed her overhearing to her own craftiness ("I found out very early that if I didn't say anything the grown people forgot there were little ears present and I could learn a lot"), her explanation is less convinc-ing on the heels of her reminiscence about learning manners.[62] At the very least, her parents must have considered the lynching an insufficiently taboo subject to require them to make sure their children were not within earshot.

What children were allowed to see within their homes was often even more powerful than what they were allowed to hear. Katharine Lumpkin of-fered one especially dramatic example in her autobiography when she de-scribed her father's beating of a black cook, which she chanced to see when she was about eight years old. As if to deny that this episode was meant to be a lesson for her, Lumpkin as author removed herself from the action with phrases like "carefully keeping my distance," just as she edged away from her father's unbearable culpability by using passive verbs. She described the cook "writhing under the blows of a descending stick wielded by the white master of the house" (not by "my father"), and she depicted herself "creeping away" from the scene, only later to ask the "hesitant question, 'What had the cook done?'" Yet this disturbing event did serve as a lesson for young Katharine, making her thereafter "fully aware of myself as a white, and of Negroes as Negroes." Significantly, her father's brutality and the fact that she had *seen* it also made this a moment that she would come back to when she later began to question Jim Crow.[63]

Whether or not her father intended or would have been pleased for Katha-rine to witness this beating is another question. Her parents stood somewhere between those who enthusiastically hoisted their children up on their shoulders at lynchings and those who taught moderation like the Smiths and the Carters. The Lumpkins clearly sheltered their children to some extent, as Katharine's earlier reflections on learning the rape-lynch myth suggest, yet they also taught the doctrine of white supremacy with particular verve — so much so that Katharine was well equipped to win a (very unusual) sixth-grade classroom debate on the question of "Are Negroes Equal to Whites?" by employing such resounding turns of phrase as "and the Bible says that they shall be hewers of wood and drawers of water forever!"[64] Perhaps most significant (and Katharine's reference to the Bible notwithstanding), Lumpkin's family seems to have approached the question of how to behave toward blacks almost entirely on social, rather than moral, terms.

"The emotional set which any good southerner is supposed to have"

Whereas a commitment to both "human" and "social" scales largely explains some whites' moderation, social referencing seems to have been primary for the majority of white southerners. Lumpkin herself suggested how this social referencing worked, noting that it "was not the custom for Southern white gentlemen to thrash their cooks, not by the early 1900s. But it was not heinous. We did not think so. It had once been right not so many years before. Apparently it still could be."[65] At least in her adult reflections, Lumpkin also insisted that the first questions she asked herself in response to this frightening scene were social, rather than moral, ones. She did not accuse her father of being a monster, as Margaret Jones Bolsterli did. Instead, she asked, What would the neighbors say? (They "said nothing.")[66] Would the sheriff come, as the cook hoped and young Katharine feared? (He did not.)

This sort of social referencing became a habit of mind for most white southerners. Writing about blacks in his 1937 study, *The Etiquette of Race Relations in the South*, sociologist Bertram Wilbur Doyle argued that "the Negro . . . 'gets along' because, when in doubt as to what is expected of him, he will ask what is customary — not what is the law."[67] White southerners, too, were taught to ask what is customary — not "what do I think" or "what is right." To put it another way, they were taught to follow racial etiquette. The extent to which this was true became clear to sociologist Olive Quinn in the early 1940s when she asked white southern high school and college students to judge whether certain scenarios involved "social equality" between blacks and whites. "In every case the individual tested the situation by a single criterion: is it accepted practice in the South?"[68]

Nevertheless, questions like "what do I think?" and "what is right?" still lingered, and so Katharine Lumpkin's family never talked about the beating of the cook within her hearing and a "strained atmosphere was present all day—a tension one came to expect whenever slight incidents of race-conflict occurred."[69] For the Lumpkins, just as for moderate families like Lillian Smith's, part of this tension resulted from the deep contradiction between whites' behavior toward blacks and their own self-image as moral, democratic, and civilized. Contradictions of this sort could weigh upon children, in ways both big and small. "I came in late to lunch one day," a young woman told Quinn. "Everyone had eaten except the cook, and I started to sit at the table with her and eat. Mother asked her to move. I didn't understand it. . . . But I was embarrassed; I didn't think Mother should have done that. She might have told me later not to do it again."[70]

As this anecdote suggests, learning and practicing racial etiquette could be uncomfortable for white children at times, not only because of moral qualms in the face of injustice, but also because racial etiquette contradicted the "good manners" they had been taught. Southerners' devotion to courtesy is legendary.[71] Nevertheless, the predominance of racial etiquette makes it clear that southern whites considered politeness—like clean railroad cars, reasonably equipped schools, and so many other of the South's best features—to be for whites only. It was a distinction that white children often failed to make until they were explicitly taught. Thus, while they relied on example and osmosis to teach most aspects of white supremacy, white parents did step in with correctives from time to time. These correctives reinforced the habit of social referencing, but they often left the kind of tension Lumpkin described unresolved as parents responded to children's questions with tautologies like "because that's the way we do things" or with silence or with the old fallback, "You're too young to understand."[72]

White parents' direct, verbal instructions in racial etiquette fall into two main categories: restrictions against too much intimacy with black people and lessons in naming and courtesy titles. Especially among the elite, white children were allowed to become fairly close to nurses and other caregivers when they were small. Yet, like the girl whose mother made the cook leave the table, these children were gradually taught to distance themselves emotionally and, to a lesser extent, physically from black people. Virginia Durr, who grew up in Alabama in the first decades of the twentieth century, summarized this process for her generation: "A great many Southern white children in those days had the experience of giving their first love to a black woman or a black man and then being taught little by little that it was a relationship they couldn't have."[73] This little-by-little teaching was largely a matter of etiquette, which encouraged white children to monitor their own behavior so that, eventually, neither they nor African Americans would have to be corrected for improper acts, many of which, like Quinn's informant's attempt to eat with the cook, might have been acceptable when the child was very young.

Even more common than restrictions against intimacy were parents' admonitions about naming and courtesy titles, especially the words "lady," "Mrs.," and "ma'am." Lewis Killian, who grew up in Georgia in the 1920s, remembered one such admonition well. "One of my most direct lessons in naming came when a black woman came begging at our front door. Still a very small boy, I rushed to the door and then hastened to the back of the house to tell Mother, 'There's a lady at the door.' When Mother returned, she said sharply to me, 'You should have told me that was a colored woman. Ladies are white!'"[74] Scenes like this one were clearly not unusual in the Jim Crow South. In fact, the Florida grandmother whom Clifton Johnson depicted was acting out a very familiar southern script. Virginia Durr recorded a condensed version in her autobiography: "I was taught by the environment and by my mother that you can't call a black woman a lady. You can't say, 'A lady's here'; you have to say, 'A woman's here.'"[75] Meanwhile, Olive Quinn quoted four different interviewees narrating similar stories. In three cases, a white mother taught the lesson that, as one put it, "There are no colored ladies"; in the fourth case, the lesson came from the informant's aunt.[76]

Sometimes black men were the subject of similar lessons and white men did the teaching, as in a humorous story told by a black southern physician: "Two white boys, nine and thirteen years old, were standing on a roadside, seeking a ride. A colored man approached, driving his own car. 'Mister, please give us a ride,' called out the younger. The car slowed down to take them aboard, when the driver overheard the older boy say, 'Didn't papa tell you not to call a nigger Mister?' The face at the wheel hardened, and the car sped away. The two-mile walk to town probably did not reconcile the boys to 'papa's' social philosophy."[77]

But even if the "social philosophy" was the same, the fact that white informants most often remember learning the rules of racial etiquette *from women* and *in relation to women* makes a great deal of sense. First, there is the fact that white children were taught to say "lady," "Mrs.," and "ma'am" even more diligently than "gentleman," "Mr.," or "Sir," which may have led them to run afoul of racial etiquette more often in relation to black women than black men. Such mistakes were all the more serious because courtesy toward white women was so very important. "Ladyhood" was the white South's most important social distinction, and "protecting" white ladies from ignorant and vicious blacks was the rationale not only for lynching but also for segregation and disfranchisement. And, while lynching and the legal maneuverings of segregation and disfranchisement were all public dramas staged primarily by white men, teaching racial etiquette was, like other aspects of child rearing, mostly women's prerogative. How fitting, then, that white women focused such lessons most often on defending their own turf—"Ladies are white!"

The Other End of the Spectrum?

Although many white parents went beyond the core curriculum of racial etiquette to encourage moderation, almost none taught racial equality. Even the handful of white southerners who dissented against white supremacy in the pre–civil rights era generally describe their parents as kindly, but conformist, and the pressures to conform were certainly great. Sociologist Arthur Raper did as much as any white southerner of his generation to improve the South's racial climate through his work with the Commission on Interracial Cooperation and through publications like *The Tragedy of Lynching* and *Preface to Peasantry*. Yet Raper and his wife worried when their children were called "nigger-lovers" by their white peers in Greene County, Georgia, in the early 1940s, and they found it necessary to accommodate racial etiquette themselves, at least to a degree. For example, when Raper was called before a Grand Jury for using courtesy titles for blacks, he suggested they "refer to his actions as 'an indiscretion'" and promised that he would "refrain from the further use of polite titles for Negroes while he was in Greene County." In his own mind, Raper meant that he would no longer use courtesy titles for anyone, black or white. One wonders, though, what he told his children about using words like "Mr." and "Mrs."[78]

No matter how strong their doubts, or even their convictions, about the immoral and unjust nature of racism, few white southerners were willing to expose their children to the censure of other whites. Ironically, Quinn even uses the word "shielding" to describe a different kind of sheltered childhood that white southern parents felt they had to provide, one that would protect their children from influences or experiences from which they "might learn behavior inappropriate to [their] position."[79] Those who did occasionally remove the shield of conformity faced not only community pressures but also the uncomfortable realization that their children's racial learning came, like all children's, from a variety of sources. Sarah Patton Boyle is a case in point. She learned most of her racial lessons from her mother, Jane Stringfellow Patton, who, in her daughter's estimation, "loved Negroes, but with the same deep tenderness she lavished on her riding horse, her dogs, and other pets"—that is, "She loved them without the slightest feeling that they were much like herself." Yet Boyle's father, Robert Williams Patton, was relatively progressive in his racial views and spent much of his career as an Episcopal clergyman working to improve educational opportunities for blacks. To his credit, Boyle's father sometimes tried to push her beyond the paternalism her mother had taught her and "even went so far as to point out occasionally . . . that the squalor of Southern Negroes resulted from poverty and other social pressures. But," Boyle concluded ruefully, "what chance had such stray thoughts against impressions gathered from our whole social pattern?"[80] That pattern, ranging from the horrors of lynching to the subtleties of naming, ensured that whites' racism would be perpetuated from one generation to the next—almost always with considerable help from Mom and Dad.

Sheltering Black Children

The South's "whole social pattern" is precisely what black parents were up against. Yet to think of black child rearing in this way is to risk overlooking the deeply personal nature of each family's efforts, like Lewis DeLaine's struggle to save his premature baby's life in a story about "sheltering" that pairs hauntingly with the one Margaret Jones Bolsterli told about her father's refusal to pay for an incubator. Told by the midwife that his third daughter, born in January 1936 on his farm in Summerton, South Carolina, was too small and weak to live, DeLaine sat up night after night heating bricks in a woodstove and placing them around the child to keep her warm. "I would say [my sister's] life is a miracle," Marguirite DeLaine, Lewis's youngest child, reflected proudly. Marguirite was also proud of the way her family lived in easier, happier moments, including the way they celebrated birthdays with a birthday cake that made each child feel special. Once when her mother was away, DeLaine's father took a hand in this as well, baking a cake for one of his girls in a pan that his wife used exclusively for cornbread. "And I thought that was so funny," Marguirite laughed. "I remember teasing [my sister] about her cornbread cake. It had no frosting on it whatsoever. But I look at my father, . . . I look back at that time and I say now you know, my father was a very sensitive man to realize his daughter would have been upset" not to have a cake.[81]

Margaret Jones Bolsterli depicted her father at one of his worst moments. Marguirite DeLaine captured her father at two of his best. Patterns of black child rearing, like patterns of white child rearing, covered a broad range of individual bests and worsts, with the difference that blacks' approaches to teaching children about race were much more self-conscious and ideologically considered, overall, than whites'. Focusing first on the black middle class in the early twentieth century, we see a well-developed ideology of child rearing that had much to do with sheltering and was rooted in a broader strategy for racial advancement through respectability and self-help. When we look beyond the middle class, however, the picture is much less clear. Middle-class sources, including a one-of-a-kind survey published by W. E. B. Du Bois and Augustus Granville Dill in 1914, clearly indicate that many poor and working-class blacks were not living up to middle-class blacks' standards of respectability in child rearing, as in a number of other aspects of life. Yet the memories of black men and women who grew up in working-class families challenge any notion that working-class black parents simply neglected their children or taught them to be subservient. Instead, we hear mixed messages from parents whose love and ambitions for their children clashed with their fear of whites—parents like Ernest Swain's father, who modeled passive acceptance of Jim Crow, on the one hand, but went out of his way to warn a "redneck" policeman to leave his two boys alone, on the other. "I was so happy he told 'em," Swain remembered, suggesting how important it was for children to see their parents stand up to whites, at least once in a while (and even if they were, like Swain's father, a little drunk at the time).[82] Holding back their emotions was hard for children, and, even under the best of circumstances, behaving "respectably" was even harder. No matter how much their parents admonished them to maintain their dignity and rise above the racism they faced, black children often responded to discrimination with anger and wanted to fight back with more straightforward and less patient methods than their parents advised. Meanwhile, black parents who taught respectability were doing their best to provide a sheltered childhood in much the same way they were using respectability as a shield for the race as a whole.

The Politics of Respectability

Confronted with terrifying racial violence, as well as disfranchisement and the legal hardening of segregation, in the late nineteenth century, blacks "dealt with the assault by turning inward" to emphasize institution-building and self-help.[83] Along with self-help came a commitment to bourgeois values such as hard work, temperance, thrift, piety, and perseverance, as well as chastity and domesticity, especially for women. Blacks practiced these values as an extension of their own religious beliefs and, in historian Glenda Gilmore's words, as "useful tools for living" in their struggle to establish themselves in business, education, and the professions after generations of enslavement.[84] Meanwhile, a commitment to morals and manners, along with some degree of education, distinguished "middle-class" from "working-class" blacks in ways that occupation and income, in a world of narrowly circumscribed economic opportunities, generally could not.[85]

Although they believed in respectability for its own sake, African Americans also hoped, reasonably enough, that their upright behavior would earn them a measure of respect from whites. For how could whites maintain the argument that blacks were naturally inferior if some blacks demonstrated that they most certainly were not? Addressed to other blacks, as well as to white racists, respectability was thus a strategy that many blacks employed in a discursive contest over black identity that was raging, especially in American popular culture, at the turn of the twentieth century. Popular imagery that depicted African Americans as lazy, immoral, and inferior and that denied that there was any such thing as a virtuous black woman served as a propaganda campaign in the very real and bloody war that white southerners were waging on black bodies, as well as black civil and political rights. Middle-class blacks hoped to counter this propaganda by behaving respectably and by encouraging other African Americans to do the same. For this reason, respectability was very much a public statement, as well as a private concern. Blacks demonstrated their morals and manners on streetcars and in other public places both from habit and belief and because they were conscious that whites, ever watchful for breaches in racial etiquette, were a highly critical but perhaps also a reachable audience.

Not a mere facade, respectability could nonetheless be a very self-conscious performance. It was also a performance best suited to elite and middle-class African Americans, who had the education and economic wherewithal to adorn their speech with polite language, to costume their bodies in tasteful clothing that did not become soiled by physical labor, and to choose the settings in which they interacted with whites. Anecdotes abound of middle-class blacks who paid close attention to clothing, hygiene, and physical appearance and who restricted their own and their children's activities to avoid encounters in which they might not be able to maintain a dignified manner. Under the circumstances, blacks' respectable self-presentation could require considerable energy and resourcefulness. Even managing one's body could be difficult in urban and small-town spaces where restrooms, water fountains, and restaurants open to blacks were sometimes few and virtually always inferior. As one Atlanta minister described it, African Americans "had to do their eating and preparations at home entirely before they went [out] so that nothing would happen to them in the physical way until they went back home."[86]

Some African Americans tried to avoid all settings in which they would have to accommodate whites' racism. For example, Atlanta University professor George A. Towns responded to the segregation of Atlanta's streetcars in 1900 first by supporting a boycott that proved unsuccessful, then by buying a bicycle, an act of resistance that reflected his relative economic advantages and that was as personally motivated as it was politically defiant. As Towns's daughter, Atlanta civic leader Grace Towns Hamilton, explained it, men like her father simply "refused to subject themselves to segregation."[87] They were too proud to submit and too fastidious—too respectable—to risk either a display of righteous anger or its consequences. Black families taught this lesson of avoidance to their children as well, encouraging them to interact with whites as little as possible and to shun segregated facilities.

Indeed, although historians have tended to study black women's and men's politics of respectability separately and mostly outside the domestic sphere, respectability must also be understood as a family strategy and one that had particular significance for children.[88] "Respectable" black parents not only sheltered their children in the ways other Americans increasingly were doing, such as keeping them in school, but also sheltered them from racism by blunting its psychological effects. In short, the same oppositional quality that made respectability appealing for black adults to practice made it absolutely vital for black children to learn.

"Respectable" Black Child Rearing

Like adult politics of respectability, respectable black child rearing emphasized the need for individual blacks to define or redefine themselves and their race in the public eye. But respectable child rearing also had an additional function: to teach children to be self-defining in their own minds. This function became all the more important as segregation became entrenched, reinforcing and codifying the lesson in racial hierarchy that racial etiquette had long taught and would continue to teach. A speech that Nannie Helen Burroughs gave before the Women's Convention of the National Baptist Convention in 1905 suggests how this preemptive socialization worked. "Men and women are not made on trains and on streetcars," Burroughs asserted. "If in our homes there is implanted in the hearts of our children . . . the thought that they are what they are, not by environment, but of themselves, this effort to teach a lesson of inferiority will be futile." Burroughs was expressing a sentiment her audience shared, namely that submission to Jim Crow required blacks to give up their civil rights but could not take away their power of self-definition.[89] Instead, if children could develop self-respect from within through their practice of respectability, they would have the power to define themselves, to develop their own sense of identity, regardless of how whites attempted to circumscribe and define them. They would possess not only the emotional strength to carry the unavoidable psychological baggage of racism but also the self-assurance and sense of purpose they needed in order to achieve in public and private life and contribute to the betterment of humanity. Mary Church Terrell expressed this optimistic viewpoint, which was universal among black clubwomen and prevalent throughout the black middle class, with rhetorical flourish: "We believe we can build the foundation of the next generation upon such a rock of morality, intelligence and strength, that the floods of proscription, prejudice and persecution may descend upon it in torrents and yet it will not be moved." While an earlier generation of black parents might have hoped that teaching their children to be respectable would dispel the clouds of racism, by the turn of the twentieth century leaders like Terrell were coming to understand that the torrents of proscription and prejudice would inevitably descend, no matter how upstanding black people and their children might be.[90] Nevertheless, respectability and self-restraint remained at the center of black child-rearing strategies throughout the first half of the twentieth century and would still be largely in place at the start of the civil rights movement, even as the look and feel of what was "respectable" changed with the decades. A young Martin Luther King Jr. did not dress or speak or act in quite the same ways in the early 1950s as an equally respectable young black man would have dressed and spoken and acted in the 1890s or the 1910s. Yet they had much in common, especially when it came to lessons learned in childhood.

A major reason for respectability's persistence is that, in the eyes of many black men and women who were raised this way, respectable black child rearing *worked*. Autobiographies and oral histories are replete with tributes to parents who taught dignity and self-respect. William J. Coker Jr. of Norfolk, Virginia, was particularly eloquent. "My father was able to shelter us from ugliness," Coker reflected. "He and my mother worked hard . . . to get us the things that they wanted us to have, to provide for us in a manner that they wanted to provide." Among these assets was a "huge house [with] plenty of space" that his father bought when they moved to Norfolk from North Carolina in 1941, when Coker was six years old. A commitment to education was also key. Even though his parents had each finished only sixth or seventh grade, other members of his family who lived nearby were "college-trained" and Coker "was raised in an environment that talked about education, pursuing education, the world, things that are going on, current events, history, literature, poems." The adults around him also discussed Jim Crow, but took care not to let Coker and his siblings hear too much "racial negativism"—either whites' negative views of blacks or blacks' negative views of whites. All of this care in his raising left Coker's inborn drive for personhood "intact." Asked if his military service in the 1950s had fueled his participation in the civil rights movement, Coker, who was a member of the Congress of Racial Equality (CORE), explained that "the desire to have equal treatment was smoothly spread throughout [his] lifetime." He continued, "Because of the things that you've heard from adults, as well as the stories they told, as well as your own need to feel your personage—I think that's a good word—it was there intact." "It's a process that takes place from the moment your parents take you out of the cradle and kiss you and coo you," Coker added. "You need to be able to stand up on your own two feet and say, 'I am,' as well as anyone else. So that was always there. I have not been whipped into thinking anything less."[91] Like Dorcas Carter's mother, who taught her children all the same lessons (though perhaps with even more emphasis on manners) a generation earlier, William Coker's family clearly "gave you feet on which to stand."[92]

For Carter as for Coker, respectability training began in infancy and incorporated many elements. Children's first lessons were about how to behave toward other blacks, not whites. Born in 1913, Dorcas Carter was old enough to remember what New Bern, North Carolina's middle-class neighborhood was like before it was destroyed by a fire in 1922:

> I felt as a girl that it was prosperous . . . because we had tailors in that community, we had butchers in that community, we had merchants in our community, we had a blacksmith in our community. . . . To me I felt as though we were almost like . . . the historic section of New Bern, on George Street particularly, that the houses were very historic and the people to me dressed . . . so modest, so cultured. When they were walking down the street you could see the men escorting the ladies by the arm and lifting them up to the street level or the curb level, all dressed with their walking canes and their derbies. These were the people whom I knew as a girl.

As the daughter of a successful building contractor and a former teacher, Carter was expected to fit in among these respectable black citizens and had to learn to do so by obeying the adults around her, chiefly her mother. Neighbors, too, "could talk to you," Carter remembered. "'Now you know [your mother] doesn't want you doing that. You get right in that house.'"[93]

Parents encouraged this community discipline by teaching children to respect their elders, both within the family and outside it. Born in 1935, Rosita Taylor of Charlotte, North Carolina, learned the same lessons black boys and girls had been taught for decades, especially in middle-class homes. Asked how she was expected to behave in front of adults, Taylor laughed, "With the utmost respect. First of all, when I saw them I was to greet them. When they spoke to me I was to speak to them with respect. You know, I was to say 'Yes, Ma'am,' 'No, Ma'am,' 'No, Sir.' I was never to challenge them. If they did something to me . . . that I thought was off-color, I just had to deal with it within myself." Adults not only stood by one another, but "during that time, everybody sort of had the same kind of principles that they upheld"—at least in her mostly middle-class neighborhood.[94] So children had little choice but to be outwardly polite and respectful, even if, inwardly, they felt that they were being unfairly treated or misunderstood.

The divide between outward demeanor and inner feelings could be all the greater because of the extent to which middle-class blacks' "principles" encompassed a whole performance of refinement. As historian Stephanie Shaw summarizes, "Cleanliness and a neat appearance were important complements to politeness. Gossiping and unnecessary borrowing were unacceptable behaviors. And woe betide one caught eating on the street."[95] Teacher and civil rights leader Septima Clark, who grew up in Charleston in the early 1900s, remembered that her mother not only forbade her from eating on the street but also spanked her on the spot when she tried to pick up a bag of candy that a white girl had dropped. "The little girl's mother was not going to let her have it, since it fell on the ground, and I was going to take it. And [my mother] knew that that would be an inferiority trait, and she whipped me," Clark recalled.[96]

Although they might think in terms of "inferiority traits," black parents focused more on family than on race to explain why respectability was so important. Norma Boyd's mother taught her that "whatever you did, you were talking about yourself. If you behaved yourself, you were saying you came from a good home. If you did anything wrong, you were saying something was wrong at home." Tied to this lesson in good behavior was a lesson in self-respect. "Another thing she instilled in us," Boyd recalled, "was that no one in all the world was any better than we were. At least the only people who were superior to us were the people whose conduct was superior to ours. So we grew up with that understanding."[97] To instill this implicitly racial "under-standing" in their children, black parents would go to considerable lengths. Henry Beard Delany, an Episcopal minister and educator and father of North Carolina–born Sarah and Elizabeth Delany, went so far as to line his ten boys and girls up for inspection each morning to make sure that their shoes were polished and their clothes and faces were clean. "He was proud of his children and I think this was just a way for him to convey this," Sarah Delany reflected. "We carried the Delany name and he wanted us to look respectable when we left the house."[98]

Just as they encouraged their children to represent their families well, black parents admonished children not to do anything that would bring shame on themselves, their families, or their race. Their gravest fears differed for boys and girls, although lessons in politeness, honesty, piety, and other virtues applied with equal force. Responding to cultural stereotypes as well as manifest dangers, black parents worried about girls' sexuality far more than boys'. Dorcas Carter's mother reminded her frequently that "the wages of sin is death and the way of the transgressor is hard." Beulah Hester's mother was much more blunt. Born in Oxford, North Carolina, in 1883 to a Baptist minister and his wife, Hester remembered her mother saying, "Beulah, I love you, but I'd rather see you in your grave than [have you] bring disgrace on me. . . . Not for the sacrifices that I made for you, but it would hurt me so that I know I couldn't stand it." One sacrifice that black families often made for their daughters—and one very important form of sheltering—was to forego their potential earnings to keep them out of household work and beyond the reach of white men. For, if girls' developing sexuality was worrisome, men's exploitative sexual appetites were more so, especially if the men were white and could not be held accountable.[99]

Parents' fears for their boys were similarly compounded by their own powerlessness in the face of white authority. Just as they feared that girls might be sexually assaulted, they feared that boys might be arrested, beaten, or worse and that they would be unable to do anything about it. Barbara Cooper, who grew up in Memphis in the 1930s, remembered that the police were "just terrible"; she felt that black "families really over-protected the boys because they were so hard on black folk, especially black boys, young men."[100] Yet, even though they understood that boys were sometimes compelled to fight and could be arrested or attacked without cause, middle-class African Americans still felt a certain shame associated with ungentlemanly behavior. As historian Willard Gatewood argues in *Aristocrats of Color*, to "run afoul of the law or to be charged with a serious crime . . . was to bring disgrace upon the family."[101] Ideally, black boys would always be able to demonstrate superior restraint and rise above degrading conflicts.

Even more important than their concern for family image was parents' belief that respectability was the key to their children's survival and success. Parents who had achieved middle-class status through hard work, upright behavior, and a commitment to education hoped that their children could build useful and prosperous lives using these same tools.

"Respectable" Child Rearing in the Black Working Class

So did many parents who had not made it quite so far. While respectability was a defining feature of the black middle class, a desire for respectability and attempts at respectable child rearing also reached across class lines. William Henry Holtzclaw's family is a good example. Aspects of Holtzclaw's childhood would have no doubt appalled many of his respectable black contemporaries. Born near the end of Reconstruction in rural Alabama, he was often left alone with his brothers and sisters while his father worked as a sharecropper and his mother cooked for their landlord's family. "At such times we children suffered an excruciating kind of pain—the pain of hunger," he recalled. "I can well remember how at night we would often cry for food until falling here and there on the floor we would sob ourselves to sleep." Late at night, his mother would return with table scraps or pot liquor from the white family's kitchen to give the children their supper. But clearly she had neither the energy nor the resources to teach them proper manners. Waking them, she "would place the pan on the floor, or on her knees, and gathering around we would eat to our satisfaction. There was neither knife, fork, nor spoon—nothing but the pan," Holtzclaw remembered. "We used our hands and sometimes in our haste dived head foremost into the pan, very much as pigs after swill." Similar to descriptions of how slave children were fed, this, surely, was the antithesis of respectability.[102]

And yet Holtzclaw's family also had its moments. His parents "had a great faith in education, and they were determined that their children should have that blessing of which they themselves had been deprived." His father called a meeting of the black men in the community, and together they constructed a schoolhouse. Holtzclaw and his siblings walked three miles each way for the two months school was in session, his oldest sister carrying him on her shoulders when his legs gave out. "At the end of the first school year there was a trying time in our family," Holtzclaw recalled in his memoir. "On this occasion the teacher ordered all the pupils to appear dressed in white. We had no white clothes, nor many of any other sort." Holtzclaw's father insisted that it would be foolish to buy white clothing for a single occasion, but his mother "was still determined that her children should look as well . . . as any of our neighbors." Staying up all night, she made suits of clothes for all three children from her white Sunday petticoat. "As there is just so much cloth in a petticoat and no more, the stuff had to be cut close . . . and as the petticoat had been worn several times and was, therefore, likely to tear, we had to be very careful how we stooped moving about the stage, lest there should be a general splitting and tearing." The Holtzclaw children made it through the school assembly with their clothes intact, coming away with a feeling of certainty that "there was no mother there who was prouder of her children than ours."[103] While not quite the same as preemptive training in middle-class respectability, this experience was, for Holtzclaw, something rather like it.

And Holtzclaw was certainly not alone. Autobiographical sources make it clear that many working-class black families taught the same morals and manners that middle-class families taught, albeit with less emphasis on the genteel performance of respectability and lessons learned from "history, literature, poems" (as Coker put it) and perhaps more emphasis on religion and on corporal punishment. Although middle-class parents used corporal punishment as well, working-class and especially rural black families seem to have used it more readily. "You can't whip children now, I guess, but Mama would be in bad shape," Ila Blue mused about her girlhood on a North Carolina farm in the 1910s. "Mama was the kind who would tell you, 'This hurts me worse than it hurts you.'"[104]

Georgia Bays's mother was another who believed in whipping children and who relied on community discipline much like what Dorcas Carter and Rosita Taylor described. "People would get together in them days. Parents, the lady people, would come together and join together about these children. All these children belonged to all of us. That's the way you was raised," Bays reflected on her childhood among Mississippi sharecroppers in the 1910s and early 1920s. For children, such cohesion among adults meant there "wasn't no getting by," Bays explained. "If I go to my neighbor's house, I'd just as well be at home, because I was taught right, you hear me, and I had to act right." If she failed to act right, the neighbor "didn't go over there and tell Mama" right away. "She just took her time and went when she got ready. When she'd tell my mama what I done done and what I said, no more talk. They didn't ask what did you do and how did you do it. They whoop[ed] you. You got two whoopings."[105]

Bays's explanation of what it meant to "act right" offers a glimpse of working-class respectability, at least for girls. Acting right meant no swearing or whistling, considered "a boy's thing," or hollering loudly, considered "too ugly . . . for a girl." More important, it meant sitting right—legs uncrossed, knees together, skirt pulled down below the knee. As she got older, Bays was warned not to flirt and never to accept money or gifts from anyone, especially men and boys, "because if you take money, that's going to cause something else." Bays's mother also told her "all about running around the house or getting off too far with boys," although it is not clear how explicit her sex education was, and her father may have had sex in mind when he insisted that she did not "know how to treat no husband" after Bays announced her plan to marry at age fourteen. (She assured him that she did know how to treat a husband and would do him "like Mama done do you.") Bays's parents' fear that she would be led into temptation by material desire encouraged them to be wary of other girls, as well as men and boys. "Learn not to want things that you see your neighbors and your neighbors' children wear," her mother told her, "because you don't know how in the world they're getting their clothes." "Oh, I'd lay around and cry. I thought it was the worst thing in the world," Bays remembered. At the time, she had felt sad and angry that she was not allowed to go to town on Saturdays with the neighbor girls, but "finally, one day it come to an end." Bays continued, "They put [the neighbor girls] in jail up at Calumet City for stealing. [My mother] said, 'Now, I told you that. That's how they get their powders and paint.'" A daughter of the same family had a child out of wedlock at thirteen and, as Bays recalled, her mother "told me about that," too.[106]

Parents tended to be less strict with their sons than with their daughters, but many of the same demands for obedience and good behavior still applied. As historian Leon Litwack summarizes, both boys and girls "were taught to demonstrate proper respect and deference in the presence of adults, particularly the elderly, and they were expected to adhere to certain moral values and standards of behavior."[107] Small crimes were not allowed to go unpunished lest they lead to larger ones, as Charles and Medgar Evers discovered when their mother "beat the stew out of" them for lying about stealing cookies. "If you lie about this you lie about somethin' else," she scolded.[108] William Henry Holtzclaw's mother taught a comparable lesson about stealing in explicitly racial terms, explaining that white people expected and even wanted blacks to steal as confirmation of their innate inferiority; therefore, "we must show them that we would not."[109]

Like Holtzclaw, working-class black children came to understand that their respectability training was about showing people, including whites,

what kind of people they were. Georgia Bays went so far as to blame the unwanted sexual attention that many black women received from white men
on some women's failure to carry themselves respectably. "There's a certain
way you can act around people and it tells [them] what not to do and what
to do, what to ask and what to say," she reflected. "So I always kept myself—
not thinking myself better, [my] flesh no better, but my ways and actions
was. I acted my place," Bays concluded, offering a seemingly transcendent
redefinition of the South's geography of social standing, "and you *better* stay
in yours."[110]

Clearly, then, "respectable" behavior served the same discursive function
for many poorer African Americans that it served for the black middle class.
Black children learned how to behave within their own communities so that
they would have an unshakable understanding of what proper behavior was.
Knowing that they were behaving properly would, in turn, protect them—at
least psychologically—from whites who treated them as if they and their behavior were improper and unworthy of respect. Even though they struggled
financially, Olivia Cherry's mother "always told [her children] that [they] were
somebody and [they] should never feel inferior or act inferior."[111] Florence
Borders recalled her father saying that "no matter what labels other people
placed on me, I determined what I was."[112] Some parents went further, encouraging their children to challenge segregation and racial etiquette. In
retrospect, Herbert Cappie thought his father was "half crazy" for insisting
that they enter segregated parks and theaters in New Orleans in the 1920s
not simply because the two of them were light enough to pass, although that
undoubtedly helped, but because they "had the right to go to these places."[113]
Similarly, Mazie Williams, who grew up in the small town of Demopolis, Alabama, during the Depression, was taught to walk out of stores if she was not
waited on quickly and to stay on the sidewalk even when whites expected
blacks to walk in the street. "The first thing I remember my grandmother
saying to me," Williams said, "was . . . that at no given time should we ever
walk in the street, that regardless of how we got through [the crowd on] the
sidewalk, that we should get through [on] the sidewalk and that she should
never be told that we didn't." Yet even Williams's outspoken grandmother
kept safety in mind, encouraging Williams to avoid fights and to use the
"colored" bathroom if she could not wait until she got home.[114]

Even if they had to accommodate to segregation and racial etiquette, however, black children who had been taught to be respectable presumably knew
within themselves that they were not the inferiors whites made them out
to be. Poet and novelist James Weldon Johnson expressed this feeling well

in an account of being thrown out of a railroad car. If the white passengers' smug looks "rose from any idea that I was having a sense of my inferiority impressed upon me, they were sadly in error," he wrote; "indeed, my sensation was the direct opposite; I felt that I was being humiliated."[115] Although being humiliated was certainly still painful, black men and women, especially but not only in the middle class, strove hard to make sure that their children—and perhaps even some whites—could see the distinction Johnson was making. Black people who behaved respectably demonstrated that blacks were not inherently inferior. Rather, they were a people who could maintain their dignity and self-respect even in the face of oppression.

"Four-fifths of the children are improperly reared"

Because it was meant, in part, to change whites' minds, respectability needed to be a unified front. Middle-class blacks did not always appreciate how hard families like Holtzclaw's and Bays's worked to instill proper morals and manners, but they could see at a glance that respectable child rearing had not taken sufficient hold throughout the working class. "Child-culture and mother-culture are the demands of the age for the race," the Atlanta-based Voice of the Negro editorialized in July 1904, in one of many articles about child rearing that appeared in the black press in the early twentieth century. "In the days of slavery we had mammies, in a day of freedom we must have 'mothers,'" the editorial insisted. "In a day of slavery we had 'topsies who just growed,' in a day of freedom we must have children who are reared and trained in home duties, home obedience, and who are trained in heart to know that virtue makes heaven, and that immorality is the mother of death." The editorial called on black women's clubs to "do something for the childhood of the race"—as, in fact, social service organizations like the Neighborhood Union were starting to do in this era.[116] Their work, like the outpourings in the black press and at conventions ranging from the massive Negro Young People's Christian and Educational Congress of 1902 to annual meetings of the NAACP, indicates the depth and breadth of middle-class blacks' concerns about how the masses of black children were being reared.[117]

Of all the articles, speeches, and other sources related to child rearing that were created by middle-class blacks in the first decades of the twentieth century, none is more interesting than a survey conducted for the Eighteenth Annual Atlanta University Conference of Negro Problems, which was the last one directed by W. E. B. Du Bois. After almost two decades of studying African American life as empirically as possible, Du Bois and the organizers of this 1913 gathering decided to take a different tack. "There is without a doubt a deep-seated feeling in the minds of many that the Negro problem is primarily a matter of morals and manners and that the real basis of color prejudice in America is the fact that the Negroes as a race are rude and thoughtless in manners and altogether quite hopeless in sexual morals, in regard for property rights and in reverence for truth," Du Bois and his co-editor Augustus Granville Dill explained in the published conference proceedings, titled "Morals and Manners Among Negro Americans." "This accusation . . . is the more easily made because manners and morals lend themselves but seldom to exact measurement." The purpose of this study, then, was to collect opinions from "trustworthy persons in various parts of the United States who ought to know of the morals and manners of Negro Americans"—that is, from preachers, teachers, social workers, artisans, and professionals, many of whom had connections with Atlanta University or other black colleges. From these opinions, Du Bois and Dill hoped to reach some conclusions about blacks' degree of civility and overall moral state that black leaders might use to counter the derogatory stereotypes that justified segregation and discrimination in whites' minds.[118]

However, when it came to answering questions about the black population's morals and manners, the men and women whose opinions Du Bois and Dill sought were deeply ambivalent. Assuming that most of the 385 people who responded to the survey were black, the commentary reprinted in "Morals and Manners" serves as something of an index of middle-class blacks' outlook on the wider black community.[119] But their impressions of what they saw there varied a great deal, and many respondents felt it necessary to qualify their statements at every turn, leading Du Bois and Dill to conclude that "the Negro race is in spiritual turmoil. It is self-conscious, self-critical, and has not yet grasped great and definite ideals."[120]

Nowhere was this spiritual turmoil and failure to grasp, or achieve, definitely held ideals more evident than on questions about child rearing among black southerners. Asked "What is the condition of colored people whom you know in regard to [the] rearing of children?" the anonymous survey respondents from the South expressed a wide range of opinions, most of them negative. "Many parents allow their children to run at large at late hours of the night," one Alabaman wrote, adding that the children "assemble in dives and hang around the corners in great numbers, especially the boys," and that "many of them are becoming gamblers and idlers." A Texan agreed that most blacks' approach to child rearing was "a complete failure," that much of the race was "lost almost without a remedy," and that it was "indeed a sad state of affairs as the children are permitted to run the streets at will." In fact, although few were quite so grim, some two-thirds of the southerners quoted in "Morals and Manners Among Negro Americans" had something negative to say about how African Americans in their communities were raising their children.[121] Less prescriptive and more descriptive than most middle-class pronouncements on child rearing, their commentary suggests not only how far middle-class blacks felt the race had yet to travel but also why, in their view, progress was so slow.

Many attributed the less than respectable behavior of many black children almost entirely to class. "Among the educated parents, the majority of the children are being beautifully reared," a Virginian wrote, adding that "there are ignorant families where the children are being neglected." This "is easy to account for," he or she concluded, perhaps referring to the lack of educational opportunities for the black population as a whole. Other respondents also seemed to find differences in child-rearing practices easy to understand. Blacks' "condition" in regard to child rearing "varies according to economic and intellectual conditions," one Alabaman wrote, while another stated simply that "better families look after children well," while "others are somewhat neglectful."[122]

While many seemed to take class differences for granted, a few of those who responded to Du Bois and Dill's survey did go on to suggest why class mattered so much. "The condition of the working people hinders them in the rearing of their children," one Georgia informant wrote. According to a South Carolinian, "Quite a number of mothers [work] in [household] service thus leaving children to care for and rear themselves during the very time they need watching. Many children attend school from such homes having to prepare themselves." Informants also recognized the inadequacy of schools and day care facilities as a problem that particularly affected the working class. "The children are neglected in many cases from lack of facilities to rear them properly, [including] inadequate schools," an Alabaman noted, citing also the "necessity of parents to work and spend little time in the home."[123]

Although they sympathized with parents whose jobs took them away from home, survey respondents were less kind in their evaluation of working-class parents' intelligence and qualifications for child rearing. Children "suffer from ignorant and incompetent parents" and "do not get proper physical, mental and moral training," a Tennessean lamented. "Most children these days get no home training and the example of their parents is such as is sure to corrupt their morals and manners," a respondent from Florida concurred. Another Floridian was even more blunt: "If there is any one thing that should be establish[ed] it is a school to teach our people how to rear their children. For God knows they don't know and don't care." Like Du Bois and Dill themselves, some informants attributed the inadequacies of black parents to their disadvantaged backgrounds in slavery and the first few decades of freedom. "Four fifths of the children are improperly reared," an informant from Alabama wrote. "The parents in equal numbers have never had proper training themselves."[124]

In general, then, the middle-class observers represented in Du Bois and Dill's survey explained failures to achieve "respectable" child-rearing ideals by pointing to the majority of black parents who were poor, uneducated, and forced to neglect their children's emotional and intellectual needs while they worked long hours at exhausting and ill-paid jobs. Recognizing these realities, some found they could hardly blame working-class families for letting their children grow up on their own. "I am not prepared to answer this question," one Alabaman wrote. "I have given this subject considerable tho[ugh]t but am still undecided as to whether the Negro of my community is rearing his children in a way that could be improved under [the] circumstances or not." "Rearing and training of children is the most difficult problem of any people," another Alabaman concluded, "and because of the colored man's financial and political status and because of having to battle with conditions which are imposed upon him[,] the work of properly rearing his children has been far from satisfactory either to himself or to his best friends."[125] Like other middle-class observers, this respondent regretted the conditions in which most black people lived but also felt he or she knew without a doubt what "proper" child rearing was.

As they lamented the conditions that made it impossible for the masses of black southerners to teach their children to be respectable, middle-class observers rarely considered that working-class blacks might be pursuing an alternative strategy rather than simply failing to live up to a middle-class standard. Perhaps the most perceptive of Du Bois and Dill's survey respondents was the South Carolinian who focused on the vast number of black mothers who worked in domestic service. These women's children not only had "to care for and rear themselves," he or she observed, but "are taught at home to defend themselves at all hazards," a lesson that clearly contradicted the "respectable" approach of rising above conflicts most, if not all, of the time.[126] Of all the survey responses from the southern states, this was the only one that even suggested that working-class African Americans might be deliberately teaching their children something other than respectability, not just failing to teach them what the black middle class wanted them to learn.

Working-Class Alternatives?

Significantly, the lesson about self-defense that this South Carolinian cited parallels a lesson that black social scientist Allison Davis described as distinctly working-class. Writing in the late 1930s, Davis was among the first generation of scholars to take on the question of how black parents prepared their children for life in the Jim Crow South. "The type of accommodation which a child is taught . . . usually depends, to a degree, upon the *social class* of his parents in the Negro society," he argued. "In lower-class families, a child is taught that he is a 'nigger' and that he must be subservient to white people, since he must work for them. He is trained to fight, however, if he is attacked." In comparison to middle- and upper-class black children who were taught to avoid contact with whites as much as possible, lower-class children were more likely "to become openly aggressive toward white people" if the normal demands for deference within the South's white supremacist society were exceeded. Otherwise, such children appeared "highly accommodated" to Jim Crow social relations on the surface while learning to adopt "certain well disguised forms of aggression" behind a mask of complacency. As Davis noted, "sabotage in one's work for white people (slowness, lack of punctuality, clumsiness) and the use of flattery, humor, secrecy, 'ignorance,' and other behavior for outwitting white people are learned at an early age."[127]

More than half a century old, Davis's work is hardly the last word on class differences in black child-rearing strategies, but it is nonetheless suggestive. Some black families clearly did teach subservience. "Honor the white folks, honor 'em, yassuh an' nosuh. You have to do that," bluesman Willie Thomas's father insisted. (At the same time, Thomas's very identity as a bluesman indicates that he also learned the arts of resistance that Davis implied were the flip side of the coin of subservience, about which more below.)[128] "Treat them right. Treat them right. Always treat white folks right," Lester "Jack" Bullock's parents admonished—a lesson that was all the more urgent whenever there was trouble anywhere near their North Carolina tobacco farm. "Don't be dogging and don't be fussing with 'em," "stay out of trouble," and "if you fight back, you might get the worstest end of it," Bullock's parents advised.[129] "A lot of black parents would tell their children, 'It's a white man's world and you just happen to be here, nigger,'" asserted Charles Evers, who grew up in Decatur, Mississippi, in the 1920s and 1930s. Evers's own father explained Jim Crow by saying, "Well, son, that's the way it is. I don't know what we can do about it. There ain't nothin' we can do about it. Because if we do anything about it, they kill you"—an all-too-prophetic lesson in the case of Charles's younger brother Medgar, who was murdered in 1963 for his civil rights activism.[130] As Leon Litwack argues, such lessons reflected a "felt urgency to acculturate black children into the difficult process of 'getting along'" that "infused much of the advice parents gave their daughters and sons: the admonitions to be alert and cautious, to act with the utmost restraint and deference, to contain their rage and resentment over insults, to do nothing that might bring into question the veracity of whites or contradict their expectations, and most important, to have as little as possible to do with whites."[131] This was, in short, the voice of black parents' fear.

And yet fear was seldom the only or even the primary emotion parents felt in relation to their children. They also felt pride, hope, ambition, love. Presumably, it was fear that made Henry Robinson want to whip his sons, James and William, for fighting back against a group of white boys who had attacked them while they were delivering laundry to a white family for whom their mother washed. Willie Belle Robinson responded differently, with a grim hope for her sons' future manhood. "They did right; they defended themselves against a gang of damn crackers," she told her husband. "They've got to learn what to expect. They're black and they'll be black until they die. And as long as they're black, they're going to be hated, scorned, cheated and persecuted. At least they can have the satisfaction of acting like men."[132]

Novelist and folklorist Zora Neale Hurston's parents were similarly divided on the question of how much to let fear shape their parental teachings. Hurston's father felt that it "did not do for Negroes to have too much spirit." Consequently, Hurston recalled, he "was always threatening to break mine or kill me in the attempt. . . . The white folks are not going to stand for it. I was going to be hung before I got grown. Somebody was going to blow me down for my sassy tongue. Mama was going to suck sorrow for not beating my temper out of me before it was too late." Even with all of her father's explicit warnings, however, the message young Zora received was decidedly mixed. Lucy Ann Hurston conceded that her daughter was "impudent and given to talking back," but she did not want to "squinch" Zora's spirit "for fear that [she] would turn out to be a mealy-mouthed rag doll by the time [she] got grown." "You leave her alone," Lucy Ann told her husband. "I'll tend to [Zora] when I figger she needs it." Meanwhile, Hurston said, she "exhorted her children at every opportunity to 'jump at de sun.' We might not land on the sun, but at least we would get off the ground."[133]

That it was Lucy Ann Hurston and Willie Belle Robinson—and not their husbands—who most encouraged their children to stand up for themselves is interesting, especially in light of "the common claim that black mothers and grandmothers in the age of Jim Crow raised their boys to show deference to white people" and thus, in the eyes of some, "emasculated" black men.[134] Based on her field work with black families in Depression-era Mississippi, Hortense Powdermaker saw things differently. "Most parents, real or adopted, are tremendously ambitious for their children," she wrote. "Usually, however, in the middle and lower classes it is the mothers who are most ambitious for their children and most unstinting in their zeal." Powdermaker explained this difference by pointing not only to the "matriarchal nature of the family"—certainly a contestable point—but also to the "more favorable position of the colored women, as contrasted to the men, [which] makes them more hopeful for the future of which their children are a symbol."[135] By the 1930s, black women did tend to have more education than black men did, and they had always been less likely to be lynched—although this fact does not alter a universe in which black women faced many other forms of violence, including not only rape but also domestic abuse at the hands of the very black men whose position was supposedly less favorable than their own.[136] Even if black mothers' optimism is hard to account for, however, Powdermaker's evidence does make it palpable. "A woman who has never been to school and has worked most of her life in the fields speaks for many when she says: 'There ain't nothing in farming and I want my child to do something else,'" Powdermaker recorded. "Another, also illiterate, says it seems like she's been working since she was born, over the washtub or in the fields, and any time she wasn't working she was just sick. She married at eighteen and has had eight children. Her husband would have been satisfied to have them just able to read and write, 'just enough so no white person could do them'; but she wants them to have all the education possible." This second mother, at least, had seen some of her hard work pay off: her oldest son had recently received his M.A. from a black college and was paying the expenses for his next oldest brother to follow in his footsteps.[137]

Still, ambition for one's children did not make it easy to decide how to teach them about race. In fact, Powdermaker suggested that it made it harder and, by implication, that the ambitious working-class mothers she described shared "respectable" middle-class blacks' anxieties to a great extent, even if they did not "recognize the problem [of acquainting their children with the inter-racial situation] as such." "That the most thoughtful parents are the ones most reluctant to broach the subject is not difficult to understand," Powdermaker argued. "Those who have a more matter-of-fact attitude toward the situation can present it to their children more easily and more naturally than those for whom it is a source of conscious and bitter inner turmoil." Yet in her own research, she found relatively little of this matter-of-fact teaching, even among those working-class families who were least able to delay, much less prevent, their children's encounters with racist whites because they themselves worked for whites as servants, tenant farmers, and the like. Most parents were reticent, and very few were "easy" or "natural" when it came to talking about race; the "usual response" to children's inevitable questions was "I don't know, that's just the way it is." None of the parents Powdermaker quoted encouraged their children to think of racism as anything other than a brutal, if inexplicable, reality; the only one who came close to naturalizing white supremacy taught her children that black and white children could not play together and that "Negroes 'must always treat white people nice and never give them any sass.' They must always remember that 'a nigger is a nigger and a White is a White.'" Other parents acknowledged whites' culpability in enforcing such an unjust system, even if a statement such as "Them's white children and if you hit them, they'll kill you" was more ambiguous and less affirming than confused black children might have liked.[138]

Perhaps it is fitting to end a discussion of working-class blacks' strategies of racial socialization with this sort of ambiguity. A different approach to the question of how working-class blacks taught their children about race might focus on working-class cultural forms, including the blues tradition alluded to above, that were part of blacks' "hidden transcripts" of resistance to white supremacy. How these elements of black culture contributed to children's racial self-understanding deserves further study. It is clear, for example, that black adults continued to pass on stories of Brer Rabbit and other tricksters long after slavery ended. As Lawrence Levine argued in his classic 1977 study *Black Culture and Black Consciousness*, "Continued Negro vulnerability—the lack of independent political and economic power bases and protracted dependence upon whites and the institutions they controlled—prolonged the need for tricksters and the lessons they had to impart."[139] But those lessons had never been simple. Often, weak characters did triumph over strong ones in slaves' folk tales, but they did so at the expense of their own morals and at considerable cost to the wider community. Moreover, tricksters sometimes got their own comeuppance, especially whenever they became too prideful. To see the trickster as a stand-in for the slave and the folk tales as mere fantasies of power reversal is therefore much too simplistic. Instead, slaves' tales embodied a fatalistic worldview. "Throughout there is a latent yearning for structure, for justice, for reason, but they are not to be had, in this world at least," Levine observed. "If the strong are not to prevail over the weak, neither shall the weak dominate the strong. Their eternal and inconclusive battle served as proof that man is part of a larger order which he scarcely under-stands and certainly does not control."[140]

As younger generations of blacks adapted slaves' tales to their own needs in the late nineteenth and early twentieth centuries, the tales themselves took on new shapes and new meanings. Levine traced two main currents of change. On the one hand, tricksters became more directly confrontational, wielding shotguns and committing murders by outright violence rather than trickery. On the other hand, storytellers became increasingly self-conscious, and even embarrassed, about their oral tradition and were more likely than slaves had been to focus on a trickster's limitations, including not only his moral failings but also his inability to prevail against enemies who, unlike the dupes of slaves' tales, frequently learned from past mistakes. Both cur-rents of change—the trickster who became violent and the trickster who failed, and often died, in the end—indicated "increasing doubts about the appropriateness or efficacy of the trickster's approach." Although Levine em-phasized that this transformation in the folklore was gradual and that the trickster's dominant characteristics of "guile and wit" maintained consider-able appeal for black audiences, one of his examples of the newer type of tale is especially interesting because of the way it was used, ironically enough, to teach a black child *not* to be duplicitous. Future anthropologist Claudia Mitchell-Kernan was a girl of seven or eight growing up in Chicago when a neighbor she did not like tried to tear her away from a storyteller's com-pany to send her on an errand. She lied, saying that her mother had told her not to go, and the storyteller, Mr. Waters, called her on it. To gain his sym-pathy, Claudia lied further, saying that she hated the neighbor because the neighbor had called Waters lazy because he did not work. Waters patiently explained that he had been laid off from his job and that, if the neighbor had called him lazy, it was out of ignorance rather than spite. "Guilt-ridden," Claudia ran the errand, and when she returned, Waters told her a story about the "Signifying Monkey," in which the monkey, a classic trickster, ended up being severely beaten by both the elephant and the lion. "I liked the story very much and righteously approved of its ending, not realizing at the time that he was *signifying* at me," Mitchell-Kernan reflected. Several days later, after she had come to understand the story's subtext while attempting to re-tell it to a friend, she sheepishly apologized to Mr. Waters for lying and was told approvingly that she "was finally getting to the age where [she] could 'hold a conversation,' i.e. understand and appreciate implications."[141] Yet if the implications of a story about the Signifying Monkey could be that lying and duplicity were wrong and that tricksters deserved to be punished, then

Mitchell-Kernan's anecdote is a good indication of just how malleable black folk traditions could be.

Like tricksters themselves, black working-class parents had to use their wits to prepare their children for life in a hostile world. Some emphasized accommodation and subservience to a greater extent than others, but more embraced respectability and the kind of dual consciousness that it could provide than the emphasis on class distinctions and conflicts in the scholarly literature on respectability and uplift might lead us to believe. Most important of all, far more were optimistic about their children's futures than a historical perspective on the longevity and durability of the Jim Crow system might deem likely. In the end, ambition and accommodation were not irreconcilable. In an age when increasing numbers of Americans were keeping their children in school longer and harboring ever greater ambitions for their futures, black parents like Willie Belle Robinson and Lucy Ann Hurston entertained hope—hope that their children could at least "get off the ground" —even if they also understood the necessity of teaching adherence to racial etiquette. "Our parents taught us [to] be wary of white folks. Leave them alone. . . . Stay in your place," Edgar Allen Hunt of Memphis told an interviewer. "My daddy was in the race riot and he done had to leave Arkansas. . . . He told us what to expect, how to expect, how to act, how to stay away from them. Don't trust them. I mean he gave us the whole ball of wax, having been in the race riot seeing some things." Yet when Hunt's father told him about "the struggles that he had" as a young man, the message was not one of subservience. Instead, his struggles had made him vow that "if he ever g[o]t any children . . . he was going to send his children to school." Hunt concluded, "With a third-grade education he had six children. He sent all of us to school. And three of us went through college. I'm not one of them. But if a man can come from that position and do what he did, then, you know, that inspires me."[142] Seeing the inspiration in a parent who taught his children to stay in their place is difficult, but at least some black children—children like Hunt, who was sixty-eight at the time of the interview—came to see it, by and by, precisely because their parents' lessons in subservience were so often mixed with admonitions to strive and assurances of love.

"I'm a little girl, but I'm going to fight that thing"

Which is not to suggest that sorting out mixed messages was easy for children, even those who grew up under the most sheltered conditions. Indeed, virtually any response to white supremacy that black parents counseled—short of anger and hatred for whites—required children to suppress their emotions in favor of keeping a cool head. And whether it was part of a bourgeois performance of refinement or rooted in a working-class family's religious and personal values, respectability required restraint above all else. Children must be polite and stay out of trouble. They must not only demonstrate their own best selves but also represent their race to a hostile and powerful white audience. They must at least try to rise above insults and turn the other cheek if attacked. Even for children who grew up in relatively comfortable circumstances, this was a lot to ask.

Like all children, the children of "respectable" black southerners had to chart a course between parental rules and the demands of their environment. They had to adapt to the rigors of respectability at the same time they reacted and adjusted to the realities of Jim Crow. Mamie Garvin Fields, born into a prominent black family in Charleston in 1888, could remember a time when she allowed her anger about South Carolina's new segregation statutes to override her parents' lessons in politeness and dignified self-restraint. Having first learned about the laws by reading the newspaper, she "got [it] into [her] head to fight that thing." The next day, when a white peddler appeared on her family's doorstep, she was ready. "Yes, my mother is here," she told him, "but this is a Jim Crow house and we got Jim Crow money, and we don't buy nothin' from no white man! So, now, get away from here!" Running next door to her aunt's house, Fields berated the peddler a second time with her cousin joining in.[143]

Fields and her cousin may not have been behaving "respectably" when they lashed out at the white peddler, but it would be hard to deny that they *were* self-defining. If the ultimate goal of respectable child rearing was, as Nannie Burroughs put it, to teach children "that they are what they are, not by environment, but of themselves," then a strict insistence on politeness and rising above conflict may have been less effective, ultimately, than an allowance for such childlike outbursts. Yet, as every black parent knew, expressions of anger or any other form of open resistance to white dominance could get children killed. Thus, a respectable restraint was necessary, as well as desirable. In short, respectability training was many black parents' best compromise between self-definition and *safety*, as well as an effort to teach their children morals and manners they genuinely believed in and considered essential to success.

In the end, even comparatively elite black parents could not deny that segregation and racism affected children, no matter how hard they tried to preempt those effects by instilling an oppositional consciousness of respect-

Shadows of Light

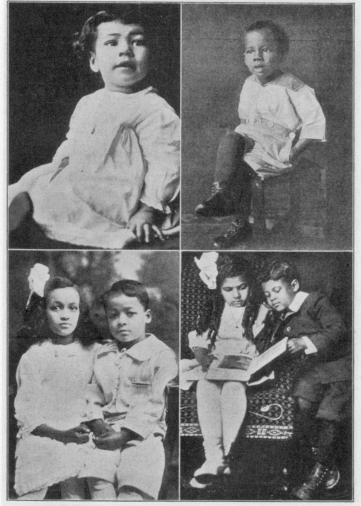

"SOULS MADE OF FIRE, AND CHILDREN OF THE SUN, WITH WHOM REVENGE IS VIRTUE"

Illustration from the Crisis, October 1916. Hundreds of readers, both North and South, answered editor W. E. B. Du Bois's request for photographs of their children to be included in the annual children's issues of the Crisis, the monthly magazine of the NAACP. Virtually all of these pictures captured the look of black middle-class respectability in the early twentieth century. The caption chosen for this illustration—"Souls made of fire, and children of the sun, with whom revenge is virtue" (a quotation from English poet and dramatist Edward Young)—is particularly suggestive of Du Bois's and other black parents' anxieties about their children's understandable, but potentially dangerous, anger toward whites.

ability in children's minds. "Men and women are not made on trains and on streetcars," Burroughs insisted, but the reality was that, to some extent, they *were*. For blacks and whites alike, living Jim Crow was a defining experience, even if that meant learning to define oneself against the racist definitions of one's society.

This was the subtext of a story Lugenia Burns Hope, founding president of Atlanta's Neighborhood Union, told about one of her sons in a 1917 speech titled "Family Life as a Determinant in Racial Attitudes of Children." Hope's point was to show how parents had "an unusual opportunity to instill ideas and thus mold attitudes" and could, if they themselves were properly educated, "direct their [children's] little minds toward a sense of brotherhood with all men." Yet the anecdote she chose belied the singular influence of home training. Explaining that she had taught her two sons to be polite to all women, regardless of class or color, Hope described an incident in which this training backfired. Riding home on a crowded, segregated streetcar, one of her boys offered his seat in the black section to a white woman who had been forced to stand. "If she had simply ignored the seat there would have been no question," Hope explained to her audience, "but she made some demonstration which the child did not understand. This raised problems in his mind which remain a complex even today, in spite of my efforts to keep the truth from him. I did not want to burden his young life because I knew it would have to come all too soon anyway. The Negro mother has to pray for patience and insight lest she forget that above all her little ones must not become embittered."[144]

Requiring enormous restraint and the suppression of justifiable emotions such as frustration and anger, respectability demanded that black children learn to shoulder the psychological burdens of Jim Crow just as their elders had before them. Yet respectability reflected not only deeply held beliefs in hard work, piety, education, and other values but also the best alternative that many blacks saw for combating segregation and racial prejudice. Indeed, middle-class observers demonstrated a remarkable degree of consensus about what constituted "proper" child rearing, as Du Bois and Dill's survey results show.

Because it represented the views of forward thinkers like Du Bois, however, "Morals and Manners Among Negro Americans" also suggested the need for black families to shift Jim Crow's psychological burdens off of black children and challenge the system itself. Having begun their study by acknowledging that many people believed the "Negro problem" to be "primarily a matter of morals and manners," Du Bois and Dill firmly rejected this hypothesis on the basis of their findings. The "hope of the future in moral up-lift" lay not in African Americans trying harder to become respectable, they argued, but in "thoro[ugh] common school training for Negro children, re-spect and protection for Negro women, widened industrial opportunity for Negro men and systematic effort to lessen race prejudice."[145] As Du Bois and Dill realized, solving the "race problem" would depend not on how black chil-dren behaved but on how much respect and opportunity American laws and American attitudes would allow them to have. Although respectability re-mained important, by the late 1930s and early 1940s, more and more black adults would come to share this more overtly political viewpoint, and a civil rights movement that was often conceived of as being *for* children (much as it was later led *by* children) would begin to take shape.

3 I Knew Then Who I Was

The night air was heavy, and all of the houses along Houston Street were dark and unusually quiet. It was shortly after sundown on September 23, 1906, and rumor had it that a white mob was gathering, ready to descend on Atlanta's Darktown, the working-class black neighborhood three or four blocks south of Walter White's childhood home. Thirteen-year-old Walter had every reason to be afraid, having witnessed the brutality of white mobs on Pryor and Marietta streets the night before. Riding along with his father, a mail collector, on his evening shift, he had been swept up in the excitement of events he did not understand. His insistence that they return home by way of Five Points, the heart of Atlanta's business district and the epicenter of the violence, had almost cost them dearly, as an undertaker's carriage with three terrified blacks crouched in the rear sped past and nearly toppled their tiny wagon. Only the sting of the driver's whip, as he alternately lashed the horses and the pursuing whites, had allowed the hearse to escape with its living riders. A lame bootblack from an exclusive, black-owned barbershop had not been so lucky. Caught out alone on Peachtree Street, he had tried to outrun the mob, only to be beaten to death before Walter's eyes. On Pryor Street, an elderly black woman had been scarcely fifty yards ahead of the mob when Walter and his father overtook her. Although he was slight of build, George White had managed to lift the woman into the speeding cart as Walter whipped their mare to a gallop.

Now, on the second night of a riot incited by race-baiting politicians and sensational headlines, Walter and his family turned out the lights and waited. Stationed at a front window in the family parlor, Walter wondered what it would be like to use the shotgun across his lap to kill a man. As midnight approached and the crash of shattering glass from the corner street lamp broke the silence, it seemed he might soon find out. With the mob surging toward his home, "there opened up within me a great awareness," White recalled in the first chapter of his 1948 autobiography, *A Man Called White*. "I knew then who I was. I was a Negro."[1]

Although gunfire from a neighboring building quickly scattered the advancing mob, this moment of self-recognition never left the boy who grew up to become executive secretary of the National Association for the Advancement of Colored People (NAACP). White's complexion was fair, his hair blond, his eyes blue—facts that helped him and his equally light father get home alive on that Saturday night in 1906—but his identity was "Negro" and he was "gripped by the knowledge" of it. "I was sick with loathing for the hatred which had flared before me that night and come so close to making me a killer," White wrote, "but I was glad I was not one of those who hated." The haters' world was made up "of contrasts in values: superior and inferior, profit and loss, cooperative and noncooperative, civilized and aboriginal, white and black." Forged in opposition to these dualities, to the idea that to be African American was to be inferior and therefore "marked for excision, expulsion, or extinction," White's identity as a Negro was "all just a feeling then, inarticulate and melancholy." And yet it was a reassuring feeling "in the way that death and sleep are reassuring": immutable, unshakable, something he would cling to for the rest of his life.[2]

Few children growing up in the Jim Crow South experienced a moment of racial self-recognition as extraordinary and striking as Walter White's. Most came to understand race more gradually and less self-consciously as they found the color of their skin determining how they were treated in a society where race meant everything. Nevertheless, White's story of the Atlanta riot is a revealing, if heightened, example of a kind of narrative about learning race that both black and white southerners tell, especially in autobiography. Titling the first chapter of his memoir "I Learn What I Am," White introduced his experience of the riot as a moment when he "was taught that there is no isolation from life," that he could not carry on his existence unaffected by the social implications of race. His socialization came on a "night when, in terror and bitterness of soul, I discovered that I was set apart by the pigmentation of my skin (invisible though it was in my case)." Other autobiographers' stories of racial socialization are more mundane but no less formative. Certain experiences stand out in their memories, just as, White explained, "the Atlanta riot naturally stands out in my memory as a shocking awakening to the cruelty of which men driven by prejudice, ignorance, and hatred can be guilty."[3] This chapter examines black and white southern autobiography for such stories of racial learning, analyzing them as both archetypal and historical—that is, as stories that both aspire to the universal and reflect the social forces shaping their specific settings in place and time.

The archetypal nature of blacks' racial learning stories is illustrated by two early examples set outside the South: W. E. B. Du Bois's and Mary Church Terrell's similar yet, mainly because of gender, different narratives of being insulted by white classmates in integrated northern schools in the 1870s. In both cases, we see expositions of a common theme in African American autobiography, what Thomas C. Holt has described as the "traumatic confrontation with the Other that *fixes* the meaning of one's self before one even has had the opportunity to *live* and *make* a self more nearly of one's own choosing."[4] Accounts of such traumas generally imply (with much justification, as I will argue) that all nonwhite individuals learn the same lessons in more or less the same way at one point or another. But the traumas themselves are historically specific. Blacks' southern, Jim Crow–era experiences of racial socialization share certain characteristics with those that Du Bois and Terrell recount, but they also differ in ways that are region- and time-sensitive. First, they include a lot more violence, whether actual or incipient, than northern archetypes. Second, in black southerners' stories, segregation matters— sometimes directly, as when Sarah and Bessie Delany are sent to the back of a Raleigh streetcar, but more often indirectly, as when an awareness of segregation principles (always more prevalent than segregation statutes) seems to embolden white antagonists, including white children, to pick on blacks.

White southerners' stories of racial learning rarely emphasize segregation. Instead, they are accounts of enforcing racial etiquette in childhood told by the small minority of whites who have come to reject racism as adults. As such, they are regionally distinctive, though not "representative," considering how few white southerners challenged Jim Crow prior to the civil rights movement. Even so, white authors, like black ones, tend to depict their childhood experiences of racial learning as typical (or archetypal), the implication being that if whites like themselves who shared all of the usual prejudices of their race and region from childhood on could change their minds, then so, too, could the rest of the white South.

If such narratives seem political or calculated, that does not make them any less "true." Another way to say that black and white southerners' stories of racial learning are both archetypal and historical is to say that they are both self-consciously constructed and remembered. They are the product of a writing process and a *remembering* process that seems to have highlighted everyday interracial encounters as little dramas of racial learning. Characterized by trauma, ambivalence, or guilt, such dramas stayed with the individuals who experienced them, prompting reflection and a reworking of events in memory. Remembering, in turn, provided these individuals with a more complete sense of their own identities and culminated, ultimately, in retrospective accounts of how they learned race that are similar to, though usually less pointed than, Walter White's "I knew then who I was."

Of course, not all black and white southerners who experienced childhood racial dramas, nor all who reflected on them, wrote and published autobiographies. I am suggesting, nonetheless, that memory and reflection underlie both individuals' sense of themselves and autobiographers' writings, creating a link between the two. For, as historian Jacquelyn Hall has argued, "we are what we remember, and as memories are reconfigured, identities are redefined." Confronted by current events and impressions, we look to how we thought, felt, and acted in the past for guidance, engaging in an act of remembering that takes place in and privileges the demands of the present. Our "ongoing reconstructions" of what we remember—our reordering of memories into useful patterns and our reinterpretation of past events to fit present needs—"help secure the identities that enable us to navigate, legitimate, or resist the present order of things."[5]

As a sustained act of reconstructing an individual past, an autobiography can serve not only as a source but also as a model for the development of an individual's sense of self. Southern autobiographies may not provide unmediated evidence of what black and white children experienced, but they do tell us a great deal about *how they remembered*, allowing us to recapture something of the process by which their racial identities were formed. In fact, autobiography is sometimes better at showing *how* authors remembered than *what* they remembered. That is, moments recorded in autobiography should not be taken at face value as historical facts. But neither should they be discounted as groundless fabrications. To do so would, first of all, be impractical. Autobiographers may misremember the past (if, indeed, there is such a thing as remembering "correctly"),[6] they may unconsciously touch up their own self-portraits, they may indulge in nostalgia, and they may even lie. But they also know things about themselves, especially themselves in childhood, that very few other historical sources allow us to see.

Beyond this pragmatic argument, though, awaits a recognition that there is also something of value to historians in autobiography's retrospective and constructed nature. In autobiography and in related forms such as oral history, men and women of an earlier time draw on inside information that only they can possibly know to offer their own interpretations of how they came to be who they are. And though these autobiographical assessments are strictly interpretations, they retain a link to the selves in question that no other person's necessarily outside observations can share.

One goal of this chapter, then, is to find a middle ground between a convenient but potentially uncritical reading of autobiography as fact, on the one hand, and a debilitating skepticism about autobiography's truthfulness, on the other. To that end, I analyze black and white southerners' autobiographical stories of racial learning first as literary tropes—"dramas of social inequality"—and then make a case for understanding them at a deeper level as well, as memory-based and identity-forming "dramas of (racial) socialization" (recognizing that autobiographers' socialization stories can also be about class or gender or sexuality or region and are often about all of these and then some, all at the same time). By reading autobiographers' "dramas" for the relationship between their constructed nature and their basis in remembered experience, we can explore both the question of how children learned race and the nature of identity itself.

Dramas of Social Inequality

Returning to Walter White's account of the Atlanta riot, we should begin by acknowledging that White's story tells us as much about his adult political consciousness as about his adolescent sense of self. Opening his autobiography with the words "I am a Negro," White was taking up a common theme in African American autobiographical writing, a theme that historian Kevin Gaines describes as "the telling of the moment, usually during childhood, at which the author learns the drama of 'social equality,' or, as James Weldon Johnson put it, 'the brutal impact of race and . . . how race prejudice permeate[s] the whole American social organism.'" Highly self-conscious, conventional, literary, sometimes lyric, these narratives are a subset of the childhood stories that black autobiographers tell. They recount "the painful socialization of young African American males and females into a negrophobic, Victorian social order," and they are inevitably shaped by autobiographers' mature political views. Often, Gaines notes, these stories minimize certain aspects of the childhood experience—such as the child's natural desire for acceptance from other human beings and the depth of the pain, fear, and confusion that accompany rejection and ill use—in favor of a reasoned commentary on the pathological nature of whiteness. Thus, Walter White supposedly achieves a global historical perspective on race relations at the age of thirteen, identifying himself as "a Negro" while distancing himself from "those who hated," "those whose story is in the history of the world, a record of bloodshed, rapine and pillage." Undoubtedly, the riot did have a significant impact on White's understanding of race and race relations in 1906. But, as Gaines concludes, "We can be more certain . . . that an accretion of subsequent experiences," including frequent episodes of mistaken identity based on his skin color and his assumption of a white persona while investigating lynchings for the NAACP, "animated White's search for the origin of his racial identity" and intensified "his desire to dissociate himself from whiteness."[7]

Gaines's observations about Walter White provide an excellent starting point for an examination of black and white southerners' autobiographical interpretations of how their racial identities were formed. Expanding on Gaines's analysis, I will argue that, although shaped by literary convention, "dramas of social equality" are meaningful not only in relation to the adult autobiographers who tell them but also in relation to the childhood selves they purport to describe. I will also suggest that much of our emphasis should be on the word "drama" and that "drama of social *inequality*" is a more appropriate term.

As historian Nell Painter explains, in southern parlance "'social equality' meant people of two races . . . sitting down together at table or on a train, sharing a smoke at a club, or belonging to the same organization" without drawing distinctions between master and servant, boss and worker, dominant and subordinate. According to the logic of white anxiety, associations of this kind were supposed to lead directly to "race mixing," that is, to sexual relations between white women and black men. This assumption led many race-proud African Americans to disavow any desire for "social equality" almost as vigorously as white demagogues denounced it. Thus, "'social equality' existed only in the negative" in the South, as a kind of association among equals that must not happen across race lines.[8] This was, of course, precisely the lesson that the youthful protagonists of black autobiographers' childhood dramas had to learn. Social *inequality*—whites' insistence on their own superiority and their resultant social distancing of blacks—is what these autobiographical stories are all about.

Time and again in late-nineteenth- and twentieth-century texts, black autobiographers make a direct connection between the experience of racism in early childhood and the beginnings of a sense of themselves as being "black" or "Negro" or "colored." Like Walter White, they resolve stories of "I Learn What I Am" with statements of "I knew then who I was," not merely "I knew what other people thought of me." In a similar vein, black activist and feminist Pauli Murray titled a chapter of her autobiography, *Song in a Weary Throat*, not "Learning About Racism," but, more profoundly, "Learning About Race."[9] Although there are regional and historical variations to consider, it is first worth noting that black autobiographers' stories of racial subjugation in childhood span many decades and are by no means limited to the South. Indeed, these "dramas of social inequality" lie at the heart of some of the most fundamental discussions of what it has meant to be black anywhere in the United States.

Appropriately enough, W. E. B. Du Bois narrated an everyday drama of this sort at the very beginning of *The Souls of Black Folk*, just a few sentences before his famous description of blacks' "double-consciousness" as Americans and as Negroes. "I remember well when the shadow swept across me," Du Bois, who was born in 1868 in Great Barrington, Massachusetts, wrote. "I was a little thing, away up in the hills of New England. . . . In a wee wooden schoolhouse, something put it into the boys' and girls' heads to buy gorgeous visiting-cards—ten cents a package—and exchange. The exchange was merry, till one girl, a tall newcomer, refused my card,—refused it peremptorily, with a glance. Then it dawned upon me with a certain suddenness that I was different from the others; or like, mayhap, in heart and life and longing, but shut out from their world by a vast veil." Like Walter White, Du Bois went on to reject the white world that had rejected him. "I had thereafter no desire to tear down that veil," he continued. "I held all beyond it in common contempt, and lived above it in a region of blue sky and great wandering shadows. That sky was bluest when I could beat my mates at examination-time, or beat them at a foot-race, or even beat their stringy heads."[10]

Nevertheless, despite "all this fine contempt," Du Bois was affected deeply by the racism he encountered. Changing his metaphor from veil to impenetrable prison walls, he acknowledged that "the shades of the prison-house closed round about us all": the "whitest" blacks as well as dark-skinned "sons of night," those who "plod darkly on in resignation," as well as those who "beat unavailing palms against the stone, or steadily, half hopelessly, watch the streak of blue above."[11] Thus, Du Bois conceded that he was unable to resist or remove himself completely from the effects of racism, and he also made a connection between his own drama of social inequality and the experiences of others who shared his prison-house and had to look longingly to the same "streak of blue" that had sustained him as a boy.

Drawing on this connection, Du Bois then presented his analysis of black identity as a perpetual sense of "two-ness." America yielded blacks "no true self-consciousness," he asserted. The nature of American society allowed African Americans to see themselves only "through the revelation of the other world. It is a peculiar sensation, this double-consciousness, this sense of always looking at one's self through the eyes of others, measuring one's soul by the tape of a world that looks on in amused contempt and pity. One ever feels his two-ness,—an American, a Negro; two souls, two thoughts, two unreconciled strivings; two warring ideals in one dark body, whose dogged strength alone keeps it from being torn asunder."[12] Like Pauli Murray and Walter White, Du Bois took the lessons of living among whites to be not merely about racism but about race. "Looking at one's self through the eyes of others" defined who one was—"an American, a Negro"—not simply what other people thought.

Other African Americans' dramas of social inequality share Du Bois's emphasis on racial identity yet sometimes differ markedly from the history of "contempt" and the struggle "to attain self-conscious manhood" that Du Bois put forth.[13] One key difference is gender. Black clubwoman and educator Mary Church Terrell's autobiography is especially revealing on this point, offering a feminine counterpart to Du Bois's at once masculine and universalizing anecdote. Writing self-consciously as *A Colored Woman in a White World*, Terrell introduced this particular drama of social inequality as "an experience which indelibly impressed my racial identity upon me and about which even to this day I do not like to think."

Like Du Bois's drama, Terrell's encounter took place in a mostly white school in the North. Born in 1863, the year of Lincoln's Emancipation Proclamation, to a successful Memphis businessman and his wife, Terrell left home at the age of six to attend a model school affiliated with Antioch College in Yellow Springs, Ohio. Going into the school cloakroom one day to get her coat, she found a group of older white girls chatting, striking poses before a mirror, and "joking about their charms." "'Behold my wonderful tresses,'" one of the girls was saying. "'But look at my sparkling eyes,'" called out another. As she was putting on her coat, Terrell heard one of the girls speak to her, and "not knowing what else to say, I imitated the young ladies, as a small girl sometimes will, by asking 'Haven't I got a pretty face too?' 'You've got a pretty black face,' said one of the young ladies, pointing her finger at me derisively." Unlike the disdainful girl who refused Du Bois's card silently, "at a glance," Terrell's antagonists did not leave it to her to figure out that she was different. "The shout of laughter that went up from that group of young women rings in my ears to this day," wrote Terrell, who was nearly eighty when she published her autobiography. "For the first time in my life I realized that I was an object of ridicule on account of the color of my skin. I was so shocked, embarrassed, and hurt I was glued to the spot."[14]

Terrell's childhood self is depicted with more emotional complexity than

Du Bois's. Rather than realizing "with a certain suddenness" that blacks and whites are alike in their humanity but separated by a societal "veil," little Mollie Church (as Terrell was then called) realized only "that these young white girls were making fun of me, were laughing at me, because I was colored"—a level of analysis that seems much more realistic for a child spurned by other children with whom she has tried to make friends. In her anecdote, Terrell described herself as "a pathetic little figure," not only "motionless" but incapable of holding onto her hat, which she let slip to the floor as she tried to process the white girls' ridicule. Only after she had "recovered sufficiently" to pick up her hat (and symbolically her pride, given hats' characteristic meaning as a social signifier), did Terrell voice any measure of the contempt that Du Bois claimed instantly to have felt. "I ran to the door," Terrell wrote, then "stopped, turned around, and hurled back defiantly, 'I don't want my face to be white like yours and look like milk. I want it nice and dark just like it is.'"[15]

A comparison of Terrell and Du Bois's anecdotes suggests some of the differences that gender can make both in children's experiences of racism and in their adult interpretations of those experiences. Terrell's drama of social inequality has an all-female cast, as well as a feminized setting. In the white girls' dialogue, racial distinctions become inextricably linked with notions of female beauty and sexual attractiveness, an adolescent preoccupation with "sparkling eyes" and "wonderful tresses" that was as new to the still-childlike Mollie Church as the idea that her skin color could make her ugly or ridiculous in someone else's eyes. Terrell's exit line challenges the white girls' very conceptions of beauty, rejecting the ideal of milky skin in favor of her own "dark" complexion, which in reality was not much darker than Walter White's or, presumably, than those of the other girls in the cloakroom. Thus, Terrell's anecdote describes a stage in her maturation as a woman, as well as in the development of her racial consciousness. At the beginning of the scene, she is simply imitating the talk of older girls "as a small girl sometimes will"; by the end, she has asserted her own, alternative definition of female beauty —merely a child's rejoinder at this point but nevertheless a strong reaction against the white girls' insult that, according to Terrell, relieved her of any future impulse to make fun of people because of the way they looked.

If Terrell's story is that of an outcast from a white female homosocial world, Du Bois's drama bears the marks of the rejected suitor, offering a subtle commentary on race and heterosexual relations. The schoolchildren's exchange of calling cards was an imitation of adult social forms, the girl's silent rejection of Du Bois's card an extreme example of "cutting" such as a refined lady of the 1870s would have practiced on a member of her own social set only in a case of "inexcusable rudeness" or "some grave misdeed."[16] By ignoring Du Bois's card, the "tall" (and, by implication, older or at least physically more mature) girl was accusing him of being presumptuous. To share a classroom with him was one thing—at least Du Bois gave no indication that she or any of the other children had ever snubbed him before. But for him to think that she might recognize him socially, the first step in a young woman's journey toward respectable marriage, was another thing entirely. That Du Bois had no interest in courtship, that he did not even understand the game of exchanging cards and did not know what had "put it into the boys' and girls' heads," mattered no more than the fact that Terrell had entered the cloakroom only to get her coat. Either in reality or in Du Bois's retelling or both, this experience "of when the shadow swept across me" was about learning the socially acceptable relationship between a white woman and a black man.

Du Bois's response to this lesson was equally as gendered as the lesson itself. It is hardly a coincidence that Du Bois mentioned beating white classmates' "stringy heads" at the conclusion of his drama of social inequality or that Walter White claimed to have experienced his most profound moment of racial self-awareness with his finger crooked on the trigger of a gun. In contrast to Terrell, whose "defiant" exit line is really rather feeble, black male autobiographers tend to emphasize their own assertiveness and efforts at self-defense. Thus, White and Du Bois find the roots of their uncompromising leadership as Race Men in the racial battles of their younger years—a self-discovery that was probably true to life for each of them but that also recalls Frederick Douglass's foundational account of winning his manhood in a one-on-one battle with the slave-breaker Edward Covey.

Meanwhile, Terrell ended her drama of social inequality not with a struggle for "self-conscious manhood" but with a monologue about endurance. Suggesting that her encounter in the cloakroom had heightened her awareness of all forms of discrimination, Terrell described her efforts to remind other black children who were in the habit of taunting Chinese immigrants that "just as they made fun of Chinese, many people made fun of us." Or, Terrell continued, "I would run up to white children and declare with too much emphasis and feeling, perhaps, that I liked the Chinaman's pretty yellow complexion better than I did their pale, white one." There "were always consequences of various kinds after such a speech, which were often decidedly unpleasant." Nevertheless, Terrell determined to "stand" the consequences, no matter what they were, because she "remembered the scene in the cloakroom."[17]

Black Southerners' Dramas of Social Inequality

The comparatively genteel setting of Terrell's drama suggests important questions about class, as well as place and time. How did the racial socialization of children who had access to such privileges as integrated, well-funded schools in the North differ from the racial socialization of those who did not? What difference did it make to grow up black entirely in the South, where nearly 80 percent of black Americans lived at the start of World War II?[18] How did dramas of social inequality experienced in the 1870s differ from ones experienced in the 1890s and 1910s (leaving aside, for the moment, changes of the 1920s and beyond)?

It is difficult to imagine an African American childhood more different from Mary Church Terrell's than Richard Wright's. As his classic autobiography, *Black Boy*, recounts, Wright learned race on the streets of Memphis and of Jackson, Mississippi—streets to which he first had to win "the right" by knocking the heads of other African American boys. Born in 1908, Wright described his mother's insistence that he learn at about the age of six "to stand up and fight for yourself." After his father abandoned them, his mother took a job as a cook in a white family's kitchen. She was often "tired and dispirited," and she depended on Richard and his younger brother to take care of themselves. One evening, she sent Richard out twice to buy groceries only to have a gang of black boys knock him down and steal his money each time. Ella Wright gave her son more money, another shopping list, and "a long heavy stick," then told him that she would whip him if he failed to complete his errand. "She slammed the door and I heard the key turn in the lock," Wright wrote. "I shook with fright. I was alone upon the dark, hostile streets." Deciding it was better to be beaten on the streets where he could defend himself rather than at home where he was helpless against his mother's punishment, Wright set out for the store. He depicted his battle against the gang as a "frenzy" in which he struck out in blind fear, chased the boys as they ran sobbing to their parents, and then shouted threats at the parents as well. On his way home, Wright kept the stick "poised for instant use," but no one approached him. He had earned the right to physical inviolability—the right not to be beaten up without someone doing something about it, in this case himself—a stage in the development of his selfhood that children who lived in a less threatening environment or had more protective parents rarely had to experience.[19]

Violence figured in Wright's first, mystifying encounter with race as well. Having learned that he was capable of protecting himself on the street, he soon fell in with a crowd of African American children who spent their days roaming the city while their parents, many of whom were household workers like his mother, were at work. "Every happening in the neighborhood, no matter how trivial, became my business," Wright recounted. "It was in this manner that I first stumbled upon the relations between whites and blacks, and what I learned frightened me." Wright claimed to have known of the existence of white people before but never to have thought much about it. "It might have been that my tardiness in learning to sense white people as 'white' people came from the fact that many of my relatives were 'white'-looking people," he mused. "And when word circulated among the black people of the neighborhood that a 'black' boy had been severely beaten by a 'white' man, I felt that the 'white' man had had a right to beat the 'black' boy, for I naively assumed that the 'white' man must have been the 'black' boy's father. And did not all fathers . . . have the right to beat their children?" Certainly, Wright's own father had often exercised a paternal right to beat him before deserting the family and leaving the job to his wife.

When Ella Wright assured him that the "white" man was not the "black" boy's father, Wright became confused. "Then why did the 'white' man whip the 'black' boy?" he asked. "The 'white' man did not *whip* the 'black' boy," his mother replied, making a distinction between whipping and beating that was perhaps especially important to a woman who relied so heavily on corporal punishment. "But why?" Wright pressed.

> "You're too young to understand."
> "I'm not going to let anybody beat me," I said stoutly.
> "Then stop running wild in the streets," my mother said.
> I brooded for a long time about the seemingly causeless beating of the "black" boy by the "white" man and the more questions I asked the more bewildering it all became.

Bewildered as he was, Wright had learned that there was something significant about whiteness that remained as yet hidden. "Whenever I saw 'white' people now," he wrote, "I stared at them, wondering what they were really like."[20]

Very soon, Wright's questions about whites developed into questions about himself. Waiting for the train that would take him and his mother and brother to their new home in Elaine, Arkansas, Wright noticed for the first time that there were two lines of people buying tickets, "a 'white' line and a 'black' line." Once on the train, he saw that the separation continued and he wanted to "go and peep at the white folks" in their separate cars. "Quit talking foolishness!" his mother snapped when he asked for permission to do so. "I had begun to notice that my mother became irritated when I questioned her about whites and blacks," Wright observed, "and I could not quite understand it. I wanted to understand these two sets of people who lived side by side and never touched, it seemed, except in violence."

Foremost in Wright's mind was his "white"-looking maternal grandmother: "Was she white? Just how white was she? What did the whites think of her whiteness?" Putting these questions to his mother on the train that night got Wright nowhere. "Did Granny become colored when she married Grandpa?" he asked. "Will you stop asking silly questions!" Wright's mother replied.

"But did she?"

"Granny didn't *become* colored," my mother said angrily. "She was *born* the color she is now."

Again I was being shut out of the secret, the thing, the reality I felt somewhere beneath all the words and silences.

"Why didn't Granny marry a white man?" I asked.

"Because she didn't want to," my mother said peevishly.

"Why don't you want to talk to me?" I asked.

She slapped me and I cried.

Grudgingly, Wright's mother explained that her mother had been a slave and had Irish, Scottish, and French, as well as African, ancestry. Learning that his father had "some white and some red and some black," Wright asked, "Then what am I?" "They'll call you a colored man when you grow up," his mother replied. "Then she turned to me and smiled mockingly and asked: 'Do you mind, Mr. Wright?'" Whether or not he recognized the double irony in his mother's use of the courtesy title "Mr." for a child who was black, Wright "was angry and did not answer." "I did not object to being called colored," he concluded, "but I knew that there was something my mother was holding back. She was not concealing facts, but feelings, attitudes, convictions which she did not want me to know." Still, knowing from the stories of other children that black people sometimes got killed for reasons he could not begin to fathom, Wright decided "it would be simple": "If anybody tried to kill me, then I would kill them first."[21]

Like White and Du Bois, Wright emphasized his own masculine readiness to fight back at the same time that he told how white aggression—even rumors of white aggression—as well as distinctly southern patterns of segregation shaped his earliest understanding of race. Unlike White and Du Bois, however, Wright did not attribute a mature viewpoint to his younger self. Just as Terrell's "pathetic little figure" in the cloakroom comprehended only that others were making fun of her, Wright's seven- or eight-year-old protagonist responded to his growing knowledge about whites with a childlike self-assertion based on the same code of get-them-before-they-get-you behavior that his mother had taught him to practice in his relations with other blacks.

Only later in his autobiography did Wright indicate how important his "spontaneous fantasies" of fighting with whites were in the development of his racial identity. At the end of his conversation with his mother on the train, Wright said only that he "did not object to being called colored," a very different statement from Walter White's affirmation, "I knew then who I was." Later, however, Wright acknowledged that his fantasies of retaliatory violence "were a moral bulwark that enabled me to feel I was keeping my emotional integrity whole." No longer "a reflection of my reaction to the white people," his fantasies were "a part of my living, of my emotional life. . . . Tension would set in at the mere mention of whites and a vast complex of emotions, involving the whole of my personality, would be aroused. . . . I had never in my life been abused by whites, but I had already become as conditioned to their existence as though I had been the victim of a thousand lynchings."[22] Thus, from his first "tardy" awakening at the age of six or seven, Wright claimed to have become fully "conditioned" to the grim realities of blackness and whiteness by the age of eight or nine.

Wright's youth, his obsession with violence, and the fact that his racial conditioning included so little direct contact with whites all bespeak the effects of his region, age, and class. Unlike Du Bois, who grew up outside the South, Wright could not have experienced a period of interracial fellowship with grade-school classmates because schools in Memphis were segregated, as were railroads and most other public facilities by the time Wright was growing up in the 1910s. Unlike the Memphis-born but far more elite Terrell, who began her autobiography with a description of her weekly visits to the white grandfather whose support helped her father become a millionaire, Wright did not have positive—or even complex—relationships with whites when he was a young child that challenged his impression that "these two sets of people who lived side by side . . . never touched . . . except in violence."

In painting this autobiographical portrait of his childhood, however, Wright did downplay some kinds of experiences with whites, never, for example, describing the white family for whom his mother cooked, despite the fact that Ella Wright sometimes took him and his brother to work with her to keep them out of trouble. Nor did he discuss his warm relationship with a white family he worked for when he was somewhat older, preferring instead to present an uncomplicated picture of a racially divided South.[23] In the brutal world of southern urban poverty, black children's interactions with whites could, in fact, be limited. On the other hand, many black children worked for whites or played with white children on a regular basis, and many cities' black neighborhoods were intermixed with white neighborhoods or were too small to constitute a wholly separate sphere. Wright's distancing of whites, like his suggestion that he was a late bloomer because he recognized the "whiteness" of white people only at about age six, may have reflected his own experiences and certainly captured the realities of some black southerners. At the same time, these aspects of his narrative served to deepen the gloom of the "Southern Night"—Wright's title for the first part of his autobiography—that he had set out to describe.

As Wright's story of his train trip suggests, even if white people were remote from a southern black child's existence, their presence, and especially the outward signs of segregation and the haunting threat of racial violence, were not. Sara Brooks, growing up in the even more isolated world of southern *rural* poverty in the 1910s, had very little to do with whites. Her father, an Alabama black belt farmer who eventually managed to buy land, seldom allowed his children to go to town, and "when we went to town," Brooks recalled, "we didn't hang around, because my father told us, 'You go into town, you tend to your own business, you turn right around and come back home.'" Occasionally, Brooks and her siblings did field work for a Mr. Garrett, the only white farmer who lived nearby, but even this contact was intermittent. Nevertheless, Brooks's interaction with the Garrett family taught her a great deal about class, as well as race, for the Garretts "didn't have no more than we had and they didn't look no better than we did—just a different color, that's all."[24]

Even before Brooks was old enough to wield a hoe for Mr. Garrett, however, she had encountered segregation and white antagonism in one of the places where Richard Wright encountered it, on a train. Born in 1911, long after the segregation of trains and other forms of public transportation had become the law of the land throughout the South, Brooks recalled her first trip to visit her grandmother a few towns away. She was very young at the time and had to be whisked away from the train tracks, where she was dancing and shouting at the arrival of the train, oblivious to the danger of being run down. In addition to noting the segregation at the depot and in the cars, Brooks remembered that the train made one stop where no African Americans got off. "That was a place they called Foxfield," and it had "a sign on a post, 'Niggers, read and run.'" Brooks's father saw the sign, "but he didn't say nothin," she continued. "And at that time we was just so glad to get on the train. We didn't say nothin and we didn't question anything"—neither the sign at Foxfield nor the signs of segregation visible in the two separate crowds on the railroad platform and the two separate cars on the train. "Nope," Brooks concluded. "We just went. But when we start thinkin, gettin older, then we'd ask each other, say, 'Wonder why?'"[25]

Comparatively well-off, educated, and far more accustomed to dealing with whites than Brooks was, Raleigh natives Sarah and Elizabeth Delany also remembered the impact of Jim Crows laws and suggested that it took little re-flection for black children to get the point. "Mama and Papa knew these laws were coming, of course," the Delany sisters, born in 1889 and 1891, recalled, "but they didn't prepare us. I guess our parents could not find the words to explain it. They did not want to fill us with hatred. They did not want us to become bitter." About five and seven years old, respectively, when Raleigh's parks and streetcars became legally segregated, Elizabeth and Sarah Delany first encountered the new laws on a Sunday afternoon when their parents, Episcopal priest and educator Henry Beard Delany and his wife, Nanny, took them to Pullen Park for a picnic. First, the trolley conductor insisted that the Delanys go to the back—a painful thing for the Delany girls, who loved to ride up front where they could feel the breeze blowing through their hair. Then, at the park, a new wooden sign had appeared in the middle of the spring where picnickers got their water, designating one dipper for "White" and the other for "Colored." "Why, what in the world was all this about? We may have been little children," the Delany sisters asserted, "but, honey, we got the message loud and clear." In perhaps her first conscious act of resistance, Bessie Delany promptly drank from the white dipper when no one was looking.[26]

Like the Delany sisters, Mamie Garvin Fields witnessed the passage of Jim Crow legislation when she was a child. Growing up in a racially mixed neighborhood in Charleston, South Carolina, Fields and her brothers and sisters had always played with the children of the Eye family, whose parents were German immigrants. The day after Governor Ben Tillman successfully pushed a series of segregation laws through the South Carolina legislature, however, the boys of the two families began to fight. "The marbles that they had played with on the ground they now used as weapons." Fields remem-bered. "If you met Kramer [Eye] in the street, he would call you 'nigger.' Then we would shout 'cracker' back. That quick the children who had been friends changed." These changes extended beyond the two houses on Short

Court, Fields added. Soon, to prevent fights, the Charleston police began to enforce an "unwritten law" that black and white children must walk home from school on opposite sides of the street.[27]

Despite her emphasis on the effects of legal segregation, Fields made it clear that southern black children's experiences of racial discrimination usually had more to do with unwritten rules than with actual laws. "All these years," Fields reflected in a chapter of her memoir titled "Forbidden Places," "I have been trying to think why a small white boy of Charleston came by my sister Ruth and myself, as we stood by the iron gate at George Street and St. Philip to say, 'Scat! Nigger, what you doin' down ya?' I wonder if he knew why he said it." As Fields explained, "down ya" was at the gates of the College of Charleston, where she and her sister had stopped to admire the well-groomed campus. No law forbade them from peering in at the gate, yet this "small white boy of Charleston" considered the college to be white territory, and despite his youth, he had the authority to enforce his views. "Frightened, we got away and got away fast," Fields recalled. "We didn't fight. We didn't know how. And anyway, our parents wouldn't like it if we did, because 'the children of Short Court' didn't fight. . . . We were 'aristocratic.'" In contrast to brother Herbert, who tussled with Kramer Eye, they were also girls.

Like Richard Wright's awakening to segregation on the train, Fields's encounter with the white boy at the gates of the College of Charleston became a moment of racial self-discovery. Running across the street to the comfort and protection of Aunt Jane, an elderly black woman who sold sweets from a basket on St. George Street, Fields and her sister got a lesson in racial identity and race pride. "Chillun," Aunt Jane said sweetly, "dat ain't fo' we. Colonel Gould Shaw put a school for we on Mary Street. Go dere, chile. Someday you chillun will go right *ya* to get schoolin', just like dat po' buckrah who talked to you so mean." Going on to tell stories about slave days and "her home 'cross the sea,'" Aunt Jane made Fields and her sister forget about the insult they had just experienced at the same time that she used narrative to incorporate the two little girls into her "we." Yet, as her memoir attests, Fields would remember even many years later her disgust at being chased away like a cat. The actions of the small white boy of Charleston, like the sign at Foxfield that Brooks saw from the train, were the sorts of day-to-day expressions of whites' racism that compelled African American children to "wonder why."[28]

Ultimately, no matter how carefully we may try to analyze their historical content, we must also accept these stories as archetypes. Neither class privilege nor the absence of formal Jim Crow legislation could prevent black children from experiencing the "wonder why" moments that got them thinking about race and themselves. In this respect, Mary Church Terrell's girlhood and Richard Wright's boyhood were not so different after all, even though their most similar childhood experiences still differed considerably as a result of gender, class, and historical moment. Another story from Terrell's autobiography illustrates this point. Taking a train trip with her father, Robert Church, a wealthy and well-connected black businessman, in the late 1860s, some forty years before Wright was born, Terrell had "the Race Problem brought directly home to me" for the first time.[29] Unlike her encounter with the white girls in the cloakroom somewhat later, this early awakening to race relations took place—and could only have taken place—in the South. In Tennessee, as in other southern states, white train conductors frequently barred black passengers from sitting in first-class coaches, despite the fact that the legal framework of segregation had not been built—not yet, anyway; Tennessee would pass the South's "first Jim Crow law," requiring separate first-class coaches for black and white passengers, in 1881.[30] Prior to this time, in the 1860s, 1870s, and even into the 1880s, self-respecting blacks like Robert Church regularly challenged racial custom by occupying the first-class seats to which their first-class tickets entitled them—a highly visible act of self-assertion that would have been unthinkable for most African Americans in the 1910s, much less for Richard Wright's impoverished single mother, who could scarcely afford to be thrown *off* of a train that she and her two young children could scarcely afford to be *on*.

Because of his wealth and unusually high social status and because race relations remained relatively fluid in the Reconstruction era, Robert Church clearly felt more confident than Ella Wright ever could have—confident enough that, during one train trip north from Memphis, he not only took first-class seats but also left his daughter, then five years old, alone in the first-class coach while he went to the smoker. When the conductor came around to take the passengers' tickets, he glared at Terrell "and asked who [she] was and what [she] was doing in that car." "I replied as well as a frightened little girl, five years old, could be expected to answer under the circumstances," Terrell recalled. "But I did not placate the irate conductor, who decided then and there to put me into the coach 'where I belonged.'" The conductor pulled Terrell roughly from her seat, demanding of another passenger, "Whose little nigger is this?" Aware of Robert Church's social standing, the passenger advised the conductor to leave Terrell alone. Meanwhile, one of Church's white friends went to the smoking car to get him. What followed was a scene that Mary Church Terrell would never forget. "In that section at that time it was customary for men to carry revolvers in their pockets," she wrote rather cryptically. "Fortunately, no one was injured and I was allowed to remain with my courageous father in the white coach."[31]

As cryptic as Terrell's account was, it clearly described a time very different from Richard Wright's era. Even a wealthy and well-liked black businessman such as Robert Church would have been unable to threaten a white man with a pistol without repercussions in the South of the early twentieth century. That Church was apparently able to do so in the 1860s, presumably with white men's support, was an anomaly of class and timing. The 1860s and 1870s were not a golden age for black southerners, but they were better than the 1890s and the early 1900s, and even though individuals like Robert Church could not predict the future, they did try to take advantage of opportunities to act as first-class citizens. By the time Richard Wright and his mother and brother took their train ride to Arkansas—to the short-term refuge of slightly better off family members rather than up North—Robert Church's argument that first-class tickets entitled blacks to first-class accommodations had been made moot by the Supreme Court's 1896 decision in *Plessy v. Ferguson* and by the widespread implementation of segregation statutes.

Nevertheless, the comparative advantages of growing up in the decades before segregation hardened made less of a difference to Terrell as a child than we might expect. Despite her rescue, the five-year-old girl was deeply troubled by the incident on the train. She was certain that she must have done something wrong for the conductor to treat her so rudely, and so she examined herself thoroughly once she was safely home: "I hadn't mussed my hair; it was brushed back and was perfectly smooth. I hadn't lost either one of the two pieces of blue ribbon which tied the little braids on each side of my head. I hadn't soiled my dress a single bit. I was sitting up 'straight and proper.'" Turning to her mother for an explanation, Terrell must have found the suggestion that "sometimes conductors on railroad trains were unkind and treated good little girls very badly" less than satisfying.[32] Although her mother's response was reassuring rather than snappish, as Wright's mother's answers often were, Terrell, like Wright, may have realized that her mother was "holding back." Thus, while differences of class, gender, and historical moment shaped children's experiences of racial subjugation, the "wonder why" questions that such experiences raised cut across class, gender, and, within the broad scope of the postbellum South, even chronological lines.

Indeed, as black children quickly learned, whites' practice of drawing distinctions between themselves and African Americans was so fundamental to postbellum southern society that it hardly required such institutional settings as trains and schools, much less did it depend on the existence of legal segregation. A passage from Sara Brooks's autobiography illustrates this point. Reiterating that their white neighbors, the Garretts, were as poor as her own family, Brooks went on to say that they still "musta thought they was more than we were because when we'd go to the spring to get water, Mr. Garrett had to drink the water first." As Brooks described it, if she or one of her siblings went for water while they were working in Garrett's fields, "Mr. Garrett wouldn't say nothing. But when you bring it back, then he's thirsty and he'd holler, 'Water boy, bring the water round. If you don't like your job, set your bucket down.' Mr. Garrett would be teasin, you know, but that mean bring it on to him. So we'd take it to him first—we knew—and then he'd drink and his kids would drink and then we'd drink." Irritated, Brooks complained to her father, betraying just the sort of childlike outspokenness that many African American parents feared. Rather than explaining Garrett's behavior or acknowledging the legitimacy of her complaint, Brooks's father reminded her over and over to keep her mouth shut around whites. It annoyed Brooks to have to bite her tongue, but she obeyed her father. She also learned to be glad when it was her turn to go for water because—out of the same impulse to resist that led Bessie Delany to drink from the "white" dipper at Pullen Park—she pointedly rejected Garrett's petty bid for precedence and learned to "drink mine at the spring."[33]

White Southerners' Dramas of Social Inequality

Garrett's insistence that he and his children drink before Brooks and her siblings drank even though they were all drinking from the same bucket in the middle of an Alabama cornfield gets at the nature of prejudice itself. Lacking other resources for a display of dominance, Garrett seized on his ability to command the Brooks children and to demand priority in the seemingly small matter of who drank before whom. Moreover, as with many white southerners, Garrett's belief in the superiority of whites and inferiority of blacks may have operated at a visceral level, his gut reaction telling him that drinking after a black person was somehow dirty and defiling.

In *Separate Pasts*, white autobiographer Melton McLaurin described a similar moment when "Negro spit" threatened, in his own mind, to contaminate his purity and erode his dominance as a white southern male. McLaurin was about thirteen years old at the time, growing up in the small town of Wade, North Carolina, in the early 1950s. He and a white friend were playing pick-up basketball with four black boys of about the same age, including twelve-year-old James Robert Fuller Jr., whom everyone called "Bobo." Stopping to air up the leaky ball, McLaurin unthinkingly took the needle from Bobo and put it in his mouth to wet it, realizing only a split second later that Bobo had just wet the needle himself a moment before. "The realization that the needle I still held in my mouth had come directly from Bobo's mouth, that it carried on it Bobo's saliva, transformed my prejudices into a physically painful experience," McLaurin wrote. Despite the fact that he had drunk from the same cup as blacks in childhood and regularly ate food prepared by black hands, to McLaurin the basketball needle had inexplicably become "the ultimate unclean object, carrier of the human degeneracy that black skin represented. It transmitted to me Bobo's black essence, an essence that degraded me and made me, like him, less than human."

McLaurin "felt compelled" to preserve his own pure-white essence at all costs, but he could not let on that his sense of racial superiority was, in fact, so fragile: "Ironically, the same prejudices that filled me with loathing and disgust also demanded that I conceal my feelings. . . . The rules of segregation which I had absorbed every waking moment of my life, and which were now an essential part of my consciousness, demanded that I retain my position as the superior, that I remain in control of the situation." Less afraid of "the poison of Bobo's saliva" than of letting Bobo see that he had "the power to cut me to the emotional quick . . . and challenge the sureties of my white world," McLaurin simultaneously suppressed his fear of being defiled and grew violently angry. He slammed the needle into the basketball and pumped it up, then flung the ball at Bobo, taking him by surprise and hitting him in the stomach. Bobo flashed anger, then cooled to puzzlement. McLaurin had asserted his dominance, a dominance to which, by refusing to fight back, Bobo had, in McLaurin's eyes, acquiesced. McLaurin's "vindication of white supremacy" was not complete, however, until he could wash away every trace of Bobo's contaminating blackness. After the other boys had gone back to the court to shoot baskets, he went to a nearby water faucet and performed a private "baptism of plain tap water" that restored his "white selfhood."[34]

McLaurin's suggestion that his very selfhood had been at issue not only explains his violent behavior but also makes it clear that there are *white* versions of the "drama of social inequality," as well as black ones. White southerners' "rage to explain" has often manifested itself in autobiographical accounts of childhood dramas much like the ones African American autobiographers tell, but with the roles reversed.[35] Rather than experiencing the pain and confusion of racial subordination, white children learned to inflict it, often first on black nurses and playmates. Like black-authored dramas, whites' stories reveal the extent to which race and other categories of identity, particularly gender and class, were inextricably linked and learned in tandem. And like black autobiography, white southern autobiography has often had an explicit political intent. For white southerners who went on to challenge all or part of the Jim Crow system as adults, usually as a result of some adult moral or political transformation, an account of their "typical" southern upbringing served not only to show how much their own racial attitudes had changed but also to suggest that if *they* could change, so could other white southerners, and so, ultimately, could the South.

Although always the product of a small minority of white dissenters, white-authored dramas of social inequality appeared with increasing frequency during and after the civil rights movement of the 1950s and 1960s.[36] Many describe post–World War II childhoods like that of McLaurin, who was born in 1941, but there are also a number of works by an older generation born in the decades before and after 1900. In these autobiographies, repentant white southerners recount their own sometimes-eager, sometimes-reluctant practice of racial etiquette, their enacting of racial scripts that put them on the other side of the stage from black counterparts in equally formative dramas of social inequality.

Katharine Du Pre Lumpkin's *Making of a Southerner*, published in 1946, offers one early and illuminating example. Born in 1897, Lumpkin recalled knowing from an early age that the streets of her small South Carolina town "were the white man's wherever he chose to walk." Blacks were supposed to yield the sidewalk, even if it meant walking in the gutter. "I could have been hardly more than eight when a little Negro girl of our age, passing a friend and me, showed a disposition to take her half of the sidewalk," Lumpkin wrote in her autobiography. "We did not give ground—we were whites!" When the black girl's arm brushed against her, Lumpkin's companion "turned on the Negro child furiously," saying "'Move over there, you dirty black nigger!'" This moment would prove memorable for Lumpkin precisely because the little girl did not move as expected but instead "flared back at us with a stinging retort." If her friend's demonstration of social superiority did not have the anticipated effect on the black child, it did have an effect on Lumpkin: in her autobiography, she used this moment to illustrate her growing awareness "of myself as a white."[37]

Born less than a decade after Lumpkin, Virginian Sarah Patton Boyle recounted a similar drama of social inequality in her 1962 autobiography, *The Desegregated Heart*. In her anecdote, though, the target of her social distancing was someone whose friendship she valued. Boyle was also older and more ambivalent about race than eight-year-old Lumpkin, and it was her mother rather than a white peer who encouraged her to act self-consciously "white." Like most elite and many middle-class white children of her generation, Boyle had an African American nurse in early childhood, and her primary playmates were the children of her family's black household workers and farmhands. When Boyle reached puberty, her parents suddenly informed her that her relations with African Americans "from now on must be formal," that it was no longer "proper" for her to be "familiar" with black children and adults. A training period followed in which her mother rewarded and punished her according to her adherence to racial etiquette. "I remember running into the house heartsick after snubbing the advances of a child of whom I was particularly fond," Boyle wrote in her autobiography. "He had skipped up to me, suggesting that I come along on some small adventure. . . . Crushing back my desire both for his company and for the fun, I answered stiffly, 'No, I can't.'" Then, "with proper Southern-lady courtesy," she inquired after the boy's well-being, a keynote of white paternalism that even this child, his head lowered, clearly understood. Watching from the porch, Boyle's mother was pleased; like Mary Church Terrell's mother in a different context, she assured her daughter that she had been "a good girl."[38]

The inverse of W. E. B. Du Bois's story of the tall white girl who rejected his card, Boyle's genteel drama of social inequality raises important questions about gender and class. That gender shaped white children's roles in the daily dramas of a racist society is obvious in Boyle's "Southern-lady courtesy," as well as in the masculine aggressiveness that McLaurin felt compelled to display. The fact that both of their dramas took place during adolescence is also significant. As Boyle suggested, her parents' insistence that she maintain social distance from African Americans had everything to do with her physical and sexual maturation. Like other white southern girls, she had to learn to think of herself as the icon of purity that the ideology of southern ladyhood demanded, eliminating the merest hint of sexual availability from her behavior, just as the tall white girl silently eliminated Du Bois from the ranks of eligible suitors by refusing his card. As Katharine Lumpkin's story indicates, white girls learned to draw such distinctions long before puberty and to treat African American girls just as disdainfully as African American boys. Nevertheless, the heightened scrutiny that Boyle and many other white southern girls encountered at adolescence reiterated the gendered nature of their racial socialization.

White boys, by contrast, learned that the demands of chivalry did not apply to black girls and women. In *The Southern Heritage*, published in 1958, South

Carolinian James McBride Dabbs remembered "no feeling against Negroes" but felt that "one event which [he had] never forgotten" indicated that he did have "the usual sense of white privilege." Walking home from school one day in the early 1900s when he was "not yet ten," he encountered "the usual crowd of Negro children also going home." "I must have been accustomed to the privilege of the path along the edge of the dirt road," Dabbs wrote, "for, suddenly, when I came face to face with a Negro girl much larger than I who apparently wasn't going to give way, I drew back and hit her hard in the stomach." His act was unusually aggressive, and a black boy on the scene even commented on his bad behavior. "That ain't good business," the boy objected. "Good enough for me," Dabbs "snorted." "I wasn't ashamed," he concluded in his memoir, "but I didn't tell Father or Mother."[39]

Dabbs's awareness that his parents would not approve suggests the constraints that families often placed on white children's behavior, especially among the middle and upper classes. For Boyle, the connection between class and behavior was even more profound. Taught to revere her family's aristocratic Virginia heritage, Boyle also learned to incorporate African Americans into an elaborate hierarchy that counted upstanding blacks as "humanly," if not socially, above less-decent whites. Nevertheless, Boyle's approach— politeness mixed with equal or greater parts of condescension—probably did little to convince blacks of her admiration and "special love." A class-based concern for "character" could make white southerners such as Boyle paternalistic at best.[40] Among children subject to peer pressure and struggling to overcome their own youthful insecurities, the demands of respectability often failed to make them even that.

In her influential 1949 autobiography, *Killers of the Dream*, Lillian Smith emphasized the subtlety and constancy with which white children were socialized into the southern racial system. "Neither the Negro nor sex was often discussed at length in our home," explained Smith, who was born in 1903 and grew up in the small town of Jasper, Florida.

We were given no formal instruction in these difficult matters but we learned our lessons well. We learned the intricate system of taboos, of renunciations and compensations, of manners, voice modulations, words, feelings, along with our prayers, our toilet habits, and our games. I do not remember how or when, but by the time I had learned that . . . all men are brothers with a common Father, I also knew that I was better than a Negro, . . . that a terrifying disaster would befall the South if ever I treated a Negro as my social equal and as terrifying a disaster would befall my family if ever I were to have a baby outside of marriage.

Obviously interwoven with lessons about gender, Smith's race training eventually came to include very specific, if often unstated, lessons about day-to-day relations with blacks. Significantly, she associated these more specific rules—the rules about eating, drinking, and shaking hands that comprised racial etiquette—with adolescence, while suggesting that a substrate of racism had been laid down in her from infancy.[41]

Along with these reflections, Smith narrated a poignant drama of social inequality. This particular "drama of the South" began when a white club-woman happened to find a little white girl living with a black family on the black side of town. Convinced that the child had been kidnapped, the white clubwomen of Jasper first questioned the black family, then, with the help of the town marshal, took the girl away from them and placed her in the Smith home. Janie "roomed with me, sat next to me at the table, . . . wore my clothes, played with my dolls and followed me around from morning to night," Smith recounted. "She was dazed by her new comforts and by the interesting activities of this big lively family; and I was as happily dazed, for her adoration was a new thing to me; and as time passed a quick, childish, and deeply felt bond grew up between us."

Three weeks later, a black orphanage called and informed the clubwomen that Janie was black. Smith described the upheaval that this news brought: "All afternoon the ladies went in and out of our house talking to Mother in tones too low for children to hear. As they passed us at play, they looked at Janie and quickly looked away again, though a few stopped and stared at her as if they could not tear their eyes from her face." While some of these white women may have been most upset by their inability to distinguish black from white, Annie Smith bore the added emotional burden of explaining to her daughter why her new friend had to return to "Colored Town" and was never to visit or play with her again. "Why?" Smith demanded over and over, until her mother, her voice "sharp" but her face "sad," finally ended discussion of the matter with the same words, ironically, that Richard Wright's mother often used to quiet her son: "You're too young to understand."

Smith herself could do no better when it came time to explain the situation to Janie. "I'm white. . . . And you're colored. And white and colored can't live together because my mother says so," she told Janie in a quiet tête-à-tête. Like Smith herself a few moments before, Janie wanted to know why. "Because they can't," Smith resolved firmly, although she knew that "something was wrong. . . . I knew that my mother who was so good to children did not believe in her heart that she was being good to this child," Smith wrote, adding that she nevertheless "felt compelled" to believe what her mother and other white adults said. It "was the only way my world could be held together."

Compelled to see her friendship with Janie in relation to the racial taboos she had been learning all her life, Smith suddenly felt guilty for becoming close to Janie at all. She went to the piano to play out her stormy feelings, as she always did when she was troubled. Undoubtedly troubled as well, Janie sat down next to her on the piano bench and tried to embrace her. "I shrank away as if my body had been uncovered," Smith recalled. "I had not said a word, I did not say one, but she knew, and tears slowly rolled down her little white face."[42] Just as surely as the white girls in the cloakroom of Mary Church Terrell's school, young Lillian Smith had drawn a social distinction designed to teach a black child who and what she was: "I'm white. . . . And you're colored."

Although Smith narrated this incident as an example of a remembered experience that contributed to her eventual renunciation of Jim Crow, it is clear that it was a formative moment in the development of her childhood racial identity as well. Looking back, Smith also saw it as a moment paradigmatic of the New South. Her specific experience with Janie was "an incident that has rarely happened to other southern children," she acknowledged. "But it was an acting-out, a private production of a little script that is written on the lives of most southern children before they know words. Though they may not have seen it staged this way, each southerner has had his own private showing."[43] Each "private production" also reflected differences of class, gender, and historical circumstance; yet the "little scripts" shaping the lives of southern children were very much the same for both blacks and whites even though blacks and whites played opposite roles.

Dramas of Socialization

Lillian Smith's analysis of southern children's racial learning as "dramas" that follow "scripts" is important because it reminds us that autobiographers' "dramas of social inequality" are *dramas of socialization* as well. That is, they are not merely literary conventions or self-conscious political statements; rather, they are a literary subset of a much larger category of narratives that embody the memories and the process of remembering that define and continually redefine individuals' sense of themselves, regardless of whether they ever write these narratives down in memoirs. In short, the somewhat conventional childhood stories that I have been calling "dramas of social inequality" are best understood as highly crafted *versions* of the usually *unwritten* stories we all tell ourselves about ourselves in an effort to understand who we are and how we fit in our world. No matter how much an autobiography may be shaped by adult concerns, the childhood stories that autobiographers tell contain a core of identity-shaping experience. They are touchstones of memory worn smooth by frequent handling. Thus, barring conscious deception, the "polished" narrative of an autobiographer does not necessarily tell us less about his or her experiences than a supposedly "unvarnished" account. Instead, if we recognize that every experience involves individuals' subjective interpretations of events, we may find that the highly interpreted stories of autobiographers tell us even more than putatively transparent texts.

In *Mastering Slavery: Women, Family, and Identity in Women's Slave Narratives*, Jennifer Fleischner accepts critic Paul John Eakin's insight that autobiography is not simply mimetic but attempts to *transform* the past, involving "a simultaneous acceptance of and refusal of the constraints of the real."[44] Autobiographers not only find themselves but create themselves in writing, and they do so with a greater self-awareness than critics have generally recognized. Even those authors most committed to telling "the truth" comprehend, at some level, that they can tell the truth only as they saw it and as they have come to understand it. Indeed, for many, the autobiographical impulse derives from a feeling that they have achieved a mature viewpoint on past events. Thus, to write an autobiography is, as Fleischner puts it, "to act on the desire to repeat one's past in order to 'supplement' it, because the past is and was 'never acceptable.'"

Building on Eakin's observations, Fleischner goes on to discuss a key psychoanalytic concept that Freud called the "compulsion to repeat," "the idea that, over the course of a life, each individual symbolically restages powerful experiences out of a complex tangle of motivations: to test, verify, and correct reality; and to master or give vent to underlying feelings of rage, fear, frustration, and pressures for revenge. In this way," Fleischner concludes, "the psychoanalytic model of the vicissitudes of remembering is consonant with . . . the autobiographical project to 'supplement' a 'never acceptable' past." Although the Freudian compulsion to repeat is presumably less conscious and perhaps also more urgent than the autobiographer's desire to retell his or her life story as literature, the analogy between these two forms of "repetition" holds, suggesting, in Fleischner's words, "that there is a continuum between unconscious and self-conscious narrative positions, along which all narrators move."[45] There is a link between individuals' narration of their memories in autobiography and their earlier and ongoing narration of the memories to themselves in an effort to determine who and what they are.

Recognizing similarities between the memory work of autobiographers and the everyday workings of memory on a conscious and subconscious level helps us to see the ways in which our experiences and the stories we tell about them do, in effect, create us. Although crafted into literary dramas of social inequality, black and white autobiographers' childhood stories often remain open-ended, retaining some part of the trauma that could make a particular moment unacceptable and thus destined for repetition in both the psychoanalytic and the narrative senses of the word. It is in the open-endedness of these dramas of social inequality that we can read southern children's dramas of socialization. And, as we shall see, dramas of socialization also appear in stories that autobiographers tell without any conscious intent to say "I knew then who I was."

Whether or not they are shaped into dramas of social inequality, dramas of socialization are marked by an irresolution and depth of emotion that suggest that a meaningful interaction between the individual and his or her culture has taken place. They are moments when one learns, to repeat Walter White's phrase, "that there is no isolation from life," that social categories impinge upon individual psychology, shaping individuals' thoughts, feelings, and convictions at a level beneath consciousness, beyond even the autobiographer's, much less the experiencing subject's, control. Thus, writing about her terrifying encounter with the white train conductor more than six decades after it happened, Mary Church Terrell left her five-year-old self looking herself up and down in confusion and guilt, despite her mother's reassurances. Similarly, Sara Brooks ended her story about the threatening sign at Foxfield with the simple question that had haunted her over the years, "Wonder why?" W. E. B. Du Bois wrote of double-consciousness, Richard Wright of "spontaneous fantasies" of retaliatory violence that were a "moral bulwark" constructed to keep his "emotional integrity whole." Melton McLaurin suggested that his angry-but-guilty reaction to Bobo Fuller's saliva taught him that "segregation was serious" but also "for the first time raised questions" about the morality of the institution in his mind.[46] Lillian Smith compared her lost sisterhood with Janie to a splinter that "worked its way . . . down to the hurt places in my memory and festered there."[47] More than forty years after snubbing her playmate, Sarah Patton Boyle ended her anecdote with a question half-submerged in a twelve-year-old's "strange combination of depression and pride": "I was a GOOD GIRL," she reflected, "But oh, what had

I *done!*"[48] It is the indeterminacy of such moments—the almost inevitable seepage of underlying feelings of rage, fear, frustration, confusion, guilt, or pain into even the most calculated narratives—that reveals their true formative power.

Even Walter White's autobiography, which begins with the most overdetermined drama of social inequality thus far considered, offers an open-ended drama of this sort. Unlike his account of the Atlanta riot, which was at least partially fictional (as White's biographer Kenneth Jankin has shown, White's mother and sisters were quite certain and repeatedly assured White that he had *not* had a gun on the night he supposedly sat ready to defend his home),[49] this story does not read like a self-conscious drama of social inequality even though it clearly recounts an important moment in the development of White's sense of himself as an African American. "At the corner of Courtland Street was a watering trough for horses," White began. "Occasionally thirsty humans patronized it also; you pressed down on a handle and contorted your body so as to get your face under the spigot." White's mother forbade her children from drinking from the fountain for fear of germs and disease and probably also from a sense that drinking from a trough was beneath them. But Walter liked to drink from this fountain nonetheless.[50]

By setting the scene in such detail, White suggested that the story he was about to tell had as much to do with boyishness as with race. Unlike other black autobiographers, for whom drinking from forbidden fountains has often served as an example of testing the limits of segregation, White did not flag this as a racial story, much less a story of "I knew then who I was." Instead, a discussion of his childhood reading led him to mention the library at the First Congregational Church, the wide, fenced lawn of which served as a playground for him and his friends. Mention of the church led him, in turn, to reflect on his boyhood tussles with whites. "We often had to do battle to protect our bailiwick from the gangs of white boys on Courtland Street," White wrote. Usually these fights were more amusing than serious; however, the situation was different for any black boy "caught alone."

Sent out for groceries one day by his mother, eight-year-old Walter stopped for a drink. While he was bent over the trough, a white boy crept up behind and shoved him, smashing his nose against the spigot and showering him with water. Furious, Walter ran after the boy, "who yelled derisive remarks about 'niggers drinking from white fountains.'" Realizing he could not catch up, Walter picked up a rock and threw it more accurately than he expected, hitting the boy on the back of the head. "I saw him stagger and clutch his head, the blood oozing between the fingers," White recalled. "My anger changed to cold terror." Suddenly, eight-year-old Walter had to think about race. "I had hit and injured a *white* boy," he abruptly realized, "and, knowing that a white policeman, judge, and jury would take his word, I saw myself being sent away to prison for a long term."[51]

Walter's fears were neither unfounded nor implausible in an intelligent child of eight, especially one who read well at an early age.[52] Every day, Atlanta's largest newspaper, the *Constitution*, ran a feature on the local recorder's court, often titled contemptuously "Judge Broyles' Matinee." There, black and white readers alike could take note of the dozens of African Americans, including young children, arrested and sentenced daily for petty crimes ranging from public drunkenness to riding bicycles on the sidewalk to throwing rocks. Even if Walter did not read the papers, he undoubtedly heard stories about chain gangs and the notoriously bad conditions at the Atlanta stockade, just as Richard Wright picked up on neighborhood gossip and thereby learned his earliest lessons about blacks and whites.

Suddenly compelled to think about the legal consequences of his actions, Walter was, in essence, confronted with race itself. Within seconds, he went from being a boy who wanted a drink of water, perhaps because he was thirsty but also because he enjoyed defying his mother's rules, to being a "black" boy drinking from a fountain that another boy arbitrarily decided to label "white." Only when he drew blood did Walter realize that the other boy actually had the power to make such distinctions—indeed, he had the force of law in the form of white policemen, white judge, and white jury, if not an actual segregation ordinance, on his side. Thus, a half-second later Walter's anger turned to terror. Because of the social implications of his blackness, he could not experience anger without an identity-forming accompaniment of fear.

That Walter's fear of white retribution cut to the marrow of self is evident in the events that followed. Forgetting his errand, he ran home crying to his mother and begged her to whip him. "Somehow or other I felt that if she did so I would thereby escape other punishment," White wrote. Walter's mother laughed, wanting to know for which of his "many misdeeds" he was asking to be punished. "Expecting a burly policeman to put in his appearance any minute," Walter had no time for details. "'Never mind what for,' I pleaded, 'just whip me—whip me quick!'"[53]

Again, Walter's childlike guesses at the way the world worked were astute. A few years later, in the same daily newspaper column that might have told him what punishment to expect from Judge Broyles, Walter could have read about Ferman Jones, an African American boy brought in for throwing rocks. Carrying a strap with her into the courtroom, Jones's mother assured City

Councilman E. W. Martin, who was acting as recorder in Broyles's absence, that if he would simply turn the boy over to her, she would, as reported in the newspaper's derisive dialect, "t'ar de hide offern him." "She was told to take the boy and 't'ar,'" the *Atlanta Constitution* announced, "and the case was dismissed."[54] Clearly, Ferman's mother's promise was a strategy for snatching her son back from the clutches of the white court, which saw her child as merely one of the eight hundred or so black children under the age of sixteen who would appear before it that year.[55] Her act was also subversive in the sense that she was not only saving her child but also recouping authority lost to the state at the moment of Ferman's arrest. Although it is impossible to know what effect either his arrest or his subsequent whipping, assuming he got one, may have had on Ferman, it is clear that his mother's strategy worked. Indeed, her performance as a "proud but distressed mamma" was so compelling to white observers eager to typecast her according to their own ideas about strong black Mammy figures that she got her small victory reported in the city's largest white newspaper for other black parents, as well as white readers, to see.[56] The fact that it was reported derisively and in dialect ought to concern us in some respects but not in others; faced with the same agonizing inability to protect their children from white authorities, most black parents, whatever their social status, would have understood.

Still, for eight-year-old Walter, begging to be whipped without explanation and before anyone had even accused him of doing anything wrong, the same self-protective strategy takes on an almost pathological air. He could, after all, have asked his mother for asylum. He could have hidden, in hopes that the storm he was expecting would blow over, or he could have put on a brave face and acted as if nothing had happened at all. Instead, mixed in with the little boy's terror must have been some measure of uncertainty, perhaps even guilt. Like five-year-old Mary Church Terrell, like that fictional race criminal Huckleberry Finn when he decided that he would rather go to hell than betray his fugitive slave friend Jim, Walter seems to have possessed an intuitive sense of justice that told him that his crime must, in fact, be great if his anticipated punishment could be so harsh.

Madeline White was not prepared to whip her son for no reason, was in fact sitting down to wipe the tears of laughter from her eyes with the corner of her apron when the doorbell rang. Hiding behind his mother's skirts, Walter saw, not the burly white policeman he had feared, but the irate mother of the boy whose head he had gashed. "I am going to have the law on that boy of yours," she shrieked—although her very appearance at the Whites' door suggests that she was not quite ready to call the police, perhaps because she believed that children's misadventures fell under women's jurisdiction or because her family, though white, was not of the social class that the Atlanta police generally served.[57] Sobering instantly, Walter's mother demanded that he tell her what he had done. She then turned to the white woman and "so vigorously defended" her son that the woman's anger cooled and Walter's fear evaporated and he began "to preen myself as something of a hero" for having had the courage to fight back. That satisfying feeling "did not last long." Relieved of the uncertainty and fear that had made him think he needed to be punished by someone, Walter now faced punishment indeed. After the white woman left, Madeline White ordered him to cut some switches from the peach tree in the back yard. "These she peeled to make their sting more memorable. Thereafter I managed to quench my thirst at home."[58]

Although White suggested in his autobiography that his mother punished him for his disobedience alone, it is hard to believe that this was all there was to it. Like all African American parents in the Jim Crow South, Madeline White knew that her ability to protect her child was severely limited. Even as she thanked God that she had been able to dissuade the white mother from calling the police, she probably also felt both anger at her son for worrying her and agony at the realization that she might not be able to save him in the future. As many African Americans' descriptions of Jim Crow–era discipline show, these complex emotions often manifested themselves in a heavy sense of responsibility to impress upon children, with the sting of a peachwood switch if necessary, the importance of staying out of trouble at all costs.[59]

Walter White did not record his reaction to the whipping, but it is certain that his emotions, too, after it as before it, were complex. Already in the course of a few minutes, perhaps half an hour, he had run an emotional gauntlet from slight mischievousness to anger, fear, uncertainty, pride, and, sent to cut switches at the moment of his victory, defeat. Like other autobiographers' dramas of socialization, this story of Walter White's remains open-ended. He could not and did not even try to summarize its meaning with the succinctness that he brought to his story of the Atlanta riot: "I knew then who I was." Suffused with emotion, all that his eight-year-old self could know for certain was that his wounds—perhaps his smashed nose, certainly the welts of his whipping—smarted.

Memorable Moments

The fact that White did not shape this anecdote into a drama of social inequality does not mean that he did not shape it at all. Inevitably, the six short paragraphs he devoted to this incident, like his account of the Atlanta riot, say as much about him as an autobiographer and about the time of his autobiography's creation as they do about his experiences as a young boy. Each of the childhood stories White told in his autobiography also represents only one formative moment of many—many that we can know about because White remembered and recorded them and many more that have been lost to history because only he *could* have recorded them and, for whatever reason, he did not.

Although autobiography can, of course, never be complete, its greatest value as a source is precisely in its focus on the moment, particularly the unsettling and therefore memorable moment, for it is *in the moment*—in the experience of the thirsting, bending, smarting body "situated in time, place, and history"—that the raw materials of identity are gathered.[60] In other words, while we may speak of the conflict between Walter and his antagonist as an everyday racial incident, we must also recognize that everyday incidents are what *make* race as far as their participants are concerned.[61] Setting out to buy groceries, bending over to take a drink of water, Walter was not black in any self-conscious or socially significant way until another boy, embracing the social and psychological privileges of whiteness, took notice of him, attacked him, and made him so. Even the white boy's epithets could make Walter black only in a social sense, as, for example, in the eyes of a passerby who might have noticed him or pondered his racial affiliation only after hearing the other boy's cries.

It took the chilling slap of fear to make Walter himself conscious of racial difference; in his autobiographical retelling, he distinguished himself as black only insofar as he expressed his "cold terror" at injuring someone who was "*white*" (emphasis in original). Drawing a white boy's blood instantly conjured a vision of trial and punishment in Walter's mind, a familiar narrative of "white policeman, judge and jury" in which race would be all-important in a way that race was not important, not even present except in the white boy's memories of previous encounters, when Walter stooped to drink. Thus, just as we need to write the history of the moment in order to see how Walter's experiences made him black (for the countless time in his young life), we must also consider the ways in which historically located experiences build on one another and are shaped by participants' knowledge of the past, as well as their speculations about the future.[62] For, without prior knowledge gained, perhaps, in the battles on Courtland Street, how could the boy who shoved him have possibly known that white-skinned Walter was anything other than "white"?

We—meaning everyone, from participants to participant-observers to historians looking back—can enter society only in the middle. There is always a past that partially determines what we will encounter in life and how we will respond to it. There are always a present to confront and a future to anticipate, shaping our sense of what is and what will be and shading our analyses of what has already been.[63] We can never truly isolate an experience from the flow of past, present, and future, nor can we legitimately identify any moment as singularly formative, as *the moment* that allowed us to say once and for all (as opposed to just temporarily), "I knew then who I was." On examination, we have to admit that other moments are also important and that the subjective meanings we give to any particular memory change from one act of remembering to the next depending on what we need the memory *for* at any given time. Meaning exists only in the present, in our perpetual reinterpretation of our memories, be they memories of childhood or of the last five minutes, both of which are irretrievably passed and continue to exist only in our own minds. As Lillian Smith noted just before recounting her story about finding and losing Janie, "to excerpt from a life and family background one incident and name it as a 'cause' of a change in one's life direction is a distortion and often an irrelevance. The hungers of a child and how they are filled have too much to do with the way in which experiences are assimilated to tear an incident out of life and look at it in isolation." And yet Smith did go on to tell her story as a snippet of experience, a coherent narrative with a beginning, a middle, and an end. Her encounter with Janie was, in her words, "a drama," "a private production of a little script that is written on the lives of most southern children before they know words."[64]

As impossible as it is for us to extract an experience from the minute-by-minute flow of existence, it is equally true that we do so all the time in our minds, imposing continuity and meaning. We think in terms of stories, marking off beginnings and endings among our experiences as if we were putting stops in a telegram, even though we know, if we think about it, that every beginning has antecedents and no ending equates to the end of a story's possible significance in our unfolding lives. In the same way, black and white southern autobiographers have long narrated their dramas of socialization, often in a highly self-conscious form as dramas of social inequality, as a way to extract meaning from the inexorable progression of their experiences. Everyday dramas were a fundamental unit of experience for black and white southerners writing about their Jim Crow childhoods. Manifestations of a "compulsion to repeat," such dramas are not merely conventions of literature but measured doses of perception and understanding. They are embodiments of what black and white children could take in, how they assimilated it, and how they remembered and repeated it throughout their lives. As such, autobiographers' dramas are also a good indication of where historians need to look if they want to begin to answer the question of how black and white southern children's racial identities were formed.

4 Playing and Fighting

In 1941, on the eve of the United States' entry into World War II, the federal government began to buy up land near Jacksonville, North Carolina, to build Marine Corps Base Camp Lejeune. Laura Donaldson's family had lived in the area for generations, and she and her siblings, recently orphaned by their father's accidental death, attended a hearing that would determine how much they would be paid for their 120 acres. Laura was about eighteen years old at the time and would remember that day for decades. "For all of this property, they wanted to give us two hundred dollars and I said no," she recalled. "I stood up and I said I refuse to accept this." "Gal, what do you mean you refuse to accept this?" the judge replied. "I said 'I refuse to accept giving away the property that my father worked so hard to leave for his children for two hundred dollars.' . . . So my brother's pulling on my dress. 'Sit down, Sis. . . . Sit down, Sis, sit down!'" Undeterred, Laura went on to tell the judge that she also refused to accept his decision to give her neighbor Mrs. Allen, a white widow with several children, only three hundred dollars, for her farm. "Well, what do you know about property?" the judge demanded. "I said, 'I know that my daddy worked too hard for it and I know that Mr. Allen worked too hard for his.' So he said, 'Well, we'll call a recess.'" The hearing ended without setting a price for Laura's family's land, but when the check came a few months later, it was "like about a thousand dollars which still wasn't enough but it was more than we would have gotten." Laura had made her point.[1]

There are a number of ways to interpret eighteen-year-old Laura Donaldson's stand, and Donaldson herself offered more than one interpretation as she looked back on it after more than fifty years. On the one hand, she saw her behavior as an act of courage that corresponded to her father's teachings. "He always told us that you are just as good as anyone and don't let anyone tell you that you are not just as good as the next person," she explained. "So

I grew up with that feeling that I was just as good." On the other hand, she recognized that her actions could well have had a very different outcome and that she should, perhaps, have listened when her older brother told her to sit down and shut up because "he knew about Jim Crow." She continued, "I was too young really to know because we . . . younger children had not been exposed as he had."[2] Or, more likely, she *had* been exposed to Jim Crow in various forms but chose to maintain her defiance, a position that was far from unusual among black teenagers.

Another intriguing aspect of Laura Donaldson's story is the fact that Mrs. Allen was the first white adult she ever remembered giving her a hug. "In our community, it wasn't as racist as some and we had grown up playing with the white children," Donaldson remembered. "But this was the first time that an adult white person had ever embraced me." Not that being hugged by a white person was necessarily a thrill: Allen dipped snuff and Laura was afraid she was going to dribble tobacco juice on her. "But she grabbed me and she said, 'Honey, thank you so much. Thank you so much. I didn't know how to talk to [the judge] like that.'"[3]

As Laura Donaldson's story reminds us, for black children growing up in the Jim Crow South, there was no equivalent to the much-mythologized relationship between white children and their dear old "Mammies" and "Uncles." Those who came from mixed-race families might know the affection of white relatives, and certainly the history of interracial sex in the South meant that many "black" family members looked "white." But unlike white southerners, who often cited their childhood relationships with black caregivers as an indication of the "love" that existed between the races despite segregation, black southerners had no white "Mammies" or "Uncles" to point to. Their closest interracial relationships were with white playmates, as Donaldson herself suggests. This chapter is about interracial play and its close companion, interracial fighting.

In 1992, Nobel Prize–winning novelist Toni Morrison published *Playing in the Dark: Whiteness and the American Literary Imagination* and, in so doing, helped to spark a continuing scholarly interest in the ways in which blackness and whiteness are both cultural constructs that depend, to a large extent, on one another.[4] When I write of interracial "play," I am mostly using the word in a colloquial sense to refer to children's games and other activities. Yet I also want to stress the element of cultural interchange that Morrison's title evokes—including its suggestion that analyses of this sort ultimately have more to tell us about whites than about blacks. As child development specialists increasingly recognize, "play" is actually serious developmental *work* for children. Through play, they attempt to gain a clearer understanding of the world by manipulating it, and their manipulations extend far beyond material objects or the rules of made-up games to include all manner of social phenomena.[5] Children play with racial concepts as much as any other aspect of their culture, especially when they encounter playmates whose differences in skin color and other physical features become all the more noticeable because of the ways those differences seem to matter to adults. Thus, the playing—and the fighting—discussed in this chapter is just as much about cultural construction as the literary "playing in the dark" Morrison examined, and it is about the shaping of individual racial identity as well.

Black and white children growing up in the Jim Crow South learned a great deal about race through their ongoing interactions with one another. Evidence of this learning is preserved in adults' reflections on their childhoods, which, like Laura Donaldson's account of the government hearing, include their own explicit and implicit analyses. In autobiographical writings and oral history interviews, both black and white southerners attribute significance to interracial contact, especially play, among children, but their interpretations of this contact differ. Black informants who played with white children when they were young often cite this fact as evidence that some whites were friendlier than others or that race relations were better where they grew up than in other parts of the region. But few describe interracial play with any great nostalgia, and most point out that black and white children eventually went their separate ways, whether as a result of adult intervention or of their own accord. Some whites also look back on interracial play less nostalgically than we might expect. They describe playing with black children as merely a fact of their childhoods without suggesting that it had any major impact on their developing racial views—an accurate reflection, perhaps, of the extent to which they learned *not to allow* childhood bonds with black playmates and caregivers to interfere with lessons in racial etiquette and white supremacy. If white informants are wistful about childhood interactions with blacks, that wistfulness most often emerges from the regrets of those who have come to question white supremacy only belatedly, as adults. They look back on childhood play with blacks as something that should have prevented them from becoming racists, even though it did not.

How did black and white southern children interact with one another in a childhood world that was, at least in part, separate from the world of grown-ups? And what did those interactions mean to their developing conceptions of race and of themselves? Obviously, play was only one aspect of children's distinctive sphere, and the children of the early twentieth century spent many more hours working than we often remember, especially the majority of black and white southerners who grew up on farms. School filled many of their hours as well, although how many varied greatly according to a child's race, class, and locale. Then there were Sunday school and church, which, like work, were a major part of many children's lives in the early twentieth century. And there were the countless hours that all children spend alone or with their siblings or parents or other relatives, in family parlors or bedrooms or haylofts or trees. In short, there is far more to the distinctive world of childhood than one could ever hope to describe.

Nevertheless, we can learn a great deal from studying children's interactions with racial "others" because it was largely through such interactions that both black and white children continued to develop an understanding of race and the impact it would have on their lives. To be sure, some white children did grow up in isolation from black children and vice versa—a fact that comes to life in a story told by one black woman whose town bordered an all-white area in the southern Appalachians. One morning, a four-year-old white boy ran up to her, grabbed her hand, "looked up very confidently into [her] face and said, 'Are you a nigger?'" She continued, "His whole face was wreathed in smiles, and he was so obviously searching for an answer to his question that one could not but be gentle with him. He skipped on down the street with me, still holding my hand while I explained the meaning of the word he had just used."[6] Clearly, this boy had already learned something about race, evident in his use of the word "nigger," before he ever met a black person. Yet even he had his first face-to-face encounter with an African American at a fairly early age, and most black and white southerners were far less isolated from one another.

Instead, black and white children interacted often, some every day, their encounters unfolding in yards, on streets, and in other spaces between the highly segregated zones of school and church and parlor. Because they faced exclusion or subordination or abuse, blacks seem to have understood the lessons—and the limitations—of interracial contact much more clearly and at an earlier age than whites did, usually well before puberty, although their comprehension also grew with time. To them, friendly play was not meaningless, but it was an exception to the workings of a society structured around white dominance. Inevitably, the day would come when black and white could no longer play together at all, much less as equals, and that day might even be marked by the imposition of codes of adult racial etiquette such as the new requirement that a white boy or girl be called "Mister" or "Miss." Interracial fighting, particularly the impersonal name-calling and rock-throwing that many black children experienced, often came to have a more honest, if infuriating, feel than the frustrating complexities of their personal relationships with the white "friends" of early childhood. Particularly by their adolescent years, black southerners generally based their attitudes toward Jim Crow more on their experiences of conflict with white peers—and on their growing awareness of racial violence and other aspects of racial oppression—than on any analysis of interracial "friendships" in childhood.

For this reason, an analytical emphasis on childhood encounters across race lines is inevitably less revealing for blacks than it is for whites. To look at blacks in relation to whites is to learn only why they *needed* a double-consciousness, not how they came to develop one. To see this, we have to turn inward, as black southerners themselves did, to the segregated black community: to the teachings of black parents discussed earlier, to changing views of children's potential role in political struggles (a focus of my conclusion), and to segregated institutions such as schools and churches. The scholarship on black institution-building in the Jim Crow era has grown tremendously in recent years. The best studies explore tensions, including intraracial class and ideological differences and the influence of white philanthropists and other allies, that make it impossible to conclude that all black institutions were simply "teaching equality" to black southerners. But many clearly were.[7] To the extent that young blacks learned to value themselves and their race and to understand their rights as citizens, their lessons came almost exclusively from other blacks.

For white children, on the other hand, interracial encounters were all the more important because whites were so unlikely to learn lessons that contradicted the conventional wisdom of white supremacy anyplace else. At least not directly. Although white adults and institutions such as schools and churches generally either reinforced racist thinking or maintained silence on racial issues or both, it is worth pointing out the inherent contradictions between core democratic and religious values of justice, equality, and brotherhood, on the one hand, and white supremacy, on the other. But such abstractions were easy to overlook.[8] As Lillian Smith observed, it was quite possible to live "the same segregated life as did other southerners" even with parents (much less teachers and ministers) who "talked in excessively Christian and democratic terms."[9] Thus, for whites, the lessons of interracial contact in childhood were very significant whenever they challenged supposedly natural racial hierarchies or made whites' failure to live up to their own moral and democratic values a little too plain. Overall, whites' descriptions of interracial play are more ambiguous and varied than blacks' descriptions, and their ac-

Children at Hill House, Mississippi, July 4, 1936 (above), and boys wrestling by the side of the road, Person County, North Carolina, July 1939 (right). Farm Security Administration photographer Dorothea Lange seems to have captured both children's play and, more unusually, children's fighting across race lines. Yet both images are ambiguous. The children at Hill House are obviously posed, telling us comparatively little about the context in which the photograph was taken. The North Carolina boys may have been acting spontaneously, but were they actually fighting or only playing, and does the black child have a smile on his face or a grimace? (Images courtesy of the Library of Congress, Prints and Photographs Division, FSA-OWI Collection, LC-USF34-009610-C and LC-USF34-020254-E.)

counts of childhood conflicts are more limited and almost always emphasize white guilt. It is from penitents like Smith that we learn the most about what childhood contacts with blacks could mean to white southerners. Such contacts were, to improvise again on C. Vann Woodward's famous phrase, "forgotten alternatives." They were forgotten alternatives in at least two senses: first, in that they were "forgotten" or repressed. Indeed, encouraging their children to "forget" that there might be more than one way for blacks and whites to relate to each other was the most personal part of adult white southerners' broad agenda of repressing any alternatives to rule by a conservative white elite.

Second, white children's interactions with blacks were forgotten alternatives in the sense that they were, at least sometimes, alternatives: the kinds of experiences that, if reconstructed in memory, could lead white southerners to question a society that separated them from people they cared about. In autobiography and oral history, a number of white southerners trace the roots of their adult decisions to challenge Jim Crow back to their childhood experiences, including interracial play and especially their forced separation from black playmates. But usually their dissenting views emerged only in adulthood, not as a direct outcome of the events of their early years. And dissenters were always a small minority. Tragically, for most white southerners, whatever "forgotten alternatives" the relatively open world of childhood interaction embodied remained forgotten as they matured into exclusively white social circles by the time they reached adolescence.

Interracial Play: Black Perspectives

To acknowledge that a study of interracial contacts in childhood reveals more about the tragic story of white forgetting than it reveals about black southerners' developing racial consciousness is not to say that such a study is without significance for blacks. Black southerners did see friendly play among children as significant and ameliorative, something they admit more readily in oral history than in autobiography. This discrepancy probably reflects black autobiographers' self-conscious political purpose of exposing and challenging racism, whereas the goals of oral history informants, most of whom have been interviewed in the less politically urgent climate of the post–civil rights era, are much more varied. In oral history, too, the interviewer plays an important role, shaping the conversation through the questions he or she asks. Nevertheless, very little of the black oral history material cited below resulted from interviewers asking specific questions about blacks' childhood encounters with whites. Rather, these stories of playing and fighting emerged from informants' memories more or less on their own or in response to a more general query—often a question along the lines of "What was it like in your area when you were growing up?" The spontaneity with which black informants remember examples of interracial *conflict* is particularly instructive. For, if looking at black children in relation to white children cannot show us how young blacks developed the double-consciousness that allowed them to survive and oppose Jim Crow, it can help us trace the deep roots of black adolescents' anger, which became a potent force for change by the middle of the twentieth century. Few black southerners ever forgot the anger and indignation they felt as children whenever they encountered injustice and abuse, even if, in maturity, they allowed memories of interracial play to soften their reflections on childhood.

Like Laura Donaldson, many black oral history informants mention interracial play as evidence that race relations were "good"—or at least better than average—in their communities when they were young. Nettie Thompson, who grew up in Brunswick, Georgia, in the 1910s, saw the fact that black and white children played together in her neighborhood as one of the elements that made her hometown "congenial."[10] Alease Brickers was even more explicit, using interracial play as a measure for comparing segregation in urban and rural environments. Brickers's family had moved from rural Seaboard, North Carolina, to Norfolk, Virginia, in the mid-1920s when she was twelve. Asked how Norfolk differed from her hometown, Brickers replied forcefully, "Oh, my goodness. Norfolk, it was a little different. People, white and black, in North Carolina, didn't use that segregation as much as they did in the city. . . . Because in the country, white people lived . . . in front of where we lived, and the children, they mixed, they went together, they played together. They didn't know nothing about, 'Don't you play with that child.' . . . We all played together. We didn't know no different."[11]

Although Brickers implied that black and white children did not play together in cities such as Norfolk, Depression-era observers such as black sociologist Charles S. Johnson considered interracial play, particularly among young children, common in both rural and urban settings in the South.[12] William Linyear grew up playing with Jewish children in Norfolk in the 1910s and 1920s.[13] Louise Bouise took it for granted that black and white children both came together to play and went their separate ways for school and other activities. "We had a black family on one side and a white family on the other side," she recalled of her New Orleans neighborhood. "My friends were white and colored, as we called them. The colored children I played with more or less looked like white children. But we did go to colored schools. . . . In the neighborhood we played together but everything else we did separately. . . . We knew that and we accepted it to the extent that it didn't make any difference in our friendship with the children in the neighborhood. . . . I don't remember that bothering me at the time."[14] Emmett Cheri also grew up in New Orleans, but in the 1920s, about a decade after Bouise. He saw his childhood as "typical" for Americans—at least working-class, urban Americans—of his era. "The blacks and the whites fought against each other in different parts of the city. We fought one another. We played together. It was just like any typical American kid. We was all the same."[15]

Cheri's matter-of-fact comments about playing *and fighting* also put such contacts into perspective. Children's play and, to some extent, even their fighting was as much or more about being a kid as it was about race. Essie Alexander, who grew up in a family of sharecroppers on a Mississippi plantation in the 1930s, certainly saw it this way. As a child, Alexander did not come into contact with a large number of whites, but she did get to know the one or two white families who sharecropped on the same plantation at any given time. The white children "would get out there and play," she recalled, "and sometimes if they got hot, they would run home and call us a nigger, and my younger brothers, they would call them rednecks or peckerwoods and that was the end of that. The next day, they was back playing again. So we never got into any big problem about that."[16] Like any other children, then, blacks and whites played and fought and made up again, and even racial epithets were sometimes simply handy and less meaningful than they may seem. In short, as we think about children historically, it is important to keep their youthfulness in mind.

Few accounts of interracial play offer rich descriptions of the play itself, but those that do present a child's-eye view that is worth appreciating. Ruth Cappie remembered opening the gate between her aunt's Mississippi backyard and a white neighbor's.[17] Ada Mae Stewart and her white playmates "had playhouses and we gathered them big green tree leaves and . . . some straw and set down and make skirts. We'd stir up mud. That was our cakes."[18] At age ten, Theresa Lyons liked to pour oil on her white best friend's hair. "I'd have her slicked down just like a cat," she remembered, laughing.[19]

Georgia Bays's story of interracial play also recaptures a child's perspective and, perhaps more important, reiterates that interracial experiences were part of children's larger experience of growing up. Born in 1914 to a sharecropping family in the Mississippi hills, Bays played with the children of white families in her rural neighborhood. It was in relation to these children that she learned one of the fundamental lessons of her childhood: thou shalt not steal. Bays knew that one white playmate "had a little more pretty things than [she] had." "So," Bays recounted, "while they was going to church, I decided while Mama was cooking dinner [to] go over there and get me some of her things. I took my little dress tail up and went over there and filled it full, toted it in my dress tail. That was all the sense I had." Bays stashed her loot under her family's house and continued playing. "I imagine Mama knowed what I was doing," Bays explained, "but she just took her time. Well, she got dinner done and she come on out. She said, 'Georgia, what's you doing?' I said, 'I'm playing, Mama.' She stepped out and looked up under the house. She seen what I had. . . . She didn't say another word. . . . She got through with her stuff and sat out on the porch." Bays's mother waited until the white family returned from church, then made Georgia gather up the white girl's things and marched her over to their house. "She said, 'Miss Violet, Georgia came over here and got some of your girl's things.' [Miss Violet] said, 'Oh, Lela.' [Mama] said, 'Uh-huh. I wanted you to see it.' And you know what?" Bays concluded. "I put that stuff down. [Mama] didn't have to whoop me. She just talked to me. And from that day to this one, I don't bother people's stuff."[20]

As Bays's story suggests, some black children's relationships with whites were intimate and meaningful on a variety of levels. Even as she neared seventy, Florence Borders could remember the Jewish girl who was her "best playmate" during her preschool years but who died when Borders was only five—perhaps her earliest exposure to the finality of death.[21] William Childs did not have a lot of contact with white children, but he does seem to have been fairly close to a boy named Nick, the son of a Greek immigrant who ran a grocery store in Childs's Wilmington, North Carolina, neighborhood. Asked if he and Nick remained friends as they got older, Childs replied, "Sure," and briefly recounted Nick's adult career as a dry cleaner, suggesting a lifelong acquaintance.[22]

Nick, the child of a Greek immigrant, and the Jewish girl who played with Florence Borders are just two of the many children of white ethnic minorities who figure prominently in black informants' memories of interracial play. Although the evidence remains anecdotal, working-class backgrounds and outsider status may have made such children more likely to play with black children than more elite and native-born white children were. Certainly, one particularly intriguing description of interracial play involves ethnicity as much as race. John Volter was born in 1929, the son of a salt miner in Weeks Island, a small town near New Iberia, Louisiana. Asked to describe the

Weeks Island community, Volter explained, "You have to remember this was company-owned property. It was Myles Salt Company . . . and they provided the houses for the workers. They were segregated. The blacks lived in one section and the whites lived in the other section. But somehow I crossed those bounds of race because I had a cousin, Nathan Volter, who worked for a Jew . . . named Nathan Levy, and Nathan Levy had a son, Nathan, Jr. and the two of us played together because it seemed as though the Caucasian kids didn't want to play with him." The two boys were soon joined in their play by a boy named Babineaux. "So the white guys would pass in their old car and they said, 'Well look, a Cajun, a nigger and a Jew,'" Volter recalled with a chuckle. "And we heard them, you know. It didn't faze us as children. We got so that we would play games where, when we'd get ready to part in the evening, . . . we would decide the next day to change roles. Say I'd be the Jew and the Jew would become the Cajun and the Cajun would become the nigger. So we went along in our own little world." Volter, Levy, and Babineaux remained friends despite the fact that Volter moved away from Weeks Island when he was nine. Even in retirement, they continued to get together from time to time to "cut up" and discuss, as Volter put it, "things we did, things we did to his daddy, things we did to my daddy." He continued, "You know how kids [are], we did little mischievous things and got by with it." Volter also attributed his own lack of racial prejudices to the openness of his childhood, in which the boys' racial and ethnic role-switching clearly played a part: "I think that I grew up with less prejudice and prejudiced ideas than the average black southerner for the simple reason that . . . I had already crossed the bounds here in New Iberia."[23]

As much as Volter's story may indicate a special bond between blacks and children of white ethnic minorities, it is also important to acknowledge that excluding and ridiculing blacks was one of the tried-and-true methods poorer and less-connected people could use to become more "white."[24] The desire for such a status gain may account for the intense fighting that broke out between Mamie Garvin Fields and her siblings and their German-immigrant neighbors immediately after South Carolina's segregation laws were passed.[25] It may also explain why Septima Clark, who was born in Charleston in 1898, a decade after Fields, felt that black and white children did not play together "as a rule," even though there were Irish, Italian, German, and African American families all living on the same street.[26] In other words, children of white ethnic minorities often had just as strong an incentive to avoid or harass black children as to befriend them.

Moreover, black informants describe many intimate relationships with whites in which the white family's ethnicity was not an issue. Growing up in

New Orleans in the 1920s, Herbert Cappie "had a little white friend called Jack" whose "parents were well-to-do." But despite his family's higher social status, Jack was as quick to defy racial conventions as John Volter's friends Babineaux and Levy were, particularly when he saw a clear advantage in it. "We were not supposed to go to any of the shows downtown," Cappie recalled, but "Jack and I would go to the neighborhood theater together quite often, and Jack would sit upstairs in the colored section with me because upstairs was a nickel and downstairs was a dime. So Jack had an extra nickel to spend for candy or whatever." Although Cappie did not indicate how old he and Jack were when they went to the movies, their friendship may have continued for some time. "We played football together and lots of other things. I was the only black there and if I would get the football and be successful in gaining some yardage somebody would holler out 'stop that nigger' and that would result in a fight." It would be interesting to know whether Jack stood by his friend when fights broke out, but it is clear that Jack's willingness to challenge segregation was not entirely one-sided. "Jack was the one who encouraged me to go to the white theaters," Cappie, who could easily pass for white, explained. "'Come on, Herb, let's go.' And we went and he started me to going. Well, when I wanted to go, I'd just go on by myself. Nobody gave a damn so I kept going as long as I wanted to. You see, in New Orleans, you have so many black-whites and so many white-blacks. Everybody's confused."[27]

Like Herbert Cappie, black informants frequently found their white playmates challenging racial etiquette. For example, many describe white children eating with them or their families, sometimes often enough to suggest that the children were not getting enough to eat at home. "They used to call us the 'uppity niggers' on our street because of the fact that we had a car and we were able to dress well and we always had food on our table," Lanetha Branch remembered of the Memphis neighborhood where her family moved when she was six. "In fact, one of my friends, Peggy—one of my white acquaintances—she'd eat at our house every single day because she'd come right at dinner time. She'd come for dinner."[28]

Racial etiquette could easily accommodate a white child eating with a black family since it was common for younger white children to eat in the kitchen with black household workers. But the relationships that grew up between black and white adults whose children played together sometimes presented fairly significant challenges to the unwritten rules of Jim Crow. Roosevelt Cuffie, who was born in 1926 in rural Cuffie Town, Georgia, described one such relationship with a family of white sharecroppers who lived nearby. The white father "was a man that we could get along with," Cuffie remembered, and the adults' relationship does appear to have been one of mutual trust and respect. The white parents even felt comfortable leaving their children with the Cuffies while they took weekend trips.[29]

Frankie V. Adams, who grew up in Danville, Kentucky, in the early 1900s, also considered early experiences with white children important because they allowed for what she called "interplay" within individuals' racial attitudes. "My father was a truck driver," Adams explained, and "one of the things that happened was that the white owner had three children; one was a girl, the others were boys. And when my mother would take on a special job with this white family, or any white family, for that matter, I went with her as a kid, and these boys and this girl comprised my 'family.' We would play like husband and play like mama to the younger children." To see black and white children pretending to be married and raising children together would have upset many adult southerners, black and white, in the early twentieth century. Yet Adams asserted that such intimacies were not only commonplace but also meaningful: "So all this is to say that you develop, this develops in the individual a certain kind of interplay that was something I just know sort of later was true in relation to the Carter family down here in Plains, Georgia"— a point of view that former president Jimmy Carter has himself espoused, emphasizing the importance of his early relationships with blacks to explain his humanitarian adult attitudes.[30]

Interracial Play: White Perspectives

Nevertheless, not every white description of interracial play fits the pattern Adams and Carter outline. Like blacks, whites often discuss playing across the color line as simply a fact of their childhoods. Margaret MacDougall, born in Yorkville, South Carolina, in 1903, vividly recalled a family cook who brought her small son to work with her. "And he slept in the woodbox. . . . You had a woodstove and then a kerosene stove. And the wood for the stove would be in the kitchen. And Sam, her little boy, would sleep in that woodbox because she didn't have anybody to leave him with." But asked if she played with the children of black household workers, MacDougall replied vaguely, "Yes, I guess I played with Sam, but I didn't live close to them and I can't remember any of their children." Instead, MacDougall's memories of childhood play centered on other whites and particularly on the fact that most of her playmates were boys who liked to play rough: "They would shock me on purpose, to see how loud I'd yell. . . . [Mother] didn't take any part, except that she did lean out the window sometimes when someone was pulling Thomas F.'s curls or hitting him or something, and she said, 'Hit him back, son, hit him back.' . . . So I grew up, I had to take it, climbed trees and everything else."[31]

Sociologist Lewis Killian also suggested that his childhood world was essentially white, "even though individual blacks moved in and out of it regularly." At the center were his family and a few close friends in his neighborhood in Macon, Georgia. "Then there were 'my kind of people'—the kids who went to my Sunday school, were invited to my birthday parties, and would become my best friends when I started school."[32] Within this white world, class would prove definitive, requiring Killian, whose family's aspirations outstripped their resources, to observe accepted forms of class interaction among whites just as carefully as he observed the etiquette of race.

Perhaps the whiteness of many whites' social worlds (which intensified with age, as the next chapter will show) explains why some white southerners have so little to say about their early experiences with blacks. Asked about her relationship with the children of her family's servants, Olive Matthews Stone, who grew up in Dadeville, Alabama, at the turn of the twentieth century, said simply, "We played with them. I was not conscious of the fact that, probably at adolescence, the friendship ended." Stone also told a story about her younger brother Jack, who was playing with the son of the family cook and some other boys in a pasture. When Jack ran to his mother saying he had shot the boy with his B.B. gun, his mother "hitched up the horse to the buggy and got the little boy and his mother and they went to the doctor immediately— it was a skin wound, didn't amount to very much, but Jack was scared out of his wits of what he might have done," Stone remembered, "and Mother was concerned too. She would never have dismissed anything that might have been dangerous." Still, this was "not really an example of tolerance," Stone concluded, refusing to see this episode as evidence of her parents' comparative kindness or, for that matter, as evidence of anything else.[33] Despite its potential, in Stone's telling this story is not a drama of socialization, racial or otherwise. Instead, she offered the story almost without comment and with no indication of what, other than the sense of tragedy averted, had led her to remember it for all those years.

Two decades younger than Stone, McNeil Smith left an element of his childhood similarly unexplored. "It was fun growing up in a little town," Smith recalled of Rowland, North Carolina, where he was born in 1918. "I had Negro boy friends. One day I remember going downtown with one of them, and people sat on the curbs, you know, by the drugstore, and would say, 'Here come the Gold Dust twins.'" How Smith felt about being compared to one of the racial caricatures in a popular soap advertisement, either as a child or later, remains uncertain. Rather than probing its significance, he moved quickly away from his own experience as a "Gold Dust twin" to a generalization about the experiences of white southerners, concluding this brief recollection with a near non sequitur: "But we nearly always had servants; most southern homes did."[34]

If some whites made little of the fact that they played with black children, others saw a great deal of significance in these experiences, either at the time or later on. Future historian Guion Johnson undoubtedly knew from the start that her relationship with two black children broke the rules of racial etiquette. Recounting the story as an example of her father's remarkable sense of fairness, Johnson explained that the janitor at her father's hardware store in Greenville, Texas, had complained about his inability to get music lessons for his son and daughter because the only teachers in town were white and would not accept black students. "My father said, 'If you would like to send your children to my house, I have one daughter who is taking violin and she will give one or both [children] violin lessons, and I have another daughter who is taking lessons in speech. I think that it is very important for a good citizen to stand on his own feet and know how to express himself. So, if you would like for them to take speech and violin, I'll be delighted to speak to my daughters and see if they would teach them, and I'm sure they will be very happy.'" Johnson's father not only persuaded his daughters to pass along their lessons but also told them how to treat their new students: "My father said, 'Now, you will have your classes in the living room, and you will give them punch and cookies or whatever they want to drink afterwards. Because I want them to enjoy their work and I want them to feel relaxed. And I want you to treat these children as if they were your brother and sister.' . . . So this went on for months and months, and perhaps years," Johnson concluded. "I don't remember just how long, but it was a situation that we enjoyed and the two Negro children seemed to enjoy it very much." Even Johnson's mother, who worried more about what people might think, "gradually came to accept my father's position."[35]

Johnson's parents were extremely unusual in their open defiance of Jim Crow—something Johnson herself noted by pointing out that "the children came very frankly in the front door, and there was no attempt to close the windows so that the neighbors would not know that we were giving these children lessons in violin and speech."[36] Other white parents, including those who were relatively progressive, toed the lines of convention, setting limits on how their children interacted with blacks and, quite often, forbidding interracial play altogether as the children matured.

Sometimes, such restrictions backfired, making children *more* likely to question southern racial orthodoxy, not less. Future University of North Carolina religious studies professor Ruel Tyson claimed to have developed a skeptical, questioning personality early on as a result of the double standards he saw in his parents' attitudes. The children of black neighbors and farmhands were the only playmates available to Tyson, an only child, on his family's eastern North Carolina farm. "My parents and my grandmother and all were very kind and solicitous to these people," Tyson remembered, "but there was one place where the line was drawn. I could not invite my friends inside my house. They could play with me on the porch. We could play underneath the house. I could go in their houses. I ate their food. Their parents were very kind to me, obviously. They had no choice, did they? But I think they would have been kind to me anyway. They were that kind of people." Tyson understood the prejudices behind this prohibition better as an adult, but even as a child, the inequality bothered him. "This was a perpetual problem for me. I think it was one of the sources of my earliest skepticism about a lot of things. Skepticism, I guess, born of wonder and not having any satisfactory answers given to me when I would ask the question." His family's treatment of his black playmates merely compounded Tyson's confusion over their attitudes toward Rose Noble, the beloved black nanny who nursed him through a six-month confinement with rheumatic fever at age six. He always had a "sense of questioning about how things were done," Tyson reflected. "I reconstruct that as being [due to the fact that, first of all, I was] forced out of the flow for a whole year at a crucial time [while he was sick] and secondly this black-white thing that I just couldn't come to terms with. I couldn't understand." Tyson could see how much his parents respected Rose. "I mean, of all the people in the world, she'd be in the Ark when there was a flood. She'd be among the elect as far as we were concerned. Yet [there was a] contradiction between that relationship and this prohibition." Like many other white southern dissenters, Tyson would draw on this contradiction noticed in childhood when he began to oppose Jim Crow as an adult.[37]

Forgotten Alternatives

The questioning Tyson described is something that many white children went through, especially if their families suddenly forbade them from playing with black children they liked. Dorothy Markey (better known in the 1930s under her pen name, Myra Page) told one such story. Born in Newport News, Virginia, at the turn of the century, Markey and her brother, like many city children, black and white, spent most of their summers on their grandparents' farm. There they befriended a black boy named Tom, whose grandmother, "Aunt Martha," worked in the kitchen. Tom "was sort of the all-around boy who . . . did farm chores, and we became very close, as kids can in the summer," Markey recalled. "We were young and we played games. Tom knew that farm, back and forth. He knew the creeks; he knew all the games, too. One game we called 'Slide.' When the water was on the banks it got slippery: the thing was to climb up; once you were up, you had earned a slide down. We kept slipping, and we really enjoyed that. We had a good friendship for two or three summers." But two or three summers were all that Markey and her playmates would be allowed. "One summer, my aunt called us in. She was a very kind person, seemingly, but without blinking an eye she said, 'You are not to play with Tom anymore.' We said, 'Why?' She said, 'Because you are getting big now. White and colored don't mix like that.' She broke it up. It was a terrible experience. She said, 'I've told Aunt Martha and Tom that if you children disobey, I will have to ask them to leave.' So Tom wouldn't play with us anymore."[38]

Although Tom probably regretted the loss of his playmates, he fared better than some black boys whose play with white children, especially white girls, was misunderstood. As late as 1958, four years after the *Brown* decision, two Monroe, North Carolina, boys, seven-year-old Fuzzy Simpson and nine-year-old Hanover Thompson, were arrested and jailed after a white girl kissed Hanover on the cheek. The girl remembered playing with Hanover when his mother had worked for her family as a maid, and she apparently kissed him simply because she was happy to see him again. But her mother was outraged and called the police. Convicted of attempted rape, Fuzzy was sentenced to twelve years and Hanover to fourteen—sentences that were eventually thrown out as a result of pressure from the Eisenhower administration but that clearly indicate how serious white southerners could be once they decided certain children were not to play together any longer or to play together in certain ways.[39]

The North Carolina boys' experience was unusual because it took place in the civil rights era and because federal authorities came to their aid. But black youths had long heard stories that encouraged them to be careful around whites, even when they were very young. A black teenager from Coahoma County, Mississippi, who was interviewed for Charles S. Johnson's 1941 book *Growing Up in the Black Belt* told a particularly horrifying tale from neighboring Bolivar County: "There was a little white girl 4 years old down in Duncan what asked a little nigger boy about 3 to pull her bloomers up for her. They was just little kids playing along together. Some old white man saw it and grabbed up the little boy and castrated him. Then he took the boy and threw him in the lake. Nobody ever did anything about that."[40] Living in a world where such things could happen, Dorothy Markey's friend Tom did not disobey the new rules that Markey's aunt and his own grandmother laid down.

Whatever Tom's feelings about the forced separation, for Markey, the sense of having suffered a devastating loss would linger. Her aunt's prohibition "was something terrible that we didn't understand, which had come down on all of us." That night she wrote her parents and asked to come home early. "Next summer when we went back, there was nobody; Tom was gone." He had left the farm after his grandmother died. "So our friendship was just ended." Like Ruel Tyson, Markey connected this adult prohibition on interracial play to her admiration for a family servant, Belle Franklin, who was treated kindly but not as an equal. "That and Belle, you see, left a deep impression, that made this drive in my life to find some solution for it, if I could, so that people could really live together as brothers." Markey would pursue this goal initially through the same avenue that a number of other white southern women of her generation chose: the Young Women's Christian Association (YWCA) and early efforts at interracial cooperation.[41]

Clearly, contact with black children and adults could be very important to white southerners' eventual moral and political development. But as autobiographers such as Sarah Patton Boyle and Lillian Smith explained in recounting their "dramas of socialization," often the seeds of early questioning, though planted deep, were quickly covered over. Jessie Daniel Ames, who went on to lead white southern women in a crusade against lynching in the 1920s and 1930s, acknowledged her early disinterest: although her "best friend," who was the daughter of the family cook, was forbidden from coming into the house just as rigorously as Ruel Tyson's playmates, Ames never noticed this restriction until many years later. "I went along," she confessed. "I wasn't very interested in race at all. I didn't see any segregation or discrimination or anything else."[42]

"Not seeing" racial discrimination is, of course, an important element of white privilege. And it is one that most white southerners learned to exercise at some point in their childhoods and that relatively few gave up of their own accord. Those who did—dissenters like Boyle, Smith, Tyson, and Ames—can often tell us a great deal about the significance they later came to see in their childhood contacts with blacks. Some can even provide a fairly clear account of when and why they stopped questioning the status quo for at least part of their lives. Boyle, for example, not only detailed her adolescent

Dorothy Gary Markey and her brother Barham Gary, 1908. Markey was unusual among early-twentieth-century white southerners in that she continued to ask questions about racial inequalities even as she reached adolescence. As a high school student, she sat in on meetings of an interracial committee formed in Newport News, Virginia. In college, she was active in early interracial work through the Young Women's Christian Association. She later joined the Communist Party and traveled throughout the South as a journalist. She also published several novels under the pen name Myra Page. (Courtesy of May Kanfer.)

training in racial etiquette but also offered the metaphor of sealed bottles of water purifier dropped in a reservoir: relationships and events, both in childhood and later, that made her question racial orthodoxy "were little centers— bottles—of genuine truth and experience which remained sealed off by my indoctrination and training, unable to permeate and purify my over-all conception of the Negro people and their situation in the South." It would take the "tidal wave" of blacks' increasingly vocal protests against Jim Crow after World War II, in combination with a personal spiritual crisis set off by marital troubles, to break open these bottles and allow Boyle to remember and reflect on the questions and emotions of her youth. She was over forty years old at the time.[43]

Prior to the civil rights movement of the 1950s and 1960s, very few white southerners returned to the childlike confusion or skepticism with which many had encountered race early on. For the vast majority, the "forgotten alternatives" of childhood interactions remained forgotten. But that such alternatives had once been available to them—that they, too, had sealed bottles of experience floating in their own personal reservoirs—seems inevitable. On occasion, even those who remained committed to white supremacy could admit that white supremacy had not *always* made sense. A white woman whom psychologist Robert Coles knew in Mississippi in the late 1950s is a case in point. "In spite of her ordinary civility and even graciousness," Coles wrote, this woman "is grimly opposed to any change in the way Negroes and whites get along with one another. She feels that others, 'outsiders,' are imposing strange and unsettling demands upon her. The strangeness of her own childhood, of her own relationship to Negroes as a child, no longer troubles her. Yes, there are memories, and if she is not pressed, not questioned with any intent to argue or even interpret but simply to learn, she will reveal them to herself as well as her listener." Among these memories were not only vague impressions of her childhood nurse but also a vivid recollection of being taught not to call a black woman "Ma'am" when she was seven or eight years old. "I had trouble making sense of that," she admitted, "and I asked my mother her reasons for being so against using 'ma'am' with the nigra. She tried to tell me that it was the way we did things in the world, but it never made sense to me. . . . I think what *did* make sense to me was that I had to obey my mother's wish. Then you grow older, and you stop trying to make sense of things like that. You just know that there are things you can do, and things you can't, and that's it." With no apparent irony, the woman went on to highlight the conventional (as opposed to "natural") character of her racial lessons even further. "My brother once tried to get my parents to explain to him why he had to wear a tie one place, and not another. It was the same thing. My daddy just said, 'Jimmie, that's the way it is, and that's the way we have to do it.'"[44]

After a certain amount of confusion, frustration, and even defiance, most children accept "the way we do things" without question, especially when "the way we do things" works to their advantage, as white supremacy worked to the advantage of whites. Interracial play and other forms of childhood racial contact did offer alternatives to a social pattern scripted by racial etiquette, but because they were stacked against the incentives of parental love and white peer-group acceptance, not to mention personal pride and other possible gains in status, the emotional attachments of childhood were fairly easy to "forget."

Moreover, as black children understood far better than white, interracial play was hardly a golden moment. There were almost always restrictions, both on play and in play, and the line between playing and fighting was often fine. Plus, the pain of separation or discrimination would always come.[45]

Never a Golden Moment

The limitations within play were many. Black children could play with some white children and not others, in some neighborhoods and not others, and almost any play anywhere could easily turn to fighting. Whenever white children got tired or hot or a black child excelled at a game, the epithets might start to fly. From an early age, black children knew that they had to be cautious when playing with whites; as one young black girl told Charles S. Johnson, "if you play with white children and hurt 'em you might get into trouble."[46] Meanwhile, whether children noticed it or not, their play was almost always limited to the interstitial spaces of white supremacy—yards, fields, creeks, kitchens, and sidewalks—because white sensibilities insisted on keeping black children out of parks, playgrounds, and all but the service-oriented areas of white homes.

White restrictions on children's play sometimes reflected community pressures as much as the views of individual parents. Sociologist Arthur Raper and his wife Martha would have liked to allow their children to play freely with the children of their household workers when they lived on a farm in Greene County, Georgia, in the early 1940s. But they found that even they had to respect conventions. Their first year in Greene County, the Rapers had done "what had seemed to be the rightful Easter thing on Easter Monday morning": they had invited all of the children "on the place," black and white, to an Easter egg hunt. But the neighbors had talked and the Rapers' sons "were called 'Nigger-lovers' at school, and teased about the egg hunt. We listened and wondered. How was it that it was all right for our children to play with the Negro children when harnessing a calf, rolling wheels, fishing in the little creek, gathering muscadines? But clearly the Easter egg hunt had gone against the grain of our white friends." As best the Rapers could determine, the problem was that the children had been invited "an hour ahead of time and that some of the Negro children came wearing clean overalls and freshly washed dresses."[47] Playing together spontaneously was one thing, but this smacked of social equality.

Other white parents imposed restrictions that outweighed general community pressures. Mildred Coy, who was born in 1899 in rural Wentworth, North Carolina, was not allowed to play with the children of her father's tenant farmers at all. "They weren't good enough," she explained flatly. "They were just beneath us, blacks and whites." Coy connected this prohibition to her father's overall attitude toward his tenants, one rooted, it seems, in his own economic struggles. "He had so little money himself [but] he felt superior. We never were friendly in a warm way. They were beneath us. We thought that we were above all these people."[48]

Presumably, at least some of the tenant families on the Coys' farm were quite happy to keep their children away from girls who were raised to have such attitudes. As one mother in Jonestown, Mississippi, explained to Charles S. Johnson, she encouraged her children "to be mannerable and stay in they place, and if they see some white children who want to be nice and play with them to go ahead and play with them; but if they are snarly and act mean to go ahead and not bother with them." Johnson suggested this view was typical of "lower-class" blacks, who also drew sharp distinctions between "white people" and "peckerwoods," or poor whites.[49]

Middle-class black parents were often even more protective, refusing to let their children play with white children at all. Shirley Walker's mother, Hattie Bijou, was one such parent. "I was a very lonely person," Walker recalled of her childhood in New Iberia, Louisiana, in the 1930s. "We lived around white people and I could not play with the little white girl next door. I didn't know why. We would play by the fence when no one was looking, but I didn't know that when that little girl grew up to be a certain age, I would have to say 'Miss Ruby' and my mama resented that." "I sure did," Hattie Bijou acknowledged.[50]

Shirley Walker's loneliness suggests the tensions that black parents' efforts to protect their children could involve. But it should not imply that all black children who were forbidden from playing with whites felt deprived. Many blacks' accounts of growing up in virtually all-black childhood worlds describe precisely the opposite: greater happiness and a sense of privilege that resulted from their protection. Josephine Dobbs Clement grew up in one of Atlanta's most elite black families in the 1920s and attributed her "happy childhood" to the fact that "we were so severely segregated. . . . My father's philosophy was that you never accepted segregation unless you absolutely had to. That meant you didn't go to theaters, you didn't go places for amusement because there was no pleasure to go in the back door there. If you had to go on the streetcar to go to school that was worth the sacrifice," but otherwise she and her siblings, like other elite black children, were taught to avoid both segregation and whites. As a result, "we were really protected from some of the more traumatic experiences that some other people had."[51]

All told, interracial play in the Jim Crow South was even more fraught with inequalities and incipient conflicts than children's play always is. Children are often mean to one another, and in an environment where meanness was racially coded and not only adult- but state-sanctioned, it is hardly surprising that play among black and white children often turned suddenly to fighting or took racially discriminatory forms. Rollin Chambliss, a young white man from southern Georgia, was unusually candid about the second-class treatment that he and his white companions reserved for blacks. In 1933, Chambliss received a scholarship given annually by the Phelps-Stokes Foundation to a University of Georgia student who would complete a master's thesis on a topic related to African American life. His study, "What Negro Newspapers of Georgia Say About Some Social Problems, 1933," must have been eye-opening, for, while it did not exactly free him from racism, it did prompt him to write a deeply reflective preface about his own childhood experiences of race. There were three or four white boys and half a dozen or more black boys in his "group," Chambliss explained. "We did chores together there on the farm, and went 'possum huntin' and to the swimming hole down on the creek and played ball and did all of those things that boys do in rural Georgia." Black and white did these things together, "and yet the Negroes were always a little apart. If we were swimming, they kept downstream. If we were playing ball, they were in the outfield and we did the batting. If we were gathering plums, the Negroes always left us the best bushes." Chambliss insists that there "was no ill feeling in this. Negroes were different. They knew it, and we knew it." And yet racism and racial etiquette were clearly in play: "In the fields we all drank from the same jug, but at the pump the Negroes cupped their hands and drank from them and would never have dared to use the cup hanging there. I never knew a Negro to come to the front door of my home, and I am sure that if one had done so, someone would have asked him if he minded stepping around to the back." That "someone" could easily have been Chambliss himself or one of his white peers: "At the age of ten I understood full well that the Negro had to be kept in his place, and I was resigned to my part in that general responsibility."

In fact, one of Chambliss's "first lessons" in racial interaction was particularly violent. "It was on a very quiet Sunday afternoon, and a group of white boys were lying on the grass beside the road eating peaches. One of the boys was a good deal older than the rest of us, and we looked to him as a leader." Perhaps because he was among younger boys who might be easily impressed, this "leader" made some "suggestive remarks" to a black girl passing along the road. A short while later, an angry young black man to whom the girl had repeated these remarks came up to the boys and, as Chambliss put it, "said more than I have ever heard a Negro say in defense of his women, or for any other cause." "We all knew him," Chambliss continued, "and it was not the first time that he had shown a disposition to argue with white folks. Our leader said nothing for a few minutes, and then he walked slowly up to my house, which was not far away, and came back with a shotgun. The Negro went away, and as the white boy lay down beside us and began eating peaches again, he remarked, 'You have to know how to handle Negroes.' I knew then, on that quiet Sunday afternoon almost twenty years ago, and I know now, that he was ready to use that gun, if necessary, to keep a Negro in his place."[52]

Chambliss's story, while dramatic, makes essentially the same point that Lewis Killian made about his own far less eventful childhood: that regardless of what roles certain blacks played at certain times in his youth, his was essentially a white social world. It was whites he must show off for, whites he would date, whites who would give him a job someday, and whites he had to compete with in school if he were ever to get ahead. The most meaningful parts of his world would only get whiter as he aged, in part because what is "meaningful" changes over time as adults and soon-to-be adults often begin to privilege success of various kinds over other values, including the affection of childhood caregivers and playmates. As Chambliss explained it, his association with black boys became even less intimate as he and his white friends approached adolescence. "We began then to talk of things which the Negro could not understand—of what we were going to do in life, of our little love affairs, of school life, of our hopes for the future. In such things the Negro had no part, and gradually we played together less and less."[53]

And yet the memories lingered, certainly for Killian and maybe even for

Chambliss. As inevitable as the separation was, it was often met with regret on one or both sides. Regret permeated William J. Coker's account of his friendship with a white girl named Orlette who lived in his neighborhood in Norfolk. At first, Coker tried to insist that their friendship never suffered, that "even in the midst of the segregation and the no-nos, [they] remained excellent friends." Coker continued, "She married a white boy in the neighborhood, and his people were just the opposite. They came from Tennessee, and they had a different set of attitudes. Even today when I run into [Orlette]— well, we stand in the middle of the . . . store just talking, talking, talking, [and] he kind of stands back." Later, Coker admitted that this white boy from Tennessee had played a bigger part in his early life than he had first let on. Although there were not "a lot of black kids playing with the white kids," Coker felt the white families in his area had accepted him and his siblings out of respect for their hard-working parents and "the uniqueness of where [their] house was" in a predominantly white neighborhood. "We played on an equal basis," Coker explained. "You were equals. There was not a negative word said . . . until these boys moved in from Tennessee. . . . And they brought their attitudes with them. Until they were taught better physically, they would stand in their yard in a little heap and shout things to you like 'nigger' and so forth." Coker and his older brother did manage to maintain their friendships with whites to a certain extent, but this was not the case with Orlette. "As I got a little older, I'll say puberty, I didn't see her as much," Coker admitted. "All those years before, she would come by the house almost any time." Later, Coker went on, "[we] only got a chance to talk to each other if we were passing or something like that." For the rest of their lives, chance conversations on the street and in stores would be all that was left of their friendship. And, although Coker was never interested in Orlette romantically or sexually ("because she was one of the guys" and because she was two years younger and, especially at puberty, that "makes the difference"), it had to hurt to see her marry one of the Tennessee race-baiters.[54]

Whether it resulted from new kids in the neighborhood who brought different attitudes, or a new prohibition on the part of their parents, or puberty in some vaguer sense, black and white children's relationships almost always ended or grew distant by their adolescent years. Rollin Chambliss might write as if whites alone pulled away into their own supposedly more interesting social world, "which the Negro could not understand," but the reality was that blacks entered their own world of school and work and dating also—a world that, except in relation to work, got blacker at and after adolescence just as whites' world got whiter. The world of black teenagers was also a much angrier world than that of black and white children, a subject for the next chapter. As an examination of fighting and other conflicts within children's own semi-separate sphere indicates, that adolescent anger often had deep roots.

Fighting: White Perspectives

Not surprisingly, African Americans have generally had more to say about racial conflicts in childhood than whites. Regretful whites do recount moments when they were mean to black children, as in the remarkably similar stories James McBride Dabbs and Katharine Du Pre Lumpkin told about demanding the right of way when they encountered unyielding black children in their paths. "Indeed, such territorial competition, reported by a number of repentant southerners, becomes nearly a convention of the racial conversion narrative," Fred Hobson writes.[55] But whites' stories often have the feel of isolated incidents and tend to depict blacks as passive victims—a view not shared in blacks' accounts. Moreover, whites' emphasis is always on their own guilt, especially in retrospect but often even in childhood. Lumpkin described her encounter as one that contributed to her developing awareness "of myself as a white," a sensibility that she was trying to shake off when she wrote her autobiography forty years later.[56] Dabbs used the incident in which he punched a black girl in the stomach as an illustration of the fact that he had "the usual sense of white privilege" and noted that he did not tell his parents what he had done.[57]

Lillian Smith's memories of fighting with black children are more complicated. Smith wrote about such conflicts in the abstract—and thus suggested that fighting was common. But her focus, like Dabbs and Lumpkin's, was on how whites mistreated blacks, allowing little room for blacks' own perspectives, and although she tried to re-create a child's consciousness, her adult understanding of the various pressures white children faced overwhelms her narrative. "Struggle. Sudden strange struggle. Hot feelings pouring over you, driving you to push hard against wiry dark quickbreathing little bodies, push hard until they are off the sidewalk, off into sandspurs and dirt, sobbing angrily, *We'll get even with you you just wait we'll get* . . . And your crowd, flushed and dazed, walk on, victors for a wan moment over something, you never know what." White children harassed black children because "you had to do something," Smith wrote, "and this thing, you knew, THEY WHO MAKE THE RULES would let you do. Though your own mother might scold you for fighting and pushing, if she knew, . . . OTHER PARENTS seem to think pushing little Negroes into sandspurs funny, like tying tin cans to a dog's tail." Most important, Smith continued, "this pushing off the sidewalk is not one of the Sins you have to worry about. . . . You know you will not go to hell if you push little colored kids into sandspurs (or later out of jobs) though you may go there if you steal a nickel or do 'bad' things or even think them."[58] And yet by even mentioning sin Smith made her point that the truth was just the opposite of what white southern children had been told. Pushing black children off the sidewalk was one of the sins that she was trying, through her narrative, to expiate. The tragedy of white southern childhood, as Mark Twain had pointed out in *Huckleberry Finn* decades before, was that white parents and the whole adult world of racial inequality had turned morality upside down.

Smith's suggestion that white children assaulted black children because they "had to do something" is intriguing. By pushing black children out of the way, "your crowd" became "victors," but you did not know what you had conquered. "For you like the colored kids. You don't really mind their walking on the sidewalk. What is a sidewalk!"[59] But as Smith well knew, a sidewalk was contested terrain (hence the importance of sidewalks in southern racial etiquette) and, no matter how much she wanted to blame adults for giving white southern children twisted morals, another key concept was "crowd." Starting with Smith, then, we can see black and white children's fighting not just as white memoirists usually depict it—as a childhood sin to be confessed and repented—but as the territorial battles between "us" and "them" that, both in fact and in most black accounts, they usually were.

Fighting: Black Perspectives

Unlike whites, blacks tend to emphasize blacks' active participation— rather than passive victimization—in racial conflicts. This is particularly true of black men, who make it clear that, although whites were almost always to blame for starting any given fight, they and other black children defended themselves physically as well as verbally, and were generally unafraid as long as only children were involved. Black women are somewhat more willing to admit to having been intimidated, but girls often describe fighting back as well.

Perhaps the most famous account of a fight between black and white children is the one Richard Wright provides in the opening paragraphs of "The Ethics of Living Jim Crow." At first, Wright suggests that children fought simply because it was fun and that any set of opponents would do. "You could always have a nice hot war with huge black cinders" from the railroad tracks that ran behind his early childhood home, Wright reflected. "All you had to do was crouch behind the brick pillars of a house with your hands full of gritty ammunition. And the first wooly black head you saw pop out from behind another row of pillars was your target." When Wright's "gang" engaged in a "war" with a gang of white boys who lived on the other side of the tracks, however, the rules and the purpose of fighting were suddenly different. The white boys responded to the black children's cinders with a barrage of broken bottles, forcing them to retreat. A milk bottle hit Wright behind the ear as he was running away, and the sight of blood pouring over his face further demoralized his companions. The wound also outraged Wright, who brooded over the injustice of it all. "It was all right to throw cinders. . . . But broken bottles were dangerous; they left you cut, bleeding, and helpless"—a helplessness that Wright would feel all the more deeply when his mother came home and beat him senseless for fighting with whites.

Although Wright suggested no direct cause for the battle—his gang merely "found itself engaged in a war with the white boys"—territory and prestige were clearly at issue. As he recovered from both the initial gash and his mother's beating, Wright dwelled on the fact that the white boys' yards offered trees and shrubs for protection, while his own barren yard provided only cinders. "Even today when I think of white folks, the hard, sharp outlines of white houses surrounded by trees, lawns, and hedges are present somewhere in the background of my mind," he wrote. "Through the years they grew into an overreaching symbol of fear"—the very opposite of the safety whites generally associate with suburbia.[60] Nevertheless, the fact that he rarely fought with whites again as a child was, Wright implies, merely the result of his family's move to an all-black neighborhood. Wherever blacks and whites encountered one another, fighting was inevitable.

Dorcas Carter, born in New Bern, North Carolina, in 1913, emphasized the inevitability of racial conflict as well but noted certain nuances of gender, age, and place. Carter herself was "passive" as a child, but her cousins fought with whites "all the time," a difference she attributed to the fact that they lived among whites while she lived in a predominantly black enclave. Plus, they were boys. "I guess boys weren't fearful because, you know, if I'd be with them, they'd know what I was going to do. I was going to run home," Carter laughed. Nevertheless, girls could be just as forceful as boys if they were used to whites and had reached a certain age. When two older schoolmates scuffled with a white girl who called them "black niggers," nine-year-old Carter was terrified. But her friends' actions also made sense. They lived downtown where they interacted with whites frequently, "and they felt they had as much privilege as anybody else did. And one was about eleven and

maybe the other was getting [to be a] teenager. They were ready for the fist."
Fighting back was all the more necessary because of whites' territorial attitudes. On the streets of New Bern, whites "would come like abreast," Carter
explained. "That meant they'd leave you about this much space. . . . They felt
sort of possessive if you were in their vicinity. And I guess maybe we did the
same way when they'd come uptown."[61]

Indeed, any encounter on the street seems to have presented the possibility of conflict—an impression that is certainly conveyed in blacks' frequent
accounts of being harassed on the way to or from school. Typically, black informants focus on the fact that the school system provided buses for whites
but not for blacks—an aspect of adult race relations that white children also
understood at some level, as the nature of their taunts indicates. "While we
were walking many mornings the white kids would pass in the school buses
and they would yell out to us 'Walk, niggers, walk,'" remembered Herbert
Cappie. "The only thing that made it, I guess, bearable is the fact that if we
hustled up an empty Coca-Cola bottle halfway to school we could stop at the
Coca-Cola plant and they'd give us a Coke to drink in return for the bottle."[62]
Charles Lewis, who generally recollected his boyhood days in Gulfport, Mississippi, with a great deal of pleasure, could not find even a small consolation
of this sort. Instead, having to walk four and a half miles each way to high
school while whites "teased" him from their buses brought home the realities of racism with new force. "I hadn't paid too much attention until then,"
Lewis attested, but this was "the thing that made me realize that there was
black and white."[63] The same was true for Hampton, Virginia, resident Olivia
Cherry after her family moved into a New Deal housing project called Aberdeen Gardens in 1937, when she was eleven years old. "Living in Aberdeen,
we had to take a school bus," Cherry reflected—in this case, a bus that was
used to take black and white children separately to their separate schools.
"This was my first real deep experience of segregation. We could not take the
bus until the bus had taken the white children to school. Then it came back
for us. Therefore we were late in class, and the teachers . . . didn't appreciate
it, and they took it out on us." Like many other black informants, Cherry also
remembered the measures she and her friends took to avoid white abuse.
"Walking home from school, the school buses would pass by us, and can you
believe, the white kids would spit out the window at us and call us 'Nigger'
and everything." Very quickly, the black children learned the bus route and
got "out of their way."[64]

Even though black children tried to minimize their exposure to white insults, being taunted and spat upon or otherwise assaulted was infuriating and

had a profound, if variable, impact on young blacks' attitudes. Looking back on a Depression-era childhood in Memphis, Edgar Allen Hunt suggested that stoic endurance was the black child's only answer: White children "used to make fun at us walking to school. . . . 'I wouldn't be a nigger,' they'd say out the window of the bus. But I mean, you get used to that after such a length of time. I had to walk to school the whole twelve years that I went over there. So it didn't bother us, you know. [Taking a bus] was just a privilege that they enjoyed that we didn't, and [there were] many other privileges that they enjoyed that we didn't. So we didn't worry about it. We just tried to exist and do what we had to do."[65] Other black children, like Charles Lewis and Olivia Cherry, developed a heightened awareness of race as a result of white children's racist remarks. Charles S. Johnson quoted a teenager whose experience had been similar: "I was just 8 or 9 years old when white children first meddled me. I don't think I'd thought anything about them before. I don't think I'd felt any difference in white and colored till that day" when "I got in a fight with some little white children and they called me 'nigger.'"[66]

For future novelist Margaret Walker Alexander, a childhood fight was equally formative. Alexander suggested that her early awareness of racial prejudice was the result of many experiences, from sitting on buses "behind the signs that were marked 'For Colored Only,'" to "hearing white men address grown Negro men as 'boys,'" to "reading about lynching." But it was the personal experiences of violence that stuck out most in Alexander's mind. "Once a group of boys, little white boys, beat me up on the street and black men didn't dare interfere," she recalled. "Once my father was late coming home one night and was chased through a white neighborhood by a white policeman who resented my father having books and a fountain pen in his pocket."[67] Segregation signs and systematic discrimination were galling, Alexander suggested, but physical attacks literally hit harder.

Almost half a century older than Walker, the anonymous author of a 1904 article in the *Independent* described the impact of white children's brutal behavior with particular eloquence. Like innumerable black autobiographers, this writer claimed to "remember very distinctly to this day" the "very first humiliation" she ever received. It came when a white playmate told her not to mention that she had eaten at her house, explaining "[My ma] would whip me if I ate with you . . . because you are colored." At first angry, then downcast, the author "threw [her]self upon the ground and cried" because, prior to this time, she "did not know that being 'colored' made a difference. . . ." She went on, "I was very young and I know now I had been shielded from all unpleasantness."

A "second shock" was even more profound and suggests how white children's meanness altered her outlook. Taking flowers to the home of a beloved Sunday school teacher, "Miss W.," who had died, the author was met "by quite a number of white boys and girls." "A girl of about fifteen years," the author recalled, "said to me, 'More flowers for that dead nigger? I never saw such a to-do made over a dead nigger before.'" Speechless with anger and grief, the author ended up running away from the white children under a hail of stones. "I remember the strongest feeling I had was one of revenge," she wrote, although frustration at her inability to do anything about the white girl's insult seems to have been equally prominent among her emotions. Her mother's response—that the white children "were heartless, but that I was even worse, and that Miss W. would be the first to condemn me could she speak"—clearly did little to ease her suffering. Instead, the encounter "made a deep impression on my childish heart," an impression she insisted was deeper than those left by any of the other "real horrors," including lynching, that she had learned of since. "My mother used to tell me if I were a good little girl everybody would love me, and if I always used nice manners it would make others show the same to me," she concluded. "I believed that literally until I entered school, when the many encounters I had with white boys and girls going to and from school made me seriously doubt that goodness and manners were needed in this world. The white children I knew grew meaner as they grew older—more capable of saying things that cut and wound."[68]

Like the *Independent* essayist, every black child who confronted white hostility in any of its many forms had to decide how he or she was going to react. Some children were naturally tougher or more timid than others, and a child's age and gender were certainly factors, although many girls were just as likely to defend themselves physically as boys. Lanetha Branch, for example, attributed her siblings' differing responses to white insults less to gender than to their very different personalities. Her older brother was not "timid," but he was also "not a person who wanted any trouble at all. And so because of his demeanor, he was often run home and threatened." Branch's sister was "just the opposite." White children "would call her sometimes 'Aunt Jemima' and, of course, she was very tomboyish. And so she'd beat them up."[69] A girl in Guthrie, Oklahoma, took things further. As the Cleveland *Gazette* reported in December 1894, she became so angry about some "odious remarks" made to her on her way home from school that she "attacked the 12-year-old son of G. W. Greathouse, tearing out his eyes and biting off one ear. She followed this up by crushing the boy's skull with a rock," killing him. Then she ran off.[70]

Undoubtedly, many black children who fled or fought back against white aggression did so in moments of passion, with little aforethought. But whether or not the children involved stopped to ponder such issues, individual circumstances also played a role both in shaping childhood conflicts and in determining what larger consequences they might have. Was the white children's attack physical or merely verbal? Even protective black parents sometimes encouraged their children to defend themselves if struck, no matter how adamantly they insisted that epithets could simply be ignored. Were the abusive white children familiar or unfamiliar? If they were to survive in the Jim Crow South, black children had to learn to anticipate whites' behavior from an early age, something that was easier to do with "friends" or acquaintances than with strangers. Was it likely that adults, black or white, might intervene? Often, black parents strengthened their admonitions against fighting with a promise that, as Dorcas Carter's parents put it, "if anybody bothers you, come home and tell us about it and we'll go to the parents and try to iron things out."[71]

Remarkably, white parents were sometimes quite responsive to such efforts. Shirley Bijou Walker remembered what happened when two white boys pushed her into a ditch, muddying her clothes. "Mama went after those white boys," she recalled. "I sure did," Hattie Bijou affirmed, picking up the story. "And did that man [the white father] beat them little boys! I had to beg him to quit beating his own children."[72]

As this story suggests, white parents' desire to raise their children well could lead them to support blacks, including black children, who stood up for themselves. Georgia Bays's oldest son, Bill, was "crazy about his hat"— perhaps because, as the child of Mississippi sharecroppers growing up during the Depression, he had little else to call his own. "So this white boy, he grabbed my boy's hat off his head, and my boy just whooped him good," Bays explained. When the white boy came home, Bays, who worked for the boy's family, was standing in the yard. "Here he come, hollering. . . . He had scratches all over his face. 'Mama, Bill done hit me,' and so and so and so and so." Bays just stood there: "Oh, I was so scared, honey. I didn't know what to do." But the white mother's response quickly allayed Bays's fears for her son's safety. She demanded to know what her son had done to Bill, certain that Bill would not have struck him without cause. When the truth came out, the white mother seemed to think that her son had simply gotten what he deserved. And that, Bays concluded, "was the end of that."[73]

Unfortunately, black children could never count on white sympathy. The absolute terror that Walter White felt after hitting a white boy in the head with a rock was an all-too-appropriate response to the actual danger that even defensive self-assertions could bring.[74] Dorcas Carter's fear of white retribution was even more overpowering, leading her to run and hide at the first sign of trouble. When her two older companions punched and shoved the white girl who insulted them, Carter "was so frightened [she] didn't know what to do." She abandoned her friends and ran three blocks to her aunt's house, where she hid under the porch. "I said," she recalled, "'Oh, Lord, I think this is going to be a lynching.' . . . Eyes this big. I know they must have been. Just shaking. . . . They had what they called a black maria then, an old paddy wagon, and they'd put you in there. This passed by my aunt's house and I knew they were seeking me." Although she remembered the pounding of her heart—"Lord, pitty-pat, pitty-pat, pitty-pat"—Carter could not remember whether or not she ever told her parents about this incident, nor did she say how long she hid under the porch. She did recall that her girlfriends "named me scary cat" and teased her for her cowardice when she saw them again. But fleeing from trouble was something that any black child might have to do some time, something that children joked about among themselves. Carter's friends even had a "little saying" about it. "We used to grow up talking about [how] we believe in cutting and shooting," she laughed. "Yeah, cutting around the corner and shooting for home."

Perhaps the most noteworthy aspect of Dorcas Carter's story is her fear of being arrested or lynched. Even though she was very young, she immediately understood her danger as part of a bigger picture of adult race relations, much as white children understood, at some level, why they had school buses to ride and black children did not. Asked if she was really afraid of being lynched—if this was "something [she] knew about at this stage"—Carter replied, "Yeah, I knew about they were lynching people." In retrospect, though, she thought she was probably even more afraid that "they were going to put [her] in that paddy car and maybe go to jail perhaps"—something she may have actually seen happen to other blacks.[75]

The Adult World We Never Left

With Dorcas Carter, then, we return from the world of childhood play and fighting to the adult world of Jim Crow in its most violent and unjust forms. Whatever the analytical value of considering children's encounters across the color line on their own terms, the reality is that children were never completely free from adults and the many, often disturbing and sometimes horrific ways in which adults thrust adult racial and sexual concerns into children's lives. Most powerful of all were white authority figures, including the policemen whose paddy wagon terrified Carter. But all whites were powerful, even children, whose accusations or tears could bring down the wrath of the adult white world at any moment. And while black adults were by no means powerless, their best efforts to shape black children's understanding of race and racism could not always soothe battered egos or calm emotional turmoil.

The result was not a loss of childhood but what Lillian Smith described as "haunted" childhoods for both blacks and whites.[76] Two stories about children and racial violence illustrate this point. Eura Bowie, born in about 1915, was the youngest of eleven children of a black tenant farm family in the Mississippi Delta. One day, probably in the mid- to late 1920s, she and her sister heard some dogs barking and went into the woods across from their house to investigate. The dogs were "just howling, howling, howling, howling across there, and they wouldn't go home," Bowie recounted, "and we were just wondering what was they howling for. So me and my sister, we two of us at home, we got a hoe. We was going over there to see about them, what was they howling for. But we didn't see anything. We finally seen one dog howling. He had his foot caught in a steel trap over there, and we just assumed that . . . somebody [was] trapping, you know. But we turned him loose." As someone who loved pets as a child, Bowie undoubtedly felt sympathy for the injured dog, but otherwise she did not give the incident much thought. Only later did she realize that the dog's presence in the woods was part of a larger and more sinister series of events, namely a murder. Bowie explained: "It was some [white] children going to pick dewberries. Dewberries is a berry just like a blackberry . . . only it was larger and, I'd say, better, too, because it growed mostly on a bush on the ground. And so some white children went over there [later] to pick berries, and [when] they come back, they said, 'We found a dead nigger. We found a dead nigger.'" The dead man turned out to be a local named Dee Griffith. Bowie never found out precisely what had happened, other than that Griffith had "got into it" with a white man, who killed him. The one thing Bowie did understand was how adults "made them hush" about finding the body, a "them" that presumably meant black children, as well as white.[77]

With howling dogs and forest shadows, Bowie's story includes some gothic elements. Eeriest of all, though, is the fact that, in describing this incident nearly seventy years later, she considered it important to make sure her interviewer knew what a dewberry was and how it grew. This sensory detail is a reminder that, like all children everywhere in a pretelevision age, Bowie and her black and white contemporaries lived close to the ground. Richard Coe, Elliott West, and other authors have focused on the sensual experiences that characterize both childhood and much writing about childhood, often in ways that, in Coe's words, make childhood a time when the world really is "magical."[78] But magic and horror mixed freely in the Jim Crow South, where both black and white children might savor the sweet juice of a freshly picked dewberry one moment and recoil at the sight of a lynching victim the next.

Indeed, as a moment from Isabella D. Harris's childhood indicates, small children could not always anticipate or distinguish what would be horrible from what was simply new and intriguing. In September 1912, seven-year-old Harris, who was white, heard some older girls talking excitedly at morning recess about the "lynched 'nigger' down town" in the courthouse square in Cumming, Georgia. "I'm ashamed to admit the request I made of the teacher," Harris wrote in a letter some seventy-five years later. "She was one of my father's older sisters. 'Aunt Lou,' I asked, 'when I go home for dinner, may I go by town to see a lynched "nigger"? I've never seen one before.'" Harris's aunt was "dismayed and furious" and told her she must go straight home and not speak with anyone. A little later, Harris began to comprehend her aunt's concern as a mob of angry white men passed her on the sidewalk. She was so frightened that, "even though [she] was always afraid of heights, [she] climbed to the top of a rail fence and clung there until these men with their horrible faces had gone by."[79]

It seems appropriate to end this chapter with a white child sitting on a fence. A black child in the same situation would have been more likely to run and hide—or to run home, as his or her parents would have wanted. But a white child, who knew that she was not the target of the mob's aggression yet was still troubled by it, had to figure out on which side of the fence to come down. It was easiest to repress and "forget" one's fear or guilt or even one's unacceptable affection for a black nurse or playmate. That was what white adults counseled, usually implicitly rather than explicitly and often by invoking racial etiquette. In a society in which adult white southerners energetically repressed any political alternatives to white supremacy, despite their own stated beliefs in Christian and democratic values, forgetting was also what made the rest of a white child's world comprehensible, his or her most important relationships with family and friends sustainable. And forgetting was the side of the fence that virtually all white southern children chose, even if a handful changed their minds later, remembering and acting on "forgotten alternatives" that, because of the prevalence of interracial play and the guilt that sometimes accompanied interracial fighting, many white children had once known.

Unlike white children, for whom forgetting was the easiest path, black children like Eura Bowie had little choice but to remember and reflect on both the terrors and the slights of their childhoods. For them, pain and fear were powerful mnemonics. In addition, they may have hoped that thinking through their experiences would help them find answers to urgent questions about how they could overcome rejection or close their ears to whites' epithets or, more urgent still, how they could avoid ending up like Dee Griffith, murdered in the woods. Black children never forgot either the possibilities of friendship embodied in interracial play or the pain and anger they felt at being mistreated or seeing others of their race brutalized. As they matured, they would find their anger growing, compounded by their fear and other troubling emotions. They would also find new frustrations awaiting them in their adolescent years.

5 *Adolescence*

On September 15, 1906, Mayor W. F. Dorsey of Athens, Georgia, fined four black girls ten dollars each for "insulting" five white girls as they all walked home from their respective, segregated schools. According to the *Atlanta Constitution*, the black girls had "stopped the white girls on the street, and said a number of things to them that were very objectionable, among others that the white women had been brought to the kitchen, and would sooner or later be brought to the washtub where they belonged." The girls' behavior was supposedly "without any provocation" and earned them a stern rebuke.[1] Dorsey not only "preach[ed] a little doctrine" about black inferiority but also recommended that the four girls be permanently expelled from the city schools. A search of school records indicates that several pupils were in fact suspended "on their conviction in the police court" as of September 24.[2]

And there the paper trail left by the four Athens girls more or less ends. Given more than a dozen paragraphs in the *Athens Banner* and covered at least briefly in the *Atlanta Constitution* and the *Augusta Chronicle*, this is one of the best-documented street-level encounters between black and white children that newspapers (or any other type of nonretrospective sources) are likely to yield. Yet what can we really know about this incident? Because the *Banner* reported the girls' names—Mattie Lumpkin, Roxanna Houston, Mattie Lou Johnson, and Annie Bonds—we can turn to city directories and the manuscript census for help. But only Mattie Lou Johnson appears in these sources regularly enough to make identification fairly certain. Born in March 1893 and thus thirteen years old in 1906, she was the eldest daughter of Lee and Georgia Johnson of Athens. Her father was a day laborer and her mother a laundress—typical occupations for black men and women in the early-twentieth-century South. That her parents were married and living together was also typical: despite the prevalence of single-mother households half a century later, scholars have found that two-parent families were the norm both before and after emancipation and that "as late as 1940 nearly four-fifths of black households were husband-wife headed."[3] Lee and Georgia Johnson had married at ages twenty-two and eighteen, respectively, and had ten children by 1910, the youngest not quite one year old. Although both were illiterate, they were making sure that Mattie Lou and her brothers and sisters learned to read and write. Significantly, the 1910 census also indicates that Mattie Lou, now seventeen, had attended school in the period since September 1, 1909, meaning that her education did not actually end in 1906, despite her suspension.[4]

The fact that Mattie Lou Johnson was able to go back to school suggests that the results of this sidewalk tussle among children were not as dire as they may at first have seemed. It also suggests how little a snapshot like that embodied in a newspaper account can really tell us about children's experiences of race. Retrospective sources such as autobiography and oral history at least capture some form of individual subjectivity, and they also benefit from the long view, beginning with an awareness of how things turned out. Nevertheless, certain elements of this newspaper story are interpretable enough to make it interesting, not only as a half-step away from the retrospective sources on which most of this book is based, but also as a place to start in considering the changing nature of black and white children's attitudes and interactions as they matured. First, the content of the girls' supposedly unprovoked insult is intriguing. As the Augusta paper had it, Annie, Roxanna, and the two Matties barraged the white girls with "taunts to the effect that the mothers of the white children had been driven to work in the kitchens and would eventually also have to preside at the wash-tub, while the Negroes enjoyed leisure and plenty of money."[5] Clearly, these four girls knew something about black and white adults' escalating struggles over household work and wages, a struggle that intensified right around September 15 every year as household workers left their jobs to make better money picking cotton in the fields just outside of town. A few years later, in 1913, T. J. Woofter Jr. would record white women's complaints about the difficulty of finding and keeping good servants in Athens both during cotton-picking season and throughout the year. "I find them all more or less dishonest, unreliable, dirty and incompetent," one typical employer declared.[6] Yet Mattie Lou Johnson, the daughter of a laundress, and her friends undoubtedly saw so-called unreliability and incompetence in a very different light. That is, they undoubtedly understood something of black household workers' strategies for resisting exploitation, their oppositional politics of everyday life.

A second interpretable element of this story lies in the details of who said what. According to the Athens paper, "The three larger girls pushed the smallest negro girl into the street and told her things to say to the white girls . . . [while] the others stood by and laughed at them. The smallest negro girl . . . was put up as a witness and she said she was told to do all she did by the older girls, and that they told her some things to say that she would not say, they were so bad."[7] As Dorcas Carter learned the day her friends punched a white girl for insulting them, older black children were generally more assertive than younger ones—they were, as Carter put it, "ready for the first"—and they also knew more about limiting their own culpability by getting others to do their bidding.[8]

Following black and white children into adolescence, we find their encounters across race lines growing more distant and their conflicts more hostile and more reflective of adult concerns. As the Athens example suggests, work and money became increasingly important issues, particularly for black children as they entered the paid labor force and confronted blacks' limited opportunities for advancement firsthand. Working for wages also exposed young blacks to a wider variety of interactions with whites and, for many, resulted in their being treated as either sexually available or sexually dangerous, in accordance with white views of black female and male sexuality, for the first time. White southerners' assumption that virtually all blacks were sexually experienced by the time they reached age fourteen or fifteen contrasted sharply with many young blacks' struggles with the physical changes of puberty and the social awkwardness of adolescence. Meanwhile, black parents tended to be uninformative and strict, providing youngsters with little help in making sense of adult sexual and racial mores. In relation to whites, young blacks' inexperience and uncertainty made sexualized forms of harassment all the more infuriating and difficult to bear, and coming to terms with the fact that they *must* bear humiliating treatment—since fighting back was rarely a viable option—merely added to the intense frustration that plagued many blacks' adolescent years.

How race shaped white southerners' adolescence is harder to summarize. If early work experiences meant greater exposure to racism for most blacks, most whites became more racially isolated as teenagers—a trend across the white child's life cycle that was deepened, decade by decade, by a growing distance between blacks and whites as blacks gradually found alternatives to work in white households and as the system of extensive and formal segregation implemented at the turn of the twentieth century matured. The white child of the 1930s "knows fewer Negroes than did the child of fifty or seventy years ago," observed Hortense Powdermaker, a fact that, to her mind, explained why younger whites "neither like nor hate nor fear the Negroes so intensely as do their elders," even though "they share their parents' beliefs." Powdermaker hoped that this "difference in intensity" would make younger generations of white southerners more amenable to black advancement. But changing white attitudes would prove far less important, ultimately, than the larger economic and social changes that Powdermaker and other contemporaries also cited to explain incipient changes in southern social relations. The impact of those changes would be felt mostly after World War II.[9]

Prior to the war and the massive out-migration of blacks and reshaping of the southern economy it precipitated, traditional patterns of racial interaction prevailed and, as always, were sensitive to age. Some white southerners, especially elite and middle-class white girls, were expressly forbidden from associating with blacks once they reached puberty. Even more common was a gradual separation—at least on an emotional level, if not in terms of physical proximity—as both blacks and whites grew into increasingly segregated social spheres. Introspective white autobiographers relate their increasing emotional distance from blacks to their growing preoccupation with all-white social activities such as high school sports and dating, which were themselves new phenomena in the decades prior to World War II. The development of a distinctive youth culture centered around high school is an important context for understanding white adolescents' experiences, even as early as the 1920s and 1930s.[10] Black southerners would participate in the new youth culture as well, but later and in smaller numbers as a result of educational inequalities. Few southern communities even provided black public high schools prior to the 1920s, and in the mid-1930s, when more than 50 percent of white southern teenagers aged fourteen to seventeen were enrolled in high school, the comparable figure for black southern teenagers was less than 20 percent (in some states less than 10).[11] Simply put, in the segregated South, the color of a teenager's skin was considerably more important than his or her family's socioeconomic status in determining whether his or her youth would include not only high school coursework but also the football games, after-school clubs, junior-senior banquets, and myriad social activities that were increasingly becoming the hallmarks of American adolescent life.

Other white adolescent "social activities" were less benign. As a few white- and many black-authored sources indicate, white teenage boys could be especially vicious toward black people as they jockeyed for position within their peer groups and tested the limits of white male privilege. Meanwhile, autobiographies by white men and women alike suggest that, as historian Melton McLaurin has argued, the "ritual of taunting and demeaning blacks was not only acceptable behavior, it was expected, indeed, practically demanded" as an "initiation rite, a sign of allegiance to the southern white racist ideal."[12] White southern teenagers who challenged that ideal were few and far between and would remain so until the early 1960s, when the example of young black civil rights activists began to take hold.

White adolescents' sexual maturation also took place in a racial context, just as much as blacks' did. A few white male autobiographers have written candidly about their sexual attraction to black women and girls, who, because of centuries of racist sexual slander, seemed infinitely more available than white girls in white boys' minds. But there is no way to know how many white teenagers actually had sex with black teenagers or adults. This, like many areas of white adolescent experience, remains mostly invisible in historical sources. Nevertheless, one thing does seem clear: somewhere between puberty and young adulthood, virtually all white southerners learned to forget whatever thoughts about nonracist alternatives might have lingered from their early childhood innocence of race.

Growing Up Working

Although they worked more as they reached adolescence, black children generally began contributing to their families' economic well-being from a very early age, particularly on southern farms. Thomas Chatmon of Coffee County, Georgia, was only four years old when his mother taught him to pick cotton, the first of many jobs he would do as an early-twentieth-century farm boy and his parents' eldest son.[13] Girls started early as well. Born in rural Arkansas in 1927, Geraldine Davidson had already been helping out around the house for quite some time when she became a regular field worker at age seven. "I had twin brothers and I had a baby brother, and [my mother] would have me staying home with them during the time when they were chopping cotton," Davidson recalled. Her other responsibility was to pump water and bring it to the field, a job from which she was all too quickly promoted. Her mother had given her a short-handled hoe so that she could kill any snakes she encountered. "While [my mother] was drinking water that particular day, I took the little hoe and I started chopping, and she stood back and she looked. She said, 'Oh, you can't stay at the house anymore. You're going to come to the field.' I said, 'Well, what's going to happen to my brothers?' She said, 'They're going to have to look after themselves.'" Even though her parents did make sure that she and her siblings got an education, Davidson felt that she had "messed my life up by doing that." She explained, "I often regretted it when I let her see that I could chop cotton. That was when I was seven years old. When I was eight years old, I picked 204 pounds of cotton. When I was seventeen, I picked about 370 pounds."[14]

Georgia-born Roosevelt Cuffie, who was just a year older than Davidson, recognized that both boys and girls worked hard but thought that the gender division of labor on most farms made life a little easier for girls. "The girls got a chance to be at school more days than the boys," he explained, "because the boys could plow the mules and it would be later before the girls had to stay out to help gather the crops."[15] Yet some girls plowed because their families needed them to, and others plowed even when their parents discouraged it. Sarah Rice persuaded her brother Albert to teach her to plow, then she and Albert exchanged clothes when they were alone in the fields so that "all anybody standing on the hill would see would be the pants plowing and the dress hoeing." Rice's father eventually found out and let her take over the plowing when Albert ran away from home. She also took corn to a gristmill all by herself when she was no more than eleven years old, riding the family cow "five miles up and down the hills with no saddle."[16]

Stories like Rice's are what lay behind historians' best efforts to explain southern black youths' patterns of work and schooling in the early twentieth century. Drawing on census data, Stewart E. Tolnay has found that nearly 80 percent of black southern farm children ages fifteen to eighteen reported occupations in 1910. By 1940, that number had dropped to about 43 percent, a change that paralleled a significant increase in school attendance, from 73.3 percent of black southern farm children, ages ten to fourteen, in 1910 to 84.6 percent in 1940. But blacks' school attendance rates peaked in this ten-to-fourteen age range and declined thereafter; thus, in 1940, only 55.6 percent of older teenage boys, ages fifteen to eighteen, whose families owned land were still in school while the rest, presumably, were working. The figure for older teenage girls of landowning families was 66.1 percent, a noticeably higher percentage that Tolnay does not explain but that probably reflects both the gender division of labor on southern farms and parents' reluctance to expose their daughters to the sexual dangers inherent in the one nonagricultural occupation that was most open to them: domestic work in white households. This gender gap in schooling persisted among older teenagers whose families did not own land, although the percentages attending school were lower for both sexes: in 1940, 44.8 percent for boys and 58.6 percent for girls. The correlation between families' economic status and children's tendency to leave school is obvious; moreover, leaving school is not the whole story. As Tolnay observes, for black children over age ten and especially for boys, the percentage attending school and the percentage reporting an occupation generally add up to more than 100 percent (in both 1910 and 1940), meaning that "it was common for these children to combine schooling and work throughout the year." If anything, census data underestimates the amount of work black farm children did, especially informally for their parents, other relatives, and neighbors, while failing to differentiate between regular school attendance and schooling that was intermittent and took a back seat to families' economic needs.[17] So, while some southern black youths did go to high school and participate in the youth culture that was developing there, it was by no means all who did so, even by 1940, when, for the United States as a whole, high school was well "on its way to becoming a typical teenage experience."[18]

High schools were more available to black youths in cities and towns than in the countryside. Yet white southerners' refusal to provide blacks with anything more than a rudimentary education meant that most southern communities lacked public high schools for blacks until well into the twentieth century. "In 1916 there were in all sixteen of the former slave states a total of only 58 public high schools for black children," historian James D. Anderson observes, and 33 of the 58 "were located in the border states of West Virginia, Tennessee, Texas, and Kentucky."[19] Meanwhile, in 1915, there were no black public high schools in New Orleans, Savannah, Charleston, and twenty other major southern cities.[20] In Atlanta, which was an important center for black higher education thanks to private funds from northern missionary societies, it took years of persistent black political pressure to get the city to build its first black public high school, Booker T. Washington, in 1924.[21]

In short, while cities and towns did offer blacks more educational opportunities than rural areas, these opportunities were still quite limited, especially in earlier decades. Work, on the other hand, was almost as central to the lives of black children in the urban South as it was to black children on farms. Some 64 percent of black southern nonfarm children, ages fifteen to eighteen, were recorded as having an occupation in the census of 1910. In 1940, the figure was 30.6 percent.[22] Like their rural counterparts, black children in towns and cities often combined work and schooling, as Gertrude Sanders did, clerking in her father's Birmingham store while she attended Industrial High School. Sanders graduated in 1932 and started working full time when she was only sixteen, earning fifty cents a day turning the frayed collars on men's shirts at the white-owned Les Dames Dry Cleaners, where her mother was employed. Having studied "beauty culture" at Industrial, she also made extra money during her lunch hour by fixing women's hair for "a quarter a head."[23]

Both as a high school graduate and as a black woman who never worked in domestic service, Sanders was somewhat unusual. Like the majority of adult black women who worked for wages outside agriculture, African American girls most often found jobs as maids, babysitters, or cooks in white homes.[24] Boys' work experiences tended to be more varied. Some boys followed in their father's footsteps, including Eddie Bryant, who dropped out of school in the second grade to help his father, a self-employed oyster fisherman in Hilton Head, South Carolina.[25] Boys were also much more likely than girls to earn money running errands, shining shoes, and selling newspapers—all jobs that exposed them to large numbers of strangers, black and white. Edward Blaise, who was born in 1925, dropped out of school at the age of twelve to support his sick mother. He earned $2.50 a week delivering groceries to white families on his bicycle, then, at sixteen, found a $3.00-a-week job at a New Iberia, Louisiana, bowling alley, where he worked for two years until he was drafted into the navy in 1943.[26] A decade older than Blaise, William Linyear also had to quit school to help his mother after his father got into some sort of "trouble" and had to leave town. His first job was to assist a one-legged black vegetable peddler on the streets of Norfolk, Virginia. "I would go out to his house, feed the horse, and hook the horse up to the wagon," Linyear explained, "and we'd go to the market and we'd purchase our vegetables. Then we would come to the white community to sell. . . . We would go door to door, and people would hear—we had a bell we would ring and they knew we was coming. Lots of times they would meet us, and we'd stop and service them." For this, Linyear earned seventy-five cents a day, which "went to the household." Later, he set up a shoeshine stand and started selling newspapers, eventually expanding his morning and evening routes so much that he had to hire several boys to help.[27]

William Linyear is just one example of an African American youth whose work exposed him to a wide range of white racial attitudes. Asked if he was ever harassed when he went into white neighborhoods to sell vegetables, he replied, "Sometimes, yes," adding that, if whites "didn't like you, they'd let you know it right on the spot."[28] Emmett Cheri, too, found that whites' behavior could be frustratingly capricious. Working as a delivery boy for a white-owned grocery store in New Orleans during the Depression, Cheri, who was born on Christmas Eve in 1924, had to maintain his composure even when

Boy selling the Washington Daily News, *November 8, 1921. Boys' work running errands, delivering groceries, selling newspapers, and shining shoes exposed them to large numbers of strangers, black and white. (Courtesy of the Library of Congress, Prints and Photographs Division, National Photo Company Collection, LC-USZ62-69050.)*

members of the same white family suddenly changed previously established rules of racial etiquette. "Some of them wouldn't allow you to come inside their house," Cheri recalled.

> Some of them wanted you to go no further than to the front door. Some didn't even want you to come to the front door. They wanted you to go to the rear. . . . One day I'd bring the groceries there and they'd tell me to bring them to the back and . . . put them in the kitchen. . . . The next time they wouldn't even let me come [in]. . . . The man would be in there and he said, "I told you I don't want you coming into my house." Now the wife done already told me what she wanted me to do. She didn't want me to come to the front door. She wanted me to come in the back. Told me over the telephone [to] put the groceries on the table. . . . The next [time] I'll knock at the back door and he'll come. "Well, boy, you know better than that. Put the groceries on the table."

As aggravating as such encounters were, Cheri saw them as something one simply "had to understand." "Most of the time I would go back to the store and I would tell the owner about it," he recalled. The white grocer told him not to pay any attention to such demeaning treatment, and Cheri always assured him, "No, it don't worry me."[29] Yet he remembered these encounters for the rest of his life.

Richard Wright's interactions with whites on the job were equally memorable—memorable enough that he mined them for material for *Black Boy* and "The Ethics of Living Jim Crow." With an absent father, a sick mother, and a generally unsympathetic extended family, Wright was even more desperate to earn money than most African American children. Born in 1908, he worked at a wide variety of jobs in Jackson, Mississippi, in the late 1910s and early 1920s, from running errands and making deliveries, to chopping wood and scrubbing floors for a white family, to caddying at a golf course and working as a water boy at a brickyard in the summer. When he was not quite sixteen, Wright got a job with an optical company. Although the boss intended for him to learn the trade, Wright quickly discovered that his white coworkers had no intention of teaching him to grind and polish lenses, which they considered "*white* man's work." "Whut yuh tryin' t' do, nigger, get smart?" the younger of the two white technicians demanded when Wright asked him for a lesson after a month of running errands and sweeping floors. The older of the two men shook his fist in Wright's face. "From then on they changed toward me," Wright wrote. "They said good morning no more. When I was just a bit slow in performing some duty, I was called a lazy black son-of-a-bitch." Afraid of what the two men might do to him if he reported their behavior to the boss, Wright did his best to hide his resentment behind a "nervous, cryptic smile." How well this strategy worked is unclear. Wright's biographer Michel Fabre found evidence to suggest that Wright was able to keep his job at the optical shop until he quit to go back to school. But Wright himself suggested otherwise. In two slightly different accounts, he described an eventual showdown between himself and his coworkers that revolved around a supposed breach of racial etiquette. Accused of having failed to call one of the two men "Mr.," Wright instantly understands that he is facing a uniquely Jim Crow dilemma: if he denies the charge, he will be calling one of the white men a liar, but if he admits to it, he will be "pleading guilty to having uttered the worst insult that a Negro can utter to a southern white man." Wright tries to answer cautiously but has hardly finished a sentence before one of the two men slaps him and the other attacks him with a steel bar. Only his promise to quit the job and leave at once saves him from a beating.[30]

Whether or not Wright actually had to leave his job at the optical shop, his on-the-job training in racial etiquette, like other blacks' early work experiences, taught him how important it was to keep his cool no matter how whites acted. But keeping cool was never easy. Working as a porter in a department store, Wright watched the white boss and his son drag a terrified black woman into a back room where they beat her for getting behind on a debt. Afterward, the son offered Wright a cigarette and lit it for him as "a gesture of kindness, indicating that, even if they had beaten the black woman, they would not beat me if I knew enough to keep my mouth shut."[31]

Certainly, Wright knew that he had to anticipate whites' expectations and act accordingly if he hoped to avoid trouble. But some encounters were unavoidable, as when the police stopped and searched him simply because a late delivery had kept him in a white neighborhood after dark.[32] Police harassment was a common problem. Edward Blaise got picked up one night as he and a coworker named Fred Lyounn walked home from their jobs at the New Iberia bowling alley. "That was about 1941," Blaise, who would have been about sixteen years old at the time, recalled. "And so the officer picked both of us up. He told Fred that some nigger, young nigger, broke into Phista's Jewelry Store." Quite a bit older than Blaise, Lyounn apparently answered the policemen's questions more convincingly—or fit their profile of the criminal as a "young nigger" less well—because he was soon released. Blaise recounted how the officers then turned their questions to him: "'Okay, boy, you broke in Phista's Jewelry Shop!' I said, 'No, sir.' I said, 'I was working with this man who ya'll just let go home, Mr. Fred Lyounn.' And they interrogated me.

. . . They interrogated me, interrogated me, interrogated me until I started crying, and I said, 'I'll tell you what, call my boss.' . . . So they called him. 'Oh yeah, that's my boy. He works at the bowling alley.' 'Okay then,'" the officers conceded. Blaise would never forget the words with which the policemen dismissed him: "Nigger, you better get out of here. . . . You'd better get out of here before we lock you up."[33]

Black Boys Becoming Men

As Edward Blaise discovered, one of the important facts about black boys' work lives was that being out on the street, whether to make deliveries or simply to get to or from a job, exposed them to white harassment. Yet John Boucree's experiences proved that black teens did not even have to be out in public to be vulnerable in a society that demonized young black men. Born in 1923 and thus just two years older than Blaise, Boucree was sitting on his family's porch in New Orleans when a police car stopped out front and a policeman asked him where he lived. "Right here," Boucree replied, but the policeman pushed him into the car anyway and drove him to a house about two blocks away that had apparently been robbed. Fortunately, the white resident recognized Boucree as a neighbor and vouched for him; in fact, as Boucree put it, she "raised hell . . . with the police for taking me off the steps like that." This was actually the second time Boucree had been picked up. The first time he had merely been walking home from the streetcar at dusk. A policeman had demanded to know what he was doing in the area, then suggested that he move to a different neighborhood so that he would not have to walk home past houses belonging to whites. "So what do you say to two policemen?" Boucree lamented. "Here you are a teenager and being stopped. Now that kind of thing gets to you. . . . You're black so you're wrong."[34]

Black boys' run-ins with the police were even more upsetting when they had a sexual cast. Herbert Cappie, born in 1917, described growing up in New Orleans as "traumatic" because, he explained, "When I was in my late teens . . . there would be cases of rape and if a white girl was raped, all black boys had to stay off the streets until the police had picked up one as a suspect. And they'd usually find them one whether he was a true suspect or not . . . and he invariably went to prison for it, not necessarily being guilty." Knowing this made it all the more terrifying when Cappie was himself picked up:

I'd been out and it was kind of late. It was about one o'clock in the morning and I was coming home along Broadway Street. I was smoking at that time and I didn't have a cigarette and I just started scratching matches, throwing them down like somebody nuts. And as I approached Fountainebleau Drive the policeman threw the lights on me. They were parked there in an automobile. I hadn't noticed. They threw the lights on me, blinded me with the lights, jumped out with machine guns and everything and said, "Where are you going!" I said, "I'm going home." Where you been and all these kinds of questions. Where do you live? I told them where I lived. "Come on get in the car!" I said oh my God, this is it. Well, they took me to my home. Fortunately I had a key and I let myself in. I said good night and my mother said, "Who was that?" [Laughing] I said that was some friends.

Had there been a rape scare that night, Cappie's story would have ended differently. "It was dangerous to be out there," he concluded, noting that he could easily "have gone to jail."[35]

Herbert Cappie could laugh about the dangers of police harassment in retrospect, but Emmett Cheri's memories betray a distinctly adolescent pain even many years after the fact. Born in 1924, Cheri was a senior in high school when a police detective stopped him on the street near a white school that happened to be on his way home. "The guy grabbed me behind my back," he recalled. "Wanted to know what I'm doing around that school like that because they were supposed to be having trouble, but I didn't even know anything about what kind of trouble they had." Indeed, Cheri never could explain precisely what the "trouble" at the white school was, although he did come to understand that it involved "run-ins and conflicts" and "white girls." But when he proclaimed his innocence and insisted that he was simply walking home from high school, the policeman refused to believe him. "He put me in that car and told me there won't no way in the world I'd be in high school . . . cause I was so small and little." A nod from his school principal was enough to get Cheri released, but the policeman's words about his stature must have stung. Cheri had faced persistent harassment in school because he was so small for his age—a mere 120 pounds "soaking wet" when he entered the military after high school in 1942. "As a matter of fact," Cheri confessed, "we had what they called a manual training period and instead of putting me in . . . carpentry and masonry, they had me in sewing and cooking." He also explained one teacher's refusal to let him take her algebra class by saying that he "was a little bitty fellow" rather than attributing it to the colorism that it most likely was. "I was the darkest fellow in the classroom," he reflected at another point, noting that most of the students at his high school "had straight hair and a fair complexion" and that the teachers "showed a lot of prejudice."[36]

Thus, when the policeman picked him up, Cheri must have found himself in a particularly ironic double bind: laughed at because of his size yet still considered dangerous because of his color and his sex.

Cheri's story is an important reminder that, whether or not they participated fully in the emerging youth culture, individual black youths experienced the Jim Crow South's sexualized racism in distinctly adolescent ways. For boys, growing up in the Jim Crow South meant confronting white stereotypes of black men as generously endowed and sexually aggressive, if not predatory and bestial. Being treated as a type rather than an individual was bad enough, but it was even more traumatic, to use Herbert Cappie's word, when one was going through (or anxiously awaiting) puberty and trying to get one's bearings in the adult heterosexual world. (How racial issues played out among homosexuals in the South is a question my sources have not allowed me to address.) The fact that black children were often exposed to sex in various forms at an early age, especially in the cramped living quarters and rougher neighborhoods of the working classes, did not necessarily mean that they were sexually precocious, much less self-confident. William Childs, who grew up in Wilmington, North Carolina, in the 1920s, thought he was typical of black boys of his generation in learning about sex primarily from his peers. "Back then when I was coming along there was what they called grown folk's talk and children's talk," he explained. "And there were certain things that grown folks talked about that they didn't want the children to be hearing and talking about." Sex was one of those things, a "taboo subject" in Childs's household. "My father did [try] without telling me what he was trying to do," Childs recalled, "bought a book and put it in my way without comment. . . . But like a lot of other parents [he] did not know how to go about it." Thus, Childs learned most of what he knew as a teenager from the talk of other boys: "They talked about what boys expect, what girls expect and how to go about it. What is expected of you as a male. And what is acceptable and what's not. That boys probably are expected to get away with a whole lot more than girls." Childs also learned what his peers' "experiences are and have been." At least among single people in their twenties, premarital sex was "a way of living" by his time, Childs thought. Unfortunately, he was less explicit about the sexual experiences of teens.[37]

Like Childs, Richard Wright learned about sex mostly from his peers. By age six, he had learned "all the four-letter words describing physiological and sex functions" from other children and from adults in a saloon that he frequented while his mother was at work. But it was quite some time before he found out what these words meant. Similarly, at age nine, Wright got his first uncomprehending glimpse inside a brothel after a female playmate teased him for being "a baby" because he did not know what the women were selling in the other half of the duplex where he and his family lived. But it was only after he began to hang around with older boys that his scattered impressions solidified into a general awareness. Although hostility toward whites was the "touchstone of fraternity" among Wright and his friends, their talk covered a wide range of topics: "Money, God, race, sex, color, war, planes, machines, trains, swimming, boxing, anything. . . . The culture of one black household was thus transmitted to another black household, and folk tradition was handed from group to group."[38]

One aspect of black culture Wright and his friends undoubtedly discussed was the idea that white women were "poison" for black men.[39] He knew about "the white death, the threat of which hung over every male black in the South" long before the murder of a friend's older brother brought it home to him when he was fifteen. The murdered man had supposedly been "fooling with" a white prostitute in a Jackson, Mississippi, hotel.[40]

Even if black adolescents knew about interracial sexual taboos and the mythology that accompanied them, their knowledge did not make sexualized forms of harassment any easier to bear. Retelling the story of the conflict in the optical shop in *Black Boy*, Wright added a sexual element that he did not include in "The Ethics of Living Jim Crow." The younger of his two white antagonists, Reynolds, asks him how big his penis is and taunts him with white wisdom about black men's sexual fortitude. Wright recognizes the stereotype, reflecting that he "had heard that whites regarded Negroes as animals in sex matters," and Reynolds's words make him angry. Keeping his cool becomes even more difficult when Pease, the older of the two white men, challenges him further, saying, "You didn't like what Reynolds just said, did you?" "Oh, it's all right," Wright responds, a forced smile barely masking his resentment.[41]

The fact that Wright told the optical shop story differently in his two published accounts makes it all the more difficult to know when he was putting words in his characters' mouths in order to make a point. But the version in *Black Boy* certainly suggests how hard it was for black teenagers to deal with racism in its most sexualized forms. Age and maturity helped, although interactions with white women were dangerous at any age. Alabama farmer Ned Cobb was about sixty when he decided that it was easier to overlook a debt than to risk "playin with the screws on my coffin" by confronting the white woman who owed him.[42] No matter how mature or self-confident a black man was, the threat of what Wright called "the white death" was palpable. Even the seemingly self-assured Herbert Cappie had his problems. Because of his light complexion, white girls often mistook him for white and "made passes" at him, leaving him uncertain how to respond. "You're scared to death to acknowledge it or show any sign that you noticed it. It's a beautiful life," he laughed, looking back.[43]

Most adolescent boys were not so self-confident, and at least some were innocent and shy. Middle- and upper-class black boys may have felt especially awkward about sexual matters, given that bourgeois respectability dictated premarital chastity for boys, as well as girls. Yet poor black boys might adhere to strict moral codes also, especially if their families were religious, or they might simply have little time or inclination for courtship. Arthur Clayborn, who grew up among sharecroppers outside Yazoo City, Mississippi, in the 1930s, said he knew nothing about "girls and stuff" until after he began serving in the Marines during World War II.[44] He was surely not alone.

Not that innocence or ignorance was any protection against white hysteria. Benjamin Adams's first cousin had to be shipped out of town at night to avoid being lynched after he was seen with a white female friend when he was in his early teens. Adams's cousin and the white girl "loved each other," but "there wasn't no sex involved," according to Adams. The girls' protestations of "You know, I love him" did nothing to restrain the would-be lynchers. In fact, they probably made matters worse.[45]

All in all, reaching physical and sexual maturity made life a lot more complicated for black boys, at least as far as their interactions with whites were concerned. The fact that their jobs took them out on the streets and into white neighborhoods at precisely the same time they were physically maturing meant that the raw nerves of adolescence—as well as boys' very lives, should a white person accuse them of rape or some other crime—were all the more exposed. A story that black educator Arthur L. Johnson told about his teenage years suggests just how hard it was for black boys to embrace their nascent adulthood in even the most basic ways without running afoul of white prejudice. Johnson was thirteen years old when he and an uncle, who was in his early twenties, were walking in downtown Birmingham behind a white couple and their five- or six-year-old daughter. The girl's parents stopped abruptly to look in a store window, causing the girl to step in front of Johnson. "I dropped my hand on her shoulder," Johnson explained. "It was the kind of thing that a thirteen-year-old boy, conscious of his being thirteen years old, would do to a younger child." But racism prevented Johnson's act from being perceived as mature and protective. "I don't really remember anything else until I was on the ground," he continued. The white man "attacked me so violently . . . that I didn't really know what happened until it was all over." Meanwhile, Johnson's uncle stood "frozen in fear," no more able to act than his battered adolescent nephew.[46]

Black Girls Becoming Women

African American girls were less likely to be beaten up on the street than African American boys, but they, too, faced new challenges at adolescence both as a result of their entry into paid work and because of their developing sexuality. Like boys, girls worked because they needed the money, either to supplement their families' incomes or for their own use. Olivia Cherry, who was born in Hampton, Virginia, in 1926, got her first job babysitting for the daughter of a black school principal when she was eleven years old. But her desire to make money became more urgent after her stepfather died when she was fifteen. "When I went to high school, I wanted a part-time job, so I could have an allowance," Cherry recalled. "Our income was really low then. We were not poor. We were making ends meet, but I wanted my own money. I just went here and there and I could not get a job because I was black."

Cherry did find odd jobs harvesting produce for white farmers in the area, but the work was irregular and at least one farmer tried to cheat her and several other black girls by giving them only half of their promised wages at the end of the day (for which Cherry and her friends retaliated the next day by filling their potato baskets with straw, hidden by a thin layer of potatoes on top).[47]

Girls who wanted to work more steadily usually had only one choice. As Cherry put it, "Basically I did domestic work because that's all I could get."[48] Indeed, if T. J. Woofter's findings for Athens, Georgia, are representative, household work is all that virtually any black southern girl who was not working in agriculture could find. Woofter counted sixty-four girls under eighteen working for wages in 1913 and implied that all of them were either child nurses, housemaids, or laundresses.[49] Even if Mattie Lumpkin, Roxanna Houston, Mattie Lou Johnson, and Annie Bonds were not expelled from school permanently in 1906, they may well have entered the ranks of black domestic workers by 1913, an irony they might have found all too bitter given the nature of the comments that had gotten them arrested in the first place.

Like boys' work making deliveries and selling newspapers, girls' work in white households exposed them to a range of white attitudes and behavior. Jessie Lee Chassion considered herself lucky because she avoided work as a domestic except when she was in high school and then the white woman who employed her was "a pretty nice person." "She treated me good and she taught me a lot about life itself," Chassion recalled. "She would explain things to me. . . . She always stressed how important it was for me to go to school." But her employer "wasn't like the rest of them," Chassion acknowledged.[50] Most whites expected their maids and babysitters to work long hours and do any number of tasks for low wages. In Athens in 1913, for example, the average wage for cooks, maids, and nurses was two to three dollars a week.[51] A household worker in Mississippi during the Depression would have been lucky to make that much: as historian Jacqueline Jones observes, average weekly wages there were less than two dollars and "some women received only carfare, clothing, or lunch for a day's work."[52] The work itself was endless. "Everything was included," and "it wasn't no such a thing as five days a week," Chassion summarized. "It was six, seven days a week. . . . It was whatever amount of days and they could tell you what time to come to work but they never told you what time to leave. Like if they say be here for seven o'clock, okay, you be there, but don't you never think you were going to leave at three. You were going to stay *until*."[53]

Girls like Chassion often had some idea of what to expect from whites even before they started work because their mothers or other relatives were employed as domestics. Cleaster Mitchell, born in 1922 to a family of Arkansas sharecroppers, recalled a few explicit lessons her mother taught her when she began working in white homes. "One thing they taught you was honesty," she remembered. "They always impressed this in you: 'Don't you take anything.' They'd tell you, 'Don't talk back.' They would tell you to do a good job and all these things." But Mitchell felt many of these lessons were unnecessary in her case. "From the time I was four or five, I went to work with my mother," she explained. "See, you grow up in this. It's not like waiting and saying, 'You're fifteen now. You can go do some work.' You done done all of this work [by the] time you get fifteen years old. You done worked for everybody in town."[54]

Even with her prior knowledge, though, Mitchell found that working for whites could be trying. She worked for a Mrs. Miller when she was "just a kid," eleven or twelve years old. "And see," she explained, "they test you to see will you steal something. So she goes in and she puts thirty-five cents down on the floor. So I goes in and I cleans the room." Mitchell never saw the money, which she must have swept through a knothole in the pine floor while she was mopping. But Miller, Mitchell continued, "just swore by all means [that] I had took the thirty-five cents, and I just cried and cried and cried." Later that day, Miller caught sight of the money through the floorboards, which led her to scold further rather than apologize. "She had really hurt me so bad about it," Mitchell remembered. "I've cried a many day. They accuse you of something, and if you try to say I didn't do it, they say you're lying. . . . I wanted to say, 'I'm going to tell my mother,' but you couldn't say that. Yeah, I cried a lot of times."[55]

Of all the problems black women and girls faced as domestics, none was more difficult than the problem of sexual exploitation by white males. Asked if her mother ever warned her about "watching out for abuses from white men in the household," Mitchell emphatically replied, "Oh, yes. That was taught to you very early, sir, because it was so—well, it was terrible at one time, and it wasn't nobody to tell, because sometimes the wife knowed it, but they was scared of their husband, too. You could go to the wife and she'd say, 'Oh, just don't pay him no attention,' . . . because she's scared." Many women and girls left their jobs "on that account," Mitchell continued, because "you had no alternative. To go to the law didn't mean anything."[56] Indeed, any number of black families felt that the only way to protect their girls from white sexual abuse was to keep them out of household work in the first place.[57]

For many black families, however, foregoing adolescent girls' income was not an option. Instead, girls had to work and protect themselves as best they could. Mitchell's mother taught her what to do, starting with early lessons about locking the door and not letting white men in the house when she and her siblings were home alone. Once she started working, Mitchell was lucky enough not to have an adult white male approach her until she was a bit more mature. She was about twenty-one years old when her employer's husband, Jim Brown, made his move. "I was putting up some glasses in the little shelf thing up there, and . . . he just walked up and he just put his arms around me," she recalled.

> I was so mad. I told him, "Listen, I been knowing you all of my life, Mr. Jim. You never knowed me to meddle you, flirt with you, or anything. I've been working here with Miss Heddy almost four years. You never seen me approach Mr. Billy or nobody, have you?"
>
> "No, I was just—"
>
> I said, "No, you wasn't playing. But don't you do that. As long as you live, don't you put your hands on me no more." I said, "I'll tell you why. Because if a black man done that to a white woman, you'd be the first to get out there and find a limb to hang him to. So if you would hang the black man about doing it, you think I'm going to let you do it to me?"

Mitchell's rebuke was effective. "From that day to this one," she concluded, "I had no trouble out of him."

Five or ten years earlier, Mitchell would not have been able to "speak up for myself" as successfully as she did to Jim Brown. But even as an adolescent, she managed to fend off the advances of white boys. "The little boys, they used to call theirself getting fresh, trying to get fresh," she explained. "I'd take care of them, too, because I didn't have much respect for them. I'd take care of them quickly. See, they was afraid to go back and tell their parents if they meddled me and I said something they didn't like because [their parents] taught them against black people." That is, white parents taught their sons that blacks were inferior and interracial sex was taboo. "So I had the advantage of that little bunch down there," Mitchell concluded. "I could tell them what I thought." [58]

Still, protecting oneself was never easy and not always possible. And, like white assumptions about black men's sexual rapacity, the cultural myths and economic realities that made black women and girls so vulnerable also made issues of sexuality all the more complicated for black adolescents. Although they rarely address the relationship between sex and white supremacy in explicit terms, black female autobiographers and interviewees often discuss their adolescent sex education in ways that reveal connections between the two.

Perhaps the clearest connection can be seen in the restrictions faced by African American girls growing up in "respectable" families. As historian Stephanie J. Shaw explains, the myth that black women were naturally lascivious, which whites used to justify sexual exploitation under slavery, "died hard and remained a point of contention well into the postbellum period. . . . Cognizant of racist and sexist slurs, parents emphasized the importance of disproving the sexual myths and stereotypes and insisted on sexual self-control," including admonitions to their daughters "not to present themselves in sexual or sensual ways." [59] For Laura Donaldson, this meant remembering how her mother told her older sisters to "always be a lady," even though her mother died of breast cancer and her sisters left home before Laura was old enough to understand what "being a lady" entailed. [60]

For Dorcas Carter, born into a comparatively elite black family in New Bern, North Carolina, in 1913, respectability meant not being allowed to date until she was well into her teens. As a junior in high school, Carter was allowed to attend a school banquet but could not stay for the dance, even though "every girl in the class" was allowed to go. "Mama said when you get [to be] a senior, you can go," Carter lamented. "I had to go home with a heavy heart with my pretty pink dress on and my brocade satin shoes." The next year, she almost missed the dance again because her father was not home to approve of her date, who had appeared at her door quite a bit early ("in the broad daytime") with a bunch of sweet peas. Carter's aunt pleaded with her mother, who finally let her go with the stipulations that she must take her younger brother as a chaperone and be home by nine o'clock. Fascinated by the band, Carter's brother may have had the best time of the three because her date "was just a little modest somebody" who did not know how to dance. After that, Carter vowed to herself that "when I get grown, I'm going to really dance the night away." But her family's lessons in respectability were too deeply ingrained. She went to only two more dances before, coming home after the second one, she walked past the church her family attended and felt guilty. "I said I can't be mixing up like this. That was the last time my feet went on the dance floor."[61]

Although Carter's respectability training was distinctly middle class, particularly in its emphasis on "ladylike" manners and refinement, poor black families often had high standards for their girls' behavior as well. Sarah Rice and her sisters were not allowed to accept "treats" from boys and had to take one of their brothers along wherever they went, day or night.[62] Ada Mae Stewart could receive potential suitors at home but they had to leave by nine o'clock. Meanwhile, she was not permitted to go out even after she and her first husband separated and she returned to her grandmother's house at age nineteen or twenty. Stewart also made it clear that even though out-of-wedlock pregnancy was fairly common in her rural Georgia community, girls who "done the things they oughtna" were automatically shunned. An unwed mother "didn't see the inside of a schoolhouse no more" and "got turned out of the church." And "nice" girls "couldn't play with them. . . . We had to leave them girls aside."[63]

To make sure their girls stayed "nice," parents warned them to abstain from premarital sex. Mainly because they had to learn about menstruation, black girls growing up in the Jim Crow South seem to have gotten considerably more direct instruction in sexual matters from their parents than boys did. Annie Mae Hunt's mother had begun menstruating at age ten and so made sure to prepare her daughter by the same age. Consequently, Hunt "wasn't afraid, like some girls were," including one of her cousins who "almost had hysterics. She thought some boy had something to do with her, and she knew no boy had had something to do with her. But she was bleeding, and she couldn't imagine what happened. . . . She was all confused, and then her mama told her afterwards."[64] Sarah Rice was more prepared than Hunt's cousin because she had seen her older sisters' bloodstained clothing. But she was also determined that such things would never happen to her, despite her mother's insistence to the contrary. "When it did happen to me," Rice recalled, "I was down on my knees saying my prayers, and Mama spotted it and said, 'Sarah.' She had a voice that told you whatever you wanted to know. The way she spoke, you knew it was something special." Although Rice was resistant, her mother seized the opportunity to tell her "all about the facts of life." Rice quickly realized that she had heard it all before from older girls but that they had told her "entirely wrong." Rice's mother also supplemented her explanations with moral lessons: "Mama said, 'Don't let a boy kiss you; don't let a boy touch you. If he does, you might get weak and get pregnant and disgrace your family.' She didn't spell it out in detail, but she said enough."[65]

In truth, though, Rice's mother did not say enough to give her daughter a clear understanding of her own sexuality. Instead, like a number of other black parents, she offered only a partial explanation that left her daughter confused. "I thought if a boy touched or kissed me, I could get pregnant from it," Rice continued. "I wasn't *about* to disgrace my family. Every time a guy tried to kiss me, I'd hit him or throw a rock at him. They called me crazy. But I was just scared I would get pregnant."[66] Sara Brooks's knowledge was equally incomplete. Her period took her by surprise at age fourteen and, while her father did pass on the folk wisdom that women should not wash their hair while they were menstruating, neither he nor her stepmother seems to have told her much more than that. He "shoulda told us, 'And don't go foolin around with boys and get pregnant, and if you do, don't take turpentine and try to do away with [the pregnancy],'" Brooks complained in her autobiography. This was "what he shoulda said to bring it out plain to us. But he just said, 'Never take turpentine—it'll kill you,'" a lesson Brooks finally understood only after a family friend explained that Brooks's mother had bled to death not long after Brooks was born when she tried to abort an unwanted pregnancy by drinking turpentine.[67]

Even in the absence of tragedies like the one that claimed Sara Brooks's mother, it is hardly surprising that parents were less than candid with their daughters. As Rice's mother's fear that she would "get weak and get pregnant" suggests, parents recognized that their daughters were sexual beings no matter how much that recognition disturbed them. Indeed, though most were painfully aware of their daughters' vulnerability, particularly in relation to whites, some found it difficult to impose strict standards on girls' behavior without implying that the girls would themselves be at fault not only if they "fell" but even if they were raped or harassed. Parents who forbade their daughters from wearing makeup or overly "womanish" clothing may have sent this message to some extent.[68] Septima Clark's parents also suggested it when they explained their unwillingness to let her do domestic work by saying that white men frequently "tempted"—rather than forced or coerced—black girls to have sex.[69] Fortunately, few parents were as insensitive as the mother and grandmother of a woman whose story John Dollard recorded in *Caste and Class in a Southern Town*. As a girl of eight or ten years, she had heard someone groaning as she walked past a field of tall cotton on her way to her grandmother's house. She went into the field to investigate and found a young black field hand who worked for her parents lying on the ground. The man grabbed her and attempted to rape her, but she screamed and fought him off until her grandmother came. Unfortunately, her grandmother interpreted the scene as a tryst rather than an assault. The girl's mother refused to believe otherwise and beat her daughter severely. "It has always made the informant angry to think of this incident," Dollard concluded. "She felt it was desperately unfair of her mother when she was trying to be good."[70]

As this woman's story suggests, black, as well as white, men could pose a threat to black women and girls, who had little protection from sexual assault regardless of the assailant's race. Black men could also "tempt" black women and girls in the same ways that Septima Clark's parents feared a white man might tempt their daughter if she went to work in a white household. It was a black man, indeed her Sunday school teacher, who tried to seduce Sarah Rice.

At thirteen or fourteen years old, Rice knew something "wasn't right" the day Mr. Brown grabbed her and kissed her. When he proposed that she meet him alone, she first told him "that's wrong" but was eventually persuaded by his promise to give her some money. "I thought about it and decided that if I got that money, I could tell Mama that I found it and we could buy food with it," she explained in her memoir. Rice arranged a game of hide-and-seek among her brothers and sisters so that she could slip off to meet Brown in the woods, but when the appointed time came, "the fear of the devil got in me," she recalled. "I got so frightened that I didn't go down where I was supposed to meet him. I got so scared that I could see babies; I feared I would disgrace my mama." Later, Rice was able to put a stop to Brown's efforts to seduce her by threatening to tell her mother on him—a strategy that would have had little impact on a white man. But the fact that she was tempted by a chance to get money to feed her family says a great deal about the pressures African American girls faced as they reached sexual maturity. More troubling still, Brown's attempt to seduce Rice took place at a time when Rice still believed that she could get pregnant from a man's mere touch.[71]

Filled with fear and confusion, Sarah Rice's story is very much a story of adolescence, a life stage when sex, above all, is new and mysterious. But, as Henry and Laura Donaldson's remarkably candid discussion of their court-ship reminds us, *desire* was a big part of adolescence as well. Laura was seven-teen years old when she moved to Wilmington, North Carolina, in 1940 to live with her older siblings after her father, a widower, was killed in a car accident.[72] Also seventeen, Henry was already well established at Williston Industrial High School, where he played football and was a "dap fellow" on campus—one of the increasing number of black southern teenagers who could participate in the new high school youth culture by the early 1940s. Donaldson's family was not well-to-do, but he was handsome and a good talker. "I didn't ever have any money," he reflected, "but I just had that mouth, that glib[ness] as they called it, and I ruled." Yet Laura still managed to catch his eye. "I had a string of girls," Henry laughed, but "thought she was the cut-est little thing I'd ever seen." Laura's naïveté was clearly part of her appeal. As a country girl, she had to learn the rules of urban adolescent social life. "In the country I knew nothing about football," she recalled, and when her employer *made* her quit work to watch a Williston game—a major community event—it never occurred to her to wait for Henry to change clothes and meet her afterward so that they could go out. "You didn't wait for me," he complained, after he finally found her in the crowd. "I said, 'Wait for you for what?'"

Once they did start dating, Henry and Laura quickly discovered that their attitudes toward premarital sex were very different. Henry was a self-described "sexpot" who would usually "have my way, what I wanted" with any girl he was seeing "or else I just didn't be with you." Laura was trying to be "a lady," as her parents had taught her, and she let Henry "know the ground rules." She said, "You can kiss me, you can hold my hand, but thus far, and no further." As a result, Henry "didn't pay too much attention" to his attraction to Laura until "after awhile it began to yearn on" him and he decided, "I'm going to get me some of that. . . . And I just sat down and we talked about it and she says 'No, I can't afford no children. If ever we get married, then I'll be yours but until that time, no.'"

Eventually, Henry and Laura married. "And it scared the devil out of me after we got married because the first time we had sex, oh my land, I thought I had killed her. She bled like everything," Henry confided. Only after they saw a doctor did Henry and Laura understand that her bleeding was a nor-mal part of losing her virginity. Apparently, none of the girls Henry had sex with in high school had been virgins. At least, as he put it, he "had never had that experience with none of them because they knew what it was all about."

Perhaps it was these same girls who had teased Laura, whose maiden name was Shepard, for being a prude. "I would hear the girls talking about 'we went this place and did this and did that,' and they started this thing about 'Un-uh, Laura Shepard is just as scared of a man as I am of a bear,'" Laura laughed, looking back. But despite all the peer pressure, Laura's respectability training won out, conquering Henry's premarital sexual desires, as well as her own.[73]

Henry and Laura Donaldson's story would be a typical, albeit unusually intimate, portrait of teenage sexuality in the World War II era were it not for the fact that they were carrying the weight of their race on their shoulders. Laura's conviction that she could not "afford" a baby was not only wise but reflected the particular wisdom of a "respectable" black woman's race and gender training. Similarly, other black adolescents' choices about sex both influenced and were influenced by the special conditions surrounding black sexuality in the Jim Crow South: the cultural myths, the economic realities, the conscious and unconscious strategies that blacks employed to challenge white dominance. Sexually, as well as racially, the Jim Crow South was a complicated world for black adolescents to grow into. And, as individuals like Cleaster Mitchell remind us, black youths often found whites paying attention to them sexually at unexpected moments, particularly as they entered the paid labor force. That Mitchell was able to fend off white men and boys' sexual advances seems all the more remarkable considering how little protection black women and girls actually had.

All in all, sexual harassment in its various forms was one trauma that few blacks could avoid as they matured. The fact that no one could or would explain southern racial and sexual relations in all of their complexity often made matters worse. Prominent black educator Benjamin Mays was twelve years old when news of the 1906 Atlanta race riot reached his South Carolina community. Outraged, he asked his future brother-in-law "why it was that white men could do anything they wanted to Negro women but Negro men were lynched and killed if they did the same to white women or even if they were merely accused and innocent." The young man responded by giving Mays "a stern lecture." Mays recalled, "He told me in positive language never to discuss that matter again. It was dangerous talk."[74] Parents were sometimes more helpful; certainly, Cleaster Mitchell's success in handling white males reflected the preparation her mother had given her even before she began household work. But, as William Childs reminds us, even the best-intentioned parents found it no easier to talk about sex in the early to mid-twentieth century than they do in the twenty-first. His father's solution was to put a book "in [his] way without comment," yet the book that could explain what Mays and other black youngsters wanted to know about rape and lynching and interracial sexual attractions and taboos had never been written. Moreover, many parents were far less forthcoming than Mitchell's or Childs's. Sarah Rice's mother offered only partial explanations of "the facts of life." Richard Wright's grandmother, aunts and uncles, and even his invalid mother routinely slapped him (or worse) in response to his questions about things that they considered worldly or felt he was "too young to understand."[75]

Meanwhile, adolescents' anger brewed. Sometimes that anger manifested itself in pointedly sexual ways, as when some young black boys whom anthropologist Hortense Powdermaker met in Indianola, Mississippi, directed three white men who had come to their neighborhood seeking prostitutes to the best *white* residential district in town. Powdermaker also recorded an incident that took place when two black Indianola youths were visiting some girls in a neighboring community: "During the evening two white men came in . . . [and] began flirting with the girls, and it was soon obvious why they were there. The colored boys, infuriated, set upon the intruders, using fists, chairs, or whatever they could lay hands on. They beat the Whites so badly that the latter were forced to leave." However, the black boys knew that their victory would be short-lived. They never visited the girls again for fear that the white men would shoot them.[76]

All too often, black adolescents' triumphs over whites were small victories won in the face of danger. Although psychologically satisfying, individual victories of this sort did little to change blacks' situation, and blacks' lack of economic opportunities was the most intractable problem of all. Like the traumas of sexual harassment, this fact was something black adolescents understood better and better as they matured.

"Crackers would take all your money"

Writing in the late 1930s, John Dollard described his conversation with a black youth who asked if she could talk to him about her "problems." "I anticipated a discussion of the difficulties which middle-class girls sometimes have with their mothers, such as not being able to go to parties," Dollard wrote. "But this was not the case. She said her worst problem is that they are so poor; she is ashamed of her mother's having only one dress, which she keeps clean but has to wear everywhere. They have nothing in the house for amusement, no piano, no radio, no books, no newspapers. She is having a hard time to get to school and her father does not give her money now." To send the girl to summer school, her mother had borrowed $19.25 and "washed it out" for a white woman at the rate of a dollar per week.[77]

Black teenagers clearly felt "pinched" by their economic situation, Dollard remarked.[78] Indeed, for youths like fourteen-year-old Roosevelt Cuffie of Worth County, Georgia, a growing awareness of their families' status and prospects was a source of intense frustration and pain. The Cuffies owned land and got along reasonably well by growing a variety of crops, but like most southern farmers at midcentury, they could not afford any setbacks. Thus, when one of their hogs rooted up half a row of a white neighbor's peanuts in about 1940, the Cuffies had a potential crisis on their hands. Cuffie's father offered to pay for the damage, but the neighbor refused, insisting that he was going to take the Cuffies' only milk cow instead. Although he was only a boy, Roosevelt was not about to let that happen. "So my father said, 'Don't say nothing,'" Cuffie remembered. "I said, 'Yeah, Dad, I'm going to tell him he's not carrying that cow. And I faced him and I told him. . . . So he looked at me and I looked at him and I repeated again, I said, 'You will not take this cow.'" Ultimately, Cuffie's father paid the white farmer more than enough to cover the damages and the matter was dropped. "But the thing is, they would go further than they had a need to," Cuffie concluded, drawing a lesson that he probably understood well even as an adolescent. "So you was oppressed."[79]

Half a dozen years older than Roosevelt Cuffie, Thomas Chatmon of Coffee County, Georgia, provides yet another example of a black teenager who was painfully aware of economic constraints. Known to his family as "Bud," Chatmon was sixteen years old when his mother died in 1936 and he was forced to drop out of school. For four years, he farmed and helped raise his six younger siblings while his father, John Chatmon, worked at a turpentine distillery. Finally, the day came when the Chatmons expected to clear all their debts and Thomas could resume his schooling in the nearby town of Ocilla. But first they had to settle up with their landlord, a white man named Thomas Harper. "So we went up to [Mr. Thomas's] house and went in the backyard as usual," Chatmon recalled, "and he came out on the back porch. [He said,] 'Well John, I guess you and Bud came to settle up today.' [My father] said, 'Yes, sir.' . . . [Harper] got his book out. Now I had kept a record myself of everything we got from that man that year and I know we didn't owe him any money and we were supposed to clear good money. So he came out on the porch and he started thumbing through his book. Finally he looked up at my father and said, 'John, you don't have any money coming, but you cleared your corn.'" Chatmon was incensed and would have liked to use his own records to prove Harper wrong. "I reached for my book and my daddy stepped on my foot because he knowed them crackers would kill you if you'd dispute their word." Instead, Chatmon and his father had to submit to Harper's thievery and, for the second time in his life, Chatmon saw his father cry. His own reaction was one of anger and disbelief: "The first thing [that] went through my mind was how could this man take all our money and my father had six other children down there, raggedy, no money, winter was coming, and he's going to take it all."[80] Chatmon had heard stories about "how crackers would take all your money," but he had never experienced such a serious injustice himself.[81]

Nevertheless, he was still determined to go to school. That very day, Thomas Chatmon stuffed what few clothes he had into a pillowcase and walked the twelve miles to Ocilla. Harper passed him on the road "in a new Ford he just had bought, and I'm sure he put some of the money he took from me in that car," Chatmon recalled. "You know he wouldn't stop and pick me up and ride me to town? And when he came back from town that night he stopped by the house, blew his horn, my Daddy came out and he asked my Daddy, 'Where is Bud? . . . Well, tell Bud when he comes back, come on [and] I'll let him have some money.'"[82] But Chatmon did not go back. He continued to help his father by working three jobs while he finished high school, then went on to graduate from Morehouse College. Ultimately, he became a successful businessman in Albany, Georgia. In the mid-1960s, when he was about forty-five years old, Chatmon went back to Coffee County and visited his former landlord. "He was still in the old home house. But this time I didn't go around to the back. I went up on his front porch and knocked on his door." Showing off his new Cadillac, Chatmon thanked Harper for giving him such a strong incentive to succeed: "I looked him in the eye and I said to him, 'Mr. Harper, the reason I came out here, I just want to thank you for taking my farm that year I worked out here so hard.' I said, 'Because if you hadn't taken all I had, I probably would have stayed out here and got married and had a bunch of children and made your children rich. But when you took all our money, I left.'" Chatmon invited Harper to visit his home in Albany, promising that he would not have to go to the back door. "Boy, that man turned all kinds of colors," Chatmon laughed. Meanwhile, a close friend of Chatmon's was "sitting out there [in the car] fully prepared" with a pistol in his lap.[83]

Unfortunately, few stories turned out as well as Thomas Chatmon's, especially in the short run. For black adolescents who perceived themselves to have almost no realistic chance of getting ahead, the frustrations of coming of age in the Jim Crow South were sometimes unbearable. Hosea Hudson remembered what it was like to give up hope in his autobiography, *Black Worker in the Deep South*. At fifteen, Hudson still believed in his grandmother's vision of Yankee soldiers returning to the South to complete the work of Re-construction. He also had faith in himself and managed to keep it for most of his teenage years. At that stage, he recalled, "plowing in the fields all by myself, with lots of time to daydream, I would imagine how it would be to get a bunch of men together and meet a lynch mob face-to-face and break it up. I would be following the old mule, doing my plowing, and I would won-der why grown folks were so afraid to take action." But maturity and reflec-tion cooled Hudson's ardor. As he remembered his grandmother's long legal battle against a dishonest landlord, as he thought about his childhood fears of wolves and mad dogs wandering in the dark, as he envisioned "the shotguns the white men carried," his fantasies of retaliation faded. "And then I knew that I, too," he wrote, "would be scared and might never be big and strong enough to confront the all-powerful white man."[84]

It would be hard to overstate the anger and frustration, even despair, that black adolescents experienced. Nevertheless, it is also important to recognize that childhood encompassed more than just what Richard Wright referred to as the "shocks of childhood." Although he was often hungry for food, as well as opportunity and acceptance, Wright still experienced the magic of early childhood discovery, which he captured in rhapsodic passages scattered across the early pages of *Black Boy* ("Each event spoke with a cryptic tongue. . . . There was the wonder I felt when I first saw a brace of mountainlike, spotted, black-and-white horses clopping down a dusty road. . . . There was the faint, cool kiss of sensuality when dew came on to my cheeks and shins as I ran down the wet green garden paths in the early morning. . . . There was the aching glory in masses of clouds burning gold and purple from an invisible sun.")[85] As a person, if not so much as the protagonist of his autobiographical writings, Wright also knew adolescent friendships, the heightened senses of sexual awakening, and all manner of joys and sorrows not immediately con-nected to his racial status. Hortense Powdermaker made the point well in *After Freedom*: "Early and late, the Negro's world of course includes concepts and practices not directly associated with the racial issue. As a child he goes to school, he plays ball, he works, he has his best girl, he likes one teacher and dislikes another. His parents are kindly and understanding, or harsh and unsympathetic; he is more identified with one than the other. He has all the problems, pleasures, and pains of any child; and all participate in forming the attitudes of his maturity."[86] The black person is, in short, a person, the black teen, a teen—a point that the intimacy of oral histories like Henry and Laura Donaldson's perhaps conveys even better than Powdermaker's assur-ances or Wright's powerful prose.

That Powdermaker had to state the seemingly obvious, however, reflects the fact that her generation of social scientists was the first to bring the emotional struggles of black southerners, including adolescents, to light. Books like Allison Davis and John Dollard's *Children of Bondage* (1940) and Charles S. Johnson's *Growing Up in the Black Belt* (1941), both of which were sponsored by the recently organized American Youth Commission of the American Council on Education, painted a particularly grim portrait.[87] Johnson, for example, found that roughly three-quarters of the more than 2,000 twelve- to twenty-year-olds he surveyed wanted to leave the South. Asked about their goals and ambitions, a substantially higher percentage of boys and girls said they *wanted* to enter the professions and skilled trades than those who said they expected to be able to do so, given their educational and financial limitations. And almost 40 percent of Johnson's youngest respondents agreed with the statement "I hate white people," as did approximately 25 percent of those in their midteens and 15.3 percent of those who were eighteen or nineteen. Black teenagers' attitudes toward their parents and other African Americans were also fairly negative. Nearly a quarter of both boys and girls agreed with the statement "My mother could do more for me if she wanted to," and 11 percent of the girls and 13.7 percent of the boys said yes to the statement "My father doesn't amount to much." Meanwhile, 80 percent were critical of ministers, who were traditionally seen as pillars of their southern black communities.[88] The "central message," as sociologist James B. McKee summarizes, "was that even rural black youth were seriously discontented with their lot and with the racial system that defined their status."[89]

In fact, Johnson's message was that rural black youth were especially discontented and that their anger was specific not only to their time and their circumstances—the Great Depression, Jim Crow—but also to their *age*. Adolescents were likely to be more critical of their families than younger children or adults, Johnson realized, simply because they were adolescents. "Family problems of adolescents in general revolve around the establishing of status as an independent adult," Johnson noted, no doubt drawing on theories of adolescence as an age of storm and stress that had been gaining currency in American culture ever since educator G. Stanley Hall's pioneering work in the first decade of the twentieth century.[90] "During this period" of life, Johnson continued, "parents shrink in the eyes of youth from omnipotent, perfect beings to ordinary stature as human beings with customary human faults. Frequently, the shock of this transition leads to the exaggeration of parental defects in the youth's thinking."[91] Something similar is probably also true of black adolescents' attitudes toward whites. Young blacks did not exaggerate the impact of racism on their lives—they didn't need to—but they did feel that impact more keenly precisely because they were in the process of trying to establish themselves as the sorts of independent adults they longed to be. Simply put, adolescence was a particularly low period in blacks' ability to cope with the Jim Crow system. This fundamental insight has implications for studies of the Jim Crow era, suggesting that we need to consider age, as well as sex and class, in our analyses of black life and particularly of accommodation and resistance. It also suggests that the teenagers of the pre–World War II era were not very different from the foot soldiers of the civil rights movement. As much as this earlier generation of black youths longed for change, however, their white peers were learning to embrace white supremacist traditions.

Growing into a Whites-Only World

Until his last two years of high school, future president Jimmy Carter spent most of his time outside the classroom working and playing with black boys his own age who lived on or near his family's Georgia farm. "I had a more intimate relationship with them than with any of my white classmates in town," Carter reflected in his autobiography. "This makes it more difficult for me to justify or explain my own attitudes and actions during the segregation era." Although he and his black companions probably grew apart gradually, Carter first noticed that something had changed one day when he was about fourteen. Walking from barn to pasture, two of his closest friends, Alonzo Davis and Edmund Hollis, opened a gate, then stepped back to let Carter go through. "I was immediately suspicious that they were playing a trick on me," Carter remembered, "but I passed through without stumbling over a trip-wire or having them slam the gate in my face." However rustic the setting, a symbolic threshold had clearly been crossed. "After that, they often treated me with some deference," Carter recalled. "The constant struggle for leadership among our small group was resolved, but a precious sense of equality had gone out of our personal relationship, and things were never again the same between them and me." Carter was "not reluctant" to assume his new, more elevated status, especially when it meant sharing some of his father's authority as landlord and boss, and he imagined that his friends accepted the change as readily as he did. "I guess all of us just assumed that this was one more step toward maturity and that we were settling into our adult roles in an unquestioned segregated society," he concluded.[92]

Carter's new preoccupations as an adolescent made it easier for him to accept a near-total loss of intimacy with his childhood friends. "Around age fourteen, I began to develop closer ties with the white community," he wrote. "I was striving for a place on the varsity basketball team and developed a stronger relationship with my classmates, including a growing interest in dating girls."[93] Segregated schools, not to mention an absolute prohibition against interracial dating and all other forms of "social equality," ensured that Carter's adolescent interests would draw him more completely into the white community. Other white southerners experienced the same thing, often considerably earlier than the fourteen-year-old Carter, who was somewhat isolated from white peers because of the location of his family's farm. Georgia-born sociologist Lewis Killian mentioned Sunday school and birthday parties as two early social activities that included only "my kind of people," that is, the white and mostly middle-class children who "would become my best friends when I started school."[94] And school itself was critical, especially since it was quickly becoming the center of adolescent social life.

A glance at three decades of yearbooks from Wilmington, North Carolina's white public high school—just across town from Williston Industrial, where Henry and Laura Donaldson pursued their courtship—reveals changes over time in the nature of white southerners' high school experiences, as well as changes with both age and historical moment in white children's implicit assessments of black people's roles in their lives. Wilmington, site of a notorious race riot in 1898, was a city of about 25,000 in 1910, with almost equal numbers of blacks and whites (and only fourteen residents who fit neither category, according to the U.S. census).[95] In 1911, the first year students published an annual, the whites-only Wilmington High School had a senior class of just twenty-two students. Senior pictures appeared two to a page and were accompanied by individual biographies and lines of verse. In a poll of sixty-six students (which must have included underclassmen), all but five indicated that they were going to college, while 62.5 percent of girls and 88 percent of boys affirmed that they had kissed a member of the opposite sex. So, while these white teenagers were perhaps not as chaste as their parents might have liked, they clearly were an elite and privileged bunch. Their sense of noblesse oblige is apparent on their yearbook's final page, which features a full-length portrait of "Uncle Mose," the school's black custodian and, as far as the yearbook indicates, the only black person in these white students' world. An older black man in work clothes pictured holding a school bell, Uncle Mose was, in these white youths' estimation, "A Gem in the Rough."[96]

"The Sandfiddler" of 1921, the next year in which Wilmington High School students published an annual, was equally patronizing. "Moses" appeared among photographs captioned "Ye Olde Tyme Scenes" and in a poem on the "Jokes" page titled "When Moses Last the Schoolyard Swept." His fidelity as bell-ringer was also noted. Nevertheless, as in 1911, his was the only black face in the yearbook. This is hardly surprising in the context of segregated schools, but the absence of other blacks does make the students' sentimental portrayal of Moses all the more significant as evidence of white adolescents' increasing emotional distance from blacks. Meanwhile, the yearbook's only other reminder that black people even existed came in the dramatis personae for a farce presented by the Girls' Athletic Association that May, which included "Aunt Paradise, the colored cook."[97]

By 1926, Moses had been replaced, at least in part, by a system of automatic bells. The recently renamed New Hanover High School now had more than ninety seniors, and photographs and commentary on school sports and other extracurricular activities, which had first appeared in the 1921 annual, continued to fill many pages, with scores, and sometimes highlights and player profiles, printed for every football, basketball, and baseball game of the year.[98] Clearly, as Carter suggested, athletics and social activities were occupying an ever larger place in students' lives.

By 1938, New Hanover High School had hundreds of students. The custodial duties that Moses had once performed had apparently been taken over by a younger, unnamed black man, whose picture appeared among a number of small candids of students hanging about campus in couples and groups. Three black kitchen workers, also unnamed, show up in an equally tiny snapshot, suggesting that the school now had a lunchroom, but also, given the size and anonymity of the photos, that the intimate paternalism that students had once felt for Moses had more or less disappeared. Whatever paternalism they may have felt was no longer so intimate, and crass forms of racist humor were increasingly in evidence, as, for example, in a 1934 drawing of a popular senior boy nicknamed "Nigger Nose Lawther" as a minstrel-show stereotype—indeed, the very stereotype that historian Kenneth W. Goings has identified as "Uncle Mose."[99]

Sports and other extracurricular activities continued to be important to New Hanover High students in the late 1930s, although these years saw greater standardization in yearbook design, eliminating the detailed descriptions of sports teams' seasons (now covered in the school newspaper) in favor of simple group photographs. With large classes and many students facing hardships because of the Great Depression, New Hanover High School was no longer the elite institution it had been in 1911. Vocational courses in metal- and wood-working were added in 1937, and a cooperative program covering a variety of occupations was instituted in 1938. The most striking innovation of the 1937–38 school year, however, was the sudden, enormous presence of the Reserve Officer Training Corps (ROTC). Virtually all of New Hanover High's boys appeared in their 1939 class pictures in uniform, a vivid illustration of the extent to which, with World War II looming, high school students now had to turn their attention to world affairs.[100] Equally vivid and striking are the similarities and differences between two cartoons that appeared just before the advertisements in the 1935 and the 1942 yearbooks, respectively. In 1935, the caption "Keep Going! See Our Ads" was accompanied by a caricature of a black man running from a ghost in a graveyard.[101] In 1942, the caption was the same, but the black caricature had been replaced by a caricature of a Japanese soldier being chased across the globe by a bayonet-wielding Uncle Sam.[102]

What a comparison of the two cartoons suggests is that young white southerners' racism was not only normative—an unquestioned part of their mental landscapes—but also imminently adaptable. Such was also the case when the developing southern interracial movement tried to make inroads in white southern high schools, offering lessons in racial understanding, in the period from 1928 to 1943. Alarmed by post–World War I race riots and the increasing numbers of blacks who were migrating to the North, a small group of prominent white southerners had gathered to found the Commission on Interracial Cooperation (CIC) in Atlanta in 1919. Directed throughout its twenty-five-year existence by Methodist minister Will Alexander, the CIC would "typify indigenous liberal initiatives to promote racial harmony." "But," historian John Egerton adds, "the CIC was hardly a radical force. Though it was an outspoken foe of the Klan, lynch mobs, and various forms of intolerance, it didn't urge and wouldn't endorse a federal statue outlawing lynching—that, the leaders insisted, was a local and state responsibility— nor did it challenge in any way the entrenched laws and customs of segregation."[103] Instead, the CIC encouraged harmony and communication within the segregated system and hoped for a gradual lessening of race prejudice. In 1928, having had some success in white southern colleges, the CIC took its message into the South's white public high schools. At the heart of the project was "America's Tenth Man," a pamphlet devoted to blacks' achievements and contributions to American history. In addition to distributing copies of this text (some 230,000 of them to high schools and colleges by 1943), the CIC provided teacher-training courses and sponsored student essay contests that drew hundreds of entries each year (including one in 1928 from Emory College student C. Vann Woodward).[104]

A report from a Biloxi, Mississippi, history teacher offers a detailed account of how the "Tenth Man" project worked. "'America's Tenth Man' was studied for one week in three sections of American history, with sixty-eight pupils, as a project in three junior home rooms with seventy pupils, and in two sections of modern European history, with fifty pupils," she noted. Seventy students then submitted essays on "The Tenth Man" for a local essay contest, the best receiving a prize. Four history classes also contrasted "the native African" with "the present-day Negro," using two sets of stereopticon slides. The junior class presented a general assembly program, including readings and music, presumably from black authors and composers. The juniors also held a "book shower," ultimately giving forty-eight books to a local black school. Thirty-two of the white students visited this school in the company of the city school superintendent, the white principal, and the white history teacher. The students were then asked to write reports on what they saw. What the teacher who accompanied them saw was "a most urgent need just now for a new Negro school equipped to care for twice the present number of students."[105] If the CIC's "Tenth Man" program worked, then a rising generation of white Biloxi residents ought to have been more willing than ever to address blacks' educational needs.

Students' submissions to CIC essay contests do suggest a certain improvement in racial attitudes; like a high school student from Clinton, Mississippi, many essayists felt that their "viewpoint on race relations" had "been broadened" by their study.[106] Yet, as historian Diana Selig has argued, the CIC's moderate approach, plus school officials' often selective implementation of the "Tenth Man" and other programs, meant that change would be limited at best. For example, a project in predominantly black Arcola, Mississippi, "aimed to furnish 'a clearer understanding of the tenant in his relation to the landowner.'" "The project included black history, religion, and music; it highlighted black scientists and inventors, poets and novelists," Selig observes. "Yet it assumed that blacks would remain in servile roles." In Atlanta, headquarters of the CIC, school superintendent Willis A. Sutton claimed to have taught white students "the attitude of cooperation with the Negro servant in the home or the Negro man who delivers the coal or the Negro child as they meet on the street."[107] Sutton's comments help to explain how an earlier Atlanta school project—a guide to the city published in 1921 by seventh graders in three dozen white public schools—could devote three full pages of praise to the city's black colleges yet almost entirely ignore blacks in the rest of its fifteen chapters (unless one counts the book's several photographs of black men and women picking cotton and doing other such poorly paid and back-breaking tasks).[108]

CIC essayists were similarly able to blend an (often patronizing) appreciation for black efforts with an unexamined commitment to established social and economic hierarchies. A Fayetteville, Arkansas, youth won one CIC essay contest with a paper that insisted that "the white man owes the black that succor and sympathy which a chivalrous strong man extends to his weaker brother." Other high school students, who had presumably been taught much the same curriculum, expressed even more baldly racist views. "What then should be our attitude?" one essayist asked in peroration. "Assimilate them? No! They are different[;] in the name of humanity[,] let them stay so."[109]

A limited success at best, the Commission on Interracial Cooperation's projects were the height of antiprejudice education in white southern schools. Prior to the late 1920s, and in schools untouched by "The Tenth Man," white students were unlikely to learn much of anything that challenged white supremacy as anything other than the world's natural order. Moreover, lessons learned in the classroom often held far less interest for students than lessons learned elsewhere on school grounds (not to mention lessons learned at home, at play, or in the street). Lewis Killian, born in 1919, felt that he learned little "that would directly influence my attitudes toward blacks" during the two and a half years he spent at a Macon, Georgia, elementary school in the fifth, sixth, and seventh grades. But he did get to know "two more beautiful black people" in addition to the maids, cooks, mail carriers, and day laborers he had known since he was small. Occupying a position much like that of Wilmington High School's Moses, "Belvin—probably his last name—was the janitor, and Ophelia, his wife, was the school maid. They were essential cogs in the smoothly operating machinery of the institution." They were also "deeply loved, southern style," by the school principal and all of the teachers, including Killian's mother. In retrospect, and perhaps as a boy, Killian could see that Belvin and Ophelia "presented strong, dignified images even while 'staying in their place.'"[110] Yet their relationship to white school officials, and even to white students, was clearly not one of social equality.

Beyond the lesson in southern-style paternalism that watching Belvin and Ophelia probably taught him, Killian also learned "indirectly, on the playground . . . more about the complexity of southern race relations. The *machismo* of some of the older, tougher, boys led them to boast loudly of their nocturnal visits to 'niggertown.' Whether their exploits were real or imagined, [Killian] first heard from them the myth that 'black pussy is tighter than white.'" Killian added bits of wisdom of this sort "to [his] store of folklore about blacks," just as, about a decade earlier, a young Sarah Patton Boyle had "treasured" a black maid's "formulas" for keeping a lover faithful "as much for the pleasure of repeating them mirthfully to white friends as for their immediate interest."[111] Learning to value black people only for the amusement they could provide was a key element in many white adolescents' racial socialization, and no subject was more interesting than sex. When Killian was somewhat older, he would add a belief "in the very large size of the sexual organ of black males" to his store of knowledge—the same bit of folk wisdom with which the technician in the optical shop tormented Richard Wright.[112]

In addition to revealing white adolescents' increasingly abstract, impersonal (which is to say *racial*, group-centered), and stereotypical views, Killian's memories of playground conversation raise important questions about young whites' sexual explorations across race lines. Unfortunately, this is an area where the historical evidence is particularly thin. John Dollard heard widespread testimony in Indianola, Mississippi, in the 1930s indicating that "many, if not most, southern boys begin their sexual experience with Negro girls, usually around the ages of fifteen or sixteen." He also recorded the memories of a white woman who had been warned as a teenager not to arouse her boyfriend by kissing him too warmly lest he "go to 'nigger town' afterward."[113] More intriguing, Charles Evers described white *girls'* advances toward blacks, insisting that he and his brother Medgar had "trouble getting away from white girls" in rural Mississippi in the mid- to late 1930s. Two young women he knew were particularly forward: "When they were fifteen and sixteen every chance they'd get they'd just pull at us and bother us. Decatur was a small, dull place, so I guess they wanted some excitement. . . . And I guess it gave them a thrill to see how scared of them we were." Another white girl who worked as a waitress in the café where he was a dishwasher would "just stand over me, and let her breasts hit me in the back," Evers remembered. "She'd pretend she was getting something and rub herself all up against me. *And I was scared to death.*"[114]

Anecdotes like Evers's are tantalizing but ultimately too rare to tell us very much about either the frequency or the significance of interracial sex among black and white teenagers. Nevertheless, we can speculate about the appeal of interracial sex from whites' point of view. As potential partners, blacks were, paradoxically, both forbidden fruit and more readily available with fewer consequences than whites. A white girl might reject a white boy's sexual advances, or, if she accepted them, she could demand a certain level of fidelity and publicly acknowledged commitment in return. Black girls could make no such public demands. Nor could they compel white males to provide for illegitimate children, and unlike white girls, black girls were not only unprotected by the laws on rape but hypersexualized in white imaginings. Growing up in small-town Mississippi in the late 1930s and early 1940s, Willie Morris "knew all about the sexual act," but, he wrote, "not until I was twelve years old did I know that it was performed with white women for pleasure; I had thought that only Negro women engaged in the act of love with white men just for fun, because they were the only ones with the animal desire to submit that way." As a result, black women and girls filled his sexual fantasies.[115] The result of such thinking was a dangerous double standard: if a white boy "succumbed" to a black girl's sex appeal, he need not feel nearly so guilty as if he "corrupted" a girl of his own race. Conversely, the white girls who bothered Charles and Medgar Evers were actually taking a smaller risk to their reputations than if they had acted equally aggressively toward white males. Because most white men hotly rejected the very idea that a white woman could be attracted to a black man, white girls like those Evers described simply had to protest their innocence and would most likely be believed. Of course, getting pregnant by a black man was a very different matter, and that fear, plus the particular force of the taboo against sex between white women and black men, probably made such behavior unusual, despite Evers's encounters. But, if they were both sufficiently daring and sufficiently cautious, white girls could indulge sexual desires without social consequences, since black men dare not speak out.

Even if we cannot know as much about interracial sex among teenagers as we might like, it is well worth remembering that sex and intimacy are not the same thing. Indeed, white adolescents' increasing awareness of blacks' sexuality as they matured may have actually fostered their increasingly abstract racial views. In a society that exaggerated black sex appeal yet prohibited openly romantic relationships across race lines, sexual objectification was often the only language available—other than silence—to express all manner of sexual feelings. In this sense, white men shared a measure of the caste-based restrictions on sexual freedom and self-expression that they so rigorously enforced for white women. Historian Melton McLaurin, who grew up in eastern North Carolina in the 1940s and 1950s, suggests as much in his memoir, *Separate Pasts*. More candid about interracial sex than most earlier autobiographers, McLaurin writes poignantly of his adolescent attraction to a black girl named Betty Jo, who, unlike a number of other black girls in his community, excited more than his lust. Yet even though they saw each other almost every day for six years while McLaurin clerked at his grandfather's store, they had only one significant conversation, which was stilted at best. Because they were separated by race and class, McLaurin could not tell Betty

High school boys on election day, Granville County, North Carolina, May 1940. Historian Melton A. McLaurin's sensitive memoir, Separate Pasts, describes the conversations of boys and men gathered in small-town stores and suggests that black women's sex appeal was a "predictable," "constant" topic. Photographer Jack Delano noted that these boys were dressed up for election day. (Courtesy of the Library of Congress, Prints and Photographs Division, FSA-OWI Collection, LC-USF34-040575-D.)

Jo what he wanted to tell her: "that [he] liked her, genuinely appreciated her for what she was as an individual, and not just because she was sexually attractive, although she certainly was that." Instead, he reflects, "The white society's restrictions on my ability to convey to her what I felt made clearer to me the sinister reality that underlay the deprecating remarks white males directed at black women." For McLaurin at least, the "sinister" nature of that reality included its barriers to human contact at a higher emotional level. His own response was to brood and keep silent—although, like Willie Morris, he did engage in vivid sexual fantasies involving black women and teenage girls. Other white males objectified black women and girls in lurid jokes and self-conscious bravado, in part, McLaurin implies, because they could never admit to feeling anything more for them than mere carnal desire.[116]

To recognize that white men and boys faced some restrictions in their emotional lives is *not* to exonerate them for the racial and sexual violence that many of them committed freely throughout the Jim Crow years. All too often, white males gratified their sexual appetites in exploitative or violent ways. White male adolescents' roles in racial and sexual violence are another aspect of adolescent experience that historians need to explore further. Much of what we do know comes from black sources. Yet some things are almost too painful to talk about. Stine George broke a long-standing silence when he told an interviewer how a white teenager raped his ten- or eleven-year-old sister while he, at age eight or nine, and a younger brother sat terrified in a wagon, then ran and hid in the woods. It was a quiet Sunday morning in their rural Georgia community, George remembered, and he and his brother and sister had hitched up the wagon to go visit their uncle:

> Of course, I was driving, and she was sitting in the wagon. So we went by this house where these white guys were and they were out there playing ball. I guess it was eight guys, you know, young white boys probably about eighteen, nineteen, twenty. . . . One of those white guys . . . ran and jumped on the wagon. He said, "I'm going to ride with you." . . . We knew him, see, and he got on the back of the wagon, and he was riding with us. When we got to [his?] house he took the mule from me and stopped the mule, . . . took the wagon from me and tied the mule to a tree in the yard. Then he made my sister get out and go in the house with him.

Frightened, Stine and his brother ran and hid, then began working their way home through the forest undergrowth. At one point they heard a wagon passing by at a run. "See, what he had done," George continued, "after he raped my sister, he told her to get in the wagon and go home. So she was driving the wagon and she went on home. She went by the house where my dad was, and all them got out and they couldn't understand where I was and what happened. They were alarmed." George's father called the sheriff, but "of course, he didn't do nothing. He did arrest this guy. But we finally came out of the woods and then we went back down to the house, and we didn't have any more trouble out of them, but they didn't never do nothing to that guy, you know, for what he did." [117]

A group of white teenagers who terrorized Benjamin Adams's family went similarly unpunished. As Adams explained, these boys liked to throw rocks and even shoot at the tin roof on his family's home in Edgefield, South Carolina. "They wasn't angry with us. They were just having fun with a bunch of niggers, so to speak." After all, they knew that Adams's family "didn't dare to fight back." And even pressure from the Adamses' white landlord could restrain them only for a few months at a time. [118] Clearly, white boys could be dangerous as they approached manhood and tried white male prerogatives on for size.

A few white male autobiographers have written candidly on this subject, although their focus has generally been on the post–World War II era. In an essay titled "Nigger Knocking," Alabama native Robert Houston cited class aspirations and peer pressure as the main reasons he engaged in random violence against blacks in Birmingham in the mid-1950s. [119] Willie Morris connected an increase in racial brutality to his and his friends' assumption of other aspects of an adult male role. "As we grew older, beyond puberty into an involvement with girls, it seemed as if our own acts took on a more specific edge of cruelty," he wrote. On Saturday nights, for example, he and other teens would cruise down a certain street where blacks sat on a concrete banister waiting for the Greyhound bus. At just the right moment, the driver would hug the curb and open his door. Then Morris and his friends "would watch while the Negroes, to avoid the car door, toppled backward off the banister like dominoes." Teenage boys' "taunts and threats" were also "harder and more cruel than anything we had done as children," Morris reflected. It all added up to an "unthinking sadism," in his view. [120]

But not all of white teenagers' sadism was unthinking. Some was quite personal and premeditated. Hortense Powdermaker recounted the chilling tale of a white teenager's retaliation after he lost a fight with a black boy who worked for his family. Both were about fifteen years old. "The white boy in revenge began spreading a rumor that the colored boy had said he was going to have intercourse with the white boy's sister," Powdermaker recorded. "A crowd began to gather and threaten." A lynching was averted only because a black woman courageously approached the white boy's father, who had no idea what was happening. Convinced that the black boy would never have said such a thing and that his own son was lying, he was able to stop the mob and save his employee's life.[121] One wonders what happened next: whether the white teenager was punished and whether he experienced any guilt over what he had done or merely continued to nurse his wounded pride.

Black autobiographer Jacob Reddix tells a similar story about the brittle nature of white adolescent males' racially and sexually coded self-esteem. Working as an errand boy at a logging camp in Mississippi in the 1910s, Reddix had a run-in with a white teenage coworker who apparently felt his status was threatened by working alongside an African American. When Reddix casually questioned something he had said, the white teenager exploded, demanding, "Nigger, do you mean to dispute my word?" Reddix stood his ground, albeit politely, and the white boy immediately lunged at him with a club "about the size of a baseball bat," shouting, "You goddamn black nigger, I'll teach you how to talk to a white man!" Reddix managed to escape, but the next day the white boy came at him again, this time with a knife. Again, his complaint was that Reddix did not know "how to talk to a white man," an assertion of manhood that is particularly significant given his age—and one that was quickly stymied when the white boss came upon the scene and threatened to have the white boy jailed. Nonetheless, it was Reddix, not the white teenager, who ended up quitting the summer job early for fear of his life.[122]

As both Powdermaker and Reddix's stories suggest, it was not unusual for an adult white southerner to intervene when adolescent violence became excessive. More common still were adult reminders not to use the word "nigger" and to treat blacks with decency or, among more pretentious or well-to-do white families such as Boyle's, with a paternalistic "noblesse oblige." Nevertheless, adolescents' abusive behavior should not be understood as a rebellion against white adult authority, for, as McLaurin argues, "white youths understood that the occasional admonitions from parents and 'respectable' community leaders to 'be good to' blacks did not express the attitudes of the larger white community. . . . They understood, in other words, that such admonitions had more to do with style than with substance, with class divisions within white society than with white attitudes about black inferiority or the rights blacks possessed that whites were obliged to respect."[123] Young whites may have liked to think of themselves as rebels against convention when they taunted and abused innocent blacks, as did the "James Dean and Elvis Presley look-alikes" (to use historian Pete Daniel's words) who were often the most vicious antagonists of the black students who first integrated the South's public schools in the late 1950s. But as Daniel has written of the guerrilla warfare over school desegregation at Central High School in Little Rock, Arkansas, young toughs of this sort actually "enforced their parents' segregationist ideology; they were rebels of a lost cause."[124]

Far more rare was someone like Dorothy Markey, whose adolescent rebelliousness fostered a nascent racial iconoclasm. Already troubled by childhood experiences, including her forced separation from a black playmate and the inequalities she witnessed as she accompanied her father, a physician, on his rounds, Markey continued to question elements of the Jim Crow system during her adolescent years as part of a broader rebellion against a social order she found personally restrictive. At the heart of her rebellion was the fact that she wanted to be a doctor like her father, a career her parents considered improper for a girl growing up in the early 1900s. Markey also felt her mother and other white southern women were too traditional and provided poor role models for their daughters. She challenged her parents' authority by wandering alone into parts of her hometown, Newport News, Virginia, that she was not supposed to visit. "I would go down, by myself, to the waterfront," she remembered. "The James River was very wide there, about seven miles wide, almost like the ocean. It had whitecaps and so on, and I loved it. I would go down there and get rid of this feeling of being tight inside. But it was supposed to be risky, and you just weren't supposed to do it."

Markey began to see parallels between the gender restrictions she faced and blacks' limitations under Jim Crow after she was punished for one of these trips to the waterfront. Sent to her room without supper, she refused to talk to anyone but Belle Franklin, her family's black cook. Belle was "the only one who understood" the way she was feeling, Markey later reflected. "Belle told me that as a girl . . . she sassed a white boy because he stoned her pet chicken" and her grandmother whipped her. "I said, 'Why did she whip you? You were right: He shouldn't stone your chicken.' 'Well, my Granny taught me, no matter what, you don't sass a white.'" The story "helped us to identify," Markey remembered, at least in "the sense of a denial of life and the injustices and the yearning for things that you didn't get." Markey would maintain this sense of identification throughout adolescence, getting involved in early interracial work even as a high school student.[125]

Still, Dorothy Markey was unusual, even among the small minority of white southerners who challenged Jim Crow at some point in their lives. Most white adolescents no longer questioned the racist status quo that some, at least, had found troubling in their early years. Whatever alternatives to white supremacy they may once have pondered were now fully forgotten.

Their racial socialization was complete. Even those who questioned white supremacy as adults almost always point to childhood, rather than adolescence, as the period that planted the seeds of uncertainty in their hearts. And very few participated in the interracial movement or other antiracist activities until they were in college or beyond.

Ultimately, the implications of white adolescents' embrace of Jim Crow were even more profound for the South as a region than they were for the individuals involved. Individuals could always change, as Sarah Patton Boyle and others did over the course of their lifetimes. But the successful socialization of each generation of white southerners meant that change could come to the South *only* at the individual level or—after World War II—through intense political struggle.

Conclusion
Children of the Sun

In the October 1919 issue of the *Crisis*, W. E. B. Du Bois announced that he and some of his colleagues were starting a new magazine. The *Brownies' Book* was to be "a little magazine for children—for all children, but especially for *ours*, 'the Children of the Sun.'" Raising African American children presented special challenges, Du Bois acknowledged. To illustrate black parents' dilemma, he quoted from a letter sent to him by a twelve-year-old girl. "I want to learn more about my race, [and] I want to begin early," she had written. *"I hate the white man just as much as he hates me and probably more!"* "Think of this from twelve little years!" Du Bois exclaimed. "And yet, can you blame the child?" Every October since 1912 the *Crisis* had published a special children's issue to celebrate black youth as the hope of the race and to entertain young readers. Yet almost every October, the editors had been compelled by their primary duty as representatives of the National Association for the Advancement of Colored People (NAACP) to denounce "some horror": the 1915 lynching of Leo Frank in Atlanta; a 1916 lynching in Gainesville, Florida; the 1917 riot and 1918 court-martial of black soldiers in Houston, Texas. "This was inevitable in our role as [a] newspaper," Du Bois explained, "but what effect must it have on our children? To educate them in human hatred is more disastrous to them than to the hated; to seek to raise them in ignorance of their racial identity and peculiar situation is inadvisable—impossible." Du Bois's solution, the *Brownies' Book*, would offer lessons in race pride along with efforts to teach black children "delicately a code of honor and action in their relations with white children." Du Bois also hoped the new magazine would "inspire" black youths "to prepare for definite occupations and duties with a broad spirit of sacrifice."[1]

In these respects, the *Brownies' Book* was a product of its time and place, the earliest days of the Harlem Renaissance. Although autobiography and oral history offer glimpses of how black children's racial socialization changed over time, it is in black intellectuals' and leaders' approaches to the race's child-rearing dilemma that historical change is most evident. Of particular concern was the question of black children's anger and the potential that they would learn to hate, which not only Du Bois but virtually all black parents considered disastrous. A brief look at how a few different black authors and activists tried to deal with children's anger at different times can tell us a great deal about how black children's racial learning changed as the twentieth century progressed—a story of change that is the opposite of whites' story of willful continuity but that ultimately had more impact on the South and the nation as a whole.

First, there is Silas Xavier Floyd, a black educator and Baptist minister from Augusta, Georgia, and author of one of the first books written specifically for black children by a black southerner. Published in Atlanta in 1905, *Floyd's Flowers; or, Duty and Beauty for Colored Children* was a model of the middle-class respectability training described in Chapter 2. Its 100 short stories, poems, biographical sketches, "Directions for Little Ladies" and "Little Gentlemen," and "Alphabet of Success" all encouraged young black readers to embrace bourgeois morals and manners with the explicit goal of building self-respect and race pride. Perhaps most indicative of Floyd's approach is one of his longer sketches, "Thanksgiving at Piney Grove," the story of a Georgia farm girl's transformation at "T—," "one of the great normal and industrial institutes for the training of the black boys and girls of the South." After a year at T—, meant to refer to Booker T. Washington's Tuskegee Institute, Grace Wilkins comes home with a toothbrush, "something which she had never had before." She combs her hair carefully and washes her face two or three times a day. She keeps her parents' house very clean and reads often from her new Bible, convincing the "ignorant and superstitious" skeptics in her community that her parents' many sacrifices to keep her in school have been worthwhile. After three more years at T—, Grace returns home to open Piney Grove Academy, the first public school for black children in the area. As a drawing by *Floyd's Flowers* illustrator John Henry Adams shows, she has now become the ideal of respectable black womanhood: educated, demure, refined, and ready to serve her people. Her primary service will be to teach race pride and bring her isolated community into the nation, as indicated by a celebration of "our national Thanksgiving Day" that she initiates. She puts together a program of selections from black poets, composers, and orators, including an excerpt from the 1895 speech in which Booker T. Washington famously "compromised" with segregation. The celebration convinces all of

Piney Grove's residents that "Miss Gracie Wilkins was one of the best women in all the world," a nod to the ideology of the "Best Men" and "Best Women"— the deserving black achievers whom whites should reward with equal treatment—that historians such as Glenda Gilmore have analyzed in their discussions of gender and black middle-class respectability in this era.[2]

Other sketches in *Floyd's Flowers* depicted black children in the urban settings of the modern South, including a number of boys whose pluck and luck in finding jobs and patrons would be worthy of Horatio Alger. But regardless of whether they started out in the streets or on the farm like Grace Wilkins, Floyd's message to black children was the same: self-help through education, hard work, and respectable morals and manners. As his admiration for Washington suggests, Floyd also advocated accommodation as blacks' only viable political strategy. In fact, he made a point of explaining his position to his young readers, whom he clearly assumed to be angry about their lot. As an extended and carefully reasoned statement directed specifically at black youth, Floyd's penultimate sketch, "The Future of the Negro," deserves to be quoted at length:

> My dear boys and girls, I have written nearly one hundred stories for this book and I have not said one word about the so-called Race Problem. I have done this on purpose. I believe that the less you think about the troubles of the race and the less you talk about them and the more time you spend in hard and honest work, believing in God and trusting him for the future, the better it will be for all concerned. I know, of course, that the sufferings which are inflicted upon the colored people in this country are many and grievous. I know that we are discriminated against in many ways— on common carriers, in public resorts and even in private life. The right to vote is being taken away from us in nearly all the Southern states. Lynchings are on the increase. Not only our men but our women also are being burned at the stake. What shall we do? There are those who say that we must strike back—use fire and torch and sword and shotgun ourselves. But I tell you plainly that we cannot afford to do that. The white people have all the courts, all the railroads, all the newspapers, all the telegraph wires, all the arms and ammunition and double the men that we have. In every race riot the negro would get the worst of it finally.

Floyd went on to explain that there was also "a higher reason" why blacks must not retaliate: "We cannot afford to do wrong. We cannot afford to lose our decency, our self-respect, our character." Instead, African Americans must wait patiently until right triumphed at last. "It is ordained of God that

GRACE BEFORE GOING TO SCHOOL.

GRACE'S GRADUATION.

Illustrations from Floyd's Flowers, *1905. In an era when American popular culture routinely caricatured blacks, illustrator John Henry Adams's sketches added greatly to the appeal of Silas X. Floyd's 1905 book. As one traveling saleswoman put it, "Here you have pictures of real colored boys and girls. You don't get these anywhere else."*

races, as well as individuals, shall rise through tribulations," he asserted. "And during this period of stress and strain through which we are passing in this country I believe that there are unseen forces marshalled in the defense of our long-suffering and much-oppressed people. . . . What should we care, then, though all the lowlands be filled with threats, if the mountains of our hope and courage and patience are filled with the horses and chariots of Divine rescue?"[3] Black children, like their parents before them, must be patient and trust in God.

"The Future of the Negro" encapsulates well the lessons that "respectable" black parents, both urban and rural, middle and (to a significant extent) working class, had been teaching their children for decades by the time *Floyd's Flowers* was published in 1905. The book's warm reception in the black press and lasting popularity with black readers suggests that Floyd's approach resonated with black parents. "To Prof. Floyd the race owes an incalculable debt," *Alexander's Magazine*, a black monthly published in Boston, enthused. "It is an heritage for which they have waited long. . . . Inspiring to the children, it is a comfort and help to parents who can place before them ideals and hopes to lead them upward to clean, sweet manhood and womanhood."[4] The *Voice of the Negro*, to which Floyd was a frequent contributor, agreed that *Floyd's Flowers* had "come to fill a long felt want" and predicted that it would "have an enormous sale among the colored people."[5] Contemporary estimates indicate that *Floyd's Flowers* did sell. Advertisements in the *Voice of the Negro* claimed that 10,000 copies sold in just five weeks, and a 1920 source affirmed that "no less than twenty thousand copies" of the book had sold in the fifteen years since it was first published—not quite on par with Washington's 1901 autobiography, *Up from Slavery*, which sold 30,000 copies in two years, but still very impressive for a book written for black children by a black author.[6] *Floyd's Flowers* was also reprinted several times, in 1909, 1920, 1922, and 1925.[7]

Although *Floyd's Flowers* remained popular in the 1920s, by then a new assertiveness was evident in some blacks' approach to child rearing. Indeed, Du Bois articulated an activist vision as early as 1912. "Our first impulse is to shield our children absolutely," he wrote, but black parents knew all too well that this was impossible: that "beyond all the disillusionment and hardening that lurk for every human soul there is that extra hurting which . . . waits on each corner to shadow the joy" of black boys and girls. Given this reality, black parents must neither shield nor indulge their children too much, nor should they "thrust them forth grimly into school or street, and let them learn as they may from brutal fact." Instead, Du Bois asked, "Why not rather face the facts and tell the truth? Your child is wiser than you think." Telling the truth meant that with "every step of dawning intelligence[,] explanation—frank, free guiding explanation—must come." Such explanations would not only be better for the child but better for the race, for "once the colored child understands the world's attitude and the shameful wrong of it," Du Bois promised, "you have furnished it with a great life motive—a power and impulse toward good, which is the mightiest thing man has." Although he, too, spoke the language of "dignity and self-respect," "breadth and accomplishment," and "human service," Du Bois made it clear that action (and not simply the patient waiting for "Divine rescue" that Floyd advocated) was necessary. Once they understood their predicament, black youths could become warriors in "the great battle of human right against poverty, against disease, against color prejudice."[8]

At what age children were to take up the fight was unclear. In 1912, Du Bois seemed to think of children primarily as future adult participants in civil rights struggles. By 1920, he could envision a role for children as children, evident in the very first issue of the *Brownies' Book*, which featured a 1917 photograph of black children in Harlem marching in silent protest against racial violence in the wake of a massacre in East St. Louis, Illinois. Throughout its two-year run, from January 1920 through December 1921, the *Brownies' Book* taught not only race pride but also political awareness. Du Bois's monthly editorials, which appeared under the title "As the Crow Flies," explained the issues of the day in terms young readers could understand. "One has here in quite simple form a survey of the main events of the world relevant to colored peoples," historian Herbert Aptheker summarizes. Most notable was Du Bois's coverage of independence struggles taking place in various parts of the world, his attention to the women's rights movement and labor activism, and his criticisms of the post–World War I Red Scare.[9] Meanwhile, the entire magazine breathed with the spirit of the Harlem Renaissance. Stories, poems, biographical sketches, and other features emphasized the beauty, intelligence, and creativity of African Americans, an emphasis that was reiterated in the dozens of drawings and photographs of black children and adults that appeared in every issue.[10]

Although the *Brownies' Book* was short-lived and attracted fewer than half of the 12,000 monthly subscribers it needed to become financially self-sustaining, black leaders' commitment to educating children for activism continued to grow.[11] In addition to the many other examples of political ferment that characterized the decade, the 1930s saw both an expansion and a significant shift in emphasis in the NAACP's long-standing youth program—

Children in the Silent Protest Parade, Harlem, July 28, 1917. The NAACP *and other groups organized a silent march to protest a race riot in East St. Louis, Illinois, in which at least forty blacks were killed, as well as recent lynchings in Waco, Texas, and Memphis, Tennessee. This photograph appeared in the first issue of W. E. B. Du Bois's children's magazine, the* Brownies' Book, *in January 1920. (Courtesy of the Photographs and Prints Division, Schomburg Center for Research in Black Culture, The New York Public Library, Astor, Lenox, and Tilden Foundations.)*

a shift that, it is important to recognize, resulted primarily from the efforts of young people themselves. No longer content to prepare young blacks for future involvement in the organization's activities, youth councils began to work toward immediate goals, particularly at the local level in northern cities, but even, to some extent, in the South. As Youth Director Juanita Jackson (herself in her twenties) put it in a letter "To the Youth Members of the NAACP" in 1936, "Remember, it is not enough to awaken; it is not enough to understand. We must act—and act now!" Often, action meant direct action, including demonstrations against lynching and organized resistance to segregation policies. Youth councils also conducted voter registration campaigns, including one in Greenville, South Carolina, that resulted in the arrest of the group's teenage president. Although historians have paid little attention to Depression-era youth protests, there is, as Rebecca de Schweinitz has recently argued, a case to be made for the mostly conservative NAACP as the birthplace of the militant youth activism that would later propel the civil rights movement.[12]

Nevertheless, young people's militancy continued to trouble many black adults both in the 1930s and beyond. "NAACP youth groups after the mid-1930s engaged in frequent and sometimes heated conflicts with adult leaders," writes de Schweinitz.[13] Many NAACP officials, not to mention many parents, remained unconvinced that activism, especially activism of a sort that could get teenagers arrested or worse, was the solution to the anger that, as all involved recognized, was fueling this nascent youth movement. Outside the activist circles of the NAACP, and particularly in the South, black parents still worried about children's safety above all.

Differing attitudes toward black youths' combative spirit were equally evident at the high tide of the civil rights movement thirty years later. Young activists working for the Student Non-Violent Coordinating Committee (SNCC) and the Congress of Racial Equality (CORE) ran up against black parents' fears as they relied on eager local teenagers to canvass their communities in voter registration drives and other organizing efforts. In Canton, Mississippi, Anne Moody and her coworkers from CORE lost all but one of their "fifty dedicated teen-age canvassers" after a local white gas station owner blasted five of them with buckshot. "I knew that their parents were responsible for most of them not coming back," Moody wrote. "From the beginning most of the parents had not approved of their participation in the voter registration drive. Several kids had told me that they came against their parents' wishes"—as, indeed, had Moody, whose mother sent her many tear-stained letters begging her to quit the movement or leave the South.[14]

Moody's own experience coming of age in Mississippi in the 1940s and 1950s is a reminder that, as much as leaders like Du Bois or activists like those in SNCC and CORE might advocate political awareness and involvement as the solution to the problem of black children's inevitable frustration and anger, ordinary black southerners still struggled to find the words that could explain race and racism. Moody, born in 1941 to a poor (and not particularly "respectable") family, was five or six years old when she first became really curious about skin color. She had met two of her mother's brothers for the first time and wanted to know why they looked white even though their mother "ain't that color and [their sister] Alberta ain't that color and you. . . ." "'Cause us daddy ain't that color!" Moody's mother interrupted. "Now you shut up! Why you gotta know so much all the time?" Like so many black children before her, Moody sulked in silence: "Mama was so mad that I was scared if I asked her anything else she might hit me, so I shut up. But she hadn't nearly satisfied my curiosity at all."[15]

A year or so later, Moody learned a bit more about race when she and her younger brother and sister got in trouble for following some white playmates into the white section of a segregated movie theater. Convinced that whites must be better than blacks because everything they had, from houses to theater lobbies, was better, Moody soon proposed a game of "Doctor" so that she could examine her white playmates' "privates" to see if the secret to their superiority might lie in the only parts of their bodies she had never seen. No more enlightened, she again turned to her mother, who again got angry.[16]

Only when it came to the issue of safety were Moody's mother's answers clear-cut: black children and teenagers had to learn to behave themselves and keep quiet. When Moody, at about age seven, asked about a lynching victim, her mother told her that an "Evil Spirit" had killed him and that "you gotta be a good girl or it will kill you too." Eight years later, when fourteen-year-old Emmett Till was murdered in the summer of 1955, Moody's mother told her not to let on to her white employer that she knew anything about Till's death. "Just do your work like you don't know nothing," she admonished, advice that Moody took when her employer, "one of the meanest white women in town," brought up the killing.[17] In this instance, Moody's mother succeeded in keeping her daughter safe, but her refusal to discuss racial matters fueled a smoldering resentment. "I was fifteen years old when I began to hate people," Moody later wrote. "I hated the white men who murdered Emmett Till. . . . But I also hated Negroes. I hated them for not standing up and doing something about the murders."[18] Without parental guidance to channel her anger, Moody had learned the debilitating lesson in hatred that Du Bois and other black leaders worried about, the lesson that Silas Floyd had feared might make blacks lose "[their] decency, [their] self-respect, [their] character."

And yet Anne Moody became an activist. Although the race training she received from her mother differed little from that of a Sara Brooks or a Richard Wright, both of similarly working-class backgrounds but born decades before her, by the 1950s other influences had grown strong. Most immediate for Moody was the willingness of a teacher, Mrs. Rice, to tell her about the NAACP and its long battle against lynching and for racial equality. Expanded access to higher education also played a role, since it was at Tougaloo College, which she was able to attend on an academic scholarship, that Moody first joined the NAACP at the invitation of her roommate.[19]

Beyond these individual circumstances, though, lay decades of effort on the part of blacks, particularly in organizations like the NAACP, as well as social, economic, and political changes in the American landscape as a whole. Among the most significant were the mechanization of southern agriculture and the steady migration of blacks out of the South from the 1910s through the 1950s, a population shift that made it impossible for northerners and westerners to pretend that racism was strictly a southern problem and that also brought different parts of the problem, such as housing discrimination in urban areas, to the fore. The New Deal also had a leavening effect, allowing some air into the South's closed society even if New Deal programs were far from perfect in reaching and helping black southerners. Most important of all was the impact of World War II, which both accelerated changes in the regional and national economies and gradually led to greater support for black equality and citizenship rights on the part of the federal government. Such historical trends seemed a world away for a girl like Anne Moody, whose daily routines focused mostly on survival. Before she learned about Emmett Till's death and thus learned to fear "being killed just because I was black," Moody's primary concerns had been much more basic: "I had known the fear of hunger, hell, and the Devil," she wrote.[20] The world outside of Wilkinson County, Mississippi, hardly registered at all. Nevertheless, it was broader historical changes, including the federal government's grudging responses to the demands of black activists, that made Moody's transformation from angry black teenager to committed civil rights worker possible. In turn, the civil rights movement that she joined in the 1960s has transformed the South in innumerable ways.

These were changes that most white southerners never wanted to see. The history of white southern children's racial learning is one marked by considerable continuity precisely because white southern adults willed it to be so. They taught their children the same time-worn scripts of racial etiquette that they themselves had learned, and they ensured that schools and churches —where children might learn about democracy and human brotherhood— not only would be segregated but would either reinforce white supremacy or maintain silence on race issues. When change did start to come to the South, and especially when the Supreme Court's May 1954 ruling in *Brown v. Board of Education* forced them to consider the prospect of integrated schools, the majority of white southerners responded with anger and, with much encouragement from the region's deeply entrenched political establishment, fought integration every step of the way.

Although she seems painfully naive in retrospect, Sarah Patton Boyle did not anticipate whites' recalcitrance, much less a campaign of massive resistance that would pit state officials against the federal government, in 1954. Instead, she believed that most white southerners were good-hearted people who simply did not realize that blacks disliked being treated as inferiors and that racism was morally wrong. She herself had awakened to these facts in 1950 when Gregory Swanson, the black plaintiff in an NAACP-sponsored lawsuit, had sought and ultimately won admission to the University of Virginia's law school. Under the tutelage of a black mentor, Charlottesville newspaper editor T. J. Sellers, who was far less sanguine than she was, Boyle made it her mission in the early 1950s to educate other whites just as the Swanson case and her conversations with Sellers had educated her. Above all, she hoped to disabuse white southerners of their conviction that "everybody else is prejudiced," which in her view prevented a silent majority from speaking out against racial injustice—the same "silent South" argument that, according to historian Morton Sosna, white southern liberals had been making in vain ever since New Orleans author George Washington Cable published *The Silent South* in 1885.[21] Boyle aimed at a wide audience with this message in the fall of 1954 when she submitted a characteristically optimistic article titled "We Are Readier Than We Think" to the *Saturday Evening Post*. The *Post* published the article, but under the incendiary title "Southerners Will *Like* Integration" and accompanied by a large photograph of Boyle smiling at two black male medical students that, perhaps unintentionally, raised the specter of interracial sex in many readers' minds.[22] The response was chastening. Together with the rising tide of massive resistance in the late 1950s, the hate mail and public attacks this article engendered plunged Boyle into a deep spiritual crisis. Only by discovering a bedrock faith in Christianity was she able to continue as an activist. As she explained years later, "I began to feel again that you just couldn't count on people anyway and I mustn't think in terms of people. My assignment was from God, what he wanted me to do, and that was what enabled me to go on."[23] Boyle did go on for much of the 1960s, writing and speaking to a variety of audiences, participating in marches and sit-ins with younger activists, and spending three days in jail in St. Augustine, Florida, for taking part in a demonstration there in June 1964. Meanwhile, her 1962 autobiography, *The Desegregated Heart*, sold more than 60,000 copies.[24]

Despite Boyle's disillusionment—despite the fact that few white southerners responded to her moral call even in the mid-1950s, when federal support for school integration ought to have made it easier for white opponents of Jim Crow to stand up and be counted—there is much truth in her conviction that white southerners could have found more humanity toward blacks within themselves than their support for massive resistance indicates. They could have tried to remember how they *learned* to think of blacks as inferiors who must be socially distanced, and they could have drawn on what I have described as "forgotten alternatives"—the ideas, impressions, and emotions that preceded and sometimes contradicted the lessons in white supremacy that their parents and the whole social world around them gradually taught. The sad reality is that, although such forgotten alternatives had existed, if only briefly, for many white southerners, they were insignificant as a moral or political catalyst in all but a very few cases. Even those whites who, like Boyle, managed to recapture some of the preracial innocence of childhood by reflecting on how that innocence was lost usually engaged in such reflections only after some adult racial conversion experience.[25] The comparative openness of childhood race relations was not enough, in itself, to encourage and sustain dissent among white southerners. Instead, the effectiveness of white adults' racial teachings and, more broadly, the completeness of Jim Crow as a social system was such that change could come only through persistent and organized effort on the part of blacks. In Boyle's case, it took a Gregory Swanson backed by the NAACP, not to mention the patient support of T. J. Sellers. In the case of the South, it took a massive civil rights movement and fundamental changes in federal law. And still, by many measures, the eradication of white supremacy is far from complete, both in the South and in the nation as a whole.

In the end, the significance of "forgotten alternatives" lies less in their impact on white southerners' racial politics either before or during the civil rights movement and more in the light they shed on how individual whites became accustomed to the racial order. This process is all the more important to understand historically because white Americans today so often think of racism as strictly an individual and largely an interpersonal phenomenon. In the four decades since the civil rights movement, it has become increasingly easy for whites to argue that American society is no longer racist, that the playing field has been leveled, that class is really the issue, that as long as individual whites don't intend to discriminate (and wouldn't dream of using the N-word) then they are not racists. Yet racial inequalities persist.

Certainly, I agree that interpersonal relations are an important aspect of race relations—indeed, a crucial aspect if the question is how children learned race and racism in the South in the early twentieth century. But I would be deeply troubled if, because of my emphasis on everyday encounters across race lines, this book were somehow seen to support whites' self-serving misconceptions of what racism is and how it works.

A major goal of this study has been to highlight connections between the individual and the social, between private and public, between children's racial learning and larger social, economic, and political decisions and trends. In the Jim Crow South, the racial etiquette white parents taught reinforced and perpetuated a system of inequality that was rooted in economic oppression and political disfranchisement, as well as discriminatory laws of all sorts. In twenty-first-century America, both personal relations between blacks and whites and the wider world of law, politics, and the economy have changed in various ways, yet private and public are no less connected than they ever were.

Nowadays, comparatively few white parents want their children to grow up to be racists. Most understand at some level that racism damages the whites, including children, who perpetrate it—something that a study of white children's racial learning in the Jim Crow South makes abundantly clear. Equally promising is the fact that white Americans are finally coming to terms with our nation's past, evident in the recent reexamination of the murders of Medgar Evers and Emmett Till, as well as other civil rights–era atrocities.

But it is far too easy to focus only on the past, to point to the South, to segregation, even to some hazy legacy of slavery, rather than turning an equally unblinking eye on present-day arrangements of race and class. It may be that the child-rearing practices of most white Americans no longer directly reinforce racism, but the fact is that, like the children of Jim Crow, children today learn race by interacting with the world around them as much as from their parents' teachings. As long as racial inequalities do persist, even the most egalitarian lessons of the most committed parents will only go so far. The parent who would never mistreat another human being on the basis of race may not be able to explain away the lessons his or her child may silently draw from comparing white and black neighborhoods, white and black schools, most whites' and blacks' occupations and incomes, and other indicators of social status. If white Americans truly hope to prevent their children from becoming racists, then they must learn to think of racism in broad societal—rather than narrow interpersonal—terms. And they must act accordingly. That is, they must learn to see and decide to redress the racial injustices built into the very structures of our society. "Not being a racist" in the sense of not using the N-word is simply not enough.

Scholars such as George Lipsitz have done much in the last decade or so to expose whites' "possessive investment in whiteness." They have described the extensive and systematic nature of whites' advantages over blacks and other minorities, even in cases where income levels are the same and, often, even when no simple or obvious intention to discriminate can be identified. Such advantages have ranged from whites' better educational opportunities and disproportionate benefits from the GI Bill, to their easier access to home loans through the Federal Housing Authority and other lenders. Meanwhile, whites' greater pull with government agencies has meant that highways and garbage dumps have gone into black rather than white neighborhoods, preserving whites'—but not blacks'—property values.[26] As historian Jacquelyn Hall observes, "In a society where a home represented most families' single most important asset, differential access to mortgages and housing markets and the racial valuation of neighborhoods translated into enormous inequalities" that have been "passed on from generation to generation" in the post-World War II decades.[27] Yet most whites remain ignorant or dismissive about how much they have benefited from the system rather than succeeding only on their own individual merits.

In the fall of 2005, as floodwaters from Hurricane Katrina recede from the city of New Orleans, there are signs that white America is awakening to problems of poverty and racism. Hurricanes may not discriminate, but the fact that far more blacks than whites lacked the transportation and wherewithal to evacuate before the storm did make a difference. What Americans will make of this and other facts emerging from New Orleans remains to be seen. Whatever happens, it will not be only the health and safety and future of black Americans that is at stake, although that ought to be enough. Rather, it will be the future of the nation and the hearts and souls of white and black children, who will or will not continue to learn damaging lessons of race.

Notes

INTRODUCTION

1. Boyle, *Desegregated Heart*, 22–23, 27–28.

2. Kasson, *Rudeness and Civility*; James C. Scott, *Domination and the Arts of Resistance*.

3. Dwight Conquergood provides a very helpful discussion of "the performance paradigm" in "Rethinking Ethnography," 187–91. His discussion of the "critical genealogy" of performance studies in "Ethnography, Rhetoric, and Performance" is also illuminating. Although my heaviest theoretical debts are to James C. Scott, I have also learned much from the works of Clifford Geertz, Erving Goffman, and Victor Turner cited in the bibliography. J. L. Austin's *How to Do Things With Words* is a fascinating work in the philosophy of language that I both enjoyed and found compatible with an overall emphasis on the constitutive, rather than merely descriptive, functions of words and other "speech-acts." More broadly, my interest in everyday life and individual social performance has led to a certain affinity for the ideas of Michel de Certeau, Pierre Bourdieu, and Judith Butler, and I suggest some parallels below. However, my use of words like "performance," "drama," and "script" is largely metaphorical and colloquial, geared toward a general audience and not dependent on, or even necessarily compatible with, these authors' use of these or other terms.

4. Goffman, "Nature of Deference and Demeanor," 55, 54, 53, 52, 53.

5. My analysis of racial etiquette both extends other historians' analyses and moves away from the thinking of the Depression-era social scientists whose discussions of racial "etiquette" seem to have been at least partially responsible for historians' later adoption of the term. The most sustained of these early studies was black sociologist Bertram Wilbur Doyle's 1937 book *The Etiquette of Race Relations in the South*. Psychologist John Dollard also used the word "etiquette" to describe the everyday workings of "caste" in the early 1930s in his influential community study *Caste and Class in a Southern Town*, and Powdermaker, *After Freedom*, and Davis, Gardner, and Gardner, *Deep South*, are also significant works in this vein. More than sixty years later, such works are still valuable, but mainly for the examples and anecdotes they provide. Analytically, Depression-era scholars (with a few notable exceptions, including pioneering black sociologist Charles S. Johnson) were too committed to the goal of cultural assimilation and too afraid of the possibilities of racial conflict to look very far beneath the surface of black and white southerners' etiquette-guided encounters. Instead, these social scientists tended to write as if the fact that most black southerners played their expected roles most of the time meant that they simply accepted

or were resigned to their inferior status. On some of the analytical weaknesses of this literature, see my further discussion in Chapter 1, plus McKee, *Sociology and the Race Problem*, and Rose, "Putting the South on the Psychological Map."

Historians' interpretations of racial etiquette have often drawn on this Depression-era work but have rarely depicted black southerners as so complacent. Instead, observers such as Neil McMillen have recognized that violence was the "instrument in reserve" that compelled black people to follow racial etiquette, at least outwardly, most of the time, no matter how demeaning—or even just confusing—whites' often idiosyncratic expectations might be (McMillen, *Dark Journey*, 28). Meanwhile, McMillen, Robin Kelley, and many others have documented black southerners' ongoing struggles against white dominance, including, in much recent scholarship, their dissemblance in the face of white authority and their oppositional politics of everyday life. For a brief but helpful review of recent historiography, see Gavins, "Literature on Jim Crow."

6. While I find the notion of a "script" useful, I do not mean to overemphasize the extent to which racial etiquette told either black or white southerners how to think, feel, and act at all times. A script is one thing; a performance is another and allows for actors' own conscious and unconscious efforts to shape the drama that, in this extended metaphor, equates to life itself. At minimum, a performance involves the *interpretation* of a script, and it can also involve improvisation or even a total departure from the lines one is expected to say—although, as I will repeatedly emphasize, such departures were never without consequences in the Jim Crow South. Some readers may find it helpful to think about these issues in terms of a structure-versus-agency debate: while I am sympathetic to the poststructuralist position of Judith Butler and others who argue that individual subjects are constructed through performance—that, as Julie Bettie explains, "there is no actor/agent who preexists the performance"— I am not ready to reject the possibility of agency completely. Bettie's allowance for both "performance" and "performativity" is more appealing. In her usage, the former refers to conscious acting on the part of agents; the latter (defined in terms of class but also applicable to race and gender) "to the fact that class subjects are the effects of the social structure of class inequality, caught in unconscious displays of cultural capital that are a consequence of class origins or habitus" (Bettie, *Women Without Class*, 52–53).

Bettie's use of the word "habitus" offers another hook on which to hang my efforts at theoretical clarity: on the one hand, my discussion of racial etiquette as a substantially internalized script learned in childhood bears much resemblance to Pierre Bourdieu's definition of habitus as the "socially constituted system of cognitive and motivating structures" that forms the outlook and sense of possibilities with which one approaches the world. On the other hand, the role of black southerners, and parents in particular, in shaping what we might think of as an alternative habitus in black children's minds cannot be emphasized enough because of the extent to which it kept possibilities for black agency open from one generation to the next. See Bourdieu, *Outline of a Theory of Practice*, 72–95, esp. 76. I am indebted to John Kasson for identifying parallels between my understanding of racial etiquette and Bourdieu's concept of habitus in his comments on my paper for the fall 2004 Porter Fortune Jr. History Symposium at the University of Mississippi. A collection of essays from the symposium, edited by Ted Ownby, is forthcoming from the University Press of Mississippi.

7. Evers, *Evers*, 29–30.

8. Neil Foley's *White Scourge*, Nancy Hewitt's *Southern Discomfort*, and other recent works have demonstrated the importance of understanding some areas of the South in multiracial rather than biracial terms. Nevertheless, throughout the period under study, southern "culture was," as Foley puts it, "black and white" and individuals who did not fit that model in their heritage were usually compelled to fit it in their behavior. See Foley, *White Scourge*, xiii.

9. Evers, *Evers*, 41. Since the early 1990s, historian David Roediger and many others working in a variety of fields have pioneered in the area of "whiteness" studies. I have found much of this work fascinating but sense that my own interest in "whiteness" as part of "white" people's self-understanding is rather narrow in comparison to the broader, and sometimes vague and contradictory, definitions of other authors. As a result, I have tried to limit my use of the term. For an early overview of whiteness studies in history, literature, and other fields, see Fishkin, "Interrogating 'Whiteness.'" For a stiff critique of this scholarship, see Eric Arnesen's "Whiteness and the Historians' Imagination" and the various responses to it in *International Labor and Working-Class History* (Fall 2001): 1–92.

10. My initial understanding of racial etiquette as part of a social process owes much to Joel Williamson's description of "the 'etiquette' of race relations" as the "process" by which "the balance between the needs and power of white people and the needs and power of black people was struck" (Williamson, *Crucible of Race*, 257). Other work that has informed my thinking in this regard includes J. William Harris, "Etiquette, Lynching, and Racial Boundaries," and Dailey, "Deference and Violence."

11. My work for the Behind the Veil: Documenting African American Life in the Jim Crow South oral history project at Duke University introduced me to a wealth of interviews focusing specifically on black life in the Jim Crow era. For information about the project, see Chafe, Gavins, and Korstad, eds., *Remembering Jim Crow*, xviii–xxxv.

Although my initial interest in an early-twentieth-century generation that was already passing dissuaded me from doing any interviews on my own, the incredible variety and intensity of the Behind the Veil materials led me to expand the project's periodization up to World War II and to explore white oral history sources, primarily those of the vast Southern Oral History Program Collection at the University of North Carolina at Chapel Hill.

12. On the tradition of white dissent, see Sosna, *In Search of the Silent South*; Egerton, *Speak Now Against the Day*; and Hobson, *But Now I See*.

13. For an up-to-date overview of autobiographical studies, as well as an argument for using literary memoirs as historical sources for the study of the segregated South, see Wallach, "Remembering Jim Crow."

14. Woodward, *Strange Career of Jim Crow*. All references are to the 1974 edition. On the Woodward thesis, the context in which it was initially presented, and the arguments of its most important critics, see Rabinowitz, "More than the Woodward Thesis"; Cell, *Highest Stage of White Supremacy*, chap. 4; Woodward, "Strange Career of a Historical Controversy"; Woodward, "*Strange Career* Critics"; and Woodward, *Thinking Back*, 81–99.

15. Boyle's article appeared in the *Saturday Evening Post* in February 1955 under the inflammatory title "Southerners Will *Like* Integration," earning her considerable enmity, as well as a measure of fame. On Boyle's conversion and civil rights activities, see Dierenfield, "One 'Desegregated Heart,'" as well as my introduction to the University Press of Virginia reprint edition of *The Desegregated Heart* and my essay "Speaking of Race."

16. Rabinowitz, "More than the Woodward Thesis," 844.

17. On the question of what aspects of life the debate over the Woodward thesis actually addressed, see Rabinowitz, "More than the Woodward Thesis," 847; and Cell, *Highest Stage of White Supremacy*, 94.

18. For the suggestion that Elizabeth Fox-Genovese's *Within the Plantation Household* made a compelling case for the white household as *the* unit of analysis for southern history, see Lebsock, "Complicity and Contention," 60–62. Recent work that focuses explicitly on the relationship between public and private in the post–Civil War South includes Edwards, *Gendered Strife and Confusion*; Bardaglio, *Reconstructing the Household*; and several of the essays in Dailey, Gilmore, and Simon, eds., *Jumpin' Jim Crow*. For earlier periods in southern history, such work is more extensive and includes Kathleen M. Brown, *Good Wives, Nasty Wenches*; Bynum, *Unruly Women*; McCurry, *Masters of Small Worlds*; Faust, *Mothers of Invention*; and Whites, *Civil War as a Crisis in Gender*.

19. Fields, "*Origins of the New South*," 813, 818, 817. Fields, of course, deserves much of the credit for sparking historians' interest in race as a social construction through her earlier essays "Slavery, Race and Ideology" and "Ideology and Race."

20. Goodwyn, "Populist Dreams and Negro Rights," 1446, 1450. I am indebted to Jacquelyn Hall for bringing this article to my attention and helping me think through the relationship between "forgetting" and "repression."

21. Goodwyn, "Populist Dreams and Negro Rights," 1446.

22. On the youth movement within the NAACP, see de Schweinitz, "'If They Could Change the World,'" chap. 5.

23. In the course of my research, I have examined a number of diaries, letters,

school papers, and other sources authored by white southern children of various ages. Most of these sources proved unhelpful on the question of how children understood race, much less the question of how they learned their racial attitudes. Nevertheless, I have listed several archival collections that contain children's writings in the bibliography for the benefit of anyone wishing to pursue future research.

24. Van Ausdale and Feagin, *First R*, 23–24. For a helpful review of major theories of child development, see pp. 4–16.

25. Lipsitz, "Struggle for Hegemony," 147. My subheading on this page is an allusion to Stuart Hall's frequently quoted observation that "hegemonizing is hard work," which Lipsitz quotes on pp. 146 and 147.

26. Dailey, Gilmore, and Simon, eds., *Jumpin' Jim Crow*, 5.

27. Hunter, *To 'Joy My Freedom*, 105.

28. Neil R. McMillen, *Dark Journey*, 23.

29. On segregation in the North and in antebellum cities, see Litwack, *North of Slavery*, and Wade, *Slavery in the Cities*. On segregation as a modern and urban phenomenon, see Cell, *Highest Stage of White Supremacy*, 82–191.

30. Thurber, "Development of the Mammy Image," 96; Hale, *Making Whiteness*, 118.

31. Jacqueline Jones describes the daily lives of the children of household workers in *Labor of Love*, 128–30. See also Hunter's discussion of laundry workers' role in community childcare in *To 'Joy My Freedom*, 62.

32. On "cultural narratives" as "generic stories that recur in a culture," see Maza, "Stories in History," 1495.

33. Hewitt, "Compounding Differences," 315.

34. Du Bois, *Souls of Black Folk*, 3.

35. Barkley Brown, "'What Has Happened Here,'" 298, 300. In a very helpful essay, Rogers Brubaker and Frederick Cooper describe the confusion surrounding the term "identity" in much scholarship and suggest replacing it with other, more straightforward terms. While I have continued to use "identity" in places, I have tried to make it clear that I am most often discussing individuals' sense of self, or what Brubaker and Cooper call both "self-understanding" and "'situated subjectivity': one's sense of who one is, of one's social location, and of how (given the first two) one is prepared to act." Significantly, Brubaker and Cooper note that, although "self-understanding" seems "to privilege cognitive awareness," in fact "self-understanding is never purely cognitive; it is always affectively tinged or charged"—an important element of the term's definition with regard to my discussion of "dramas of socialization" in Chapter 3. See Brubaker and Cooper, "Beyond 'Identity,'" 17–18.

36. Hall, *Revolt Against Chivalry*, 142.

37. Fleischner, *Mastering Slavery*, 20.

CHAPTER ONE

1. The story of Taylor and Mosley's bike ride appeared in the Winston *Free Press* and was reprinted in the Raleigh *News and Observer*, Sept. 22, 1898, p. 3. See also Gilmore, *Gender and Jim Crow*, 102–4 (quotes on 103). On the number of blacks elected to political office in 1896, see p. 78 and p. 260 n. 82.

2. James C. Scott, *Domination and the Arts of Resistance*, p. 2 and passim. See also James C. Scott, *Weapons of the Weak*.

3. Kelley, "'We are Not What We Seem,'" 78.

4. Coclanis, "Slavery, African-American Agency," 882.

5. Dailey, "Deference and Violence," 586.

6. J. William Harris, "Etiquette, Lynching, and Racial Boundaries," 388.

7. Both Reconstruction and disfranchisement have been the subjects of entire scholarly literatures, but some of the most important works include Foner, *Reconstruction*; Kousser, *Shaping of Southern Politics*; and Perman, *Struggle for Mastery*.

8. Atlanta's black population rose from 1,939 in 1860 to 28,098 in 1890, and the percentage of blacks in the city's population rose from 20 to 43 percent. In Nashville, the increases in this period were from 3,945 to 29,395 black residents and from 23 to 39 percent. See Rabinowitz, *Race Relations in the Urban South*, 18–19.

9. Litwack, *Trouble in Mind*, 482.

10. Migration and population statistics are from Dernoral Davis, "Toward a Socio-Historical and Demographic Portrait," 10–11.

11. J. William Harris, "Etiquette, Lynching, and Racial Boundaries," 390.

12. Kyriakoudes, "'Lookin' for Better All the Time,'" 21–22.

13. In fact, I would argue that there is no such thing as a perfect or truly effective form of hegemony. I tend to agree with James Scott's critique of hegemony as a concept. Scott acknowledges that subordinate groups' failure to challenge authority in organized and systematic ways may make it seem that they either consent to or are resigned to their oppression. The fact that subordinates' protests are limited does not, however, mean that their sense of grievance is also limited. Instead, unless they are willing to declare all-out war on their oppressors, they deliberately couch even direct opposition to authority in strategic terms "in the realistic expectation that the central features of the form of domination will remain intact" (James C. Scott, *Domination and the Arts of Resistance*, 70–107; quotation on 92). Also helpful is Lipsitz, "Struggle for Hegemony."

14. "Carleton" to *Boston Journal*, February 13, 1865, reprinted in *National Freedman* 1 (April 1, 1865): 83; quoted in Litwack, *Been in the Storm So Long*, 255.

15. Reid, *After the War*, 84.

16. Rawick, ed., *American Slave*, pt. 1, 351.

17. Forten, *Journal of Charlotte Forten*, 157.

18. Litwack, *Been in the Storm So Long*, 252.

19. Chesnut, *Diary from Dixie*, 532.
20. Eliza Frances Andrews, *War-Time Journal of a Georgia Girl*, 346–47.
21. On the increased use of "nigger," see Litwack, *Been in the Storm So Long*, 254–55.
22. Bertram Wilbur Doyle's *Etiquette of Race Relations* remains the most comprehensive overview of the codes of racial etiquette both during and after slavery. I am, for the most part, following Doyle's descriptions, which were based on travelers' reports, memoirs, and other writings. However, I have found it essential to go back to Doyle's original sources whenever possible because he was not always careful to distinguish between slaveholders and nonslaveholders, southerners and northerners, slaves and free blacks. I also disagree with his interpretations of evidence in many respects, some of which are noted in this chapter. Doyle discusses racial etiquette during slavery on pp. 1–108.

   Historical works that have influenced my thinking on racial etiquette and/or guided me to valuable primary sources include the articles by J. William Harris and Jane Dailey cited above and Genovese, *Roll, Jordan, Roll*; Litwack, *Been in the Storm So Long*; Litwack, *Trouble in Mind*; Neil R. McMillen, *Dark Journey*; Hall, *Revolt Against Chivalry*; Gilmore, *Gender and Jim Crow*; and Williamson, *Crucible of Race*. I have also learned much from Depression-era social science literature, cited below.
23. Olmsted, *Journey in the Back Country*, 168.
24. Kasson, *Rudeness and Civility*, 182.
25. Clayton, *White and Black*, 65–66.
26. Doyle, *Etiquette of Race Relations*, 2.
27. Douglass, *Narrative*, 40.
28. All three examples can be found in Osofsky, *Puttin' on Ole Massa*, 22–23. On slaves' practice of dissemblance, see also Levine, *Black Culture and Black Consciousness*.
29. On slaves' ambivalence toward troublemakers, see Genovese, *Roll, Jordan, Roll*, 625–30.
30. Wilma King, *Stolen Childhood*, 70–71. On slaves' childhoods, see also Schwartz, *Born in Bondage*, and Mintz, *Huck's Raft*, chap. 5.
31. Painter, "Soul Murder and Slavery," 133–34.
32. Genovese, *Roll, Jordan, Roll*, 511. Litwack makes a similar point about good manners as respect for all elders, black and white, in *Trouble in Mind*, 42.
33. Douglass, *Narrative*, 53–54.
34. Berlin, *Slaves Without Masters*, 320.
35. Lebsock, *Free Women of Petersburg*, 93.
36. Lane, *Narrative*, 31.
37. On free blacks' vulnerability and whites' fears, see Berlin, *Slaves Without Masters*, esp. 188–89; and Lebsock, *Free Women of Petersburg*, 92–93.
38. Litwack, *Been in the Storm So Long*, 257.
39. Reid, *After the War*, 419–20.

40. Ibid., 420 n.

41. Dr. James Watson of Rockbridge County, Virginia, murdered a black man who accidentally drove into his buggy. After brooding about the accident for a day, Watson sought the man out with the intention of beating him with his cane, a punishment he considered appropriate for an inferior. The man refused to accept the beating and ran. Watson then shot him. See Taylor, *Negro in the Reconstruction of Virginia*, 25–26, 83.

42. Reid, *After the War*, 352; Taylor, *Negro in the Reconstruction of Virginia*, 83.

43. Hall, *Revolt Against Chivalry*, 141–42, 148 (quote on 142).

44. Clifton Johnson, *Highways and Byways*, 331.

45. Neil R. McMillen, *Dark Journey*, 24.

46. Litwack, *Been in the Storm So Long*, 253.

47. Reid, *After the War*, 568–69.

48. William Wells Brown, *My Southern Home*, 245–46.

49. Neil R. McMillen, *Dark Journey*, 24.

50. Mays, *Born to Rebel*, 8.

51. Blassingame, ed., *Slave Testimony*, 653.

52. William Wells Brown, *My Southern Home*, 246–47.

53. On the "notoriously low" official estimates of the number killed in the Atlanta riot, see Godshalk, "In the Wake of Riot," 39. On the riot in general, see two new books: Godshalk's *Veiled Visions* and Mixon, *Atlanta Riot*.

54. Baker, *Following the Color Line*, 8.

55. Rosengarten, *All God's Dangers*, 425.

56. On antebellum white southerners' greater tolerance for sexual relations between white women and black men, see Genovese, *Roll, Jordan, Roll*, 422; Hodes, *White Women, Black Men*; and Rothman, *Notorious in the Neighborhood*. Two recent books, Charles F. Robinson's *Dangerous Liaisons* and Lisa Lindquist Dorr's *White Women, Rape, and the Power of Race*, argue persuasively that whites' enforcement of prohibitions against interracial sex, including their enforcement of rape laws in cases involving white women and black men, was less absolute even in the postbellum South than whites' own rape-lynch mythology would have us believe. Much depended on circumstances, such as the degree of openness in an established relationship or the class and character of the alleged rape victim and her alleged assailant. Nevertheless, that the taboo against interracial sex grew stronger after emancipation is not in dispute.

57. Clifton Johnson, *Highways and Byways*, 352.

58. For example, see Hunter, *To 'Joy My Freedom*, 105.

59. Clayton, *White and Black*, 171–72.

60. Charles S. Johnson, *Growing Up in the Black Belt*, 319. For an earlier example of relationships that challenged racial etiquette, see Beulah S. Hester's description of black-white relations in Oxford, North Carolina, in the 1910s in Hill, ed., *Black Women Oral History Project*, 5:340–43. For a discussion of rural black and

white women's interpersonal relations, see Jones, "Encounters, Likely and Unlikely."

61. White Springs *Messenger*, reprinted in *The Crisis* 1 (November 1910): 8.

62. For examples of white restaurants and lunch counters selling to blacks, see Doyle, *Etiquette of Race Relations*, 146–47.

63. My discussion of blacks' experiences as consumers owes much to Hale, *Making Whiteness*, 168–97. On country stores, see pp. 172–76.

64. Davis, Gardner, and Gardner, *Deep South*, 22–23.

65. Quoted in Porter, "Black Atlanta," 21–22. See also Doyle, *Etiquette of Race Relations*, 153; and Hale, *Making Whiteness*, 190–91.

66. Bauman, "Youthful Musings," 46. On some blacks' patronage of Chinese merchants, see Hale, *Making Whiteness*, 189.

67. Both quotes are from Porter, "Black Atlanta," 20–21.

68. Charles S. Johnson, *Patterns of Negro Segregation*, 65.

69. Doyle, *Etiquette of Race Relations*, 145.

70. Baker, *Following the Color Line*, 64.

71. Doyle, *Etiquette of Race Relations*, 145.

72. Clifton Johnson, *Highways and Byways*, 352.

73. Williamson, *Crucible of Race*, 350–51.

74. Bailey, *Race Orthodoxy in the South*, 368.

75. Quoted in Litwack, *Been in the Storm So Long*, 254.

76. Quoted in Litwack, *Trouble in Mind*, 333.

77. For Blake's story, see William Pickens to Rev. James M. Hinton, July 27, 1939, in *Papers of the NAACP*, pt. 12, 530–31.

78. Arthur F. and Martha J. Raper, "Two Years to Remember," unpublished typescript, box 32, vol. 12, pp. 71–72, in the Arthur Franklin Raper Papers #3966, Southern Historical Collection, Wilson Library, University of North Carolina at Chapel Hill. Thanks to Cliff Kuhn for directing me to this source.

79. For examples of whites forcing well-dressed black men to change clothes, see Doyle, *Etiquette of Race Relations*, 155; and Litwack, *Trouble in Mind*, 331.

80. Mamie Garvin Fields, *Lemon Swamp*, 72.

81. Litwack, *Trouble in Mind*, 335.

82. Quoted in Neil R. McMillen, *Dark Journey*, 25.

83. Wright, "Ethics of Living Jim Crow," 14–15.

84. Boyle, *Desegregated Heart*, 26.

85. Genovese, *Roll, Jordan, Roll*, 115.

86. Evers, *Evers*, 169–70. See also Neil R. McMillen, *Dark Journey*, 26–27.

87. On Doyle's belief in the "race relations cycle" outlined by Robert E. Park and Ernest W. Burgess, see Jaworski, "Park, Doyle, and Hughes," 162–65. James B. McKee emphasizes sociologists' strong preference for accommodation over conflict, noting that Park was an exception but most of his students were not. See McKee, *Sociology and the Race Problem*, esp. 134–37.

88. Doyle was born in Lowndesboro, Alabama, on July 3, 1897. He served as an instructor of sociology and psychology at various black colleges in the 1920s and 1930s and received a Ph.D. in sociology from the University of Chicago in 1934. He was also an ordained minister of the Colored Methodist Episcopal Church. For biographical information, see Yenser, ed., *Who's Who in Colored America*, 165; and Burkett, Burkett, and Gates, eds., *Black Biography*, 370.

89. Doyle, *Etiquette of Race Relations*, 144, 157–58, 159.

90. Wright, *Black Boy*, 218.

91. Ayers, *Promise of the New South*, 155, 158.

92. Neil R. McMillen, *Dark Journey*, 29.

93. Cell, *Highest Stage of White Supremacy*, 133.

94. Clifton Johnson, *Highways and Byways*, 352.

95. Powdermaker, *After Freedom*, 43, 44, 45, 51.

96. On the relationship between Powdermaker and Dollard, see Rose, "Putting the South on the Psychological Map," 346–50, and Fraser, "Race, Class, and Difference," 404, 413 n. 2. On Dollard's time in Mississippi, see Ferris, "John Dollard." My discussion of Dollard's greater influence on sociological scholarship also owes much to McKee, *Sociology and the Race Problem*, chap. 4.

97. Dollard, *Caste and Class*, 185, 343.

98. McKee (*Sociology and the Race Problem*, 173) notes that "*Caste and Class in a Southern Town* and *Deep South*, in that order, were the more influential" of the community studies published in the late 1930s and early 1940s.

99. Davis, Gardner, and Gardner, *Deep South*, chap. 21.

100. Charles S. Johnson, *Growing Up in the Black Belt*, 326–27. Johnson developed his perspective on racial conflict and the probability of change in a number of works, including *Shadow of the Plantation* and *Patterns of Negro Segregation*. On Johnson, see McKee, *Sociology and the Race Problem*, 149–51, 170–71, 192–94, 224.

101. Powdermaker, *After Freedom*, esp. chap. 16.

102. Dollard, *Caste and Class*, 9, 349–50. Rose notes that Dollard "seemed overwhelmed by the South." See Rose, "Putting the South on the Psychological Map," 352.

103. That Powdermaker identified more fully with blacks than whites during her stay in Indianola seems to be the import of Patricia Aylward Farr's oral history research in "Key Informants in Cottonville." See also Rose, "Putting the South on the Psychological Map," 340–41.

CHAPTER TWO

1. Clifton Johnson, *Highways and Byways*, 331–32. The title of this chapter comes from "You've Got To Be Carefully Taught," the title of a satirical song about racism from the musical *South Pacific*, music by Richard Rodgers and lyrics by Oscar Hammerstein II (1949).

2. Quinn, "Transmission of Racial Attitudes," 45.

3. Boyle, *Desegregated Heart*, 28.

4. See Higginbotham, *Righteous Discontent*. Higginbotham deserves much of the credit for the recent interest in respectability and racial "uplift" in African American history. As Michele Mitchell argues in a helpful review essay, even though other scholars "had already written on the significance of controlled morality to the black elite and to nationalists, it was Higginbotham who provided analytical language that would guide future work" (Mitchell, "Silences Broken, Silences Kept," 437).

5. Gaines, *Uplifting the Race*, xiv.

6. For more favorable views of black middle-class respectability, see Higginbotham, *Righteous Discontent*; Gilmore, *Gender and Jim Crow*; and Shaw, *What a Woman Ought to Be*.

7. Taking a pragmatic view, I appreciate the insights of Deborah Gray White (*Too Heavy a Load*, 270 n. 11), who wisely emphasizes the material and political consequences of the other-directed ideology of racial "uplift" rather than focusing on "respectability," which I think is best understood as a self-directed strategy and set of beliefs held by individuals and groups. The ideology of racial uplift was "as heartening as it was crippling," White argues. "On the one hand, uplift stressed racial solidarity, where those with means helped those without it. . . . However, as heroic as was this emphasis on self-reliance, uplift also marked a capitulation to racism. When black people picked up the burdens that white racism, violence, and negative stereotypes thrust upon them, they accommodated white exclusionary practices. They tacitly, and perhaps unwittingly, surrendered not only those basic civil and political rights enjoyed by white Americans but rights that were needed to maintain economic self-sufficiency."

8. Ryan, *Cradle of the Middle Class*. For a concise discussion of the shift to the "sheltered childhood" ideal, see Macleod, *Age of the Child*, as well as Mintz, *Huck's Raft*, chap. 4. The literature in the history of childhood is growing steadily. For a useful review essay that crosses national borders, see Cunningham, "Histories of Childhood." On p. 1206, Cunningham describes the general trend I am discussing as "the most fundamental shift in the experience of childhood, from one where nearly all children expected to contribute to the family economy at an early age to one where they were a net drain on that economy throughout their childhood and youth."

9. Zelizer, *Pricing the Priceless Child*, 11.

10. Mintz, *Huck's Raft*, 76–79.

11. Macleod, *Age of the Child*, 31.

12. On regional differences in family size, see Macleod, *Age of the Child*, 4–5. For a recent work on the struggle to end child labor in southern textile mills, see Sallee, *Whiteness of Child Labor Reform*. Mill workers and other industrial child laborers were, of course, a small minority in the South compared to the number of children who worked on farms. Unfortunately, census figures provide little

clue as to how large the total number of child workers actually was, since, as Macleod observes,

> the census counted no workers under age 10, nor did it count children who attended school, even though most spent far more time at farm work. Setting the 1900 and 1910 census dates for April . . . guaranteed that enumerators would fail to count many children about to embark on months of hard work. Instructions in 1900 and 1910 not to count "children working for their parents at chores, errands, or general housework" invited enumerators to dismiss girls' efforts as "housework" and boys' as "chores." . . . The safest conclusion is that child labor in the sense of reasonably hard, sustained work was much more widespread than the census recognized. (Macleod, *Age of the Child*, 110–11)

For more on black and white southern children's work experiences, see Chapter 5.

13. Dernoral Davis, "Toward a Socio-Historical and Demographic Portrait," 11.
14. For examples of blacks citing education for their children as a motivation for migrating, see Grossman, *Land of Hope*, 36.
15. Margo, *Race and Schooling in the South*, 9–18. Quotations are from p. 11 and p. 13.
16. The literature on women's associations in this period is extensive. For an introduction, see Anne Firor Scott, *Natural Allies*. Scott stresses the similarities between southern women's organizations and those in other parts of the country, arguing, "There is no case to be made for southern exceptionalism from the voluntary association evidence" (195 n. 32). On women's extension of conventional gender roles into the public sphere, see Paula Baker, "Domestication of Politics."
17. Roth, *Matronage*, 5. In *To Raise Up the South*, Sally G. McMillen describes the Sunday school movement in the post–Civil War South as part of the same trend toward greater emphasis on education and the sheltered childhood.
18. "Mrs. Walker's Fine Work," *Atlanta Constitution*, April 11, 1925, clipping in series 3, box 44, no. 461, Laura Spelman Rockefeller Memorial Papers, Rockefeller Archive Center, North Tarrytown, N.Y. Box 44 also contains transcripts of radio talks given by Martha I. McAlpine, the child study specialist hired for the program, and a 1929 report on her work.
19. Hagood, *Mothers of the South*, 137.
20. Quoted in Macleod, *Age of the Child*, 53.
21. Quoted in Grant, *Raising Baby by the Book*, 80.
22. *Atlanta University Publications*, no. 3, "Some Efforts of American Negroes for Their Own Social Betterment," 46.
23. On the Neighborhood Union, see Rouse, *Lugenia Burns Hope*; Shivery, "History of Organized Social Work"; Ross, "Black Heritage in Social Welfare"; Neverdon-Morton, *Afro-American Women of the South*, 139–63; and Lasch-Quinn, *Black Neighbors*, 113–26.

24. Lasch-Quinn, *Black Neighbors*, 120.

25. Bolsterli, *Born in the Delta*, 74–75.

26. Smith, *Killers of the Dream*, 26.

27. Johnston, "I Met a Little Blue-Eyed Girl."

28. Wilkins, "Two Against 5,000," 169.

29. Catledge, "My Life and 'The Times,'" 83–84.

30. Coralie Cook, "The Problem of the Colored Child," speech given at the Annual Meeting of the NAACP, May 4, 1914, in *Papers of the NAACP*, pt. 1, reel 8, frames 0249–69; Du Bois, "True Brownies"; Martin Luther King Jr., *Why We Can't Wait*, 69.

31. Sallee, *Whiteness of Child Labor Reform*, 4, 99.

32. Cox, *Dixie's Daughters*, 123.

33. Fred Arthur Bailey, "Textbooks of the 'Lost Cause,'" 508.

34. For an introduction to scholarship on antiblack racism in children's literature, see Broderick, *Image of the Black in Children's Fiction*; MacCann, *White Supremacy in Children's Literature*; and MacCann and Woodard, eds., *Black American in Books for Children*.

35. Sally G. McMillen, *To Raise Up the South*, 247–48. On the history of black Sunday school publishing, see esp. pp. 96–99.

36. Thomas Pearce Bailey, *Race Orthodoxy in the South*, 86.

37. Lasker, *Race Attitudes in Children*, 35.

38. Powdermaker, *After Freedom*, 31.

39. Thomas Pearce Bailey, *Race Orthodoxy in the South*, 86.

40. Maddox, *Speaking Out*, 2.

41. Quotations are from Dorothy Markey interview, from the Southern Oral History Program Collection, Manuscripts Department, Southern Historical Collection, University of North Carolina at Chapel Hill (hereafter SOHP); transcript, 14, 19. For one example of a white southerner who describes his parents as being free of racial prejudice, see Eugene Epperson Barnett, "As I Look Back: Recollections of Growing Up in America's Southland and of Twenty-Six Years in Pre-Communist China, 1888–1936," in Eugene Epperson Barnett Papers, #3669-z, Southern Historical Collection, Wilson Library, University of North Carolina at Chapel Hill; typescript, 21.

42. Smith, *Killers of the Dream*, 28.

43. On Smith's "southern-Calvinistic" upbringing, see Loveland, *Lillian Smith*, 6. Other quotations in this paragraph are from Smith, *Killers of the Dream*, 87, 90, 31, 32.

44. Boyle, *Desegregated Heart*, 23 and chap. 3 passim.

45. Ibid., 34, 35.

46. Carter, *Hour Before Daylight*, 20.

47. Holsey, "Learning How to Be Black," 423.

48. See Allen et al., *Without Sanctuary*. Based on Allen's notes on the plates, the 98

photographs in this volume represent 63 separate lynchings, at least 28 of which took place in the South (defined as the eleven states of the former Confederacy) between 1889 and 1960. All but 5 of these 28 took place before 1920, although several of the dates are approximate. White children appear in photographs 9, 10, 20, 22, 23, 24, 54, and 56. Figures in photographs 12 and 93 also appear to be quite young but were not counted as children. It is also worth noting that white children appear in photographs of 5 lynchings that took place outside the South in Oklahoma, Montana, Illinois, and Nebraska; see photographs 18, 33, 38, 49, 51, 52, and 97. Three photographs from unknown locations also include white children; see photographs 2 (possibly from Texas), 15 (possibly from Georgia), and 79.

49. Allen et al., *Without Sanctuary*, photograph 57 and notes, p. 185. Note that photograph 57 is a mirror image of the photograph that appears on p. 73. My source for the photograph included text, indicating its proper orientation. I cannot account for why the *Without Sanctuary* photograph appears in reverse.

50. My account of the Stacey lynching, including the spelling of Stacey's and Jones's names, follows Howard, *Lynchings*, 74–81. Quotations are on p. 75.

51. Lumpkin, *Making of a Southerner*, 86–87.

52. Ovington, "Revisiting the South," 61. Ovington's anecdote was drawn from her earlier visit, circa 1906.

53. Clipping from Florence, S.C., *Times*, reprinted in *Atlanta University Publications*, no. 18, "Morals and Manners Among Negro Americans," n.p.

54. Johnston, "I Met a Little Blue-Eyed Girl."

55. Litwack, *Trouble in Mind*, 287–88.

56. Allen et al., *Without Sanctuary*, photograph 25 and notes, pp. 173–74 and 187–90. On the lynching of Jesse Washington, see Bernstein, *First Waco Horror*.

57. Dollard, *Caste and Class*, 342.

58. On the door-to-door sale of lynching postcards, see Allen et al., *Without Sanctuary*, 180.

59. Mell Marshall Barrett, "Recollections of My Boyhood: The Picnic at Pitman's Mill," quoted in Ayers, *Promise of the New South*, 159.

60. Quinn, "Transmission of Racial Attitudes," 43–44.

61. Ibid., 43.

62. Jesse Daniel Ames interview, SOHP; transcript, 1.

63. Lumpkin, *Making of a Southerner*, 132–33.

64. Ibid., 137.

65. Ibid., 132.

66. Ibid., 132.

67. Doyle, *Etiquette of Race Relations in the South*, 161.

68. Quinn, "Transmission of Racial Attitudes," 46 n. 5.

69. Lumpkin, *Making of a Southerner*, 132.

70. Quinn, "Transmission of Racial Attitudes," 43.

71. On southerners' devotion to courtesy, see Wilson, "Manners," 634–37. On manners and white southern child rearing, see Cook, "Growing Up White."

72. I am paraphrasing parental explanations that appear in Coles, "It's the Same, but It's Different," 1117; and in Quinn, "Transmission of Racial Attitudes," 42–43. There are, of course, other examples I could cite.

73. Barnard, ed., *Outside the Magic Circle*, 18.

74. Killian, *Black and White*, 9.

75. Barnard, ed., *Outside the Magic Circle*, 19.

76. Quinn, "Transmission of Racial Attitudes," 42–43.

77. Lasker, *Race Attitudes in Children*, 111.

78. Arthur F. and Martha J. Raper, "Two Years to Remember," unpublished typescript, box 32, vol. 12, pp. 103, 71–72, in Arthur Franklin Raper Papers #3966, Southern Historical Collection, Wilson Library, University of North Carolina at Chapel Hill.

79. Quinn, "Transmission of Racial Attitudes," 46.

80. Boyle, *Desegregated Heart*, 14.

81. Marguirite DeLaine interview from Behind the Veil: Documenting African-American Life in the Jim Crow South Collection, Center for Documentary Studies at Duke University, Rare Book, Manuscript, and Special Collections Library, Duke University, Durham, N.C. (hereafter BTV), transcript, 17. Note that all direct quotations from Behind the Veil interviews are based on the audio tapes; quotation from the transcripts is prohibited because the transcripts have not been verified. Nonetheless, because the transcripts are also available in the Duke University collection, I have provided transcript page numbers for the convenience of anyone wishing to pursue further research in these sources. In cases where transcript pages were not numbered, I have added page numbers, counting title pages (if included) as page one.

82. Ernest Swain interview, BTV; transcript, 32–33.

83. White, *Too Heavy a Load*, 26.

84. Gilmore, *Gender and Jim Crow*, xix.

85. On the complexities of defining class among African Americans in the late nineteenth and early twentieth centuries, see Gilmore, *Gender and Jim Crow*, xviii–xix. I tend to use "middle-class" broadly to describe both the "educated, middling black men and women" whom Gilmore defines as middle-class and the "talented tenth" or "aristocrats of color" whom some studies usefully distinguish as an "elite" or "upper-class" group.

86. Quoted in Porter, "Black Atlanta," 21. For another black family's strategy for handling the lack of public bathrooms and other facilities, see Mae Massie Eberhardt, interview by Marcia M. Greenlee, in Hill, ed., *Black Women Oral History Project*, 3:262–63.

87. Dittmer, *Black Georgia in the Progressive Era*, 17. On the Atlanta streetcar boycott, see Meier and Rudwick, "Boycott Movement."

88. The literature on black middle-class respectability and racial uplift has grown considerably in recent years. See Higginbotham, *Righteous Discontent*; Shaw, *What a Woman Ought to Be*; Gaines, *Uplifting the Race*; White, *Too Heavy a Load*; and Summers, *Manliness and Its Discontents*.

89. Higginbotham quotes Burroughs and makes essentially the same point about self-definition, though without the emphasis on children, in *Righteous Discontent*, 191.

90. Quoted in Giddings, *When and Where I Enter*, 100. Giddings points out that the worsened situation of blacks at the turn of the twentieth century made club-women less optimistic about their ability to end racism by raising respectable children than black leaders such as Maria Stewart had been decades before.

91. William J. Coker Jr. interview, BTV; transcript, 20, 6, 28, 18–19, 38. See also Chafe, Gavins, and Korstad, eds., *Remembering Jim Crow*, 133.

92. Dorcas Carter interview, BTV; transcript, 21.

93. Ibid., 2, 63.

94. Rosita Taylor interview, BTV; transcript, 23.

95. Shaw, *What a Woman Ought to Be*, 16.

96. Septima Clark interview, SOHP; transcript, 18.

97. Norma Boyd, interview by A. Lillian Thompson, in Hill, ed., *Black Women Oral History*, 2:241. See also Shaw, *What a Woman Ought to Be*, 17.

98. Delany and Delany, *Having Our Say*, 72.

99. Dorcas Carter interview, BTV; transcript, 21; Beulah Hester, interview by Felicia Bowen, in Hill, ed., *Black Women Oral History Project*, 5:361. For an excellent discussion of black adults' concerns about their daughter's sexuality and the danger of sexual exploitation, see Shaw, *What a Woman Ought to Be*, 23–26.

100. Barbara Cooper, joint interview with Edgar Allen Hunt and John David Cooper, BTV; transcript, 6.

101. Gatewood, *Aristocrats of Color*, 191.

102. Holtzclaw, *Black Man's Burden*, 18–19. On how slave children were fed, see Genovese, *Roll, Jordan, Roll*, 507.

103. Holtzclaw, *Black Man's Burden*, 25, 28.

104. Ila Blue interview, BTV; transcript, 22.

105. Georgia Bays interview, BTV; transcript, 51, 10.

106. Ibid., 50–62. Quotations are from 56–57, 54, 62, 58, 59, 61.

107. Litwack, *Trouble in Mind*, 42.

108. Evers, *Evers*, 52.

109. Holtzclaw, *Black Man's Burden*, 21–24.

110. Georgia Bays, BTV; transcript, 49.

111. Olivia Cherry interview, BTV; transcript, 17.

112. Florence Borders interview, BTV; transcript, 6.

113. Herbert Cappie interview, BTV; transcript, 2.

114. Mazie Williams interview, BTV; transcript, 8–10.

115. Quoted in Litwack, *Been in the Storm So Long*, 10.

116. "National Association of Colored Women," 311.

117. On the Negro Young People's Christian and Educational Congress, which attracted some 7,000 delegates to Atlanta in 1902, see Matthews, "Dilemma of Negro Leadership." Matthews is mistaken when he says that the NYPCE Congress met only once. It met again in Washington, D.C., in 1906. See I. Garland Penn, *Souvenir; Official Program and Music of the Negro Young People's Christian and Educational Congress* (Washington, D.C.: n.p., 1906), in Schomburg Center for Research in Black Culture, New York Public Library.

118. *Atlanta University Publications*, no. 18, "Morals and Manners Among Negro Americans," 135, 5, 12.

119. Although it does provide an occupational breakdown, "Morals and Manners Among Negro Americans" does not identify the survey respondents by race, nor do Du Bois and Dill indicate whether the 4,000 surveys they initially sent out went only or mostly to blacks. However, some internal evidence suggests that the majority of the respondents were black or at least that Du Bois and Dill felt justified in using the survey as an index of black attitudes, and in this I have followed their lead. For example, Du Bois and Dill's conclusion describes the race as "self-conscious" and "self-critical" on the basis of the study's evidence. Also, some survey responses include such phrases as "our people," indicating the respondent's race. Nevertheless, the evidence is less clear than I would like.

120. "Morals and Manners Among Negro Americans," 135.

121. Ibid., 82, 89. Du Bois and Dill printed responses from ten of the eleven former Confederate states, excluding North Carolina. Assuming that each indented line in their text represented a separate response, there were 87 responses, of which 59 included some sort of negative content.

122. Ibid., 90, 82.

123. Ibid., 85, 88, 82.

124. Ibid., 89, 84, 82.

125. Ibid., 82–83.

126. Ibid., 88.

127. Allison Davis, "Socialization of the American Negro Child," 270.

128. Quoted in Litwack, *Trouble in Mind*, 37.

129. Lester "Jack" Bullock interview, BTV; transcript, 39.

130. Evers, *Evers*, 29, 39.

131. Litwack, *Trouble in Mind*, 37.

132. Quoted in Litwack, *Trouble in Mind*, 40.

133. Hurston, *Dust Tracks on a Road*, 13–14.

134. Kelley, "'We Are Not What We Seem,'" 82.

135. Powdermaker, *After Freedom*, 210–12.

136. Margo (*Race and Schooling*, 9, 11) notes that, in the early twentieth century, black girls attended school more frequently than black boys and young black

females' literacy rate was higher than young black males', reversing the trend seen among older blacks.

137. Powdermaker, *After Freedom*, 212.
138. Ibid., 215, 218–19, 216.
139. Levine, *Black Culture and Black Consciousness*, 370.
140. Ibid., 120.
141. Ibid., 379–80.
142. Edgar Allen Hunt, joint interview with Barbara Cooper and John David Cooper, BTV; transcript, 5, 169–70.
143. Mamie Garvin Fields, *Lemon Swamp*, 46.
144. Lugenia Burns Hope, "Family Life as a Determinant in Racial Attitudes of Children," typescript speech in the Neighborhood Union Collection, Woodruff Library, Atlanta University Center, Atlanta. See also Rouse, *Lugenia Burns Hope*, 32–33.
145. "Morals and Manners Among Negro Americans," 7–8.

CHAPTER THREE

1. Walter White, *Man Called White*, 11.
2. Ibid., 11–12.
3. Ibid., 5, 13.
4. Holt, "Marking," 2.
5. Hall, "'You Must Remember This,'" 440.
6. Presumably, one cannot remember "correctly" that which one experienced partially and subjectively in the first place. See Joan Scott, "Evidence of Experience," and Hall, "'You Must Remember This,'" 440.
7. Gaines, *Uplifting the Race*, 47, 51; White, *Man Called White*, 12.
8. Painter, "'Social Equality,'" 53.
9. Murray, *Song in a Weary Throat*, 28–36.
10. Du Bois, *Souls of Black Folk*, 2.
11. Ibid., 2–3.
12. Ibid., 3.
13. Ibid., 4.
14. Terrell, *Colored Woman in a White World*, 22–23.
15. Ibid., 23. J. William Harris briefly discusses the symbolism of hats and offers a number of references in "Etiquette, Lynching, and Racial Boundaries," 391 n. 21.
16. On "cutting," see Kasson, *Rudeness and Civility*, 145.
17. Terrell, *Colored Woman in a White World*, 23.
18. Dernoral Davis, "Toward a Socio-Historical and Demographic Portrait," 11.
19. Wright, *Black Boy*, 18–21.
20. Ibid., 27–28.
21. Ibid., 54–57.
22. Ibid., 86–87.

23. Wright biographer Michel Fabre notes that "Although *Black Boy* was designed to describe the effects of racism on a black child, which meant omitting incidents tending to exonerate white persons in any way, there is no doubt that the Walls were liberal and generous employers. . . . Since they respected his qualities as an individual, [Wright] sometimes submitted his problems and plans to them and soon considered their house a second home where he met with more understanding than from his own family" (*Unfinished Quest*, 46–47).

24. Simonsen, ed., *You May Plow Here*, 131, 91–92.

25. Ibid., 62–63.

26. Delaney and Delaney, *Having Our Say*, 95–96.

27. Mamie Garvin Fields, *Lemon Swamp*, 47–48.

28. Ibid., 51–52.

29. Terrell, *Colored Woman in a White World*, 15.

30. In fact, as Stanley J. Folmsbee pointed out in a 1949 article, what is often described as the South's first Jim Crow law was actually less discriminatory, in some ways, than the 1875 law it replaced. That law had released "innkeepers, common carriers, and proprietors of places of amusement" from "any obligation to entertain, carry or admit, any person, whom [they] shall for any reason whatever, choose not to entertain, carry or admit." In 1880 in a case involving a Memphis railroad, a federal circuit court found this 1875 law to be unconstitutional in areas where it conflicted with federal regulation of interstate commerce. The four black members of the Tennessee House of Representatives then initiated a repeal effort in the 1881 session but failed to achieve their goal. Meanwhile, a bill originating in the Senate passed, requiring "separate cars, or portions of cars cut off by partition walls" in which blacks who purchased first-class tickets were supposed to find "the same conveniences" and enforcement of "the same rules governing other first-class cars, preventing smoking and obscene language." See Folmsbee, "Origin of the First 'Jim Crow' Law." Quotations are from 236, 240.

31. Terrell, *Colored Woman in a White World*, 15–16.

32. Ibid., 16.

33. Simonsen, ed., *You May Plow Here*, 90–91.

34. McLaurin, *Separate Pasts*, 36–41.

35. On white southerners' "rage to explain," see Hobson, *Tell About the South*.

36. Melton McLaurin points out that the majority of southern autobiographies, black and white, that have appeared from national and academic presses since 1940 "rejected racism." Exceptions are Percy's *Lanterns on the Levee* and Robertson's *Red Hills and Cotton*. See McLaurin, "Rituals of Initiation and Rebellion," 24 n. 4.

37. Lumpkin, *Making of a Southerner*, 133–34.

38. Boyle, *Desegregated Heart*, 22.

39. Dabbs, *Southern Heritage*, 11.

40. Boyle, *Desegregated Heart*, 35.

41. Smith, *Killers of the Dream*, 27–28.
42. Ibid., 34–38. Smith recounted the same story, calling the African American girl "Julie" rather than "Janie," in "Growing Into Freedom," 50–51.
43. Smith, *Killers of the Dream*, 30.
44. For more on this point, see Eakin, *Touching the World*, 30.
45. Fleischner, *Mastering Slavery*, 20–21.
46. McLaurin, *Separate Pasts*, 41.
47. Smith, *Killers of the Dream*, 38.
48. Boyle, *Desegregated Heart*, 22.
49. Janken, *White*, 17–18.
50. Walter White, *Man Called White*, 19.
51. Ibid., 19–20.
52. In his autobiography, White noted that, by the age of twelve or thirteen, he had read and reread his family's small collection of books, which included Shakespeare, Dickens, Thackeray, Trollope, and some of the Harvard Classics. See Walter White, *Man Called White*, 18.
53. Ibid., 20.
54. *Atlanta Constitution*, August 10, 1906.
55. Ray Stannard Baker reported that 1,011 boys and girls under the age of sixteen were arrested in 1905. Of those, 819 were African Americans. For 1906, Baker found that 578 boys and girls under the age of twelve stood trial, including one six-year-old boy. Most of the 578 were black. See Baker, *Following the Color Line*, 50–51.
56. *Atlanta Constitution*, August 10, 1906.
57. Walter White, *Man Called White*, 20. The fact that they lived near the Whites is a good indication that this white family was not well-to-do. In his autobiography, White noted that his neighborhood was "deteriorating" and that his family were the only ones who kept their house painted, their fences repaired, and their yard trimmed, resulting "in sullen envy among some of our white neighbors" (*Man Called White*, 5).
58. Ibid., 20.
59. On parental discipline and observers' differing views on how it affected black males, see Kelley, "'We Are Not What We Seem,'" 82.
60. For the idea that "performance-centered research takes as both its subject matter and method the experiencing body situated in time, place, and history," see Conquergood, "Rethinking Ethnography," 187.
61. Thomas Holt offers some parallel thoughts on the development of racial consciousness and the role of the "everyday" in "Marking," esp. 7–14.
62. For the idea that we need to "historicize experience," see Joan W. Scott, "Evidence of Experience," 790–97.
63. For the idea that we "create the units of experience and meaning from the continuity of life," see Bruner, "Experience and Its Expressions," 7. My argument

that "dramas of socialization" are a fundamental unit of experience for autobiographers owes much to Bruner's essay.

64. Smith, *Killers of the Dream*, 30.

CHAPTER FOUR

1. Laura Donaldson, joint interview with Henry Donaldson, BTV; transcript, 53–54. In these and the next several quotations from this interview, I have silently trimmed Donaldson's account for some of its conversational wordiness. In one instance, I also rearranged her wording for clarity. For another retelling of Donaldson's story, see Chafe, Gavins, and Korstad, eds., *Remembering Jim Crow*, 86–88.

2. Laura Donaldson, joint interview with Henry Donaldson, BTV; transcript, 54–55.

3. Ibid., 54.

4. Morrison, *Playing in the Dark*. For an early evaluation of this growing body of scholarship that emphasizes Morrison's influence, see Fishkin, "Interrogating 'Whiteness,'" 428–66, esp. 430.

5. For a discussion of changing views on children's play, see Van Ausdale and Feagin, *First R*, 24.

6. Lasker, *Race Attitudes in Children*, 5.

7. Adam Fairclough's *Teaching Equality* has been criticized for eliding differences among black schools to suggest that all were not only progressive but shared an integrationist vision. Nevertheless, the phrase "teaching equality" is apt in many cases. The scholarship on black schools and churches is extensive. One good starting point on schools is Anderson, *Education of Blacks in the South*. On churches, see Montgomery, *Under Their Own Vine and Fig Tree*.

8. Two studies that emphasize the ways in which white schools and churches ignored contradictions and reinforced white supremacy are Leloudis, *Schooling the New South*, and Sally G. McMillen, *To Raise Up the South*.

9. Smith, *Killers of the Dream*, 32.

10. Nettie Thompson interview, BTV; transcript, 2.

11. Alease Brickers interview, BTV; transcript, 14.

12. For a discussion of how often children played together in rural versus urban settings, as well as how long such relationships tended to last, see Charles S. Johnson, *Patterns of Negro Segregation*, 146. Also relevant is Charles S. Johnson, *Growing Up in the Black Belt*, 292.

13. William Linyear interview, BTV; transcript, 30–31.

14. Louise Bouise interview, BTV; transcript, 9, 17–18.

15. Emmett Cheri interview, BTV; transcript, 25–26.

16. Essie Alexander interview, BTV; transcript, 14.

17. Herbert Cappie, joint interview with Ruth Cappie, BTV; transcript, 14.

18. Ada Mae Stewart interview, BTV; transcript, 32.

19. Theresa Lyons interview, BTV; transcript, 5.
20. Georgia Bays interview, BTV; transcript, 10–11.
21. Florence Borders interview, BTV; transcript, 6.
22. William Childs interview, BTV; transcript, 16.
23. John Volter interview, BTV; transcript, 8–9.
24. For a critique of recent scholarship on how some immigrant groups became "white," see Arnesen, "Whiteness and the Historians' Imagination."
25. Mamie Garvin Fields, *Lemon Swamp*, 47–48.
26. Septima Clark interview, SOHP; transcript, 12–13.
27. Herbert Cappie, joint interview with Ruth Cappie, BTV; transcript, 2, 48.
28. Lanetha Branch interview, BTV; transcript, 22, 5. I silently cut Branch's repetition of Peggy's name ("one of my white acquaintances, Peggy") in the first quotation, but it is striking how, both there and later in the interview, Branch changed the word "friends" to something less intimate: "acquaintances," "playmates."
29. Roosevelt Cuffie interview, BTV; transcript, 43–44.
30. Frankie V. Adams interview in Hill, ed., *Black Women Oral History Project*, 1:111. Adams goes on to say that the interaction she experienced with these white children was "pretty characteristic of the life experience we gave to one another in the period of which I'm talking." In his memoirs, Jimmy Carter emphasized most his relationships with adult black role models, but he also discussed childhood companions and games. See Carter, *Hour Before Daylight*, esp. 73–107 and 270.
31. Margaret McDow MacDougall interview, SOHP; transcript, 31–32.
32. Killian, *Black and White*, 4.
33. Olive Matthews Stone interview, SOHP; transcript, 18–19.
34. McNeill Smith interview, SOHP; transcript, 12.
35. Guion Griffis Johnson interview, SOHP; transcript, 8–9.
36. Ibid., 9.
37. Ruel Tyson interview, SOHP; transcript, 11–12.
38. Dorothy Markey interview, SOHP; transcript, 124–25. On Markey's life and writings, see Christina Looper Baker, *In a Generous Spirit*.
39. Randall Kennedy discusses this incident in *Interracial Intimacies*, 196–97. I first learned of the incident from Nicholas D. Kristof, "Blacks, Whites and Love," *New York Times*, April 24, 2005.
40. Charles S. Johnson, *Growing Up in the Black Belt*, 5–6.
41. Dorothy Markey interview, SOHP; transcript, 124–25.
42. Jessie Daniel Ames interview, SOHP; transcript, 1.
43. Boyle, *Desegregated Heart*, 43, 49. On Boyle's personal life as a catalyst for her activism, see my introduction to the University Press of Virginia reprint edition of her book, pp. xi–xii.
44. Coles, "It's the Same, but It's Different," 1117–18.
45. Occasionally, a black or white southerner suggested that his or her interracial

friendships persisted unchanged into adulthood. See, for example, Charles S. Johnson, *Growing Up in the Black Belt*, 293–94. It is difficult to know how much to credit such statements, especially where details are lacking. Johnson himself asserted that playing with white children "begins to become taboo for Negro children at about the age of 10," that youths "older than 15 only associate with whites in an employer-employee relationship," and that in the "few cases" where childhood friendships were "preserved," it was "usually on a basis of distant friendliness. Negro youth may greet white friends in the street, but they do not visit each other's homes" (320).

46. Ibid., 294.
47. Arthur F. and Martha J. Raper, "Two Years to Remember," unpublished type-script, box 32, vol. 12, p. 103, in Arthur Franklin Raper Papers #3966, Southern Historical Collection, Wilson Library, University of North Carolina at Chapel Hill.
48. Mildred Price Coy interview, SOHP; transcript, 14, 6.
49. Charles S. Johnson, *Patterns of Negro Segregation*, 247.
50. Hattie Bijou and Shirley Bijou Walker interview, BTV; transcript, 20.
51. Josephine Dobbs Clement, joint interview with William Clement, SOHP; transcript, 25.
52. Chambliss, "What Negro Newspapers of Georgia Say," 4–5, 7–8.
53. Ibid., 5.
54. William J. Coker Jr. interview, BTV; transcript, 19, 31–33.
55. Hobson, *But Now I See*, 54.
56. Lumpkin, *Making of a Southerner*, 133–34.
57. Dabbs, *Southern Heritage*, 11.
58. Smith, *Killers of the Dream*, 91–92.
59. Ibid., 91.
60. Wright, "Ethics of Living Jim Crow," 3–5.
61. Dorcas Carter interview, BTV; transcript, 73–74, 70–71, 75.
62. Herbert Cappie, joint interview with Ruth Cappie, BTV; transcript, 1.
63. Charles Lewis interview, BTV; transcript, 3.
64. Olivia Cherry interview, BTV; transcript, 3.
65. Edgar Allen Hunt, joint interview with Barbara Cooper and John David Cooper, BTV; transcript, 76–77.
66. Charles S. Johnson, *Growing Up in the Black Belt*, 287. Unfortunately, Johnson does not provide any details about this informant's age, sex, or background.
67. Margaret Walker Alexander interview in Hill, ed., *Black Women Oral History Project*, 2:45.
68. "Race Problem," 588–89.
69. Lanetha Branch interview, BTV; transcript, 5–6.
70. "Killed a White Boy."
71. Dorcas Carter interview, BTV; transcript, 72.

72. Hattie Bijou and Shirley Bijou Walker interview, BTV; transcript, 39, 41.

73. Georgia Bays interview, BTV; transcript, 37–38.

74. Walter White's story is discussed in Chapter 3. See also Walter White, *Man Called White*, 19–20.

75. Dorcas Carter interview, BTV; transcript, 70–71.

76. Smith, *Killers of the Dream*, 25.

77. Eura Bowie interview, BTV; transcript, 14–15. Bowie was vague on dates and did not indicate how old she was when this incident took place. However, her family moved to the Delta when she was nine, ca. 1924, and she married in about 1929, so the murder most likely occurred in the mid- to late 1920s. The dog's role in the story was never made clear in the interview.

78. See West, *Growing Up with the Country*, esp. 30–32, 42–45, 103, and 130–32; and Coe, *When the Grass Was Taller*. Coe explains what he means by "magical" on pp. xii–xiii, 102–3.

79. Isabella D. Harris to Max Gilstrap, January 28, 1987, Ms2687(m), Special Collections, Hargrett Rare Book and Manuscript Library, University of Georgia, Athens.

CHAPTER FIVE

1. "Five Negro Girls Heavily Fined," *Atlanta Constitution*, September 17, 1906. The *Constitution* headline is in error; only four girls were fined.

2. "Negro Girls Were Fined and Given a Lecture," *Athens Weekly Banner*, September 21, 1906. For the suspension of several unidentified students, see Minutes, September 24, 1906, p. 61, Board of Education Minute Book 2, Clarke County School District, Athens, Ga.

3. Dernoral Davis, "Toward a Socio-Historical and Demographic Portrait," 9.

4. Johnson is listed in the 1900 census as Mattie L. and in the 1910 census as Mattie Lee. However, the 1909 Athens city directory provides separate listings for her and four of her teenage brothers under the same address given for Lee and Georgia Johnson. There she is listed as Mattie Lou.

   I was unable to identify Annie Bonds or Roxanna Houston in the census or in city directories, although there was an Anna Houston who seems like a possibility. She was the daughter of a laundress and a railroad laborer and just one year younger than Mattie Lou Johnson. The 1900 census notes that the Houstons owned their home, suggesting a somewhat higher class status than that of the Johnsons, who rented and moved several times. The 1904 Athens city directory identifies Albert Houston as a porter.

   I found a Mattie Lumpkin in the 1900 census who might have been the fourth girl involved in this incident. She was born in January 1892 and was the daughter of Mariah Lumpkin, a widow who worked as a cook. However, neither Mariah nor Mattie Lumpkin is listed in either the 1904 or 1909 Athens city directory or in the 1910 census. See Manuscript Census Returns, Twelfth Census of the United States, 1900, and Thirteenth Census of the United States, 1910, Clarke County, Georgia, Georgia Department of Archives and History, Atlanta; *Athens City Directory* (1904); and Athens Directory Co., *Directory, City of Athens* (1909).

5. "Racial Remarks," *Augusta Chronicle*, September 17, 1906.

6. Woofter, "Negroes of Athens, Georgia," 61. Woofter mentions white women's difficulty in keeping servants during cotton-picking season on p. 46.

7. "Negro Girls."

8. Dorcas Carter's story is discussed in Chapter 4. See also Dorcas Carter interview, BTV; transcript, 70–71.

9. Powdermaker, *After Freedom*, 31, 34–35. Charles S. Johnson is another contemporary observer who anticipated change. See, for example, *Growing Up in the Black Belt*, 326–27. Olive Westbrooke Quinn's discussion of younger whites' greater distance from blacks parallels Powdermaker's but with more emphasis on economic change. See Quinn, "Transmission of Racial Attitudes," 46–47.

10. On the development of youth culture and, more broadly, developing notions of adolescence as a distinct period of life, see Palladino, *Teenagers*, and Kett, *Rites of Passage*.

11. Anderson, *Education of Blacks in the South*, 187–88. I am summarizing Anderson's figures for 1934.

12. McLaurin, "Rituals of Initiation and Rebellion," 13.

13. Thomas Chatmon interview, BTV; transcript, 2.

14. Geraldine Davidson interview, BTV; transcript, 13–14.

15. Roosevelt Cuffie interview, BTV; transcript, 12.

16. Westling, ed., *He Included Me*, 20.

17. Tolnay, *Bottom Rung*, 45–47. On the limitations of census data, see p. 195 nn. 35 and 37 and p. 196 n. 39. I also discuss this issue in Chapter 2, note 12.

18. Palladino, *Teenagers*, 5.

19. Anderson, *Education of Blacks in the South*, 197.

20. Ibid., 193–95.

21. On school politics in Atlanta, see Rouse, *Lugenia Burns Hope*, 74–79; Plank and Turner, "Contrasting Patterns in Black School Politics," 203–18; and Bayor, *Race and the Shaping of Twentieth-Century Atlanta*, 198–205.

22. Tolnay, *Bottom Rung*, 45.

23. Gertrude Sanders interview, BTV; transcript, 11, 26.

24. David M. Katzman traces the extent to which "black women disproportionately formed a servant class" in the early twentieth century in *Seven Days a Week*, esp. 72–79, 184–222, and app. 1. According to his estimates, "approximately three-quarters of black women wage earners worked as domestic servants or washerwomen" in 1910 and "41 percent still worked as servants and 30 percent as laundresses in 1920" (pp. 72, 74). Figures on adolescent girls are harder to come by, but Katzman does indicate that ten- to fifteen-year-olds made up 9.4 percent

of all black women in service in 1900 and 3 percent in 1920 (app. 1, table A-16). He also notes that the number of elite black families employing domestic workers was small (p. 58). Thus, the usual dynamic was, as one of his chapter titles indicates, "White Mistress and Black Servant."

25. Eddie Bryant interview, BTV; transcript, 4.

26. Edward Blaise interview, BTV; transcript, 4–7, 86.

27. William Linyear interview, BTV; transcript, 10–12.

28. Ibid., 13–14.

29. Emmett Cheri interview, BTV; transcript, 54–55.

30. Richard Wright told this story in both *Black Boy* and "The Ethics of Living Jim Crow," with variations in the two accounts. All of the quotations in this paragraph are from the latter, except for the one about Wright's "nervous, cryptic smile." See "The Ethics of Living Jim Crow," 5–8, and *Black Boy*, 220–25. For evidence that Wright was able to keep this job—and that this incident must therefore be somewhat fictional—see Fabre, *Unfinished Quest*, 52, 536 n. 21.

31. Wright, *Black Boy*, 212–13, 215–16. Fabre notes that Wright worked in a clothing store run by W. J. Farley until he was fired in September 1925. See Fabre, *Unfinished Quest*, 57.

32. Wright, *Black Boy*, 215.

33. Edward Blaise interview, BTV; transcript, 61–64. I have trimmed Blaise's account slightly and omitted the interviewer's questions.

34. John Harold Boucree interview, BTV; transcript, 63–64.

35. Herbert Cappie, joint interview with Ruth Cappie, BTV; transcript, 248–49.

36. Emmett Cheri interview, BTV; transcript, 81–84.

37. William Childs interview, BTV; transcript, 4, 48–49.

38. Wright, *Black Boy*, 28, 73, 91, 95.

39. On black southerners' use of the word "poison" in relation to white women, see Mays, *Born to Rebel*, 29.

40. Wright, *Black Boy*, 202–3.

41. Ibid., 222–23.

42. Rosengarten, *All God's Dangers*, 424–25.

43. Herbert Cappie, joint interview with Ruth Cappie, BTV; transcript, 53.

44. Arthur Clayborn Jr. interview, BTV; transcript, 52.

45. Benjamin Adams interview, BTV; transcript, 24.

46. Quoted in Mays, *Born to Rebel*, 27.

47. Olivia Cherry interview, BTV; transcript, 4–7. See also Chafe, Gavins, and Korstad, eds., *Remembering Jim Crow*, 296–303.

48. Olivia Cherry interview, BTV; transcript, 4.

49. Woofter, "Negroes of Athens, Georgia," 39.

50. Jessie Lee Chassion interview, BTV; transcript, 13.

51. Woofter, "Negroes of Athens, Georgia," 47. On domestic workers' wages, see

also Hunter, *To 'Joy My Freedom*, 52–53 and 256–57 n. 25; and Katzman, *Seven Days a Week*, esp. app. 3.

52. Jones, *Labor of Love*, 206.
53. Jessie Lee Chassion interview, BTV; transcript, 10–11.
54. Cleaster Mitchell interview, BTV; transcript, 18. Mitchell's interview is excerpted in Chafe, Gavins, and Korstad, eds., *Remembering Jim Crow*, 211–16.
55. Cleaster Mitchell interview, BTV; transcript, 11–12.
56. Ibid., 22–23.
57. On this point, see Shaw, *What a Woman Ought to Be*, 1, 14, 24.
58. Cleaster Mitchell interview, BTV; transcript, 25–27.
59. Shaw, *What a Woman Ought to Be*, 23–24.
60. Laura Donaldson, joint interview with Henry Donaldson, BTV; transcript, 42.
61. Dorcas Carter interview, BTV; transcript, 53–54.
62. Westling, ed., *He Included Me*, 65.
63. Ada Mae Stewart interview, BTV; transcript, 48. For similar comments about community attitudes toward out-of-wedlock pregnancies, see Simonsen, ed., *You May Plow Here*, 126.
64. Hunt, *I Am Annie Mae*, 47.
65. Westling, ed., *He Included Me*, 63.
66. Ibid.
67. Simonsen, ed., *You May Plow Here*, 160.
68. Stephanie Shaw discusses parental restrictions on "womanish" clothing and makeup and notes parents' awareness that their daughters "were sensual and even sexual beings." See *What a Woman Ought to Be*, 24–25, 257 n. 29.
69. Clark, *Echo in My Soul*, 23, 28–29.
70. Dollard, *Caste and Class*, 159.
71. Westling, ed., *He Included Me*, 63–64.
72. Laura Donaldson, joint interview with Henry Donaldson, BTV. In the interview, the Donaldsons said Laura moved to Wilmington in 1941, but 1940 seems more likely since she moved soon after her father was killed, which was shortly before her seventeenth birthday on July 1, 1940.
73. Laura Donaldson, joint interview with Henry Donaldson, BTV; transcript, 40–46.
74. Mays, *Born to Rebel*, 18.
75. For examples of Wright's family's reticence, see *Black Boy*, 27–28, 54–57.
76. Powdermaker, *After Freedom*, 191–92.
77. Dollard, *Caste and Class*, 105.
78. Ibid.
79. Roosevelt Cuffie interview, BTV; transcript, 22–23.
80. Thomas Chatmon interview, BTV; transcript, 10–11. Chatmon considered the episode between his father and Harper so important in deciding his life course

that he wanted to write a memoir titled "John, You Cleared Your Corn." Chatmon's interview is excerpted in Chafe, Gavins, and Korstad, eds., *Remembering Jim Crow*, 223–27.

81. Thomas Chatmon interview, BTV; transcript, 23.
82. Ibid., 16, 11.
83. Ibid., 12–13.
84. Hudson, *Black Worker*, 12–13.
85. Wright, *Black Boy*, 43, 8–9.
86. Powdermaker, *After Freedom*, 337–38.
87. On the Depression-era discovery of America's "forgotten" black youth by groups such as the American Council on Education, see de Schweinitz, "'If They Could Change the World,'" esp. chap. 2.
88. Charles S. Johnson, *Growing Up in the Black Belt*, 68, 201, 324, 67, 151. Powdermaker noted a similar lack of respect for ministers in *After Freedom*, 269–70.
89. McKee, *Sociology and the Race Problem*, 193.
90. Charles S. Johnson, *Growing Up in the Black Belt*, 65. On G. Stanley Hall and the notion that adolescence is a life stage marked by storm and stress, see Kett, *Rites of Passage*, 216–21, and Bederman, *Manliness and Civilization*, 77–120.
91. Charles S. Johnson, *Growing Up in the Black Belt*, 65.
92. Carter, *Hour Before Daylight*, 229–30.
93. Ibid., 229.
94. Killian, *Black and White*, 4.
95. To be precise, Wilmington's 1910 population was 25,748, with 12,107 blacks and 13,627 whites. See U.S. Bureau of the Census, *Thirteenth Census*, 312. On the Wilmington massacre, see Cecelski and Tyson, eds., *Democracy Betrayed*, and Gilmore, *Gender and Jim Crow*, 105–17.
96. Wilmington High School, "Sand Fiddler" (1911). Survey results appear on p. 66.
97. Wilmington High School, "Sandfiddler" (1921). The photograph of Moses appears on p. 14, the poem on p. 78, a reference to Moses as bell-ringer on p. 72, and the dramatis personae on pp. 68–69. Interestingly, Aunt Paradise is actually listed as "the colored cook *lady*" (emphasis added), a surprising linguistic construction to find in a white southern source.
98. New Hanover High School, "Sandfiddler." A summary of the school year titled "Calendar" indicates that, on November 24, 1926, the school's bells were out of order and ringing at random.
99. New Hanover High School, "Wildcat" (1934). On the "Uncle Mose" stereotype, see Goings, *Mammy and Uncle Mose*. It is worth noting that Wilmington yearbooks contain several references to minstrel shows performed by white high school students, although the nature of these shows—and whether or not they were done in blackface—is not clear.
100. New Hanover High School, "Hanoverian," vols. 2–4.
101. New Hanover High School, "Wildcat" (1935).

102. New Hanover High School, "Hanoverian" (1942).
103. Egerton, *Speak Now Against the Day*, 47–49.
104. Selig, "Next Generation in the South," 6. I am indebted to Diana Selig for bring-ing these efforts to my attention, and much of my analysis relies on her research.
105. Quoted in Alexander, "Southern White Schools Study Race Questions," 141.
106. Quoted in Selig, "Next Generation in the South," 5.
107. Ibid., 8–9.
108. *City of Atlanta by Seventh Grade Pupils*.
109. Quoted in Selig, "Next Generation in the South," 8–9.
110. Killian, *Black and White*, 13.
111. Ibid., 14; Boyle, *Desegregated Heart*, 37–38.
112. Killian, *Black and White*, 14.
113. Dollard, *Caste and Class*, 139–40.
114. Evers, *Evers*, 68.
115. Morris, *North Toward Home*, 79.
116. McLaurin, *Separate Pasts*, 82–85.
117. Stine and Doris George interview, BTV; transcript, 164–67. George's story also appears in Chafe, Gavins, and Korstad, eds., *Remembering Jim Crow*, 14–15.
118. Benjamin Adams interview, BTV; transcript, 20.
119. Houston, "Nigger Knocking," 94–95.
120. Morris, *North Toward Home*, 89–90.
121. Powdermaker, *After Freedom*, 33.
122. Reddix, *Voice Crying in the Wilderness*, 70–72.
123. McLaurin, "Rituals of Initiation and Rebellion," 22.
124. Daniel, *Lost Revolutions*, 271–72.
125. Dorothy Markey interview, SOHP; transcript, 20–21. In the interview, Markey notes that she told the story of her punishment differently in an unpublished autobiographical novel. In that account, she was punished because, to get back at her brother who was teasing her for wanting to be a doctor, she made a horse run away with the two of them in the family buggy. This is also how Christina Looper Baker tells the story in *In a Generous Spirit*, 16–18.

CONCLUSION

1. Du Bois, "True Brownies."
2. Floyd, *Floyd's Flowers*, 37–46. On "Best Men" and "Best Women," see Gilmore, *Gender and Jim Crow*, 62–63, 75–76.
3. Floyd, *Floyd's Flowers*, 321–22.
4. *Floyd's Flowers* review.
5. "Floyd's Flowers."
6. The advertisements appeared on the back covers of the November and Decem-ber 1905 issues of the *Voice of the Negro*. For the 20,000 figure, see Caldwell, *History of the American Negro*, 133. The sales figure on *Up from Slavery* is from

Harlan, ed., *Autobiographical Writings*, xxxiv. My evaluation of Floyd's sales as impressive is also based on a comparison with W. E. B. Du Bois's *Souls of Black Folk*, which sold 9,595 copies in the first five years after it was published in 1903, a figure Du Bois's biographer, David Levering Lewis, calls "exceptional" under the circumstances. See Lewis, *W. E. B. Du Bois*, 291.

7. Reprint editions include a *Floyd's Flowers* published by Chicago's Howard, Chandler Company in 1909; *Silas X. Floyd's Short Stories for Colored People Both Young and Old* (Washington, D.C.: Austin Jenkins, 1920), which was bound with Edward S. Green's *National Capital Code of Etiquette*; *The New Floyd's Flowers: Short Stories for Colored People Old and Young* (Washington, D.C.: Austin Jenkins, 1922); and *Charming Stories for Young and Old* (Washington, D.C.: Austin Jenkins, 1925).

8. Du Bois, "Editorial."

9. Aptheker, introduction to *Complete Published Works of W. E. B. Du Bois*, 3.

10. On the *Brownies' Book*, see Sinnette, "*Brownies' Book*"; Violet Joyce Harris, "Brownies' Book"; and Vaughn-Roberson and Hill, "*Brownies' Book*."

11. The *Brownies' Book* did reach more than 5,000 subscribers before its demise. See Violet Joyce Harris, "African American Children's Literature," 547.

12. My discussion of NAACP youth activism in the 1930s is based on de Schweinitz, "'If They Could Change the World,'" chap. 5, esp. 299–318. For Juanita Jackson's words, see p. 302.

13. De Schweinitz, "'If They Could Change the World,'" 311.

14. Moody, *Coming of Age in Mississippi*, 287, 293.

15. Ibid., 31.

16. Ibid., 38–40.

17. Ibid., 121, 123, 121.

18. Ibid., 129.

19. Ibid., 127–28, 247–48.

20. Ibid., 125.

21. "Everybody Else Is Prejudiced" is a chapter title in Boyle's *Desegregated Heart*. On white liberals' belief in a "silent South," see Sosna, *In Search of the Silent South*.

22. Boyle, "Southerners Will *Like* Integration," 25, 133–34.

23. Sarah Patton Boyle interview, tape recording in author's possession.

24. On Boyle's life and activism, see Dierenfield, "One 'Desegregated Heart,'" and Gillespie, "Sarah Patton Boyle's Desegregated Heart," as well as my introduction to the University Press of Virginia reprint edition of *The Desegregated Heart* and my article "Speaking of Race."

25. On white southerners' racial conversion experiences, see Hobson, *But Now I See*.

26. Lipsitz, "Possessive Investment in Whiteness." For a synthesis of much scholarship in this vein, see Hall, "Long Civil Rights Movement," esp. 1240–42.

27. Hall, "Long Civil Rights Movement," 1242.

Bibliography

MANUSCRIPT SOURCES
Athens, Georgia
    Clarke County School District
        Board of Education Minute Book 2
    Hargrett Rare Book and Manuscript Library, University of Georgia
        Athens-Clarke Heritage Foundation Oral History Project Interviews
        C. D. Flanigen Papers
        Isabella D. Harris Letter
Atlanta, Georgia
    Atlanta History Center
        Child Service and Family Counseling Papers
        Children of the Confederacy Papers
        Living Atlanta Collection
        Sheltering Arms Day Nursery Papers
    Robert W. Woodruff Library, Atlanta University Center
        Atlanta Race Riot Clippings File
        Atlanta University Papers
        Commission on Interracial Cooperation Papers
        John and Lugenia Burns Hope Papers (microfilm)
        Elizabeth and Irvin McDuffie Collection
        Neighborhood Union Collection
        George Alexander Towns Collection
    Georgia Department of Archives and History (now in Morrow, Georgia)
        Manuscript Census Returns, Twelfth Census of the United States, 1900
            (microfilm)
        Manuscript Census Returns, Thirteenth Census of the United States, 1910
            (microfilm)
        Rhoda Kaufman Papers
        Speer Family Papers
Chapel Hill, North Carolina
    Southern Historical Collection, Wilson Library, University of North Carolina
        Anne Archbell Diary, Lillie Vause Archbell Papers
        Eugene Epperson Barnett Papers
        Elsie H. Booker Papers
        Cobb Family Papers
        E. Walker Duvall Papers
        Lizzie Chambers Hall Papers

        Henry T. and Mary Ann Harris Papers
        Joseph Piper Jones Papers
        Antonina Hansell Looker Papers
        William Dygnum Moss Papers
        Arthur Franklin Raper Papers
        Loula Ayres Rockwell Papers
        Sarah Lois Wadley Papers
Charlottesville, Virginia
    Manuscripts Department, University of Virginia Library
        Lily Heth Dabney Papers
        Meade-Funsten Family Papers
New York, New York
    Schomburg Center for Research in Black Culture, New York Public Library
        Smith/Shivery Family Papers
North Tarrytown, New York
    Rockefeller Archive Center
        General Education Board Archives
        Laura Spelman Rockefeller Memorial Papers

INTERVIEWS

From the Behind the Veil: Documenting African-American Life in the Jim Crow South Collection, Center for Documentary Studies at Duke University, Rare Book, Manuscript, and Special Collections Library, Duke University, Durham, N.C.

Adams, Benjamin E. Interview by Charles H. Houston Jr. Orangeburg, S.C., subseries, July 20, 1994.

Alexander, Essie. Interview by Paul Ortiz. LeFlore County, Miss., subseries, August 10, 1995.

Bays, Georgia. Interview by Doris Dixon. LeFlore County, Miss., subseries, August 1, 1995.

Bijou, Hattie, and Shirley Bijou Walker. Interview by Felix Armfield. New Iberia, La., subseries, August 11, 1994.

Blaise, Edward C. Interview by Aaron Bastian and Felix Armfield. New Iberia, La., subseries, August 1, 1994.

Blue, Ila J. Interview by Kisha Turner and Blair Murphy. Durham, N.C., subseries, June 2, 1995.

Borders, Florence. Interview by Michele Mitchell and Kate Ellis. New Orleans, La., subseries, June 20 and August 12, 1994.

Boucree, John Harold. Interview by Kate Ellis. New Orleans, La., subseries, July 5, 1994.

Bouise, Louise. Interview by Kate Ellis. New Orleans, La., subseries, June 20, 1994.

Bowie, Eura. Interview by Paul Ortiz. LeFlore Co., Miss., subseries, n.d.

Branch, Lanetha. Interview by Doris G. Dixon. Memphis subseries, June 16, 1995.

Brickers, Alease. Interview by Blair L. Murphy. Norfolk, Va., subseries, July 26, 1995.

Bryant, Eddie. Interview by Tunga White. St. Helena, S.C., subseries, August 13, 1994.

Bullock, Lester "Jack." Interview by Karen Ferguson. Enfield, N.C., subseries, June 29, 1993.

Cappie, Herbert, joint interview with Ruth Cappie. Interview by Michele Mitchell. New Orleans, La., subseries, June 22 and 29, 1996.

Carter, Dorcas. Interview by Karen Ferguson. New Bern, N.C., subseries, n.d.

Chassion, Jessie Lee. Interview by Michele Mitchell. New Iberia, La., subseries, August 2, 1994.

Chatmon, Thomas. Interview by Charles H. Houston Jr. Albany, Ga., subseries, June 23, 1994.

Cheri, Emmett. Interview by Kate Ellis. New Orleans, La., subseries, June 23, 1994.

Cherry, Olivia. Interview by Blair L. Murphy. Norfolk, Va., subseries, August 10, 1995.

Childs, William. Interview by Rhonda Mawhood. Wilmington, N.C., subseries, n.d.

Clayborn, Arthur, Jr. Interview by Mausiki Scales and Doris Dixon. LeFlore Co., Miss., subseries, August 8, 1995.

Coker, William J., Jr. Interview by Mary Hebert. Norfolk, Va., subseries, n.d.

Cooper, Barbara, joint interview with Edgar Allen Hunt and John David Cooper. Interview by Paul Ortiz. Memphis, Tenn., subseries, June 29–July 7, 1995.

Cuffie, Roosevelt. Interview by Tunga White. Albany, Ga., subseries, June 29, 1994.

Davidson, Geraldine. Interview by Paul Ortiz. Arkansas subseries, 1995.

DeLaine, Marguirite. Interview by Kisha Turner. Summerton, S.C., subseries, July 8, 1995.

Donaldson, Laura, joint interview with Henry Donaldson. Interview by Rhonda Mawhood. Wilmington, N.C., subseries, n.d.

George, Stine and Doris. Interview by Sally Graham. Albany, Ga., subseries, June 28, 1994.

Lewis, Charles. Interview by Doris G. Dixon. Memphis, Tenn., subseries, July 4, 1995.

Linyear, William. Interview by Mary Hebert. Norfolk, Va., subseries, August 7, 1995.

Lyons, Theresa. Interview by Leslie Brown. Durham, N.C., subseries, August 16, 1995.

Mitchell, Cleaster. Interview by Paul Ortiz. Arkansas subseries, July 16, 1995.

Sanders, Gertrude. Interview by Mausiki Stacey Scales. Birmingham, Ala., subseries, June 21, 1994.

Stewart, Ada Mae. Interview by Tunga White. Albany, Ga., subseries, July 6, 1994.

Swain, Ernest. Interview by Karen Ferguson. Wilmington, N.C., subseries, July 16, 1993.

Taylor, Rosita. Interview by Karen Ferguson. Charlotte, N.C., subseries, June 10, 1993.

Thompson, Nettie. Interview by Charles H. Houston. Orangeburg, S.C., subseries, July 20, 1994.

Volter, John. Interview by Kate Ellis. New Iberia, La., subseries, August 1, 1994.

Williams, Mazie. Interview by Paul Ortiz. Birmingham, Ala., subseries, July 1, 1994.

From the Southern Oral History Program Collection, Manuscripts Department, Southern Historical Collection, the University of North Carolina at Chapel Hill

Adamson, Mary Price. Interview by Mary Frederickson, April 19, 1976. Interview G-001, transcript.

Alexander Ralston, Elreta N. Interview by Anna Barbara Perez. February 18, 1993, and March 4, 1993. Interview J-018, transcript.

Ames, Jessie Daniel. Interview by Pat Waters, [1965–66?]. Interview G-003, transcript.

Bates, J. Leonard. Interview by Dewey Grantham, August 12, 1983. Interview L-079, transcript.

Berry, Lisbon C., Jr. Interview by Terrence S. Hines, October 3 and 10, 1994. Interview J-058, transcript.

Burgwyn, William Hyslop Summer, Jr. Interview by Nancy Williams Warren, February 4, 1994. Interview J-012, transcript.

Cahoon, Robert S. Interview by Michael Grossman, September 27 and 29, 1994. Interview J-024, transcript.

Camp, Miriam Bonner. Interview by Mary Frederickson, April 15, 1976. Interview G-013, transcript.

Clark, Septima Poinsette. Interview by Jacquelyn Hall, July 25, 1976. Interview G-016, transcript.

Clement, Josephine Dobbs, joint interview with William Clement. Interview by Walter Weare, June 19, 1986. Interview C-031, transcript.

Coy, Mildred Price. Interview by Mary Frederickson, April 26, 1976. Interview G-020, transcript.

Dees, William A. Interview by Margaret R. Westbrook, September 24, 1995. Interview J-064, transcript.

Ervin, Sam J., III. Interview by Hilary L. Arnold, February 24, 1993. Interview J-003, transcript.

Everett, Kathrine Robinson. Interview by Pamela Dean, January 21, 1986. Interview C-006, transcript.

Evitt, Alice. Interview by James Leloudis, July 18, 1979. Interview H-162, transcript.

Johnson, Guion Griffis. Interview by Mary Frederickson, May 28, 1978. Interview G-029-3, transcript.

MacDougall, Margaret McDow. Interview by Mary Frederickson, April 1977. Interview G-037, transcript.

Markey, Dorothy. Interview by Mary Frederickson, July 12, 1975. Interview G-042, transcript.

McKissick, Floyd B., Sr. Interview by Bruce H. Kalk, May 31, 1989. Interview L-040, transcript.

McMillan, James B. Interview by Walter H. Bennett Jr., November 1, 1991. Interview by Glenda Gilmore, October 11, 1989. Interview C-098, transcripts.

Olive, Billy Brown. Interview by Jennifer Marsico, January 27 and February 15, 1994. Interview J-017, transcript.

Simkins, Modjeska. Interview by Jacquelyn Hall, November 15, 1974. Interview G-056-1, transcript.

Smith, McNeill. Interview by Jay Mebane, February 18, 1994. Interview J-049, transcript.

Stone, Olive Matthews. Interview by Sherna Gluck, March 6, 1975. Interview G-059-1, transcript.

Turner, Viola. Interview by Walter Weare, April 15, 1979. Interview C-015, transcript.

Tyson, Ruel. Interview by Jacquelyn Hall and Della Pollock, October 9, 1997. In process, transcript.

Other

Sarah Patton Boyle. Interview by author, January 7, 1994, Arlington, Va. Tape recording in author's possession.

PERIODICALS
Athens (Ga.) Banner
Atlanta Constitution
Augusta (Ga.) Chronicle
The Brownies' Book
Colored American Magazine
The Crisis
The Voice of the Negro

AUTOBIOGRAPHIES AND OTHER PUBLISHED PRIMARY SOURCES
Abbott, Dorothy, ed. *Mississippi Writers: Reflections of Childhood and Youth.* Vol. 2, *Nonfiction.* Jackson: University Press of Mississippi, 1986.

Alexander, Will W. "Southern White Schools Study Race Questions." *Journal of Negro Education* 2 (April 1933): 139–46.

Andrews, Eliza Frances. *The War-Time Journal of a Georgia Girl, 1864–1865*. Lincoln: University of Nebraska Press, 1997.

Athens City Directory. Athens, Ga.: Athens Banner Publishers, 1904.

Athens Directory Co. *Directory, City of Athens, Georgia (1909)*. Athens, Ga.: Banner Job Print, 1909.

The Atlanta University Publications. Atlanta: Atlanta University Press, 1896–1914. Reprint of nos. 1–2, 4, 8–9, 11, 13–18. New York: Arno Press, 1968.

The Atlanta University Publications. Atlanta: Atlanta University Press, 1898–1917. Reprint of nos. 3, 5–7, 10, 12, 19, 20. New York: Arno Press, 1969.

Bailey, Thomas Pearce. *Race Orthodoxy in the South and Other Aspects of the Negro Question*. New York: Neale, 1914.

Baker, Ray Stannard. *Following the Color Line: American Negro Citizenship in the Progressive Era*. New York: Harper & Row, 1964.

Barnard, Hollinger F., ed. *Outside the Magic Circle: The Autobiography of Virginia Foster Durr*. Tuscaloosa: University of Alabama Press, 1985.

Beam, Lura. *He Called Them by the Lightning: A Teacher's Odyssey in the Negro South, 1908–1919*. Indianapolis: Bobbs-Merrill, 1967.

Beatty, Blanche A. "The Negro Child in the Rural Community." *Opportunity* 2 (October 1924): 301–2.

Blassingame, John W., ed. *Slave Testimony: Two Centuries of Letters, Speeches, Interviews, and Autobiographies*. Baton Rouge: Louisiana State University Press, 1977.

Bolsterli, Margaret Jones. *Born in the Delta: Reflections on the Making of a Southern White Sensibility*. Knoxville: University of Tennessee Press, 1991.

Boyle, Sarah Patton. *The Desegregated Heart: A Virginian's Stand in Time of Transition*. 1962. Reprint, Charlottesville: University Press of Virginia, 2001.

———. *For Human Beings Only: A Primer of Human Understanding*. New York: Seabury Press, 1964.

———. "Southerners Will *Like* Integration." *Saturday Evening Post*, February 19, 1955, 25, 133–34.

Brown, William Wells. *My Southern Home; or, The South and Its People*. In *From Fugitive Slave to Free Man: The Autobiographies of William Wells Brown*, edited by William L. Andrews. New York: Mentor, 1993.

Carter, Jimmy. *An Hour Before Daylight: Memories of a Rural Boyhood*. New York: Touchstone, 2001.

Catledge, Turner. "My Life and 'The Times.'" In *Mississippi Writers: Reflections of Childhood and Youth*. Vol. 2, edited by Dorothy Abbott. Jackson: University Press of Mississippi, 1986.

Chambliss, Rollin. "What Negro Newspapers of Georgia Say About Some Social Problems, 1933." Master's thesis, University of Georgia, 1934.

Chesnut, Mary Boykin. *A Diary from Dixie*. Edited by Ben Ames Williams. Cambridge, Mass.: Harvard University Press, 1980.

City of Atlanta by Seventh Grade Pupils of Atlanta Public Schools. Atlanta, Ga.: Tech High School Press, 1921.

Clark, Septima Poinsette, with LeGette Bythe. *Echo in My Soul.* New York: Dutton, 1962.

Clayton, Victoria V. *White and Black under the Old Regime.* Milwaukee: Young Churchman Co., 1899.

Dabbs, James McBride. *The Southern Heritage.* New York: Alfred A. Knopf, 1958.

Davis, Benjamin J. *Communist Councilman from Harlem: Autobiographical Notes Written in a Federal Penitentiary.* New York: International Publishers, 1969.

Delany, Sarah, and A. Elizabeth Delany, with Amy Hill Hearth. *Having Our Say: The Delany Sisters' First 100 Years.* New York: Dell, 1995.

Douglass, Frederick. *Narrative of the Life of Frederick Douglass, An American Slave, Written by Himself.* Edited by William L. Andrews and William G. McFeely. New York: Norton, 1997.

Du Bois, W. E. B. "Editorial." *The Crisis* 4 (October 1912): 287–89.

———. *The Souls of Black Folk: Essays and Sketches.* 3d ed. Chicago: A. C. McClurg, 1903.

———. "The True Brownies." *The Crisis* 18 (October 1919): 285–86.

Evers, Charles. *Evers.* New York: World Publishing, 1971.

"Experiences of the Race Problem, by a Southern White Woman." *Independent,* March 17, 1904, 590–94.

Faust, Drew Gilpin. "Living History." *Harvard Magazine,* May–June 2003, 38–46, 82–83.

Fields, Mamie Garvin, with Karen Fields. *Lemon Swamp and Other Places: A Carolina Memoir.* New York: Free Press, 1983.

Floyd, Silas X. *Floyd's Flowers; or, Duty and Beauty for Colored Children, Being One Hundred Short Stories Gleaned from the Storehouse of Human Knowledge and Experience.* Atlanta: Hertel, Jenkins, 1905.

"Floyd's Flowers; or, Duty and Beauty." *Voice of the Negro* 2 (October 1905): 722.

Floyd's Flowers review. *Alexander's Magazine* 1 (December 1905): 59.

Forten, Charlotte L. *The Journal of Charlotte Forten: A Free Negro in the Slave Era.* Edited by Ray Allen Billington. New York: W. W. Norton, 1953.

Harlan, Louis R., ed. *The Autobiographical Writings.* Vol. 1 of *The Booker T. Washington Papers.* Urbana: University of Illinois Press, 1972.

Hill, Ruth Edmonds, ed. *Black Women Oral History Project from the Arthur and Elizabeth Schlesinger Library on the History of Women in America, Radcliffe College.* 10 vols. Westport, Conn.: Meckler, 1991.

Holliday, Carl. "The Young Southerner and the Negro." *South Atlantic Quarterly* 8 (April 1909): 117–31.

Holsey, Albon L. "Learning How to Be Black." *American Mercury* 16 (April 1929): 421–25.

Holtzclaw, William Henry. *The Black Man's Burden*. New York: Neale, 1915.

Hornsby, Alton, Jr., ed. *In the Cage: Eyewitness Accounts of the Freed Negro in Southern Society, 1877–1929*. Chicago: Quadrangle, 1971.

Houston, Robert. "Nigger Knocking." *Southern Exposure* 8 (Fall 1980): 94–95.

Hudson, Hosea. *Black Worker in the Deep South: A Personal Record*. New York: International Publishers, 1972.

Hunt, Annie Mae. *I Am Annie Mae: An Extraordinary Woman in Her Own Words, The Personal Story of a Black Texas Woman*. Austin, Tex.: Rosegarden Press, 1983.

Hurston, Zora Neale. *Dust Tracks on a Road*. New York: HarperPerennial, 1991.

"Is a Race Clash Unavoidable?" *Winston Free Press*. Reprinted in *Raleigh News and Observer*, September 22, 1898, 3.

Johnson, Clifton. *Highways and Byways of the South*. 1904. Reprint, New York: Macmillan, 1905.

Johnston, Bertha. "I Met a Little Blue-Eyed Girl." *The Crisis* 4 (July 1912): 147.

Keenan, Hugh T., ed. *Dearest Chums and Partners: Joel Chandler Harris's Letters to His Children: A Domestic Biography*. Athens: University of Georgia Press, 1993.

"Killed a White Boy." Cleveland *Gazette*, December 22, 1894, 1, <http://dbs .ohiohistory.org/africanam/page1.cfm?ItemID=18251> (accessed June 24, 2005).

Killian, Lewis M. *Black and White: Reflections of a White Southern Sociologist*. Dix Hills, N.Y.: General Hall, 1994.

King, Martin Luther, Jr. *Why We Can't Wait*. New York: Signet, 2000.

Kristof, Nicholas D. "Blacks, Whites and Love." *New York Times*, April 24, 2005.

Lane, Lunsford. *The Narrative of Lunsford Lane, Formerly of Raleigh, North Carolina, Embracing an Account of His Early Life, the Redemption by Purchase of Himself and His Family from Slavery, and His Banishment from the Place of His Birth for the Crime of Wearing a Colored Skin*. Boston: J. G. Torrey, 1842.

Le Guin, Charles A., ed. *A Home-Concealed Woman: The Diaries of Magnolia Wynn Le Guin, 1901–1913*. Athens: University of Georgia Press, 1990.

Lumpkin, Katharine Du Pre. *The Making of a Southerner*. 1946. Reprint, Athens: University of Georgia Press, 1981.

Maddox, Lester. *Speaking Out: The Autobiography of Lester Garfield Maddox*. Garden City, N.Y.: Doubleday, 1975.

Mays, Benjamin E. *Born to Rebel: An Autobiography*. New York: Charles Scribner's Sons, 1971.

McLaurin, Melton. *Separate Pasts: Growing Up White in the Segregated South*. Athens: University of Georgia Press, 1987.

Moody, Anne. *Coming of Age in Mississippi*. New York: Dell, 1976.

"More Slavery at the South, by a Negro Nurse." *Independent*, January 11, 1912, 196–200.

Morris, Willie. *North Toward Home*. Boston: Houghton Mifflin, 1967.

Murray, Pauli. *Song in a Weary Throat: An American Pilgrimage*. New York: Harper & Row, 1987.

"National Association of Colored Women, The." *Voice of the Negro* 1 (July 1904): 310–11.

New Hanover High School. "The Hanoverian." Vols. 1–7. Wilmington, N.C.: Wilmington Stamp and Printing Co., 1936–42.

———. "The Sandfiddler." Wilmington, N.C.: Wilmington Stamp and Printing Co., 1927.

———. "The Wildcat." Wilmington, N.C.: Wilmington Stamp and Printing Co., 1934.

———. "The Wildcat." Wilmington, N.C.: Wilmington Stamp and Printing Co., 1935.

Olmsted, Frederick Law. *A Journey in the Back Country, in the Winter of 1853–1854.* New York: G. P. Putnam's Sons, 1907.

Ovington, Mary White. "Revisiting the South: Changes in Twenty-One Years." *The Crisis* 34 (April 1927): 42–43, 60–61.

———. "Selling Race Pride." *Publisher's Weekly*, January 10, 1925, 111–14.

The Papers of the NAACP. Part 1, Meetings of the Board of Directors, Records of Annual Conferences, Major Speeches, and Special Reports, 1909–50. Frederick, Md.: University Publications of America, 1982, microfilm.

The Papers of the NAACP. Part 12, Selected Branch Files, 1913–39. Series A. The South. Frederick, Md.: University Publications of America, 1982, microfilm.

Percy, William Alexander. *Lanterns on the Levee.* New York: Alfred A. Knopf, 1941.

"The Race Problem—An Autobiography by a Southern Colored Woman." *Independent*, March 17, 1904, 586–89.

Rawick, George P., ed. *The American Slave: A Composite Autobiography.* Vol. 12, Georgia Narratives, Parts 1 and 2. Westport, Conn.: Greenwood, 1972.

Reddix, Jacob L. *A Voice Crying in the Wilderness: The Memoir of Jacob L. Reddix.* Jackson: University of Mississippi Press, 1974.

Reid, Whitelaw. *After the War: A Tour of the South, 1865–1866.* 1866. Reprint, New York: Harper & Row, 1965.

Robertson, Ben. *Red Hills and Cotton: An Upcountry Memory.* Columbia: University of South Carolina Press, 1942.

Rosengarten, Theodore. *All God's Dangers: The Life of Nate Shaw.* 1974. Reprint, New York: Vintage, 1989.

Silone-Yeates, Josephine. "The National Association of Colored Women." *Voice of the Negro* 1 (July 1904): 283–87.

Simonsen, Thordis, ed. *You May Plow Here: The Narrative of Sara Brooks.* New York: W. W. Norton, 1986.

Smith, Lillian. "Growing Into Freedom." *Common Ground* 4 (Autumn 1943): 50–51.

———. *Killers of the Dream.* New York: W. W. Norton, 1994.

Taylor, Alrutheus Ambush. *The Negro in the Reconstruction of Virginia.* Washington, D.C.: The Association for the Study of Negro Life and History, 1926.

Terrell, Mary Church. *A Colored Woman in a White World.* Washington, D.C.: Ransdell, 1940.

Tucker, Annie E. "Formation of Child Character." *Colored American Magazine* 2 (February 1901): 258–61.

Tuttle, William M., Jr., ed. "W. E. B. Du Bois'[s] Confrontation with White Liberalism During the Progressive Era: A Phylon Document." *Phylon* 35 (September 1974): 241–58.

U.S. Bureau of the Census. *Thirteenth Census of the United States Taken in the Year 1910.* Vol. 3, *Reports by States.* Washington, D.C.: Government Printing Office, 1913.

Waring, Martha Gallaudet, and Mary Alston Waring. "Impressions of the Eighties Upon a Child of Georgia." *Georgia Historical Quarterly* 17 (March 1933): 40–52.

Weatherford, W. D., ed. *A Survey of the Negro Boy in Nashville, Tennessee.* New York: YMCA Association Press, 1932.

Westling, Ruth, ed. *He Included Me: The Autobiography of Sarah Rice.* Athens: University of Georgia Press, 1989.

White, Walter. *A Man Called White.* 1948. Reprint, Athens: University of Georgia Press, 1995.

Wilkins, Roy. "Two Against 5,000." *The Crisis* 43 (June 1936): 169–70.

Williams, Sylvanie Francaz. "The Social Status of the Negro Woman." *The Voice of the Negro* 1 (July 1904): 298–300.

Wilmington High School. "The Sand Fiddler." Vol. 1. Raleigh, N.C.: Edwards and Broughton, 1911.

———. "The Sandfiddler." Nashville: Benson Printing Co., 1921.

Woofter, T. J., Jr. "The Negroes of Athens, Georgia." Phelps-Stokes Fellowship Studies No. 1, *Bulletin of the University of Georgia* 14 (December 1913): 1–62.

Wright, Richard. *Black Boy (American Hunger): A Record of Childhood and Youth.* New York: HarperPerennial, 1993.

———. "The Ethics of Living Jim Crow." In *Uncle Tom's Children.* New York: Harper & Row, 1940.

SECONDARY SOURCES

Allen, James, Hilton Als, John Lewis, and Leon F. Litwack. *Without Sanctuary: Lynching Photography in America.* Santa Fe, N.M.: Twin Palms, 2000.

Anderson, C. Arnold, and Mary Jean Bowman. "The Vanishing Servant and the Contemporary Status System of the American South." *American Journal of Sociology* 59 (November 1953): 215–30.

Anderson, James D. *The Education of Blacks in the South, 1860–1935.* Chapel Hill: University of North Carolina Press, 1988.

Andrews, William L. "In Search of a Common Identity: The Self and the South in Four Mississippi Autobiographies." *The Southern Review* 24 (Winter 1988): 47–64.

Aptheker, Herbert. Introduction to *The Complete Published Works of W. E. B. Du Bois: Writings in Periodicals Edited by W. E. B. Du Bois: Selections from the Brownies' Book*, 1–4. Millwood, N.Y.: Kraus-Thomson, 1980.

Arnesen, Eric. "Whiteness and the Historians' Imagination." *International Labor and Working-Class History* 60 (Fall 2001): 3–32.

Austin, J. L. *How to Do Things With Words*. 2d ed. Cambridge, Mass.: Harvard University Press, 1975.

Ayers, Edward L. *The Promise of the New South: Life After Reconstruction*. New York: Oxford University Press, 1992.

Bailey, Fred Arthur. "The Textbooks of the 'Lost Cause': Censorship and the Creation of Southern State Histories." *Georgia Historical Quarterly* 75 (Fall 1991): 507–33.

Baker, Christina Looper. *In a Generous Spirit: A First-Person Biography of Myra Page*. Urbana: University of Illinois Press, 1996.

Baker, Paula. "The Domestication of Politics: Women and American Political Society, 1780–1920." *American Historical Review* 89 (June 1984): 620–47.

Bardaglio, Peter W. *Reconstructing the Household: Families, Sex, and the Law in the Nineteenth-Century South*. Chapel Hill: University of North Carolina Press, 1995.

Barkley Brown, Elsa. "'What Has Happened Here': The Politics of Difference in Women's History and Feminist Politics." *Feminist Studies* 18 (Summer 1992): 295–312.

Bauman, Mark K. "The Youthful Musings of a Jewish Community Activist: Josephine Joel Heyman." *Atlanta History* 39 (Summer 1995): 46–50.

Bayor, Ronald H. *Race and the Shaping of Twentieth-Century Atlanta*. Chapel Hill: University of North Carolina Press, 1996.

Bederman, Gail. *Manliness and Civilization: A Cultural History of Gender and Race in the United States, 1880–1917*. Chicago: University of Chicago Press, 1995.

Berlin, Ira. *Slaves Without Masters: The Free Negro in the Antebellum South*. New York: Pantheon, 1975.

Bernstein, Patricia. *The First Waco Horror: The Lynching of Jesse Washington and the Rise of the NAACP*. College Station: Texas A&M University Press, 2005.

Bettie, Julie. *Women Without Class: Girls, Race, and Identity*. Berkeley: University of California Press, 2003.

Bloom, Lynn Z. "Coming of Age in the Segregated South: Autobiographies of Twentieth-Century Childhoods, Black and White." In *Home Ground: Southern Autobiography*, edited by J. Bill Berry, 110–22. Columbia: University of Missouri Press, 1991.

Bourdieu, Pierre. *Outline of a Theory of Practice*. Translated by Richard Nice. New York: Cambridge University Press, 1977.

Broderick, Dorothy M. *Image of the Black in Children's Fiction*. New York: R. R. Bowker, 1973.

Brown, Kathleen M. *Good Wives, Nasty Wenches, and Anxious Patriarchs: Gender,*

Race, and Power in Colonial Virginia. Chapel Hill: University of North Carolina Press, 1996.

Brubaker, Rogers, and Frederick Cooper. "Beyond 'Identity.'" *Theory and Society* 29 (February 2000): 1–47.

Bruner, Edward M. "Experience and Its Expressions." In *The Anthropology of Experience*, edited by Victor W. Turner and Edward M. Bruner, 3–30. Urbana: University of Illinois Press, 1986.

Burkett, Randall K., Nancy Hall Burkett, and Henry Louis Gates Jr., eds. *Black Biography, 1790–1950.* Vol. 1. Alexandria, Va.: Chadwyck-Healey, 1991.

Butler, Judith P. *Gender Trouble: Feminism and the Subversion of Identity.* New York: Routledge, 1989.

Bynum, Victoria E. *Unruly Women: The Politics of Social and Sexual Control in the Old South.* Chapel Hill: University of North Carolina Press, 1992.

Caldwell, Arthur Bunyan, ed. *History of the American Negro and His Institutions.* Georgia edition. Atlanta, Ga.: A. B. Caldwell Publishing, 1920.

Cecelski, David S., and Timothy B. Tyson, eds. *Democracy Betrayed: The Wilmington Race Riot of 1898 and Its Legacy.* Chapel Hill: University of North Carolina Press, 1998.

Cell, John W. *The Highest Stage of White Supremacy: The Origins of Segregation in South Africa and the American South.* Cambridge, United Kingdom: Cambridge University Press, 1982.

Certeau, Michel de. *The Practice of Everyday Life.* Translated by Steven Rendall. Berkeley: University of California Press, 1984.

Chafe, William H., Raymond Gavins, and Robert Korstad, eds. *Remembering Jim Crow: African Americans Tell About Life in the Segregated South.* New York: New Press, 2001.

Clark, Kenneth B., and Mamie K. Clark. "The Development of Consciousness of Self and the Emergence of Racial Identification in Negro Preschool Children." *Journal of Social Psychology, S.P.S.S.I. Bulletin* 10 (November 1939): 591–99.

Coclanis, Peter. "Slavery, African-American Agency, and the World We Have Lost." *Georgia Historical Quarterly* 79 (Winter 1995): 873–84.

Coe, Richard N. *When the Grass Was Taller: Autobiography and the Experience of Childhood.* New Haven: Yale University Press, 1984.

Coles, Robert. "It's the Same, but It's Different." *Daedalus* 94 (Fall 1965): 1107–32.

Conquergood, Dwight. "Ethnography, Rhetoric, and Performance." *Quarterly Journal of Speech* 78 (February 1992): 80–123.

———. "Rethinking Ethnography: Towards a Critical Cultural Politics." *Communication Monographs* 58 (June 1991): 179–94.

Cook, Florence Elliott. "Growing Up White, Genteel, and Female in a Changing South, 1865–1915." Ph.D. diss., University of California, Berkeley, 1992.

Cox, Karen L. *Dixie's Daughters: The United Daughters of the Confederacy and the Preservation of Confederate Culture.* Gainesville: University Press of Florida, 2003.

Cunningham, Hugh. "Histories of Childhood." *American Historical Review* 103 (October 1998): 1195–1208.

Dailey, Jane. "Deference and Violence in the Postbellum Urban South: Manners and Massacres in Danville, Virginia." *Journal of Southern History* 63 (August 1997): 553–90.

Dailey, Jane, Glenda Elizabeth Gilmore, and Bryant Simon, eds. *Jumpin' Jim Crow: Southern Politics from Civil War to Civil Rights.* Princeton, N.J.: Princeton University Press, 2000.

Daniel, Pete. *Lost Revolutions: The South in the 1950s.* Chapel Hill: University of North Carolina Press, 2000.

Davis, Allison. "The Socialization of the American Negro Child and Adolescent." *Journal of Negro Education* 8 (July 1939): 264–74.

Davis, Allison, and John Dollard. *Children of Bondage: The Personality Development of Negro Youth in the Urban South.* Washington, D.C.: American Council on Education, 1940.

Davis, Allison, Burleigh B. Gardner, and Mary R. Gardner. *Deep South: A Social Anthropological Study of Caste and Class.* Chicago: University of Chicago Press, 1941.

Davis, Dernoral. "Toward a Socio-Historical and Demographic Portrait of Twentieth-Century African-Americans." In *Black Exodus: The Great Migration from the American South,* edited by Alferdteen Harrison, 1–19. Jackson: University Press of Mississippi, 1991.

Dierenfield, Kathleen Murphy. "One 'Desegregated Heart': Sarah Patton Boyle and the Crusade for Civil Rights in Virginia." *Virginia Magazine of History and Biography* 104 (Spring 1996): 251–84.

Dittmer, John. *Black Georgia in the Progressive Era, 1900–1920.* Urbana: University of Illinois Press, 1977.

Dollard, John. *Caste and Class in a Southern Town.* 3d ed. Garden City, N.Y.: Doubleday Anchor, 1957.

Dorr, Lisa Lindquist. *White Women, Rape, and the Power of Race in Virginia, 1900–1960.* Chapel Hill: University of North Carolina Press, 2004.

Doyle, Bertram Wilbur. *The Etiquette of Race Relations in the South: A Study in Social Control.* Chicago: University of Chicago Press, 1937.

Eakin, Paul John. *Touching the World: Reference in Autobiography.* Princeton, N.J.: Princeton University Press, 1992.

Edwards, Laura F. *Gendered Strife and Confusion: The Political Culture of Reconstruction.* Urbana: University of Illinois Press, 1997.

Egerton, John. *Speak Now Against the Day: The Generation Before the Civil Rights Movement in the South.* New York: Alfred A. Knopf, 1994.

Elkins, Stanley M. *Slavery: A Problem in American Institutional and Intellectual Life.* 3d ed. Chicago: University of Chicago Press, 1976.

Ellison, Ralph. "Richard Wright's Blues." In *Shadow and Act*. New York: Random House, 1953.

Fabre, Michel. *The Unfinished Quest of Richard Wright*. 2d ed. Translated by Isabel Barzun. Urbana: University of Illinois Press, 1993.

Fairclough, Adam. *Teaching Equality: Black Schools in the Age of Jim Crow*. Athens: University of Georgia Press, 2001.

Farr, Patricia Aylward. "Key Informants in Cottonville: Revisiting Powdermaker's Mississippi." *Journal of Anthropological Research* 47 (Winter 1991), 389–401.

Faust, Drew Gilpin. *Mothers of Invention: Women of the Slaveholding South in the American Civil War*. Chapel Hill: University of North Carolina Press, 1996.

Ferris, William R. "John Dollard: Caste and Class Revisited." *Southern Cultures* 10 (Summer 2004): 7–18.

Fields, Barbara J. "Ideology and Race in American History." In *Region, Race, and Reconstruction: Essays in Honor of C. Vann Woodard*, edited by J. Morgan Kousser and James M. McPherson, 143–77. New York: Oxford University Press, 1982.

———. *"Origins of the New South* and the Negro Question." *Journal of Southern History* 67 (November 2001): 811–26.

———. "Slavery, Race and Ideology in the United States." *New Left Review* 181 (June/July 1990): 95–118.

———. "Whiteness, Racism, and Identity." *International Labor and Working-Class History* 60 (Fall 2001): 48–56.

Fishkin, Shelly Fisher. "Interrogating 'Whiteness,' Complicating 'Blackness': Remapping American Culture." *American Quarterly* 47 (September 1995): 428–66.

Fleischner, Jennifer. *Mastering Slavery: Memory, Family, and Identity in Women's Slave Narratives*. New York: New York University Press, 1996.

Foley, Neil. *The White Scourge: Mexicans, Blacks, and Poor Whites in Texas Cotton Culture*. Berkeley: University of California Press, 1997.

Folmsbee, Stanley J. "The Origins of the First 'Jim Crow' Law." *Journal of Southern History* 15 (May 1949): 235–47.

Foner, Eric. *Reconstruction: America's Unfinished Revolution, 1863–1877*. New York: Harper & Row, 1988.

Foster, Frances Smith. "Parents and Children in Autobiography by Southern Afro-American Writers." In *Home Ground: Southern Autobiography*, edited by J. Bill Berry, 98–109. Columbia: University of Missouri Press, 1991.

Fox-Genovese, Elizabeth. *Within the Plantation Household: Black and White Women of the Old South*. Chapel Hill: University of North Carolina Press, 1988.

Fraser, Gertrude. "Race, Class, and Difference in Hortense Powdermaker's *After Freedom: A Cultural Study in the Deep South*." *Journal of Anthropological Research* 47 (Winter 1991): 403–15.

Fredrickson, George. *The Black Image in the White Mind: The Debate on Afro-American Character and Destiny, 1817–1914*. New York: Harper & Row, 1971.

Gaines, Kevin K. *Uplifting the Race: Black Leadership, Politics, and Culture in the Twentieth Century.* Chapel Hill: University of North Carolina Press, 1996.

Gates, Henry Louis, Jr. "The Trope of the New Negro and the Reconstruction of the Image of the Black." *Representations* 24 (Fall 1988): 141–43.

Gatewood, Willard B. *Aristocrats of Color: The Black Elite, 1880–1920.* Bloomington: University of Indiana Press, 1990.

Gavins, Raymond. "Literature on Jim Crow." *OAH Magazine of History* 18 (January 2004): 13–16.

Geertz, Clifford. "Deep Play: Notes on the Balinese Cockfight." In *The Interpretation of Cultures: Selected Essays,* 412–53. New York: Basic Books, 1973.

———. "Found in Translation: On the Social History of the Moral Imagination." In *Local Knowledge: Further Essays in Interpretative Anthropology,* 36–54. New York: Basic Books, 1983.

———. "Thick Description: Toward an Interpretive Theory of Culture." In *The Interpretation of Cultures: Selected Essays,* 3–30. New York: Basic Books, 1973.

Genovese, Eugene D. *Roll, Jordan, Roll: The World the Slaves Made.* New York: Vintage, 1976.

Giddings, Paula. *When and Where I Enter: The Impact of Black Women on Race and Sex in America.* 1984. Reprint, New York: Bantam, 1985.

Gillespie, Joanna Bowen. "Sarah Patton Boyle's Desegregated Heart." In *Beyond Image and Convention: Explorations in Southern Women's History,* edited by Janet L. Coryell, Martha H. Swain, Sandra Gioia Treadway, and Elizabeth Hayes Turner, 158–83. Columbia: University of Missouri Press, 1998.

Gilmore, Glenda Elizabeth. *Gender and Jim Crow: Women and the Politics of White Supremacy in North Carolina, 1896–1920.* Chapel Hill: University of North Carolina Press, 1996.

Godshalk, David Fort. "In the Wake of Riot: Atlanta's Struggle for Order, 1899–1919." Ph.D. diss., Yale University, 1992.

———. *Veiled Visions: The 1906 Atlanta Race Riot and the Reshaping of American Race Relations.* Chapel Hill: University of North Carolina Press, 2005.

Goffman, Erving. "The Nature of Deference and Demeanor." In *Interaction Ritual: Essays on Face-to-Face Behavior,* 47–95. New York: Pantheon Books, 1967.

———. *The Presentation of Self in Everyday Life.* Garden City, N.Y.: Doubleday Anchor, 1959.

Goings, Kenneth W. *Mammy and Uncle Mose: Black Collectibles and American Stereotyping.* Bloomington: Indiana University Press, 1994.

Goodwyn, Lawrence C. "Populist Dreams and Negro Rights: East Texas as a Case Study." *American Historical Review* 76 (December 1971): 1435–56.

Grant, Julia. *Raising Baby by the Book: The Education of American Mothers.* New Haven: Yale University Press, 1998.

Grossman, James R. *Land of Hope: Chicago, Black Southerners, and the Great Migration.* Chicago: University of Chicago Press, 1989.

Hagood, Margaret Jarman. *Mothers of the South: Portraiture of the White Tenant Farm Woman.* 1939. Reprint, Charlottesville: University Press of Virginia, 1996.

Hale, Grace Elizabeth. *Making Whiteness: The Culture of Segregation in the South, 1890–1940.* New York: Pantheon, 1998.

Hall, Jacquelyn Dowd. "The Long Civil Rights Movement and the Political Uses of the Past." *Journal of American History* 91 (March 2005): 1233–63.

———. *Revolt Against Chivalry: Jessie Daniel Ames and the Women's Campaign Against Lynching.* Rev. ed. New York: Columbia University Press, 1993.

———. "'You Must Remember This': Autobiography as Social Critique." *Journal of American History* 85 (September 1998): 439–65.

Harris, J. William. "Etiquette, Lynching, and Racial Boundaries in Southern History: A Mississippi Example." *American Historical Review* 100 (April 1995): 387–410.

Harris, Violet Joyce. "African American Children's Literature: The First One Hundred Years." *Journal of Negro Education* 59 (Fall 1990): 546–47.

———. "The Brownies' Book: Challenge to the Selective Tradition in Children's Literature." Ph.D. diss., University of Georgia, 1986.

Hewitt, Nancy A. "Compounding Differences." *Feminist Studies* 18 (Summer 1992): 313–26.

———. *Southern Discomfort: Women's Activism in Tampa, Florida, 1880s–1920s.* Urbana: University of Illinois Press, 2001.

Higginbotham, Evelyn Brooks. *Righteous Discontent: The Women's Movement in the Black Baptist Church, 1880–1920.* Cambridge, Mass.: Harvard University Press, 1993.

Hobson, Fred. *But Now I See: The White Southern Racial Conversion Narrative.* Baton Rouge: Louisiana State University Press, 1999.

———. *Tell About the South: The Southern Rage to Explain.* Baton Rouge: Louisiana State University Press, 1983.

Hodes, Martha Elizabeth. *White Women, Black Men: Illicit Sex in the Nineteenth-Century South.* New Haven: Yale University Press, 1997.

Holt, Thomas C. "Marking: Race, Race-making, and the Writing of History." *American Historical Review* 100 (February 1995): 1–20.

Howard, Walter T. *Lynchings: Extralegal Violence in Florida during the 1930s.* Cranbury, N.J.: Associated University Presses, 1995.

Hunter, Tera W. *To 'Joy My Freedom: Southern Black Women's Lives and Labors after the Civil War.* Cambridge, Mass.: Harvard University Press, 1997.

Janken, Kenneth Robert. *White: The Biography of Walter White, Mr. NAACP.* New York: New Press, 2003.

Jaworski, Gary D. "Park, Doyle, and Hughes: Neglected Antecedents of Goffman's Theory of Ceremony." *Sociological Inquiry* 66 (May 1996): 160–74.

Johnson, Charles S. *Growing Up in the Black Belt: Negro Youth in the Rural South.* 1941. Reprint, New York: Schocken Books, 1967.

————. *Patterns of Negro Segregation*. New York: Harper & Brothers, 1943.

————. *Shadow of the Plantation*. Chicago: University of Chicago Press, 1934.

Johnson-Feelings, Dianne. *The Best of the Brownies' Book*. New York: Oxford University Press, 1996.

————. "Children's and Young Adult Literature." In *The Oxford Companion to African American Literature*, edited by William L. Andrews, Frances Smith Foster, and Trudier Harris, 133–40. New York: Oxford University Press, 1997.

Jones, Jacqueline. "Encounters, Likely and Unlikely, Between Black and Poor White Women in the Rural South, 1865–1940." *Georgia Historical Quarterly* 76 (Summer 1992): 333–53.

————. *Labor of Love, Labor of Sorrow: Black Women, Work, and the Family, from Slavery to the Present*. New York: Vintage, 1985.

Kasson, John F. *Rudeness and Civility: Manners in Nineteenth-Century Urban America*. New York: Hill & Wang, 1990.

Katzman, David M. *Seven Days a Week: Women and Domestic Service in Industrializing America*. New York: Oxford University Press, 1978.

Kelley, Robin D. G. "'We Are Not What We Seem': Rethinking Black Working-Class Opposition in the Jim Crow South." *Journal of American History* 80 (June 1993): 75–112.

Kennedy, Randall. *Interracial Intimacies: Sex, Marriage, Identity, and Adoption*. New York: Pantheon, 2003.

Kett, Joseph F. *Rites of Passage: Adolescence in America, 1790 to the Present*. New York: Basic Books, 1977.

King, Wilma. *Stolen Childhood: Slave Youth in Nineteenth-Century America*. Bloomington: Indiana University Press, 1995.

Kousser, J. Morgan. *The Shaping of Southern Politics: Suffrage Restriction and the Establishment of the One-Party South, 1880–1910*. New Haven: Yale University Press, 1974.

Kyriakoudes, Louis M. "'Lookin' for Better All the Time': Rural Migration and Urbanization in the South, 1900–1950." In *African American Life in the Rural South, 1900–1950*, edited by R. Douglas Hurt, 10–26. Columbia: University of Missouri Press, 2003.

Lasch-Quinn, Elisabeth. *Black Neighbors: Race and the Limits of Reform in the American Settlement House Movement, 1890–1945*. Chapel Hill: University of North Carolina Press, 1993.

Lasker, Bruno. *Race Attitudes in Children*. New York: Henry Holt, 1929.

Lebsock, Suzanne. "Complicity and Contention: Women in the Plantation South." *Georgia Historical Quarterly* 74 (Spring 1990): 59–83.

————. *The Free Women of Petersburg: Status and Culture in a Southern Town, 1784–1860*. New York: W. W. Norton, 1984.

————. *A Murder in Virginia: Southern Justice on Trial*. New York: W. W. Norton, 2003.

Leloudis, James L. *Schooling the New South: Pedagogy, Self, and Society in North Carolina, 1880–1920.* Chapel Hill: University of North Carolina Press, 1996.

Levine, Lawrence W. *Black Culture and Black Consciousness: Afro-American Folk Thought from Slavery to Freedom.* New York: Oxford University Press, 1977.

Lewis, David Levering. *W. E. B. Du Bois: Biography of a Race, 1868–1919.* New York: Henry Holt, 1993.

Lipsitz, George. "The Possessive Investment in Whiteness: Racialized Social Democracy and the 'White' Problem in American Studies." *American Quarterly* 47 (September 1995): 369–87.

———. "The Struggle for Hegemony." *Journal of American History* 75 (June 1988): 146–50.

Litwack, Leon F. *Been in the Storm So Long: The Aftermath of Slavery.* New York: Alfred A. Knopf, 1979.

———. *North of Slavery: The Negro in the Free States, 1790–1860.* Chicago: University of Chicago Press, 1961.

———. *Trouble in Mind: Black Southerners in the Age of Jim Crow.* New York: Alfred A. Knopf, 1998.

Lott, Eric. *Love and Theft: Blackface Minstrelsy and the American Working Class.* New York: Oxford University Press, 1993.

Loveland, Anne C. *Lillian Smith: A Southerner Confronting the South, A Biography.* Baton Rouge: Louisiana State University Press, 1986.

MacCann, Donnarae. *White Supremacy in Children's Literature: Characterizations of African Americans, 1830–1900.* New York: Garland, 1998.

MacCann, Donnarae, and Gloria Woodard, eds. *The Black American in Books for Children: Readings in Racism.* 2d ed. Metuchen, N.J.: Scarecrow Press, 1985.

Macleod, David I. *The Age of the Child: Children in America, 1890–1920.* New York: Twayne, 1998.

Margo, Robert A. *Race and Schooling in the South, 1880–1950: An Economic History.* Chicago: University of Chicago Press, 1990.

Mather, Frank Lincoln, ed. *Who's Who of the Colored Race: A General Biographical Dictionary of Men and Women of African Descent.* Vol. 1. Chicago: F. L. Mather, 1915.

Matthews, John Michael. "The Dilemma of Negro Leadership in the New South: The Case of the Negro Young People's Congress of 1902." *South Atlantic Quarterly* 73 (Winter 1974): 130–44.

Maza, Sarah. "Stories in History: Cultural Narratives in Recent Works in European History." *American Historical Review* 101 (December 1996): 1493–1515.

McCurry, Stephanie. *Masters of Small Worlds: Yeoman Households, Gender Relations, and the Political Culture of the Antebellum South Carolina Low Country.* New York: Oxford University Press, 1995.

McKee, James B. *Sociology and the Race Problem: The Failure of a Perspective.* Urbana: University of Illinois Press, 1993.

McLaurin, Melton. "Rituals of Initiation and Rebellion: Adolescent Responses to Segregation in Southern Autobiography." *Southern Cultures* 3 (Summer 1997): 5–24.

———. "Southern Autobiography and the Problem of Race." In *Looking South: Chapters in the Story of an American Region*, edited by Winfred B. Moore Jr. and Joseph F. Tripp, 65–76. New York: Greenwood, 1989.

McMillen, Neil R. *Dark Journey: Black Mississippians in the Age of Jim Crow*. Urbana: University of Illinois Press, 1989.

McMillen, Sally G. *To Raise Up the South: Sunday Schools in Black and White Churches, 1865–1915*. Baton Rouge: Louisiana State University Press, 2002.

Meier, August, and Elliott Rudwick. "The Boycott Movement Against Jim Crow Streetcars in the South, 1900–1906." *Journal of American History* 55 (March 1969): 756–75.

Mintz, Steven. *Huck's Raft: A History of American Childhood*. Cambridge, Mass.: Belknap Press of Harvard University Press, 2004.

Mitchell, Michele. "Silences Broken, Silences Kept: Gender and Sexuality in African-American History." *Gender and History* 11 (November 1999): 433–44.

Mixon, Gregory. *The Atlanta Riot: Race, Class, and Violence in a New South City*. Gainesville: University Press of Florida, 2005.

Montgomery, William E. *Under Their Own Vine and Fig Tree: The African-American Church in the South, 1865–1900*. Baton Rouge: Louisiana State University Press, 1993.

Morrison, Toni. *Playing in the Dark: Whiteness and the Literary Imagination*. New York: Vintage, 1993.

Myrdal, Gunnar. *An American Dilemma: The Negro Problem and Modern Democracy*. New York: Harper & Brothers, 1944.

Neverdon-Morton, Cynthia. *Afro-American Women of the South and the Advancement of the Race, 1895–1925*. Knoxville: University of Tennessee Press, 1989.

Nichols, J. L., and William H. Crogman, eds. *Progress of a Race; or, The Remarkable Advancement of the American Negro*. Naperville, Ill.: J. L. Nichols & Co., 1929.

Olney, James. "Autobiographical Traditions Black and White." In *Located Lives: Place and Idea in Southern Autobiography*, edited by J. Bill Berry, 66–77. Athens: University of Georgia Press, 1990.

Osofsky, Gilbert, ed. *Puttin' on Ole Massa: The Slave Narratives of Henry Bibb, William Wells Brown, and Solomon Northup*. New York: Harper & Row, 1969.

Painter, Nell Irvin. "'Social Equality,' Miscegenation, Labor, and Power." In *The Evolution of Southern Culture*, edited by Numan V. Bartley, 47–67. Athens: University of Georgia Press, 1988.

———. "Soul Murder and Slavery: Toward a Fully Loaded Cost Accounting." In *U.S. History as Women's History: New Feminist Essays*, edited by Linda K. Kerber, Alice Kessler-Harris, and Kathryn Kish Sklar, 125–46. Chapel Hill: University of North Carolina Press, 1995.

Palladino, Grace. *Teenagers: An American History*. New York: Basic Books, 1996.

Perman, Michael. *Struggle for Mastery: Disfranchisement in the South, 1888–1908*. Chapel Hill: University of North Carolina Press, 2001.

Pinckney, Darryl. "Aristocrats." *New York Review of Books*, May 11, 1995, 27–34.

———. "Professionals." *New York Review of Books*, April 20, 1995, 34, 43–49.

———. "Promissory Notes." *New York Review of Books*, April 6, 1995, 41–46.

Plank, David N., and Marcia E. Turner. "Contrasting Patterns in Black School Politics: Atlanta and Memphis, 1865–1985." *Journal of Negro Education* 60 (Spring 1991): 203–18.

Porter, Michael Leroy. "Black Atlanta: An Interdisciplinary Study of Blacks on the East Side of Atlanta, 1890–1930." Ph.D. diss., Emory University, 1974.

Powdermaker, Hortense. *After Freedom: A Cultural Study of the Deep South*. 1939. Reprint, Madison: University of Wisconsin Press, 1993.

Quinn, Olive Westbrooke. "The Transmission of Racial Attitudes Among White Southerners." *Social Forces* 33 (October 1954): 41–47.

Rabinowitz, Howard N. "More than the Woodward Thesis: Assessing *The Strange Career of Jim Crow*." *Journal of American History* 75 (December 1988): 842–68.

———. *Race Relations in the Urban South, 1865–1890*. Urbana: University of Illinois Press, 1980.

Reddick, Lawrence D. "Racial Attitudes in American History Textbooks of the South." *Journal of Negro History* 19 (July 1934): 225–65.

Ritterhouse, Jennifer. "Speaking of Race: Sarah Patton Boyle and the 'T. J. Sellers Course for Backward Southern Whites.'" In *Sex, Love, Race: Crossing Boundaries in North American History*, edited by Martha Hodes, 491–513. New York: New York University Press, 1999.

Robinson, Charles F. *Dangerous Liaisons: Sex and Love in the Segregated South*. Fayetteville: University of Arkansas Press, 2003.

Roediger, David R. *The Wages of Whiteness: Race and the Making of the American Working Class*. New York: Verso, 1991.

Rose, Anne C. "Putting the South on the Psychological Map: The Impact of Region and Race on the Human Sciences during the 1930s." *Journal of Southern History* 71 (May 2005): 321–56.

Ross, Edyth L. "Black Heritage in Social Welfare: A Case Study of Atlanta." *Phylon* 37 (Winter 1976): 297–307.

Roth, Darlene Rebecca. *Matronage: Patterns in Women's Organizations, Atlanta, Georgia, 1890–1940*. Brooklyn, N.Y.: Carlson, 1994.

Rothman, Joshua D. *Notorious in the Neighborhood: Sex and Families Across the Color Line in Virginia, 1787–1861*. Chapel Hill: University of North Carolina Press, 2003.

Rouse, Jacqueline Anne. *Lugenia Burns Hope: Black Southern Reformer*. Athens: University of Georgia Press, 1989.

Rudwick, Elliott M. "W. E. B. Du Bois and the Atlanta University Studies on the Negro." *Journal of Negro Education* 26 (Fall 1957): 466–76.

Ryan, Mary P. *Cradle of the Middle Class: The Family in Oneida County, New York, 1790–1865.* Cambridge, United Kingdom: Cambridge University Press, 1981.

Sallee, Shelley. *The Whiteness of Child Labor Reform in the New South.* Athens: University of Georgia Press, 2004.

Schwartz, Marie Jenkins. *Born in Bondage: Growing Up Enslaved in the Antebellum South.* Cambridge, Mass.: Harvard University Press, 2000.

Schweinitz, Rebecca Lyn de. "'If They Could Change the World': Children, Childhood, and African-American Civil Rights Politics." Ph.D. diss., University of Virginia, 2004.

——. "'We do not have a dream, we have a plan': Young People in the Civil Rights Movement." Paper presented at the Organization of American Historians Annual Meeting, Boston, Mass., March 2004. In author's possession.

Scott, Anne Firor. *Natural Allies: Women's Associations in American History.* Urbana: University of Illinois Press, 1991.

Scott, James C. *Domination and the Arts of Resistance: Hidden Transcripts.* New Haven: Yale University Press, 1990.

——. *Weapons of the Weak: Everyday Forms of Peasant Resistance.* New Haven: Yale University Press, 1985.

Scott, Joan W. "The Evidence of Experience." *Critical Inquiry* 17 (Summer 1991): 773–97.

Selig, Diana. "Cultural Gifts: American Liberals, Childhood, and the Origins of Multiculturalism, 1924–1939." Ph.D. diss., University of California–Berkeley, 2001.

——. "The Next Generation in the South: The Commission on Interracial Cooperation in the Schools." Paper presented at the Organization of American Historians Annual Meeting, Boston, Mass., March 2004. In author's possession.

Shaw, Stephanie J. *What a Woman Ought to Be and to Do: Black Professional Women Workers During the Jim Crow Era.* Chicago: University of Chicago Press, 1996.

Shivery, Louie D. "The History of Organized Social Work Among Atlanta Negroes, 1890–1935." Master's thesis, Atlanta University, 1936.

Sinnette, Elinor Desverney. "The Brownies' Book: A Pioneer Publication for Children." *Freedomways* (Winter 1965): 133–42.

Sosna, Morton. *In Search of the Silent South: Southern Liberals and the Race Issue.* New York: Columbia University Press, 1977.

Summers, Martin. *Manliness and Its Discontents: The Black Middle Class and the Transformation of Masculinity, 1900–1930.* Chapel Hill: University of North Carolina Press, 2004.

Thurber, Cheryl. "The Development of the Mammy Image and Mythology." In *Southern Women: Histories and Identities,* edited by Virginia Bernhard, Betty

Brandon, Elizabeth Fox-Genovese, and Theda Perdue, 87–108. Columbia: University of Missouri Press, 1992.

Thurmond, Michael L. *A Story Untold: Black Men and Women in Athens History.* Edited by Dorothy Sparer. Athens, Ga.: Clarke County School District, 1978.

Tolnay, Stewart E. *The Bottom Rung: African American Family Life on Southern Farms.* Urbana: University of Illinois Press, 1999.

Turner, Marcia E. "Black School Politics in Atlanta, Georgia, 1869–1943." In *Southern Cities, Southern Schools: Public Education in the Urban South,* edited by David N. Plank and Rich Ginsberg, 177–97. New York: Greenwood Press, 1990.

Turner, Victor. *From Ritual to Theatre: The Human Seriousness of Play.* New York: Performing Arts Journal Publications, 1982.

Van Ausdale, Debra, and Joe R. Feagin. *The First R: How Children Learn Race and Racism.* Lanham, Md.: Rowman & Littlefield, 2001.

Vaughn-Roberson, Courtney, and Brenda Hill. "*The Brownies' Book* and *Ebony, Jr.!:* Literature as a Mirror of the Afro-American Experience." *Journal of Negro Education* 58 (1989): 494–510.

Wade, Richard C. *Slavery in the Cities: The South, 1820–1860.* New York: Oxford University Press, 1964.

Wallach, Jennifer Jensen. "Remembering Jim Crow: The Literary Memoir as Historical Source Material." Ph.D. diss., University of Massachusetts–Amherst, 2004.

West, Elliott. *Growing Up with the Country: Childhood on the Far-Western Frontier.* Albuquerque: University of New Mexico Press, 1989.

White, Deborah Gray. "The Cost of Club Work, the Price of Black Feminism." In *Visible Women: New Essays on American Activism,* edited by Nancy A. Hewitt and Suzanne Lebsock, 247–69. Urbana: University of Illinois Press, 1993.

———. *Too Heavy a Load: Black Women in Defense of Themselves, 1894–1994.* New York: W. W. Norton, 1999.

Whites, LeeAnn. *The Civil War as a Crisis in Gender: Augusta, Georgia, 1860–1890.* Athens: University of Georgia Press, 1995.

Williamson, Joel. *The Crucible of Race: Black-White Relations in the American South Since Emancipation.* New York: Oxford University Press, 1984.

Wilson, Charles Reagan. "Manners." In *Encyclopedia of Southern Culture,* edited by Charles Reagan Wilson and William Ferris. Chapel Hill: University of North Carolina Press, 1989.

Woodward, C. Vann. *Origins of the New South, 1877–1913.* Baton Rouge: Louisiana State University Press, 1951.

———. "*Strange Career* Critics: Long May They Persevere." *Journal of American History* 75 (December 1988): 857–68.

———. "The Strange Career of a Historical Controversy." In *American Counterpoint: Slavery and Racism in the North-South Dialogue.* Boston: Little, Brown, 1971.

———. *The Strange Career of Jim Crow.* 3d rev. ed. New York: Oxford University Press, 1974.

———. *Thinking Back: The Perils of Writing History.* Baton Rouge: Louisiana State University Press, 1986.

Yenser, Thomas, ed. *Who's Who in Colored America: A Biographical Dictionary of Notable Living Persons of African Descent in America.* 6th ed. Brooklyn, N.Y.: Thomas Yenser, 1944.

Zelizer, Viviana A. *Pricing the Priceless Child: The Changing Social Value of Children.* 1985. Reprint, Princeton, N.J.: Princeton University Press, 1994.

Index

Chatmon, John, 206–7
Chatmon, Thomas, 184, 206–7
Cheri, Emmett, 152, 187, 189, 192–93
Cherry, Olivia, 93, 172, 173, 196
Chesnut, Mary, 29
Child labor, 59, 65, 249–50 (n. 12)
Child rearing: by black parents, 6, 32–33, 56–58, 62–63, 65, 82–107, 224–31; respectability as focus of, 17, 19–20, 83–94, 97, 103, 104–7, 225–26, 228; and racial etiquette instruction, 54, 55–56, 79–81, 234; by white parents, 54, 55–58, 61–82, 233–34; northern approach to, 58; and "sheltered childhood" ideal, 58–63, 82–83, 85; new ideals of, 61; expert advice on, 61–62; and protection from racism, 63, 65, 85, 87; and exposure to racism, 63–68, 71–78; moderate white approach to, 68–71, 78, 79, 81–82; overprotective, 89, 165; blacks' criticism of other blacks', 94–97; and black mothers' ambitions, 100
Children: and resistance to white domination, 11, 19, 20, 83, 93, 98, 103–4, 123, 127; and hate, 11, 104, 224, 225, 232–33; and "race" and "racism" concepts, 12–13, 20, 118–29, 132–33, 146, 173; racial socialization of, 13, 32–33, 57–58, 68, 101, 109–42, 233–34; post–Civil War situation of, 16–17; double-consciousness of, 18; lynching attendance by, 19, 64, 71–78; and anger, 20, 83, 104, 136–37, 151, 225, 232; and "sheltered childhood" ideal, 58–63, 82–83, 85; and interracial relationships, 79–80, 132–33, 141, 144–69, 154, 155, 178, 179; and contacts with whites, 121–27, 146–47; and interracial fighting, 144, 146–47,

152, 154, 164, 166, 169–76, 170–76, 178, 179; work experiences of, 182, 184–91, 196–98; and *Brownies' Book*, 224–25, 229–30; activist training of, 228–31; political awareness of, 229–32. *See also* Adolescents; Education; Racial etiquette
Children of Bondage (Davis and Dollard), 209
Children of the Confederacy, 66
Children's literature, 66–67
Childs, William, 153, 193, 204–5
Child welfare laws, 65
Church, Mollie. *See* Terrell, Mary Church
Church, Robert, 125–26
Churches and Sunday schools, 66–67, 146, 147, 234, 250 (n. 17)
CIC. *See* Commission on Interracial Cooperation
Cities. *See* Urban life
Citizenship, 26, 233
Civility, 25, 70, 95
Civil rights movement, 7–8, 11, 15, 27, 53, 86, 107, 129, 184, 229–35
Civil War, 15, 26, 28
Clark, Septima, 88, 154, 202
Class, 5, 25, 88–103, 106, 118, 165; and status, 4, 15, 34, 37, 48, 69–70, 154; and respectability, 6, 17, 19–20, 56–57, 83–94, 103, 195, 199–200, 200, 225–26; and paternalism, 29, 81–82, 130, 131, 212, 215, 221; and racial etiquette, 44–45, 69–70, 130, 131; and black self-esteem, 52–53, 54; and child rearing, 59, 62, 94–97, 98, 100–101; and white southerners, 64–67; and child welfare laws, 65; and gender, 115–16, 130; and social inequality, 130, 131. *See also* Middle class; Upper class; Working class
Clayborn, Arthur, 195

Fourteenth Amendment, 26
Fox-Genovese, Elizabeth, 8
Frank, Leo, 224
Franklin, Belle, 161, 222
Freud, Sigmund, 134
Friendships, interracial, 132–33, 141,
    144–45, 150, 154, 155, 160–61, 168
Frustration, 20, 207–8, 232
Fuller, James Robert, Jr. (Bobo), 127–
    28, 135

Gaines, Frances, 5–6
Gaines, Kevin K., 57, 112, 113
Gardner, Burleigh, 44, 53
Gardner, Mary, 44, 53
Garrett family, 122, 127
Garvin, Herbert, 124
Garvin, Ruth, 124
Gatewood, Willard, 89–90
Gender: and racial etiquette, 25, 30,
    55–56, 80–81, 130; and voting rights,
    26; and white violence, 40–41;
    and black male–white female rela-
    tionships, 40–42, 113, 117, 160–61,
    194–95, 204–5, 216; and sexual
    impropriety concerns, 40–42, 160–
    61; and black clubwomen, 61, 62,
    65, 86, 94; and black women's
    optimism, 86, 99–100; and black
    women's sexual availability, 89, 182,
    184, 216–17; and black education
    level, 100, 185, 255–56 (n. 136); and
    racism, 115–16; and class, 115–16,
    130; and social inequality, 115–16,
    130, 211; and black women's beauty
    ideal, 116; and restrictions on white
    adolescent girls, 130, 131–32, 160–
    61, 168, 183, 222; and black male
    sexuality, 182, 193–96, 203–4; and
    farm work, 184–85, 196; and black
    male maturation, 191–96; and black
    female maturation, 196–205; and

sexual exploitation, 198–99, 202
    (see also Rape); and black women's
    sexuality, 200–201, 203–4, 216, 217
Gender analysis, 7
Genovese, Eugene, 48–49
George, Stine, 219, 220
Georgia State College of Agriculture,
    61
GI Bill, 237
Gilmore, Glenda, 13, 22–24, 83–84,
    226
Girls. See Gender
Goffman, Erving, 3–4
Goings, Kenneth W., 212
Goodwyn, Lawrence C., 9, 10–11, 13
Great Depression, 45, 209
Great Migration, 26–27, 60, 233
Griffith, Dee, 177, 179
Grimes County, Texas, 9–11
Grossman, James, 60
Growing Up in the Black Belt (Johnson),
    53, 209
Guilt, 150, 169, 178

Hagood, Margaret Jarman, 61
Hale, Grace Elizabeth, 16
Hall, G. Stanley, 209
Hall, Jacquelyn, 19, 111, 237
Hamilton, Grace Towns, 85
Hard work: valuation of, 56, 83, 106,
    226
Harlem Renaissance, 224, 229
Harper, Thomas, 206–7
Harris, Isabella D., 178
Harris, J. William, 26, 27
Hate: children and, 11, 104, 224, 225,
    232–33
Hays, Florence, 40
Hester, Beulah, 89
Heyman, Josephine Joel, 44
Higginbotham, Evelyn Brooks, 56
Hobson, Fred, 169

Rabinowitz, Howard N., 8, 50

Race, 2, 4–6, 100–101, 103, 139, 232–33; social construction of, 9–11; children's understanding of, 12–13, 20, 118–33, 146, 147, 173; southern white moderate approach to, 68–71; contemporary perspectives on, 236–37. *See also* Racial etiquette

Race riots, 41, 108–9, 112–13, 139, 140, 204, 211, 229

Racial equality, 81, 87; and dramas of inequality, 112–33; teaching of, 147, 259 (n. 7). *See also* Segregation; Social inequality

Racial etiquette, 1–6, 16, 22–55, 78; and forms of address, 1, 31, 37–38, 40, 44, 45–46, 52, 55, 80–81, 146; and white southerners, 1–3, 14, 16, 18–19, 24–56, 68–69, 78, 79–81, 110, 129, 130, 155, 166–67, 234, 236; and segregation, 1–3, 16, 24, 28, 43, 50–51, 85, 234; and racial violence, 4, 24, 25, 27, 33–37, 50; as social control, 4, 48, 239–40 (n. 5); children's experiences with, 4–5, 17–19, 26, 32–33, 54, 55–56, 69, 79–81, 93, 110, 129, 130, 146, 155, 166–67, 234, 236; black challenges to, 5, 17, 22–23, 29, 31–32, 37, 46, 49, 50, 51, 54, 93, 127, 129, 131, 180–82; and double-consciousness, 18, 114–15, 135, 147, 151; role of, 25–28; and emancipated slaves, 28–37; and slaves, 30–32; and dining, 30–31, 42, 43, 52, 79, 80, 155; changes and continuities in, 37–47, 53; and retail interactions, 43–45, 53; caste as defining feature of, 51; social scientists' views on, 51–54; as attack on black self-esteem, 52–53; and white moderates, 68–71, 78, 79; and social boundaries, 69–70; black parents' teaching of, 98–99, 100,

101, 103; psychological burdens of, 106; white challenges to, 155, 158; and black workers, 189, 190. *See also* Socialization, racial

Racial identity, 9, 224, 243 (n. 35); development of, 15, 111–42; and relational difference, 17–19; and double-consciousness, 18, 114–15, 135, 147, 151; and interracial play, 145

Racial pride, 224, 225, 229; of whites, 65. *See also* Respectability

Racial roles, learning of. *See* Socialization, racial

Racial uplift, 103, 249 (n. 7). *See also* Respectability

Racial violence. *See* Lynchings; Violence

Racism, 9, 11, 20, 82, 166, 182; teaching about, 6, 65, 86, 98–101, 103, 232–33; sense of self and, 9, 112–17; children's understanding of, 12–13, 20, 124, 126–27; children's protection from, 63, 65, 85, 87, 166; children's exposure to, 63–64, 71–78, 104, 106; in children's literature and schoolbooks, 66–67; northern, 110, 115–17, 118, 121; personal experiences with, 112–36, 141; sexualized, 193, 194–95, 215–16; contemporary perspectives on, 236–37. *See also* Racial etiquette; Segregation; White supremacy

Randolph, Peter, 31–32

Rape, 4, 36, 41, 72–74, 78, 160, 191, 202, 219–220, 246 (n. 56)

Raper, Arthur, 46, 81, 164–65

Raper, Martha, 164–65

Reconstruction, 15, 26, 28–29, 35–37, 76–77, 125

Reddix, Jacob, 221

Reed, Paul, 75

Reid, Whitelaw, 28, 35, 36, 37–38

Relational difference, 17–19

black parents' concerns about, 89, 185, 199–205; and black stereotypes, 182, 193, 194–96, 199, 215–20; and threat of "white death," 194–95; instruction of black girls about, 200–201

Shaw, Stephanie J., 88, 199

"Sheltered childhood" ideal, 58–63, 82–83, 85

Shopping: racial etiquette of, 43–45, 53

Silent South, The (Cable), 234

Simon, Bryant, 13

Simpson, Fuzzy, 160

Slave resistance, 24

Slavery, 24, 28–34, 53, 94

Slaves' tales, 101–2

Smith, Annie, 132

Smith, Lillian: on white moderates' racial etiquette, 68–69, 70, 71, 78, 79; on racial socialization, 131–33, 135, 141, 147, 150, 161; on fighting with black children, 169–70; on racial violence, 177

Smith, McNeil, 157–58

SNCC. *See* Student Non-Violent Coordinating Committee

Social boundaries, 69–71, 130, 131, 135–36. *See also* Paternalism; Racial etiquette

Social class. *See* Class; Status

Social control, 4, 16, 48

Socialization, racial, 2, 5, 12–14, 32–33, 57–58, 68, 101, 109–42; and black southerners, 109–10, 118–27; and northern blacks, 110, 114–18; and white southerners, 110, 127–33, 135, 141, 147, 150, 161, 163, 223, 233–34; and adolescents, 130, 132, 223; dramas of, 133–39; and sexuality, 215–16; and effectiveness of whites' teachings, 235; contemporary issues of, 236–37. *See also* Racial etiquette

Social referencing, 78, 79

Social service organizations, 62, 94

Sosna, Morton, 234

Southern Heritage, The (Dabbs), 130–31

Stacey, Reuben, 71–72

Status, 4, 15, 34, 37, 48, 69–70, 154

Stealing, 92, 197

Stewart, Ada Mae, 152, 200

Stone, Olive Matthews, 157

Storekeepers, 43–45, 53

Strange Career of Jim Crow (Woodward), 7, 8

Student Non-Violent Coordinating Committee (SNCC), 231, 232

Submissiveness, 32–33

Subordination, 25, 27, 31, 43, 47, 51

Subservience, 98, 103

Substantive rules, 3

Sunday schools, 66–67, 146, 250 (n. 17)

Supreme Court, U.S., 7, 126, 234

Sutton, Willis A., 214

Swain, Ernest, 83

Swanson, Gregory, 234, 235

Tatom, Charity, 29, 37

Taylor, Rosita, 88, 91

Teenage pregnancy, 200, 201, 216, 217

Teenagers. *See* Adolescents

Temperance, valuation of, 56, 83

Terrell, Mary Church (Mollie Church): optimism of, 86; and northern racism, 110, 115–16, 117, 118, 121; childhood segregation experience of, 125–26, 135; and racial socialization, 130, 133, 135, 138

Territorialism, 169, 170, 171, 172

Thomas, Mark, 49

Thomas, Willie, 98

Thompson, Hanover, 160

Thompson, Nettie, 151

Thrift: valuation of, 56, 83

Thurber, Cheryl, 16

Till, Emmett, 232, 233, 236

Tillman, Ben, 123

Titles. *See* Forms of address

Tolnay, Stewart E., 185, 186

Towns, George A., 85

Trains. *See* Public-transportation segregation

Transcripts: "hidden," 23–24, 25, 36, 47–51, 101; "public," 23–24, 25, 28, 36

Tricksters, 101–3

Tucker, Thomas, 34

Tuskegee Institute, 225

Twain, Mark, 170

Two-parent households, 180–81

Tyson, Ruel, 159, 161

United Daughters of the Confederacy (UDC), 66

University of Georgia, Athens, 61

University of Virginia, 8, 234

Unwed mothers, 200

Up from Slavery (Washington), 225

Upper class, 56, 84, 195, 199–200

Urban life: and racial etiquette, 34, 43, 44, 54; and segregation, 50–51; and child rearing, 59; and interracial play, 151–52; and black educational opportunities, 186; and housing discrimination, 233

"Useful child" ideal, 58

Van Ausdale, Debra, 12–13

Vardaman, James K., 63

Violence, 176–79; and racial etiquette, 4, 24, 25, 27, 33–37, 50; and political repression, 9–10; and adolescents, 21, 219–21; and murder of blacks, 35–36, 41, 47, 177, 179; women as cause of, 40–41, 167; and race riots, 41, 108–9, 112–13, 139, 140, 204, 211,

229; whites' fear of, 52; as Great Migration cause, 60; children's exposure to, 64, 71–78, 176–78; Wright's experiences with, 118–22, 135. *See also* Lynchings; Rape

Voice of the Negro (magazine), 94, 228

Volter, John, 153–54

Volter, Nathan, 154

Voting rights, 26; registration drives, 231

Walker, Shirley Bijou, 165, 175

Warren, John, 40

Washington, Booker T., 45, 225, 226, 228

Washington, Jesse, 75

Watson, James, 246 (n. 41)

"We are Readier Than We Think" (Boyle), 8, 234

West, Elliott, 177–78

Whipping, 33, 34, 91, 119

White, Deborah Gray, 249 (n. 7)

White, George, 108

White, Madeline, 138–39

"White," sense of being, 2, 20, 129–33, 169

White, Walter: on Atlanta race riot, 108–9; on racial identity, 111, 112–13, 115, 117, 120, 121; on racial socialization, 135, 136–37, 138–40; childhood interracial fighting, experience of, 136–37, 175–76

White Man's Union, 10

"Whiteness" studies, 241 (n. 9)

White supremacy, 6, 18, 78, 145, 199; white dissenters from, 6, 81, 129, 150, 159, 161–63, 234–35; and social construction of race, 9, 10–11; black resistance to, 11, 13, 19, 20, 21, 49–50, 83, 85, 93, 98, 101, 103–4, 123, 127, 210; children's and adolescent's questioning of, 11–12, 20,